DIGITAL
PHOTOGRAPHER'S
HANDBOOK

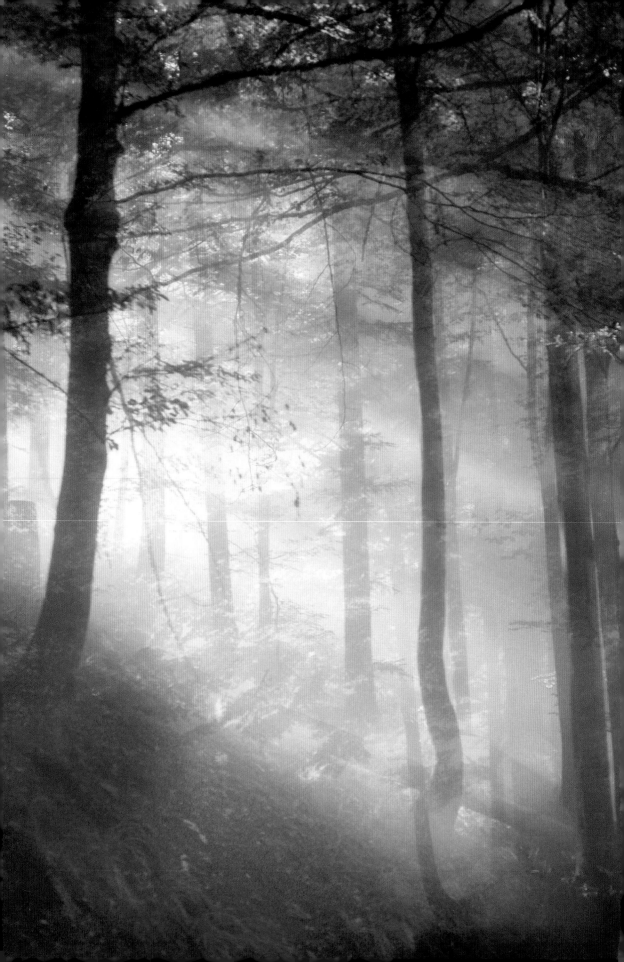

DIGITAL
PHOTOGRAPHER'S
HANDBOOK

TOMANG

 Penguin
Random
House

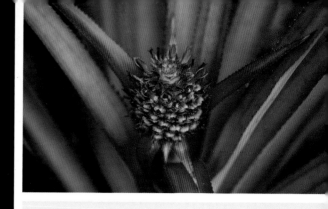

For Wendy

Senior Editor Nicky Munro
Designer Joanne Clark
US Senior Editors Rebecca Warren, Margaret Parrish
Jacket Designer Mark Cavanagh
Production Editor Ben Marcus
Production Controller Mandy Inness

Managing Editor Stephanie Farrow
Senior Managing Art Editor Lee Griffiths

This edition produced on behalf of
Dorling Kindersley by
Sands Publishing Solutions
4 Jenner Way, Eccles, Aylesford, Kent ME20 7SQ, UK
Editorial Partners David & Sylvia Tombesi-Walton
Design Partner Simon Murrell

First American Edition, 2012
This edition published in the United States in 2016 by
DK Publishing, 345 Hudson Street
New York, New York 10014

CONTENTS

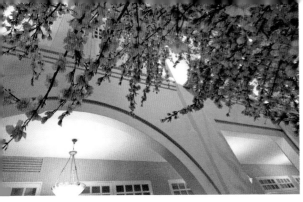
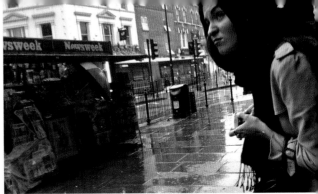

1 CORE SKILLS

2 PHOTOGRAPHY PROJECTS

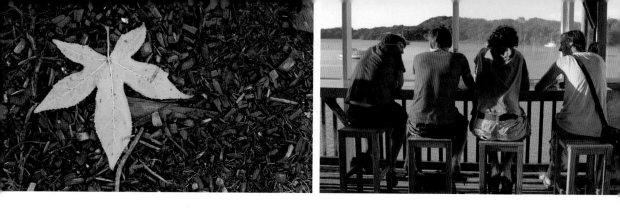

3 IMAGE DEVELOPMENT

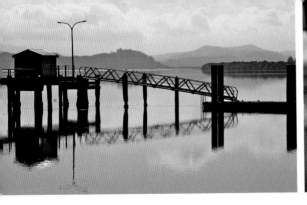
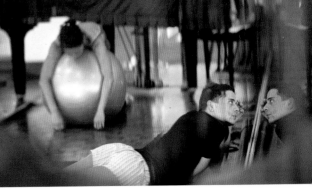

4 SHOWING AND SHARING

5 BUYING GUIDE

6 GOING FURTHER

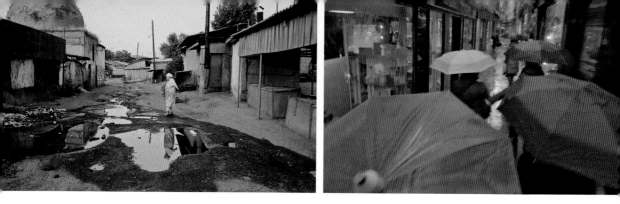

INTRODUCTION

This is the sixth edition of the *Digital Photographer's Handbook*, celebrating fourteen years in print. In that time, while few of the fundamentals of image-making have changed, digital technologies have transformed much of photography almost beyond recognition. The steady rise of photographers' skills as access to photography has spread to literally billions of people all over the world is itself a remarkable social and artistic phenomenon. One result is the bewildering explosion in the number of photographs being made: the total has passed a trillion images per year, and by the next edition we should not be surprised to learn that the 2-trillion mark has been reached.

While the steady improvement in photographic abilities is attributable in part to technology's ingeniously adept mediation, it is evident that skills and understanding of photography have genuinely grown and continue to blossom. Nonetheless, the hunger for photographic knowledge has also exploded, which drives the continuing demand for—and appeal of—this book.

We have responded to the latest developments with numerous updates to the *Digital Photographer's Handbook*. We have taken account, for example, of the rise of the interchangeable lens compact and the diversification of image manipulation and management. In the process, our sections on film and scanning have finally had to be removed. In their place, we have introduced several spreads on which we examine images to understand the theory behind their impact.

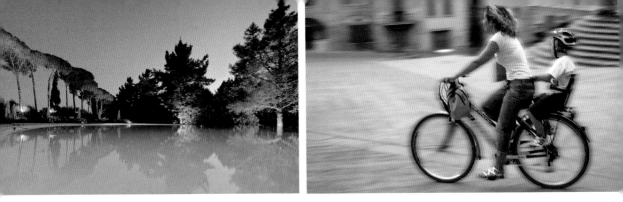

With this sixth edition, we find photography approaching a turning point. Core practices such as photojournalism are under siege from changing economic, political, and ideological forces. The dominance of social media has driven sweeping changes in the nature of the photographic subject, pushing formerly trivial subjects such as the self, the mundane, and daily meals to center stage.

Major technologies are now fully mature, so the computer errors, crashes, and corrupted files that made digital photography such a time-consuming process are no longer daily occurrences. The power of the internet and the ability to send a still image to a million places around the planet in seconds are now taken for granted. In short, the camera in your hand is the most elaborate and potent visual tool ever invented. You can enjoy enormous fun with it. You can have your life hugely enriched by its creative returns, and you can make a difference to the world. That is photography's strength—that is its gift to you. And it is yours to give back through your own humanity, artistry, and creativity.

May the light be with you!

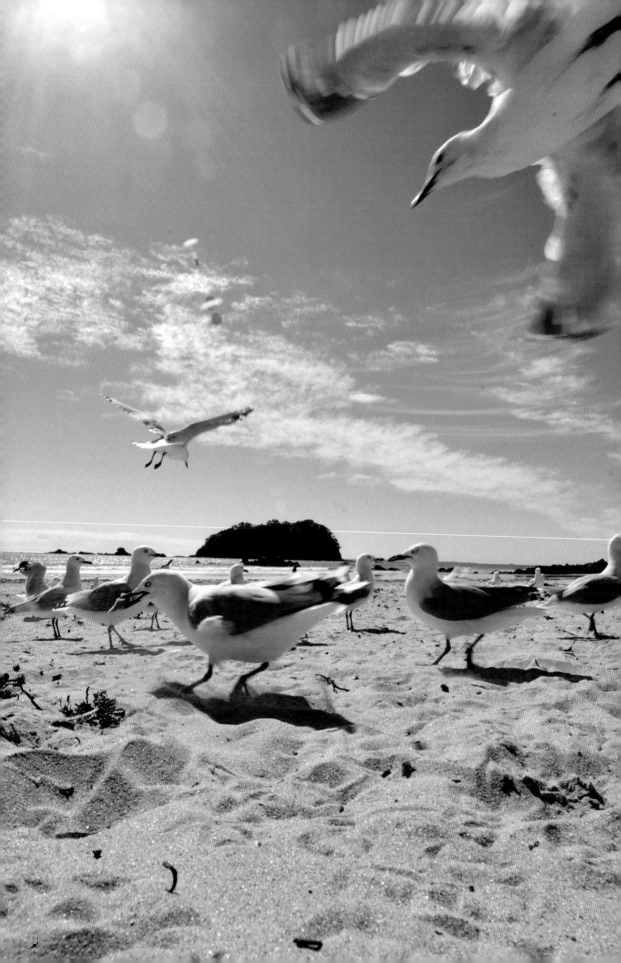

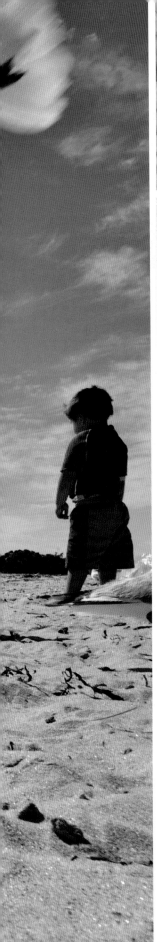
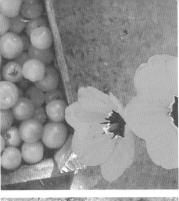
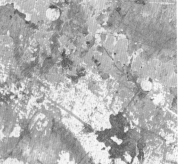
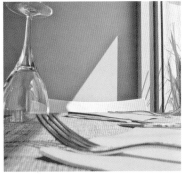
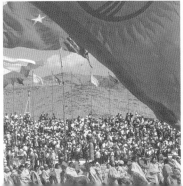

1 CORE SKILLS

HANDLING CAMERAS

The key requirement for handling cameras is to hold steadily during exposure. In addition, your grip on the camera should enable you to reach all the important and constantly used controls easily: this means it needs to be firm enough to hold the camera safely, but not so tight as to inhibit use—exactly the same principle as holding a tennis racket or a golf club.

Steady and steadfast

Whatever kind of camera you have, there are some simple pointers to ensure a stable position for sharp pictures. Many cameras are equipped with image stabilization, nonetheless, the more steadily you hold a camera, the sharper will your image be.

- Try holding the camera in different positions to find which is most comfortable for you; you do not have to hold it the same way as everyone else.
- Lean or prop yourself on any stable support that is available—a table, railing, wall, boulder, tree.
- Support your camera at three points, that is, in both hands and resting against your forehand, if possible. Avoid holding the camera in only one hand.

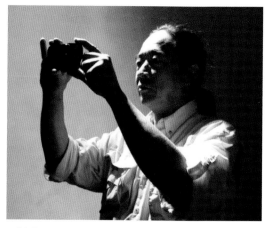

▲ **Using a camera phone**
Hold securely and steadily in both hands, using the wrist-strap, if available. Where possible, make exposures using button, rather than touch-screen, controls.

- Keep your elbows touching your body for the most stable hold.
- Support large lenses such as zooms for SLRs with an underarm grip: palm upward and placed under the lens. This not only stops the lens from "drooping" downward, but also eases strain on your wrist.

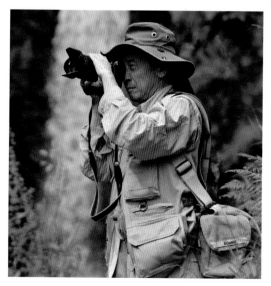

▲ **Unsupported imbalance**
Avoid this scenario: a shoulder-slung bag tending to twist the body; failure to support the weight of the camera in the left hand from underneath; and camera-strap not in use in a location where dropping the camera is almost certain to be disastrous.

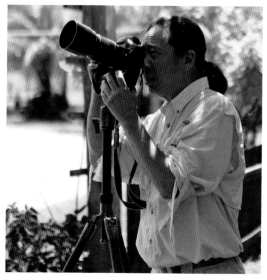

▲ **Using a tripod**
Work close to the tripod for steadiness and hold it down to make the set-up more rigid and resistant to vibration. Extend the central column only if you need to obtain the full height of the tripod. Do not hang the neck-strap around your neck in case you absent-mindedly walk away.

Camera ergonomics

Larger cameras, such as super zoom compacts (*see p. 337*) and SLRs, are all designed to be highly ergonomic: fitting the hand well, with controls positioned for ease of use. Smaller point-and-shoot cameras tend to be designed with the compact dimensions as a priority, with ease of use a secondary consideration—this can be a drawback for those with larger hands who may find it tricky to use small buttons and touch-screen areas. Virtually all cameras are designed for right-handed people.

- Heavy SLR cameras are easier to hold if you use a wrist strap for the right hand.
- A large interchangeable tripod plate fixed under the camera can help give a steady hold.
- A shoulder mount or similar rig is useful for very heavy equipment, or when you wish to shoot video with your SLR.

Camera controls

Using your camera without taking pictures is rather like practicing tennis or golf swings without hitting a ball. It familiarizes you with the feel of core actions such as selecting shutter or aperture settings, and zoom techniques. Such mastery of your camera controls allows you to keep your eye on the action, rather than the camera, the better to concentrate on your photography. A secure grip is part of the picture: always use the wrist-strap with compact cameras, or the neck-strap for larger models, so you need never fear dropping precious equipment.

TRY THIS

Rehearse taking pictures with your camera so that it becomes second nature. Learn how to adjust all the controls without looking at them—for example, there may be two clicks to the left between the two modes you use most often. Do you know—without looking—which way to turn the focusing ring to focus more closely? Or how to zoom in? Learn how to lock focus and hold the exposure entirely by feel. Hold the camera in a variety of positions to find the one that is most comfortable and stable. Only when you really know your way around your camera with your eyes closed can you concentrate fully on whatever it is you are photographing.

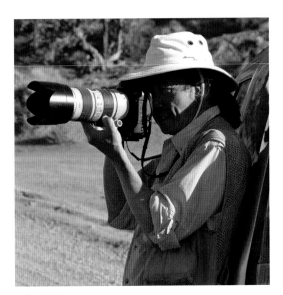

▲ Body lean
Whenever you use long focal settings on a zoom or a long lens, take advantage of any support that is available—a tree, lamp post, or car—that will help to steady the camera while you aim and shoot. Be aware that passing traffic can shake a car for a second or two.

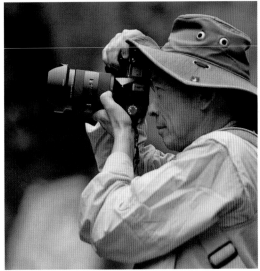

▲ Portrait format hold
Almost all cameras are easier to hold for landscape format shots than portrait: practice to establish a hold that is comfortable for you. Support the camera from below, keep your elbows tucked in to stablize the hold, and ensure that you can release the shutter and make control settings easily.

YOUR FIRST PICTURES

Photography first became truly popular when photographers no longer had to be personally responsible for processing their pictures. In the digital era, you can simply press the button and your camera or computer does all the rest. Indeed, with many cameras you can start snapping away the moment you take it out of the box. There is no need to hold back, and certainly no immediate call for the instruction book.

First date

After the initial fun, however, it is worth making a few conscious decisions. It is a good idea to set at least the date and time before you begin any serious photography. If you are going on vacation, remember to change to local time—and if you are traveling with friends or family it helps if you synchronize your cameras' clocks, as this makes it easier to sort and sequence images later.

Quality or ease

The default, or "out-of-the-box" settings will be designed to help you use the camera easily and also to give a good impression of its abilities. You may find that, for this early stage of experimentation,

the image files are unnecessarily large. Change the image size to the smallest while you are learning to use the camera.

You can, and should, shoot freely with the camera. Try out all the different modes and scene settings, different sensitivities, and color settings to see what results they produce. Try the camera indoors, on friends and family, take it outdoors, use it in bright light, and in darkened places. While at this stage of learning, it is OK to make a quick review of the images you capture. However, the best way to assess images properly is by using a computer monitor (*see pp. 356–7*).

Regaining control

You can leave all settings on automatic, thereby putting the camera in control. You may be able to teach yourself the basics of composition with this set up, but the finer points of exposure and color control will be in camera's hands, not yours. In short, you will not be making the most of your camera.

When you have an idea what each mode and setting does to your images, adopt a group of settings—for example aperture priority, high ISO, no flash, black-and-white, high sharpening—and

▶ **Unlikely beauty**
Photography has a unique talent for turning the unattractive into an intriguing image. The unlikeliest subjects, such as rusting doors, peeling paint and, as here in New Zealand, the worn bottom of a boat, can yield patterns of colors and textures that entertain the eye.

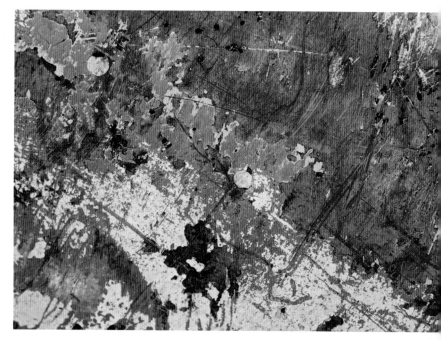

use it to make a whole series of images. This is a good way to learn all about your camera.

Chimping is for chumps

Chimping is short for "checking image preview" and seems very appropriate for photographers who exclaim "Oo! Oo! Ah! Aah!" while reviewing their images on the camera's LCD screen. If you allow yourself to be distracted by the preview image, you will miss many shots. It also breaks the rhythm of shooting, and interrupts the concentration you should be applying to the subject.

Try to reserve your reviewing to rest breaks and moments when you are sure nothing is going on. You do not have to go as far as some photographers, who tape up their camera screens to wean themselves off the habit, but turn off the preview and you will find you photograph more, and become more attuned to your subject.

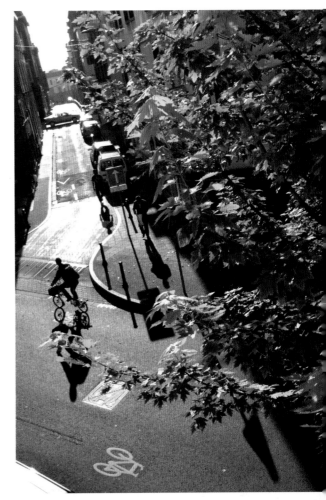

▶ Out of the window
If you have a window, you have a source for images: there will be changes in the light, and there may be ever-changing activity in the street. Keep watch and pictures will present themselves.

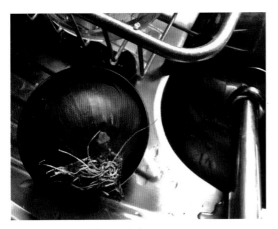

▲ Even the kitchen sink
With its usual jumble of bright metallic pots and pans, colorful food, and areas of plain surface, a kitchen is a surprisingly rich source of images. Contrast colorful dishes with steel utensils, and place natural forms against machined surfaces. Take time to explore details with the camera set to close-up mode, with the flash turned off. Wait for sunny days to obtain the most light indoors.

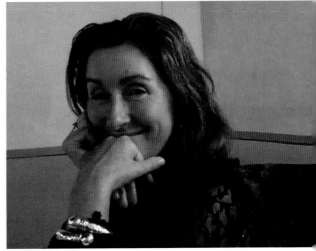

▲ Family snaps
Do not hold back from pointing the camera at members of the family. Catch them at relaxed times with any camera—here with a cameraphone at a restaurant—for portraits that capture their character.

PICTURE COMPOSITION

Photographers have the good fortune to be able to build on the experience of centuries of painting and graphic art with the unique visual tools of photography. Photographic composition arises through the joining of elements such as angle of view, perspective, depth of field, color, and tone with the visual structures that generations of artists have found effective in their work.

Any photographic composition can be said to work if the arrangement of the subject elements communicates effectively to the image's intended viewers. Often, the best way to ensure a striking composition is to look for the key ingredients of a scene and then organize your camera position and exposure controls to draw those elements out from the clutter of visual information that, if left competing with each other, would weaken the photograph's impact. Composition is not only about how you frame the picture; it is also how you use aperture to control depth of field, focus to lead the viewer's attention, and expose to use light and shade to shape the image.

If you are new to photography, it may help to concentrate your attention on the scene's overall structure rather than thinking too hard about very specific details; these are often of only superficial importance to the overall composition. Look for the lines that lead through the image. Are there any repeated elements, any arrangements that make a pattern? Try squinting or half-closing your eyes when evaluating a scene; this helps reduce the details and reveal the scene's core structure.

Explore each situation or opportunity by moving around the subject as much as possible, trying out different angles from as high and low as you can. When you feel the image looks right, make the exposure without further thought. If you are slave to the same rules as everyone else, your pictures will look like all the others. The fastest way to learn is to experiment freely.

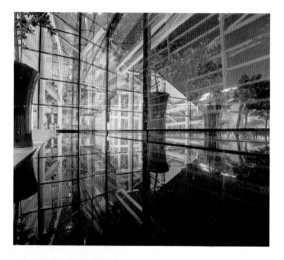

▶ Symmetry
Symmetrical compositions are effective for images that contain elaborate detail, such as this resort interior in Singapore. As a composition strategy, symmetry also works very well for subjects of the utmost simplicity, such as portraits against a plain background.

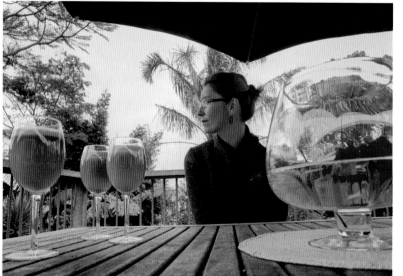

◀ Radial
Radial compositions are those in which key elements spread out from the center. This imparts a lively feeling, even if the subject is static. In this portrait, made in New Zealand, actual and implied lines radiate away from the central subject, pointing to the portrait sitter at the same time as leading away to all the other elements.

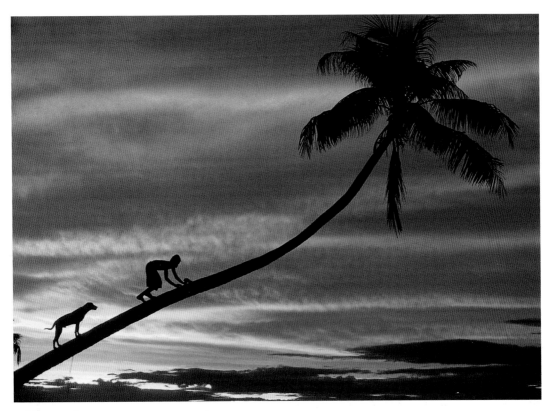

▲ Diagonal

Diagonal lines that lead the eye from one part of an image to another will impart more energy than horizontal lines. In this example, made in Taveuni, Fiji, it is not only the curve of the palm's trunk, but also the movement of the boy and his dog along it that encourage the viewer to scan the entire picture, sweeping naturally from the strongly backlit bottom left-hand corner to the top, thus engaging with the textures of the sky.

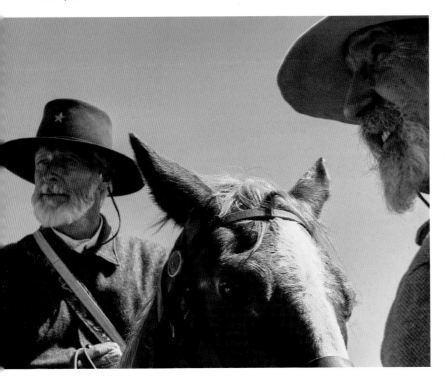

◄ Overlapping

Subject elements that overlap indicate increasing depth, as do the relative sizes of objects of known dimensions. We can tell that the man on the right is closer, because he is larger than the horse, while the man on the left must be farther away; not only is he smaller than the other man, but he is also behind the horse. These elements work together to articulate the three dimensions in this photograph, taken during an American Civil War reenactment in the United States.

▶ The golden spiral and golden section

This image has been overlaid with a golden spiral based on the golden section, as well as with a grid dividing the picture area into phi ratios. This demonstrates that, even with a fleeting shot, photographers compose instinctively, to fit elements to harmonious proportions.

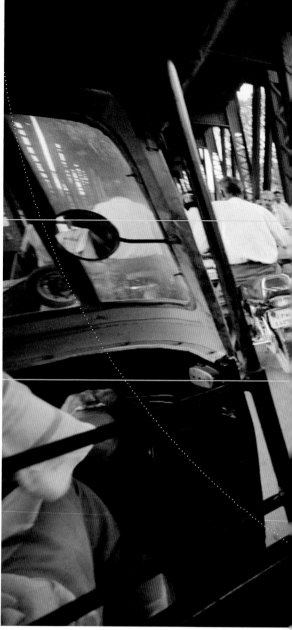

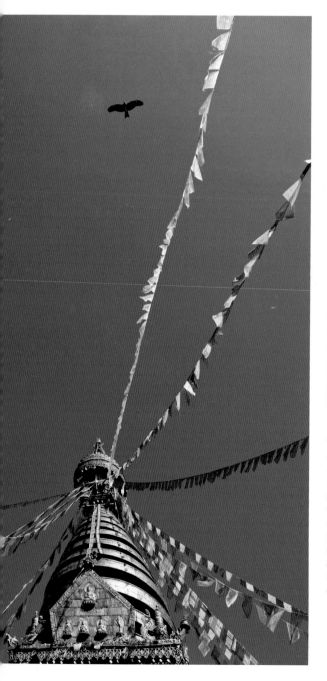

◀ Tall crop

The opposite of a letterbox composition (*right*) is a tall and narrow crop, which emphasizes an upward sweeping panorama—a view that can be taken in only by lifting the head and looking up. As with all crops based on a high aspect ratio, it usefully removes a lot of unwanted detail around the edges.

▶ Letterbox composition

A wide and narrow letterbox framing suits some subjects, such as these prayer flags in Bhutan, perfectly. Such a crop concentrates the attention on the sweep of colors and detail, cutting out unwanted—and visually irrelevant—material at the top and bottom of the image.

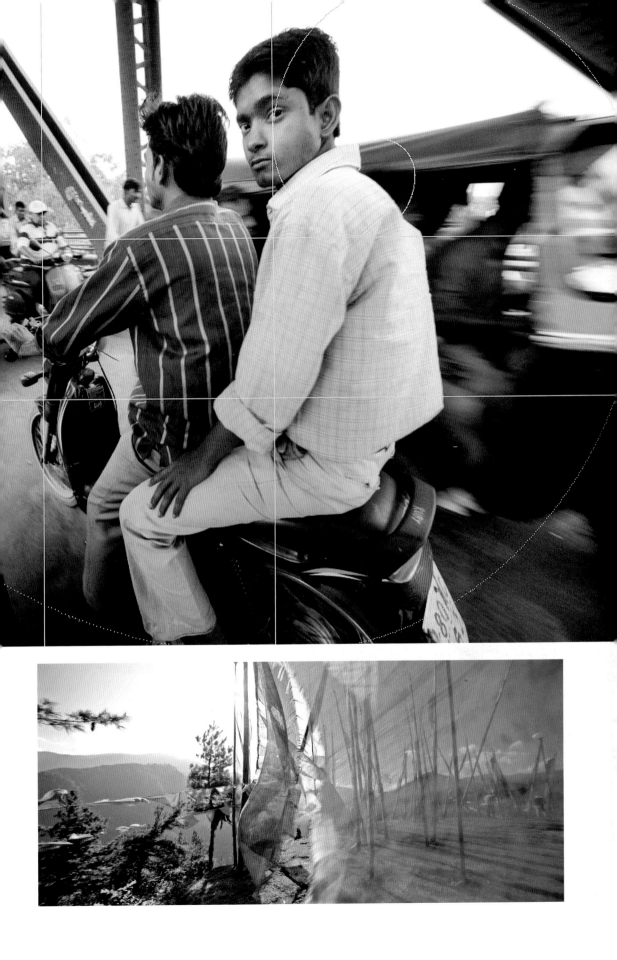

PICTURE COMPOSITION CONTINUED

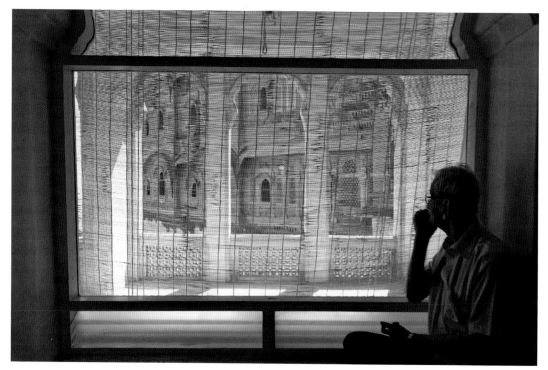

▲ Framing

The frame within a frame is a painterly device often exploited in photography. Not only does it concentrate the viewer's attention on the subject, but it also often hints at the wider context of the subject's setting. Through overlap, the frame also describes the space receding into the distance as here, in Jodhpur, India.

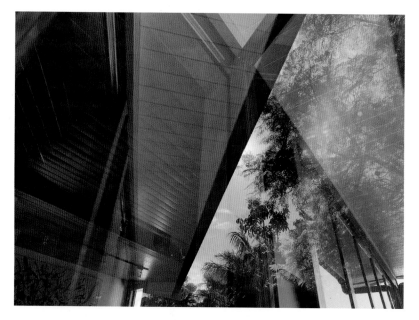

◄ Geometric patterns

Geometrical shapes, such as triangles and rectangles, lend themselves to photographic composition because of the way they interact with the rectangle of the picture frame. Here, in a 19th-century villa in Auckland, New Zealand, shapes from narrow strips to sharply acute triangles are all at work to make this an eye-catching composition. Colour contrasts between the warm reds of the wood and sky also contribute.

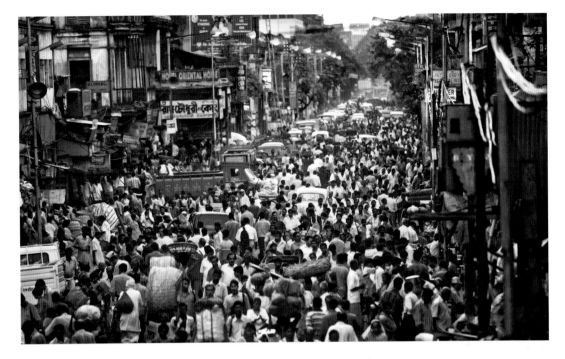

▲ Massed pattern

Even the massive crowds in this street in Kolkata, India, are organized. The receding parallel of the road, the glint in power lines, and the differences in scale of people can all be used to make sense of what initially appears to be chaos.

▼ Rhythmic elements

The ghostly silhouettes of trees in Palaia, near Pisa in Italy, organize the space into an irregular but discernible rhythm of lights and darks, with the more or less regular negative spaces between the trunks. Seen together, they create an ambivalent mood—mysterious, yet calm.

TRY THIS

Look out for patterns whenever you have a camera to hand. When you find an interesting example, take several shots, shifting your position slightly for each. Examine the pictures carefully and you may find that the shot you thought most promising does not give the best result. Often, this is because our response to a scene is an entire experience, while photographs have to work within the proportions of the format.

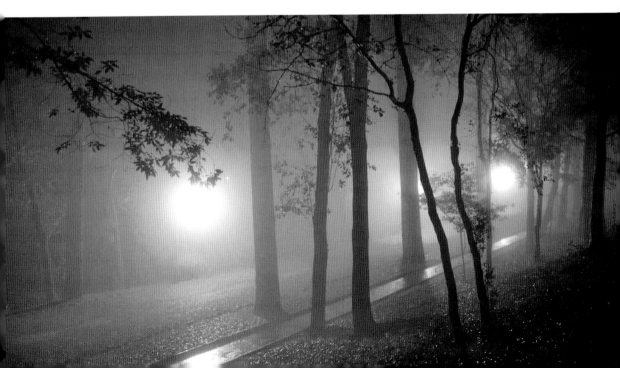

PICTURE COMPOSITION CONTINUED

This view of the Taj Mahal, in Agra, India, was made with an ultra-wide-angle lens to place the monument in the context of the surrounding river and open spaces. The hero is the mood, the late evening calm, not the monument itself. While it is visually a simple image, there were tough technical demands. Lighting across the image must be even, and the subtle changes of tone captured in a way to preserve smooth transitions. The bright spot of light should not be allowed to cause ghosting or flare.

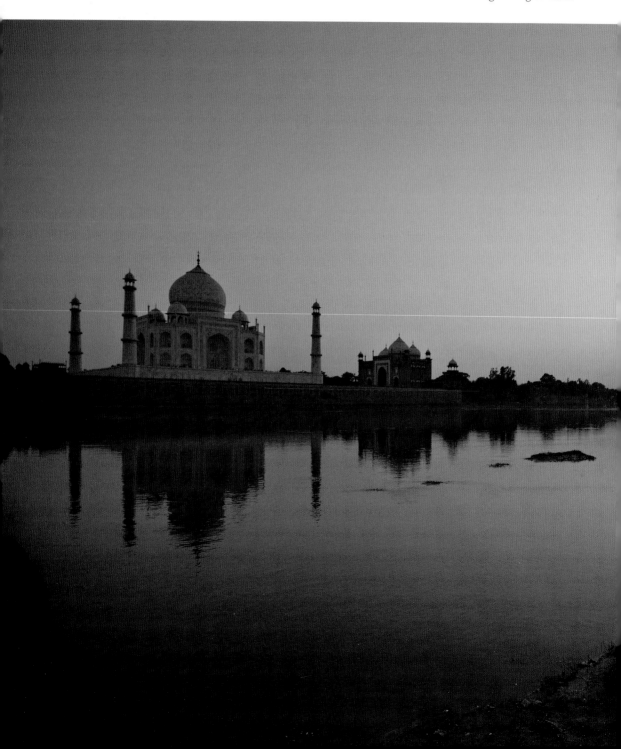

TECHNICAL INFO

CAMERA
Canon EOS-1Ds Mark II

LENS
Sigma 12–24 mm at 12 mm

SETTINGS
ISO 100 • f/8 • ¹⁄₈₀ sec

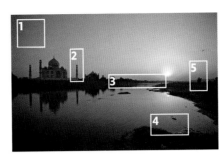

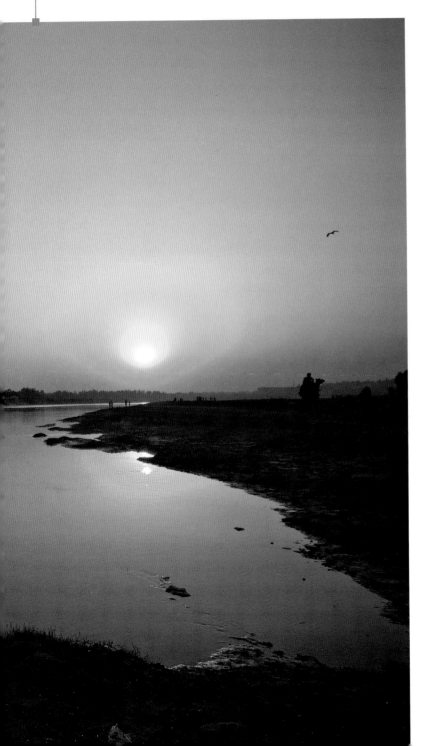

1 **Light fall-off**
The natural light falloff darkens the corners, providing a soft frame to the composition.

2 **Vertical uprights**
The towers are used as important punctuation points. They work best when perfectly vertical, not converging. To achieve this effect, the camera must be aimed directly at the horizon.

3 **Receding lines**
The uneven but steadily converging lines on the horizon and river lead to the setting sun and give the viewer a sense of increasing distance.

4 **Foreground movement**
Some activity, such as a hint of reflection in wet mud, animates the lower part of the image. If this corner were devoid of movement, the image would feel incomplete.

5 **Edge activity**
A camel waits to offer tourists a clichéd photo opportunity. Keeping the animal very small in the image helps set the scene and scale without creating a predictable, posed picture. Projection effects of the ultra-wide angle render the camel wider than is natural, which is helpful here, since it appears larger in the final image.

FOCUSING AND DEPTH OF FIELD

Depth of field is the space in front of and behind the plane of best focus, within which objects appear acceptably sharp (*see opposite*). Though accurate, this definition tells you nothing about the power that depth of field has in helping you communicate your visual ideas. You can, for example, vary depth of field to imply space, to suggest being inside the action, or to emphasize the separation between elements within the picture area.

Varying depth of field

Your chief control over depth of field is the lens aperture: as you set smaller apertures (using f/11 instead of f/4, for example), depth of field increases. This increase is greater the shorter the lens's focal length, so that the depth of field at f/11 on a 28 mm lens is greater than it would be at f/11 on a 300 mm lens at the same working distance. Depth of field also increases as the subject being focused on moves farther away from the camera. Meanwhile, at close focusing distances, depth of field is very limited.

Using depth of field

An extensive depth of field (resulting from using a small lens aperture, a wide-angle lens, distant focusing, or a combination of these factors) is often used for the following types of subject:

■ Landscapes, such as wide-angle, general views.
■ Architecture, in which the foregrounds to buildings are important features.
■ Interiors, including nearby furniture or other objects, and far windows and similar features.
As a by-product, smaller apertures tend to reduce lens flare and improve lens performance.

A shallow depth of field (resulting from a wide lens aperture, a long focal length lens, focusing close-up, or a combination of these) renders only a small portion of the image sharp, and is often used for:

■ Portraiture, to help concentrate viewer attention.
■ Reducing the distraction from elements that cannot be removed from the lens's field of view.
■ Isolating a subject from the distracting visual clutter of its surroundings.

LENS FOCUSING

Spreading light reflected from or emitted by every point of a subject radiates outward, and those rays captured by the camera lens are projected onto the focal plane to produce an upside-down image. The subject only appears sharp, however, if these rays of light intersect precisely on the sensor plane (achieved by adjusting the lens's focus control). If not, the rays are recorded not as points, but rather as blurred dots. If the image is reproduced at a small enough size, then even dots may appear as points, but as a subject's image diverges farther from the sensor plane, so the dots recorded by the camera become larger and larger, until, at a certain point, the image appears out of focus—the points have become large enough to be seen as blurred dots.

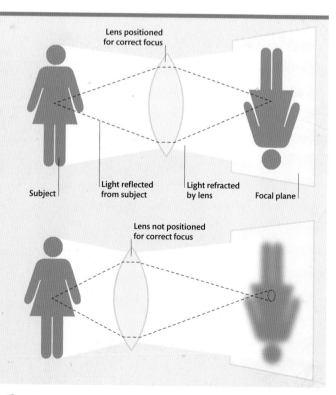

Lens positioned for correct focus

Subject | Light reflected from subject | Light refracted by lens | Focal plane

Lens not positioned for correct focus

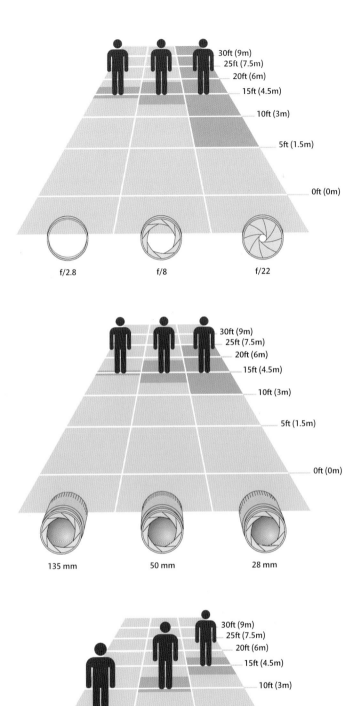

| f/2.8 | f/8 | f/22 |

◀ Effects of lens aperture

The main reason for changing lens aperture is to adjust camera exposure: a smaller aperture restricts the beam of light passing through the lens. However, the aperture also alters depth of field. As you set smaller apertures, the cone of light passing through the lens becomes slimmer and more needlelike. As a result, even when it is not perfectly focused, light from the subject is not as spread out as it would be if a larger aperture were used. Thus, more of the scene within the field of view appears sharp. In this illustration, lens focal length and focus distance remain the same, and depth of field at f/2.8 covers just the depth of a person, whereas at f/8 it increases to 6ft (2m) in extent. At f/22, depth of field extends from 5ft (1.5m) to infinity.

| 135 mm | 50 mm | 28 mm |

◀ Effects of lens focal length

Variations in depth of field resulting from focal length alone are due to image magnification. With our figure at a constant distance from the camera, a long focal length (135mm) will record him at a larger size than does a standard lens (50mm), which, in turn, creates a larger image than the wide-angle (28mm). To the eye, the figure is the same size, but on the sensor or film, the figure's size varies directly with focal length. Where details are rendered smaller in the image, it is more difficult to make out what is sharp and what is not. As a result, depth of field appears to increase. Conversely, longer focal length lenses magnify the image, so magnifying differences in focus. Thus, depth of field appears to be greatly reduced.

| 5ft (1.5m) | 5ft (1.5m) | 15ft (4.5m) |

◀ Effects of focus distance

Two effects contribute to the great reduction in depth of field as you focus more and more closely to the camera, even when there is no change in lens focal length or aperture. The main effect is due to the increased magnification of the image: as it looms larger in the viewfinder, so small differences in the depth of the subject call for the lens to be focused at varying distances from the sensor or film. Notice that you must turn a lens more when it is focused on close-up subjects than when it is focused on distant ones. Another slight but important reason for the change in depth of field is that effective focal length increases slightly when the lens is set farther from the focal plane—in other words, when it is focused on subjects close-up.

FOCUSING AND DEPTH OF FIELD CONTINUED

Autofocusing (AF)

Cameras are able to focus automatically on your photographic subject by using one of two systems. The active system, which uses a beam of infrared (IR), is now largely obsolete but was formerly much used in compact AF cameras. In the passive system, however, sensors analyze the image to determine whether it is in focus and, if not, how best to bring it into focus.

One passive method detects the contrast of fine detail in the image: unfocused images present as low-contrast, because they lack detail. The lens is then made to change focus so that contrast is at a peak, corresponding with a sharp image. This method requires good light levels to work well.

Another passive method samples a part of the image, then splits it into two beams. When these beams fall on certain reference points in the sensor (the beams are "in phase"), the lens is considered to be in focus. The crucial property of this method is that the phase differences vary, depending on whether the lens is focused in front of or behind the plane of best focus. This information enables the system to work very rapidly, even continuously.

For best results, note the following:

■ For off-center subjects, aim the focusing area at your subject, "hold" the focus with light pressure on the shutter or focus-lock button, then reframe.

■ Extremely bright objects in the focusing region—sparkling reflections on polished metal, for instance—could confuse the sensor and reduce accuracy.

■ Photographing beyond objects that are close to the lens—for example, through a bush or between the gaps in a fence—can confuse the autofocus system.

■ Restless subjects, such as children or flowers in a light breeze, may be best kept in focus by setting a distance manually and then adjusting your position backward and forward to maintain focus.

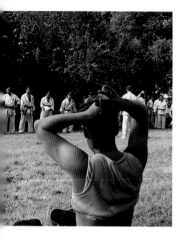

◀ Mimicking depth
While a narrow field of view usually yields a shallow depth of field, you can simulate a more generous zone of sharp focus linked with a narrow field of view by cropping a wide-angle image. Here, a 28mm view has been cropped to that of a 200mm lens, and the scene appears sharp from foreground to background.

▶ Selective focus
A telephoto shot (135 mm) taken with the lens aperture wide open (f/1.8) throws the model in the background well out of focus while the porcupine spines of her necklace are rendered pin sharp. Although almost nothing is sharp in this image, its power comes from the suggestiveness of the blurred image: it is perfectly clear what the subject is about.

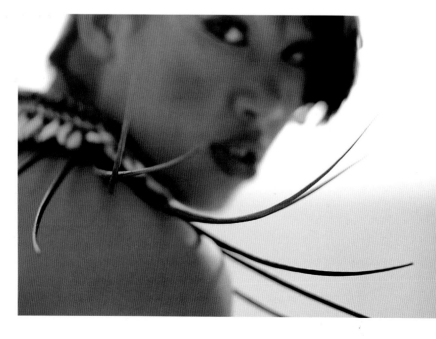

■ With very rapidly moving subjects, it may be better to focus on a set distance and then wait for the subject to reach that point before shooting.

Hyperfocal distance

The hyperfocal distance is the focus setting that provides maximum depth of field for any given aperture. It is the distance to the nearest point that appears sharp when the lens is set at infinity, and it is the nearest distance at which an object can be focused on while infinity appears sharp. The larger the aperture, the farther this point is away from you.

This is useful when the scene is changing so rapidly that you cannot keep focus on your subjects. With very rapid autofocus cameras, its utility is limited. It is better to focus on a subject than to hope depth of field will render it sharp enough.

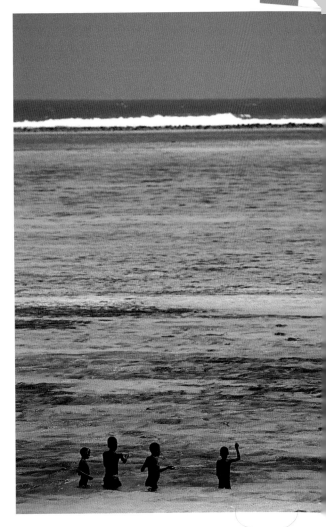

▶ Off-center subjects

With off-center subjects, as here, you may need to ensure your camera does not focus on the middle of the frame. Modern systems may recognize the main subject and focus accordingly. For this image, I focused on the boys, locked the setting, and recomposed the shot. Even in bright conditions and focusing at a distance, depth of field is limited because of the very long (400 mm) focal length.

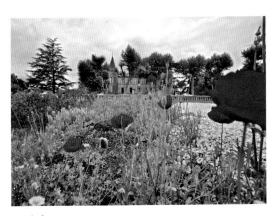

▲ Right aperture

Even an ultra wide-angle lens will offer insufficient depth of field when objects are close to the lens and very distant unless a small aperture is used. In this shot, the charm of the scene would have been lost had either the château or foreground flowers been unsharp. The smallest aperture on this lens was set to give maximum sharpness, but the long shutter time needed meant that a tripod was necessary.

PERCEIVED DEPTH OF FIELD

Acceptable sharpness varies according to how much blur a viewer is prepared accept. This, in turn, depends on how much detail a viewer can discern in the image, which, in turn, depends on the final size of the image (as seen on a screen or as a paper print). As a small print, an image may display great depth of field; however, as the image is progressively enlarged, it then becomes more and more obvious where the unsharpness begins, thereby making the depth of field appear increasingly more limited.

IMAGE ORIENTATION

Since most camera formats produce rectangular pictures, you can change the way you hold the camera to give either horizontal or vertical results. Image orientation produces different emphases and so can alter the whole dynamic of a shot.

Picture shape should normally be dictated by the natural arrangement of subject elements—in other words, by the subject's own orientation. In portraits, for example, the subject will usually be sitting or standing, and so the camera most often is turned on its side to give vertical framing. As a consequence, vertical picture orientation is often called "portrait." Landscape scenes, however, with their usually horizontal orientation, have given their name to horizontally framed pictures.

Landscape-shaped images tend to emphasize the relationship between subject elements on the left and right of the frame, while portrait-shaped pictures tend to relate foreground and background subject elements. And bear in mind that picture shape strongly influences what is included at the periphery of a scene, so you can use image orientation as a useful cropping device.

Breaking the "rules"

If you decide to move away from these accepted framing conventions, or "rules," you then have an opportunity to express more of an individual vision.

Simply by turning the camera on its side you could create a more striking picture—perhaps by increasing the sense of energy and movement inherent in the scene, for example. Using an unconventional picture orientation may, therefore, reveal to the viewer that you are engaging more directly with the subject, rather than merely reacting to it.

Think ahead

Another factor to consider is that since most printed publications are vertical in format, pictures are more likely to be used full-size if they are vertically framed. As a safeguard, commercial photographers often take vertically framed versions of important views or events, even if an image's natural orientation is horizontal.

A potential problem with vertical framing occurs when using cameras with swiveling LCD screens. Even if the camera has a viewfinder, if you attach any type of lens accessory you then have to use the LCD screen exclusively for viewing and framing.

If, however, your images are intended for publication on the web, you need to bear in mind that the monitor's format is more horizontal in shape, and so appropriately framed images will then be easier to use at full-size.

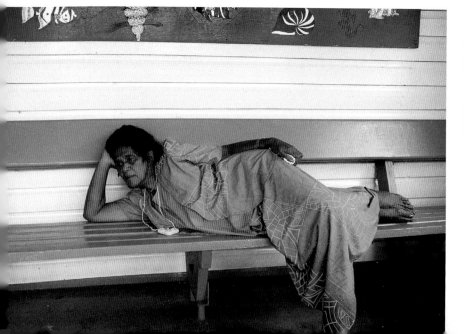

◄ Reclining figure
The strong horizontal lines of both the bench and the metal cladding on the wall behind, as well as the elegant, reclining pose of this Fijian woman, all suggest that horizontal framing is appropriate here.

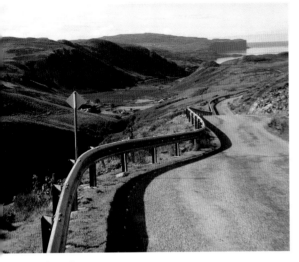

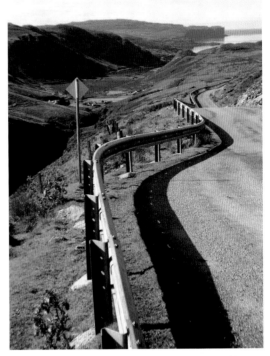

▲ Landscape scenery

A horizontal, or "landscape," view (*above*) is often an obvious choice for a landscape subject. However, vertical, or "portrait," framing (*right*) can effectively suggest space, especially when some natural feature in the scene—the snaking crash barrier in this example—leads the eye right from the foreground through to the background.

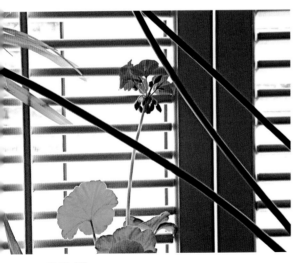

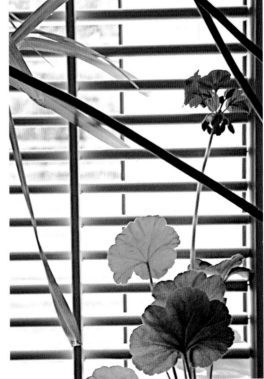

▲ Still-life

Different sets of lines that may be contained within a picture can be given additional prominence, depending on the framing you decide to adopt. Horizontal orientation (*above*) allows the strong, diagonally slanting plant stems to make a visual statement, while the vertical image orientation (*right*) makes more of the parallel slats of the blind.

IMAGE PROPORTIONS

As you take more pictures you may start to notice that the proportions of an image have a subtle effect on the picture's ability to communicate. A square image, for example, more often than not evokes a sense of stability and balance. However, an image that is just slightly rectangular can communicate a sense of indecision or make subject matter look uncomfortable within its frame. This type of framing is, therefore, best avoided unless you have clear reasons for it.

Panoramas

The "panoramic" picture was popularized most recently by the obsolescent APS (Advanced Photo System) cameras launched in 1996. In reality, this system simply cropped the top and bottom off an ordinary image, changing it into a narrow one, and so it is not a true panoramic image.

Digital cameras, however, can produce true panoramas (in which the camera swings through the scene, from side to side or up and down), so

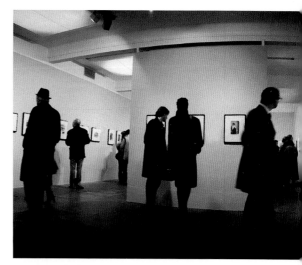

▲ **True panorama**
A true panoramic camera uses a swinging lens to project its image onto a curved piece of film. The movement of the lens causes the typical curvature of lines away from the middle of the frame, as you can see in this example taken at an exhibition in a picture gallery.

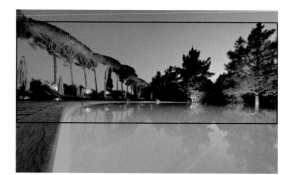

◀ **Letterbox crop**
The points of interest in many images center on the horizon, but there is sometimes a problem of too much empty sky or distracting foreground. A crop that drastically reduces sky and foreground is excellent for land- or cityscapes as it simplifies compositional problems.

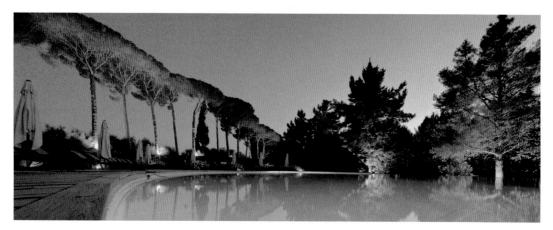

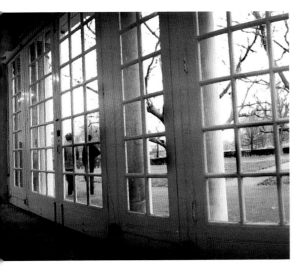

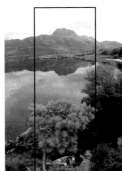

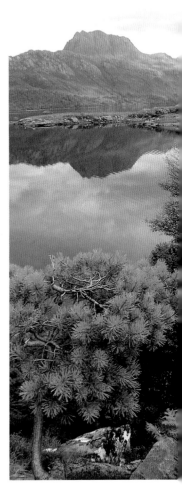

▲ Vertical cropping

An attractively framed, if conventional, shot of a lake in Scotland (*above*) has been transformed into a sharper, more challenging composition (*right*) simply by cropping it into a narrower, more vertical shape, in imitation of a traditional silk wall hanging.

that the field of view of the image is greater than the field of view of the lens. This is achieved by taking a number of pictures that overlap and "sewing" them together (*see pp. 298–9*).

To achieve best results, pivot the camera around a fixed point, such as a tripod, so that as you rotate the camera the image does not appear to move. To aid you, some digital cameras have a "panorama function," which indicates where the next pictures should be taken by showing you on the LCD screen the previous image as a guide.

Taking time to select the right view to experiment with really pays dividends with panoramic images. For example, you need to be aware that panoramas made up of individual pictures that include subjects positioned close to the camera, or even in the near middle-distance, will show a perspective distortion that makes the scene appear bow-shaped once images are combined.

Exposure is another consideration when taking panoramas. If you swing your camera across a scene, you will see that the exposure settings in the viewfinder read-out alter as different areas of light and shade influence the changing picture area. If you were to take your panorama like this, you may find that, say, the foreground area fluctuates between dark and light from frame to frame. To prevent this occurring, take the camera off automatic and set the exposure manually.

CROPPING

One of the simplest, and often one of the most effective, changes you can make to image proportions is to crop them—in other words, slicing portions from the sides, top, or bottom of the picture area. This can change the whole emphasis of a shot by, for example, removing unnecessary or unwanted subject matter or by changing the relationship between various subject elements and the borders of the frame. This can turn a mediocre picture into a truly arresting image.

COMPOSITION AND ZOOMS

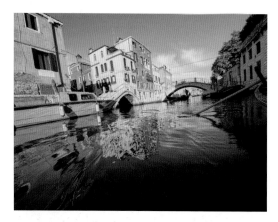

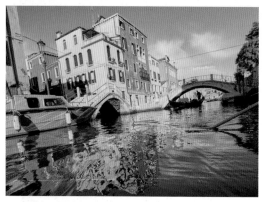

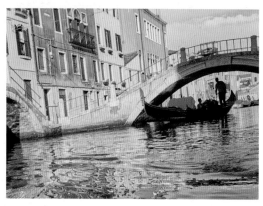

▲ Zooms for framing
Zoom lenses come into their own when you are stuck in position, as on a boat in the canals of Venice, Italy. They are also handy when it is difficult or too time-consuming to change lenses, since they allow you to introduce variety into what would otherwise be similarly framed images. Remember to keep the autofocus on or to re-focus after zooming for sharp results.

Zoom lenses are optics whose focal length you can alter while keeping the image in focus, resulting in a change in the lens's field of view. Expressed another way, zoom lenses allow you to change the magnification of an image without having to swap lenses (*see pp. 342–5*). When the field of view is widened (to take in more of the subject), the image must be reduced in order to fill the sensor area. This is the result of setting a short focal-length lens or a wide angle on a zoom. Conversely, when the field of view is narrowed (to take in less of the subject), the image must be magnified, again in order to fill the sensor area. This is the result of using a long focal-length lens setting on the zoom, often called its telephoto setting.

Working with zooms

The most efficient way to use a zoom is to set it to the focal length you feel will produce the sort of effect you are aiming for, then frame up the composition. This method of working encourages you to think about the scene before even raising the camera to your eye to compose the shot. It also offers smoother technique than zooming in and out of a scene searching for a setting that works. This is because a zoom always changes the angle of view around the central axis, but your subject may be off axis, which means you have to re-compose the image with every change of zoom setting.

Professional methods

Many professional photographers use zooms as if they were multiple fixed-focal-length lenses, often setting only the widest end or the longest end, and occasionally the middle setting. They then use the zoom control only to make fine adjustments to the framing if needed.

This is the fastest way to use these optics, simply to take in more of the scene or to turn your attention to a smaller part. Zooms operate at their slowest when used to find and finesse the composition. This is because the best way to finalize a composition is to make small adjustments in the perspective—that is, by moving around—rather than by turning the zoom from a fixed position.

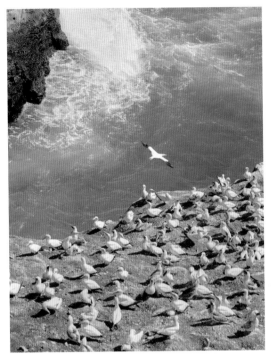

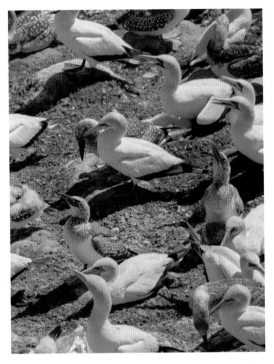

▲ Zooms for composition

Zooming from one position has the effect of cropping into the view. Note that zooming alone does not change the perspective unless there is also a change in position. Nonetheless, as here, at the Muriwai Gannet Colony, New Zealand, images at varying zoom settings can feel markedly different. The 80 mm view (*above left*) is spacious and brings the nesting birds into context with the sea. But the 400 mm view (*above*) is more than merely a small part of the 80 mm view; rather, it takes us into the colony and gives an idea of its crowded conditions.

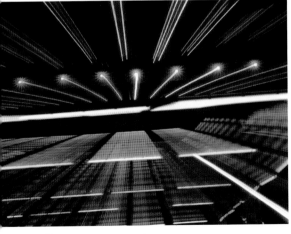

▲ Zoom movement

Colors explode out from this photograph of a store display—an effect achieved by turning the zoom ring to increase the lens's focal length during a relatively long exposure, causing lights to smear across the sensor. The slow start to the zoom gives the brighter end of the light trail.

POINTS TO CONSIDER

- **Distortion:** Most zoom lenses distort the image by making straight lines look curved. This is especially the case at wide-angle settings.
- **Camera shake:** At the very long effective focal lengths some digital cameras offer—such as a 35 mm equivalent of 350 mm—there is a great danger that camera shake during exposure will reduce image quality. Make sure you hold the camera steady, preferably supported or braced, and use a short shutter time.
- **Lens speed:** As you set longer focal lengths, the widest available aperture becomes smaller. Even in bright conditions, it may then not be possible to set short shutter times with long focal lengths.
- **Lens movement:** Some lenses may take a few seconds to zoom to their maximum or to retract to their minimum settings. Don't be tempted to rush the action by pushing or pulling at the lens.

MOVEMENT BLUR

The generally accepted advice is that you should hold the camera steady when capturing pictures. Any movement during exposure causes the image to move across the sensor. If that movement is visible, it is seen as a blur, which causes the image to look unsharp at best and, at worse, quite unrecognizable. Nonetheless, there is certainly a place for pictures that display a thoughtful or expressive use of subject blur.

Try it and see

The effects of exposure during movement are unique, and no other recording medium represents the blur of movement in quite the same way as a camera. However, since what you capture in the image will vary with the level of movement of the subject and with distance, its effects are hard to predict. Experiment freely with different settings and evaluate results on a computer monitor, rather than the camera's review panel.

With experimentation and experience, you will find that brighter areas quickly become too bright when overlapped. At the same time, dark areas tend to be reduced by overlapping with lighter areas. The net result is a tendency to overexpose. You can exploit this to create high-key images or set exposure overrides to force tones to be darker, which helps to maintain intense colors (*see pp. 70–1 and 72–3*). The tendency to overexpose also means that results are best in dull light with a limited number of light-sources.

Contrasting blur

The appearance of blur is usually enhanced when it is seen in contrast against sharply defined forms or shapes. By the same token, sharpness appears

▼ **Moving camera**
The blur produced by taking a photograph from a speeding car streaks and blends the rich evening light in a very evocative and painterly fashion in this example. To the eye at the time of taking, the scene was much darker and less colorful than you can see here. It is always worth taking a chance in photography, as you never know what might come of it.

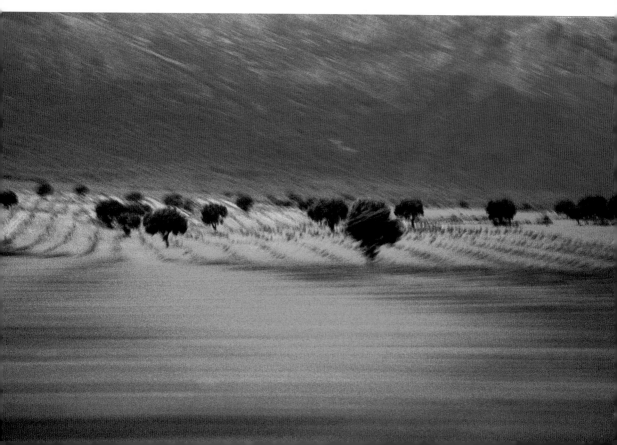

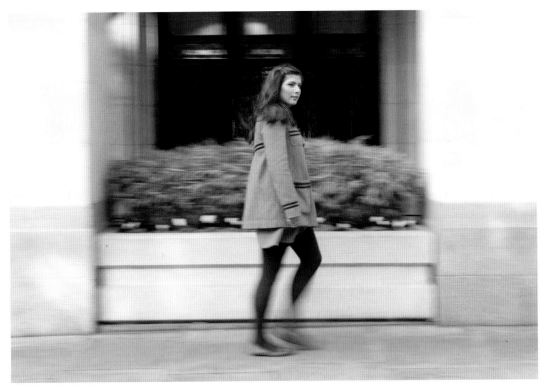

▲ Pan handling

Following the movement of a subject during exposure—panning—exploits the fact that different speeds of movement produce different levels of blur. Parts of the image that are relatively stationary in the image—such as the girl's face—appear sharper than elements that move more rapidly, such as her legs or the background.

greater where it contrasts with blur, so it is worth arranging for some part of the scene to remain sharp. This may call for the use of a tripod. Start with exposure times not longer than ⅛ sec with a normal lens. Very long exposures cause so much blur that it becomes difficult to identify the subject. They are also a lot more difficult to control.

Quality blur

It may seem unnecessary to bother with focus since you are working with blur, but you will find that it is worth focusing as carefully as you would if you were aiming for a sharp image. By doing this you produce a solid "core" to the image, against which the viewer can more readily appreciate the blur.

For similar reasons, it is just as important to maintain image quality as ever. Movement blur produces smooth or milky tones, so any break-up of the image either from resolution that is too low for the output size (see pp. 180–1), or noise caused by high sensitivity (high ISO) settings can detract from the overall effect.

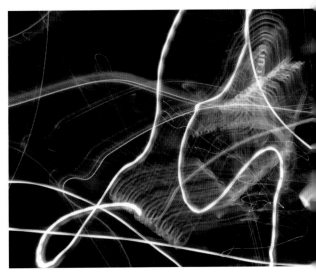

▲ Tossing the camera

This is a technique that can be huge fun and totally unpredictable: set shutter priority with an exposure time of 1 or more seconds. Hold on to the camera strap, press the shutter button, then toss the camera into the air with a spinning action (ensuring that the camera does not hit the ground). For the best results, try this at night with street lights or neon signs.

Funky zoom
Three movements combined in a single shot produced this result entirely in camera. There was movement up an escalator at the Atomium, Brussels. The camera was rotated around the lens while I held the zoom ring, which also caused a zoom (*see also p. 33*). A long exposure of 2 seconds was needed to allow time for all the effects to come together.

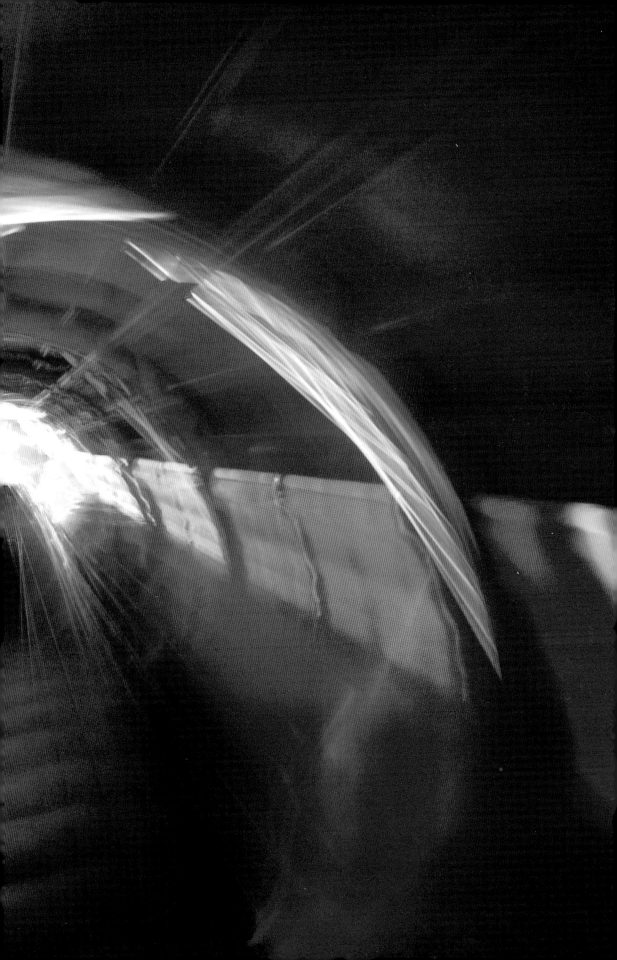

CLOSE-UPS

Close-up photography is the act of making images of subjects that are within touching distance. In the past, this unique category of picture-taking required special equipment, but these days most compact cameras and camera phones readily focus to within 6 in (15 cm) and closer.

There are two ways to get close to your subject: either you approach physically, or you increase the focal length of your lens—that is, you approach optically. Both increase the size, or magnification, of your main subject and, at the same time, cut out the background. Physically moving changes your perspective on the subject, while approaching optically zooms toward the subject.

As you move closer, you can see more details in your subject—the furry surface of a flower, the dots on a spider's back—but at the same time, you can see less: the depth of field reduces dramatically. You may either exploit this and produce images with considerable blur in the background (see the dragonfly opposite) or use the smallest possible aperture to increase the depth of field. To help you obtain sharp images, you may also need to increase the ISO setting to allow brief exposure times, or use flash to provide the lighting.

When you need to keep a distance between yourself and your subject, set the longest focal length on your zoom lens before focusing close-up. You can improve the close-up range by attaching supplementary close-up lenses. For serious work, use extension tubes that fit between the lens and camera to allow higher magnifications.

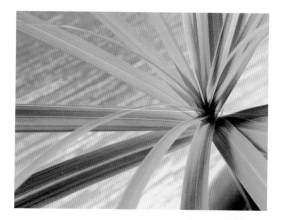

◄ Simple subjects
Learning just what to include and what to leave out of a picture is a useful skill to master—not only is the image itself usually stronger for being simpler in visual content, as in the example shown here, but it is also often easier to use it for a range of purposes, such as compositing (*see pp. 276–83*). Subject movement is always a problem with close-ups, especially plants outdoors where they can be affected by even the slightest breeze. If you cannot effectively shield the plant from air currents, then set the shortest exposure time possible, consistent with exposing the image accurately, to freeze any subject movement.

► Avoiding highlights
One of the secrets underlying good close-up photography is avoiding unwanted highlights. These usually appear as insignificant, out-of-focus bright spots when you frame the shot, but in the final image they can appear more prominent and distracting. For this shot, I moved around the subject, keeping my eye on the screen, and released the shutter only when the brightest area was positioned just as I wanted.

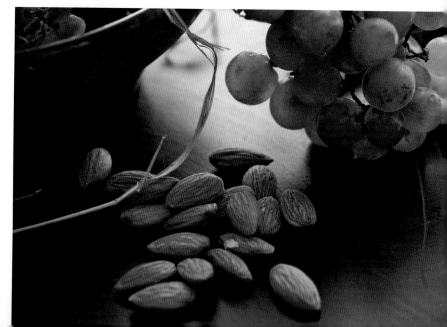

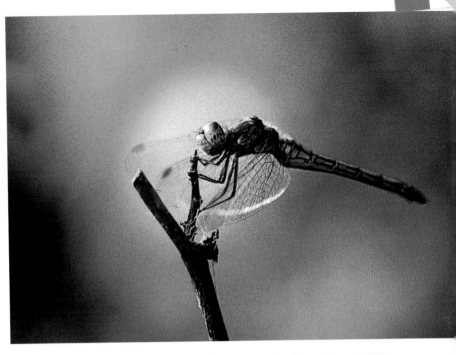

▶ Long close-up

A long focal-length lens with close-focusing ability allows you to get close to small, easily disturbed subjects such as this dragonfly, and so obtain a useful image size. In addition, the extremely shallow depth of field with such a lens throws even nearby image elements well out of focus. The central bright spot is, in fact, a flower.

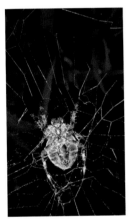

◀ Normal close-up

With static or slow-moving subjects, a normal focal-length lens used at its macro setting will suffice.

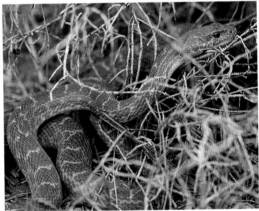

▶ Safe distance

It was dangerous to get too close to this constrictor, so a close-focusing, long lens was the best way to obtain good magnification.

TIPS CLOSE-UP

The combination of shallow depth of field at close distances with the need for high magnifications offers many technical challenges. Here are some ideas to help you:

- Set focusing to manual. This is often faster and more accurate than auto-focus: when it misses its mark, it may focus all the way to infinity and back again in search of the subject.

- Once focus is found, it may be easier to keep the subject in focus by moving backward and forward with it, instead of follow focusing.

- Set very small apertures to maximize depth of field:

f/11 or f/16 are good, but avoid the smallest, such as f/22 or f/32, as image quality will be reduced.

- If you are not using flash, set the highest ISO available: it is usually preferable to have a sharp but noisy image than a blurred noise-free image.

- Image stabilization systems are a big help in ensuring sharp images, assuming the subject does not move during exposure.

- The best way to prevent blur from movement is to use electronic flash: at short distances this is immensely powerful, and the very brief exposures freeze all but the fastest movements.

EXTREME LENSES

Lenses with special capabilities—such as the ability to take ultra wide-angle views or greatly magnify distant subjects—call for extra care in their use, since they make special demands on photo technique.

Ultra-wide angles

Wide-angle lenses with a 35 mm equivalent focal length of down to around 28 mm are easy to use, but when focal lengths become shorter than 21 mm, successful results are less certain because they exaggerate perspectives, making close objects appear much larger compared to distant ones.

■ Avoid having very recognizable shapes—a face or a vase—near the edges of the frame. It will appear distorted to one side when the image is viewed at a small size (*see below*).

■ To ensure the image is evenly lit (all wide-angle lenses project significantly more light onto the center of the image than the edges), try to use smaller apertures with evenly lit subjects, such as landscapes with open skies.

■ To keep accessories such as filters from intruding into the lens's field of view, do not use more than one filter at a time. Also, make sure scallop-shaped lens-hoods are fitted correctly.

■ Ultra wide-angle lenses can catch a bright source of light, such as the sun, within the picture area,

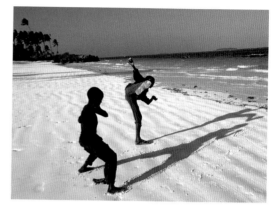

▲ Problem horizons

In the hurry to record this scene on a beach on Zanzibar, the slight tilt of the camera, which went unnoticed while using the 17mm setting on the lens, has produced an uncomfortable looking horizon. Though far from a disaster, the picture would have benefited from a moment's extra thought before shooting.

causing flares or strong reflections within the lens barrel. You can minimize the likelihood of flare by setting smaller apertures.

■ The extensive depth of field of ultra wide-angle lenses causes dust and drops of water on the lens to show up easily—so keep the lens very clean.

■ Line up wide-angle lenses very carefully with the horizon or some other prominent feature, since the

▶ Wide-angle "distortion"

An ultra wide-angle lens encompassed both the stall holder and her produce, but not only does she appear very distorted by being projected to the corner of the frame, so, too, are the tomatoes in the bottom right-hand corner. If, however, you were to make a large print of this image and view it from close up, the apparent distortion disappears.

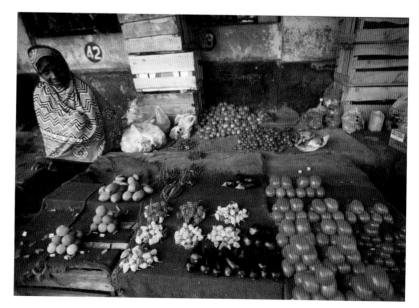

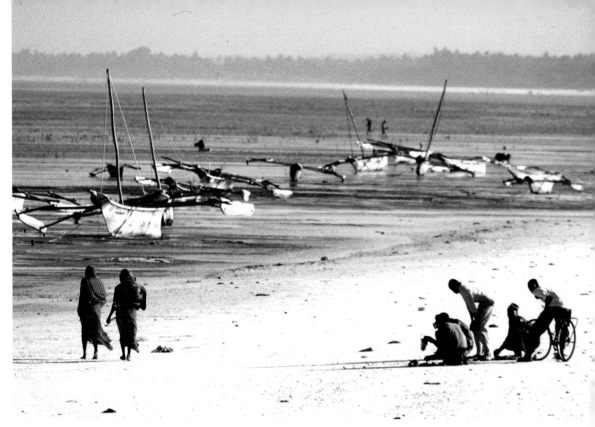

▲ Long telephoto

In this version of the scene shown on the right, the zoom lens was set to 400mm and a 1.4x extender was also used, giving an effective focal length setting of 560mm.

broad sweep of view will exaggerate the slightest error in picture alignment.

■ Do not use the minimum aperture: you rarely need the depth of field produced, and image quality is likely to be degraded. However, selecting a small aperture may improve image quality when focusing on very close subjects.

Wide-ranging zooms

Zooms that offer a wide range of focal length settings, such as 28–300 mm or 24–720mm, are attractive in theory, but in practice may require special handling.

■ The wide-angle setting is likely to show a lot of light fall-off, with the corners of the image being recorded darker than the middle, so steer clear of images that require even lighting to be effective.

■ At the longer focal lengths, give the camera time to achieve focus and hold the camera as steadily as possible to record sharp images.

■ Image distortion is always the price you pay for a wide range of focal lengths, so avoid photographing buildings and items with clearly defined sides

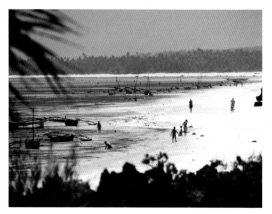

▲ Short telephoto

This view shows a beach scene on Zanzibar as imaged by a moderate 100mm telephoto setting. At this magnification, the lens shows the general scene but not any of the activity or recognizable subject details (*compare this with the top image*).

and straight lines. There will be a setting, usually around the middle of the range, where distortion is minimized; but even here, straight lines may appear very slightly wavy.

■ As you set longer and longer focal lengths on a zoom lens, the maximum available aperture may become smaller and smaller. To obtain the best results, use the longer focal lengths only in brightly lit conditions.

QUICK FIX OPTICAL PROBLEMS

Distortion occurs when straight lines in the subject are rendered curved in the photograph. In general photography, distortion is not problem if it is not obvious at first glance. However, images of architecture, documents, and natural features such as the horizon often need to be free of distortion.

Problem: When using a zoom or wide-angle lens, or an accessory lens for increasing the field of view, the straight lines in the image of any subject elements—such as the sides of buildings, the horizon, or room interiors—appear to be bowed or curved. This distortion is not the same as converging verticals (*see p. 208*) or the squashing effect of extreme wide-angle lenses on objects placed near the edge of the frame; these are both artifacts due to the way the image is projected.

Analysis: Distortion is caused by slight changes in magnification of the image across the picture frame. Asymmetrically constructed lenses –that is, where the elements on either side of the aperture are not similar—are prone to this type of imaging distortion. The majority of wide-angle and zoom lenses are highly asymmetric in construction.

Solution: The best solution is to use lens profiles specifically designed for your lens in image-manipulation software such as DxO Optics or Capture One. These make automatic corrections based on actual lens settings—for example, the zoom setting and camera in which it is used. If you do not have these tools, use a lens-correction filter in your image-manipulation software; this will include a geometric distortion control. Failing that, try using distortion filters to reverse the effect—for example, applying a Spherize distortion to counteract the lens distortion.

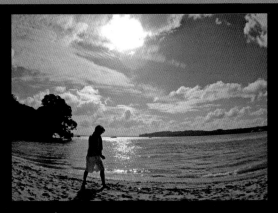

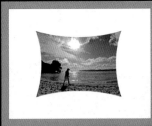

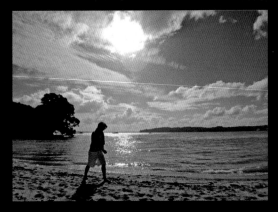

▲ **Barrel distortion**
In the original shot (*top*), a wide-angle attachment led to barrel distortion. This is easily corrected with a geometrical distortion control in a lens-correction filter. Failing that, use a Spherize filter with the image on a large canvas (*middle*) to squeeze it from all sides to fix the barrel shape (*above*).

HOW TO AVOID THE PROBLEM

- Avoid placing straight lines, such as the horizon or a junction of two walls, near the frame edges.
- Avoid using extreme focal lengths—either the ultra-wide or the ultra-long end—of a zoom range.
- Choose a focal length setting that offers the least distortion, usually around the middle of the range.
- Place important straight lines in the middle of the image—this is where distortion is usually minimal.

Although many optical problems can be solved, or at least minimized, using appropriate software, prevention is always better than cure.

Problem: The image looks unsharp, blurred, or smudged. Contrast is not high and the highlights are smeared.

Analysis: A dirty lens or lens filter, lack of sharp focus, damaged optics, camera shake, or subject movement may separately, or in combination, be the cause of blurred pictures.

Solution: You can increase contrast to improve image appearance using the Levels or Curves controls of image-manipulation software. Applying a Sharpen or Unsharp Mask filter is also likely to improve the image. The main subject can be made to appear adequately sharp if the background is made to look more blurred. To do this, select areas around the main subject and apply a Blur filter.

▶ Specks on lens

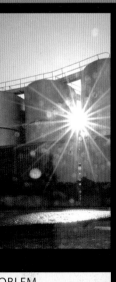

Drops of water on the lens have caused light to be refracted in the water, causing unwanted spots of light in the image. These can be removed by repairing or cloning, but it is better to keep the lens clean in the first place. Note that these spots are not caused by flare (*below*).

HOW TO AVOID THE PROBLEM

Clean the lens or lens filter if it is marked; use a tripod to steady the camera for long shutter times or when using a telephoto lens or setting; if available, use an image-stabilization lens.

Problem: Bright spots of light—variously colored, fringed, blurred, or sharp—can be seen in the image. Spots can be single occurrences or appear in a row, and stretch away from a bright point source of light in the scene. Similarly, a bright, fuzzily edged patch of light, known as veiling flare, fills part of the image area.

Analysis: These types of fault are most likely the result of internal light reflections within the lens. Stray light entering the lens from a bright light source has reflected around the lens and then been picked up by the sensor.

Solution: Working with a digital file, small spots of light can easily be removed by cloning or rubber-stamping adjacent unaffected areas of the image onto them. Large areas of flare—such as in the example shown—are more difficult to correct, since they cover a significant area of the picture and contain no information to work with.

▶ Flare

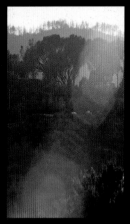

An unobstructed sun in the frame causes light to reflect within the lens, resulting in flare. By changing camera position, it was possible to mask the sun with a column of the building, while allowing a little flare through to suggest the brilliance of the light. Some of the reflections may be removed, but probably not all of them.

HOW TO AVOID THE PROBLEM

Use a correctly designed lens hood to reduce the amount of light entering the periphery of the lens; and avoid pointing the lens directly toward bright light sources. If the shot demands that you include an intense light source in the image, set a small lens aperture to reduce the size of any internal reflections.

QUICK FIX OPTICAL PROBLEMS CONTINUED

Even if you compose your shot and capture a scene beautifully, you may need to address subtle technical image issues.

Problem: Images viewed at high magnification are marred by colored fringes on sharply defined lines, such as branches against skies, most obviously where objects are near the image periphery. This reduces the sharpness of the image.

Analysis: The colored fringes may be caused by lens aberrations that focus light of different colors to different points. This results in, for example, the red image being slightly larger than the blue, causing fringes to be visible. Defects may also result from errors in digital color interpolation at high-contrast edges. Or both defects may occur at the same time.

Solution: The defects can be reduced by equalizing the size of the different-colored images. This is most easily done by applying specific lens profiles in software such as DxO Optics or Capture One. Manual adjustments may be needed to remove the defects entirely. You can repair the defect with standard image-manipulation software using the lens-correction modules: view your image at high magnification, then manipulate the sliders until the defects disappear.

HOW TO AVOID THE PROBLEM

Set smaller apertures to reduce color-related aberrations. Use fixed-focal-length lenses that give the highest level of correction. Use professional-quality zoom lenses, which offer less aberration than less expensive lenses.

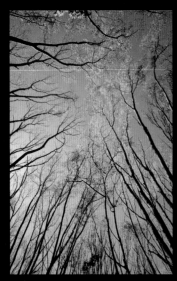

1 Original image
Looking up at the fresh shoots of spring against a clear blue sky, this image is acceptably sharp and detailed when seen at a small size. This is thanks in part to high-contrast elements within the composition, such as the branches and the sky.

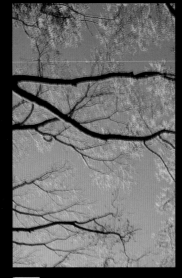

2 Magnified view
If a large print were to be made, however, the defects would become apparent: the branches are ringed on one side with magenta and blue, and on the other with green. The result is a reduction in detail and the breakup of detail in the leaves.

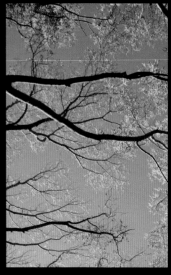

3 Aberration correction
By manipulating the red/cyan and green/magenta controls in a lens-correction module, much of the color fringing can be removed. This results in a much sharper image with clean details.

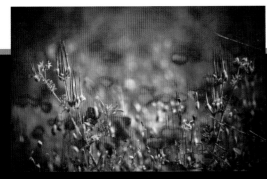

▲ Darkened corners

This image results from using a full aperture with a long zoom lens. Darkened corners can help frame the center of the image, exploiting a technical fault for its effect.

HOW TO AVOID THE PROBLEM

Vignetting is easy to avoid if you are careful with your filters and lens hoods. Use slimline filters with very wide-angle lenses. Do not fit another filter on top of the first. Use the correct lens hood, and ensure it is aligned correctly.

Problem: The middle portion of the image appears significantly brighter than the periphery. More seriously, corners of the image are clipped, with a blurred, darkened edge.

Analysis: Images with corners that are darker than the center are suffering from light falloff, where less light reaches the outer edges. This may also be caused by vignetting: the light is obstructed by something that shadows the light path. This could be caused by one or more screw-in filters whose rim is too deep for use with a wide-angle lens. It may also be caused by using an incorrectly fitted or aligned lens hood.

Solution: Light falloff can be corrected by using software tools. Corners made black with vignetting are best cropped off the image.

Problem: The quality of images taken at the closest focusing distances is disappointing; they are not sharp or lack contrast.

Analysis: Lenses usually perform best at medium or long distances: the degree of close-up correction depends on lens design.

Solution: Poor image sharpness may be improved by applying Sharpness or Unsharp Mask filters. Contrast will be improved with Levels or Curves. Try localized burning-in to improve contrast, which will also increase apparent sharpness without increasing visual noise.

HOW TO AVOID THE PROBLEM

Small apertures are likely to improve sharpness. Try using different focus and zoom settings—there will be a combination that gives the best possible quality. An alternative solution is to attach a close-up lens to the main lens. This acts as a magnifying glass and can improve close-up performance.

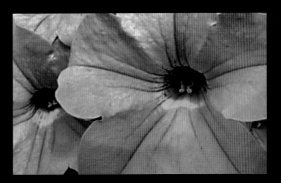

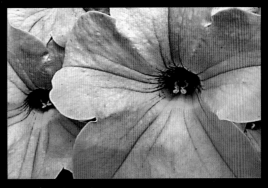

▲ Improving close-ups

The original image (*top*) shows the features characteristic of a low-quality close-up: poor sharpness and reduced contrast. Applying an Unsharp Mask filter and an increase in contrast significantly improves results (*above*).

INFLUENCING PERSPECTIVE

You can exercise control over the perspective of a photograph by changing your camera position. This is because perspective is the view that you have of the subject from wherever it is you decide to shoot. Perspective, however, is not affected by any changes in lens focal length—it may appear to be so but, in fact, all focal length does is determine how much of the view you record.

Professional photographers know perspective has a powerful effect on an image, yet it is one of the easiest things to control. This is why when you watch professionals at work, you often see them constantly moving around the subject—sometimes bending down to the ground or climbing onto the nearest perch; approaching very close and moving further away again. Taking a lead from this, your work could be transformed if you simply become more mobile, observing the world through the camera from a series of changing positions rather than a single, static viewpoint.

Bear in mind that with some subjects—still lifes, for example, and interiors or portraits—the tiny change in perspective between observing the subject with your own eyes and seeing it through the camera lens, which is just a little lower than your eyes, can make a difference to the composition. This difference in perspective is far more pronounced if you are using a studio camera or waist-level finder on a medium-format camera.

Using zooms effectively

One way to approach changes in perspective is to appreciate the effect that lens focal length has on your photography. A short focal length gives a

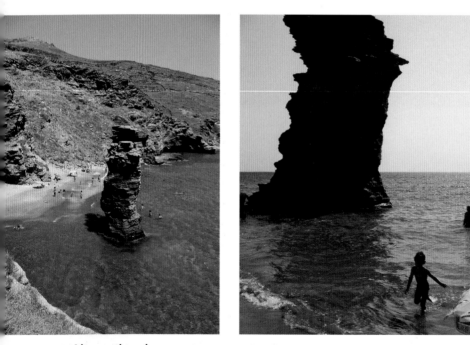

▲ Alternative views

This wide-angle view (*above left*), shows an unremarkable snapshot of a beach, in Andros, Greece. It is a simple image of the place, but it lacks an engaging interpretation or inventive viewpoint of the scene. Once on the beach, the temptation is to take in a wide shot that summarizes the whole scene. Instead, a low viewpoint that takes in the corner of a parasol gives a more intimate and involving feel: by using the parasol to balance the large rock, the picture is almost complete. Waiting for the right moment—a child running into the foreground—brings the whole perspective to life.

perspective that allows you to approach a subject closely yet record much of the background. If you step back a little, you can take in much more of the scene, but then the generous depth of field of a wide-angle tends to make links between separate subject elements, as there is little, if any, difference in sharpness between them.

A long lens allows a more distant perspective. You can look closely at a face without being nearby. Long lenses tend to pull together disparate objects—in an urban scene viewed from a distance, buildings that are several blocks apart might appear to crowd in on top of each other. However, the shallow depth of field of a long lens used at close subject distances tends to separate out objects that may actually be close together by showing some sharp and others blurred.

PERSPECTIVE EFFECTS

Wide-angle lenses

- Take in more background or foreground.
- Exaggerate the size of near subjects when used in close-up photography.
- Exaggerate any differences in distance or position between subjects.
- Give greater apparent depth of field and link the subject to its background.

Telephoto lenses

- Compress spatial separation.
- Magnify the main subject.
- Reduce depth of field to separate the subject from its background.

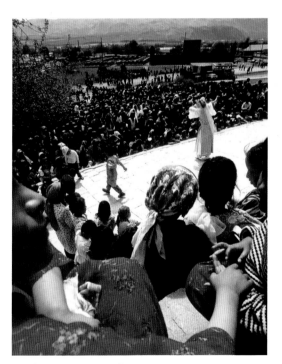

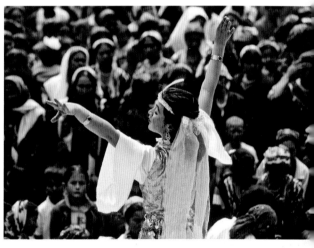

▲ Distant perspectives

Overlooking the action there is a sense of the crush of people at this festival in mountainous Tajikistan (*above*). Two children holding hands complete the scene. The long focal length version (*above right*) focuses attention on the dancer, but excludes all sense of setting beyond the crowd watching the traditional performance.

TRY THIS

For this exercise, leave your zoom lens at its shortest focal length setting. Look for pictures that work best with this focal length—ignore any others and don't be tempted to change the lens setting. This will help to sharpen your sense of what a wide-angle lens does. You may find yourself approaching subjects—including people—more closely than you would normally dare. The lens is making you get closer because you cannot use the zoom to make the move for you. Next, repeat the exercise with the lens at its longest focal length setting.

CHANGING VIEWPOINTS

Always be on the look-out for viewpoints that give a new slant to your work. Don't ignore the simple devices, such as shooting down at a building instead of up at it, or trying to see a street scene from a child's viewpoint rather than an adult's.

Your choice of viewpoint communicates subtle messages that say as much about you as they do your subject. Take a picture of someone from a distance, for example, and the image carries a sense that you, too, were distant from that person. If you photograph a scene of poverty from the viewpoint of a bystander, the picture will again have that distant look of having been taken by an aloof observer. Lively markets are popular photographic subjects, but what do they look like from a stallholder's position? If you enjoy sports, shoot from within the action, not from the sidelines.

Practical points

Higher viewpoints enable you to reduce the amount of foreground and increase the area of background recorded by a lens. From a high vantage point, a street or river scene lies at a less acute angle than when seen from street or water level. This reduces the amount of depth of field required to show the scene in sharp focus.

However, from a low camera position subjects may be glimpsed through a sea of grass or legs. And if you look upward from a low position, you see less background and more sky, making it easier to separate your subject from its surroundings.

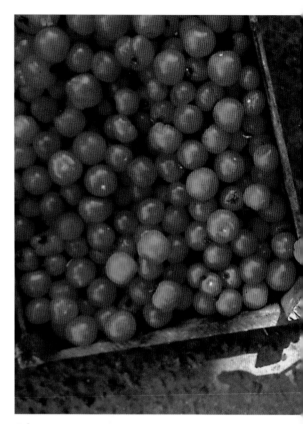

▲ **Less can say more**
At markets and similar types of location, all the activity can be overwhelming—and the temptation is often to try to record the entire busy, colorful scene. However, if you look around you, there could be images at your feet showing much less but saying so much more. In Uzbekistan I noticed next to a fruit stall a lady who had nothing to sell but these few sad tulips.

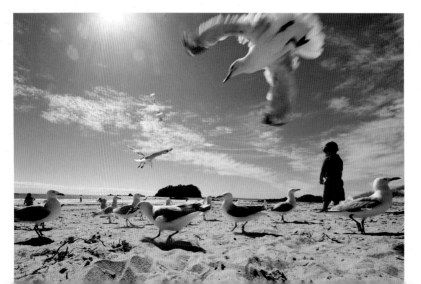

◄ **Child's eye view**
From almost ground level, the swooping gulls feel quite threatening and pull the viewer into the action. At the same time, looking upward gives the viewer a sense of open skies—this would be lost with the gaze directed downward.

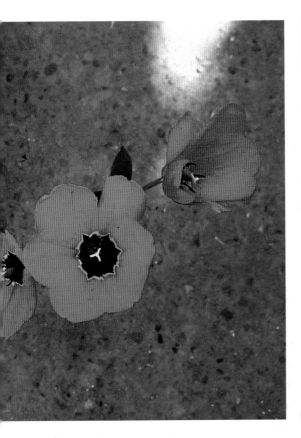

- In some parts of the world, it is a good idea to avoid drawing attention to your presence. Your search for an unusual camera viewpoint could attract the unwanted interest of officialdom. Even climbing onto a wall could land you in trouble in places where strangers are not a common sight or photographers are regarded with suspicion.
- As well as being discourteous, it might also be illegal to enter a private building without permission in order to take photographs. You may be surprised at how cooperative people generally are if you explain what you are doing and why, and then ask for their assistance.
- Try to be open and friendly with people you encounter—a pleasant smile or an acknowledging wave is often the easiest, and cheapest, way to elicit a helpful response from strangers.
- Prepare your equipment before making your move. Balancing on the top of a wall is not the best place to change lenses. With manual cameras, preset the approximately correct aperture and shutter time so that if you snatch a shot, exposure will be about right.

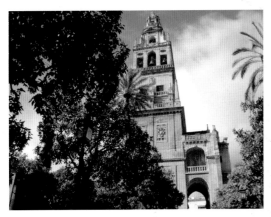

▲ Changing viewpoint

This conventional view of the Mesquita of Cordoba, Spain (*above*), works well as a record shot, but it is not the product of careful observation. Looking down from the same shooting position, I noticed the tower of the building reflected in a puddle of water. Placing the camera nearly in the water, a wholly more intriguing viewpoint was revealed (*right*). An advantage of using a digital camera with an LCD screen is that awkward shooting positions are not the impossibility they would be with a film-based camera.

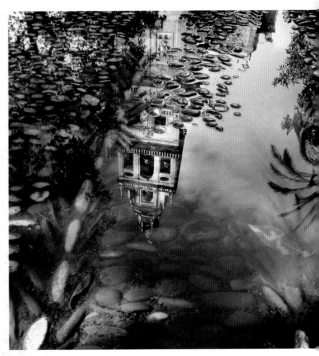

Caterpillar views
An SLR with an ultra-wide angle lens used at a low angle produces an intriguing composition, with the organized chaos of leaves and light creating a complex of lines, frames within frames, and contrasts of scale. Use a polarizing filter to reduce leaf shine, which dilutes colors.

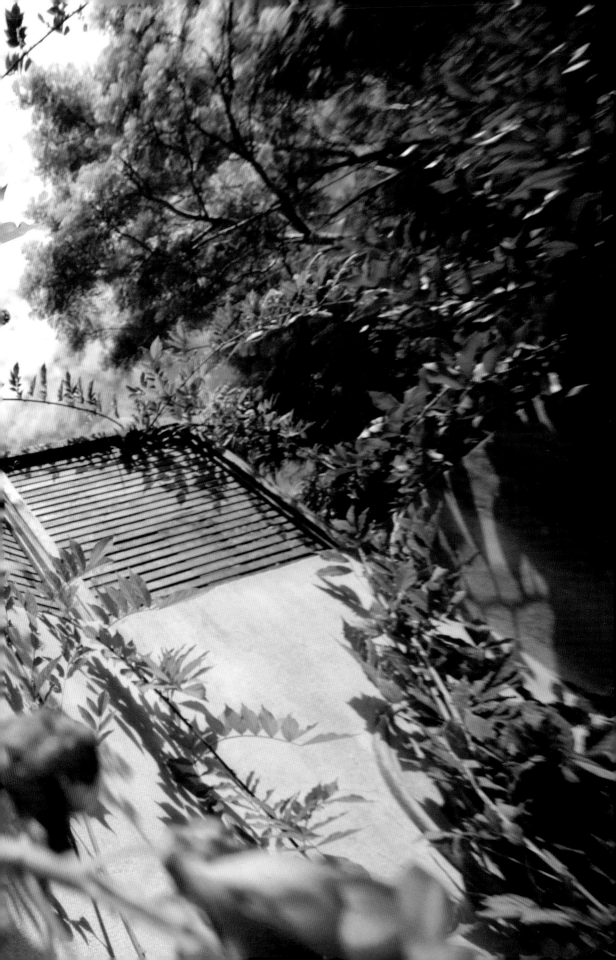

QUICK FIX LEANING BUILDINGS

Buildings and architectural features are always popular photographic subjects, but they can cause problems of distortion that are tricky to rectify.

Problem: Tall subjects—such as buildings, lampposts, trees, or even people standing close by and above you—appear to lean backward or as if they are about to topple over. Extreme wide-angle views are particularly prone to this effect.

Analysis: This distortion occurs if you tilt the camera upward to take the picture because you are trying to avoid taking in too much of the foreground and not enough of the height of the building. The top of the building is farther away, so it appears smaller, causing the whole image to lean backward.

Solution: Stand farther back, and keep the camera level. You will still take in too much of the foreground, but you can crop the image later.

- Use a wider-angle lens or zoom setting, hold the camera precisely level, then crop off the foreground in image-manipulation software.
- Take the picture anyway and try to correct some or all of the distortion by manipulating the image later.
- Use a shift lens. Such equipment is expensive, but it provides the technically best solution.

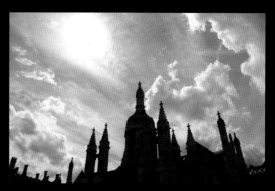

▲ Tilting the camera
An upward-looking view of the spires of Cambridge, England, makes the buildings lean backward. The visual effect can be exploited for drama.

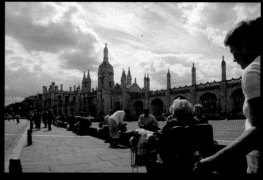

▲ Using the foreground
By choosing the right camera position, you can keep the camera level and include foreground elements that add to the shot.

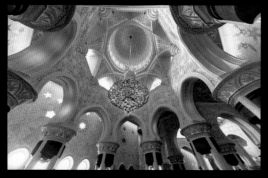

▲ Looking up
The awe-inspiring Grand Mosque in Abu Dhabi, United Arab Emirates, invites ultra-wide-angle views of the columns and ceilings. But in a small image, the strong convergences appear too exaggerated and extreme.

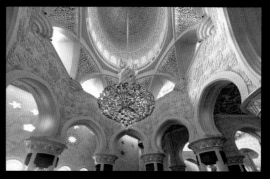

▲ Partial correction
By using the viewpoint or perspective features in image-manipulation software, it is possible to reduce the converging lines and give a more natural look. Such a result is not possible using only a lens.

QUICK FIX FACIAL DISTORTION

Distorted facial features, such as an overly large nose, is often the reason that a portrait is unattractive. It is the consequence of moving in close to make the subject's face as large as possible within the frame.

Problem: Portraits of people taken close-up with normal lenses will exaggerate certain facial features, such as noses, cheeks, or foreheads.

Analysis: The cause is a perspective distortion. When an image is viewed from too far away for its magnification, the impression of perspective is not correctly formed (*see also p. 40*). This is why at the time you took the photograph, your subject's nose appeared fine, but in the print or on screen it looks disproportionately large.

Solution: Use a lens setting longer than a 35 mm equivalent of 50 mm—that is, about 70 mm or more. This helps ensure that for an average-sized screen from a normal viewing distance the perspective looks correct.

- Work at the longer end of your zoom lens.
- If you have to work close-up, try taking a profile instead of a full face (*see below*).
- void using wide-angle lenses close to a face, unless you want a distorted view.
- Don't fill the frame with a face at the time of shooting. Instead, rely on cropping at a later stage if you need the frame filled (*see pp. 30–1*).
- Don't assume you will be able to correct facial distortions later on with image-manipulation software. It is hard to produce convincing results.
- Don't worry too much about distortions: the expression and lighting give a greater visual impact.

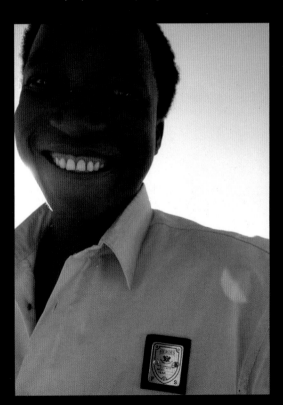

▲ Face-on
To emphasize the friendly character of this man, several "rules" were broken: a wide-angle lens was used close-up; the shot was taken looking upward; and the face was placed off in one corner, thus exaggerating the distortion already present.

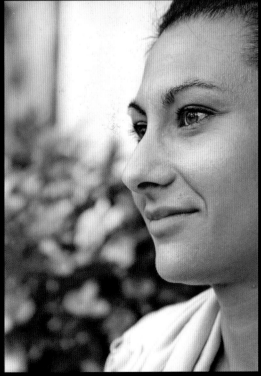

▲ Wide-angle profile
If forced to take a portrait close-up with a wide-angle lens—35 mm in this instance—it is best to look for a profile, since this avoids many of the problems associated with distortion in face-on shots. Make sure you focus carefully on the eye.

COLOR COMPOSITION

Color can be used to express emotion in an image. Pale, soft colors are restful and tranquil, while rich, vibrant colors burst with energy and demand attention. Color is integral to visual experience, but in photography it is almost a separate subject in itself. The basis of successful color photography is to use color in its own right, instead of merely capturing the many hues of a scene.

Color as subject

One approach is to photograph colors themselves rather than the objects they imbue—that is, to try to treat the subject as if it were the incidental feature in the scene. You do not need to learn to see in color, but you do need to learn to see colors for themselves—entirely separate from the thing that displays the color.

This change of mental focus could radically transform the entire way you photograph. You evaluate a scene not in terms of whether it is a marvelous vista but in color analytic terms. You will observe that colors vary not only with hue—the name given to a color—but also with intensity, or saturation. Soon, you will appreciate another quality: the value, or brightness, of a color. With more experience, you will appreciate that certain colors can be captured in their full richness, whereas others will appear weaker. Understanding each dimension adds to your ability to compose with color.

Color wheel

The colors of the rainbow can be arranged in a circle (the "color wheel"): the basic primary colors are red, blue, and yellow. In between these are placed violet, green, and orange, and between these are all the intermediate colors. A hue that is directly to the left or right of a color on the wheel is said to be an analogous, or adjacent, color—such as light and dark green with yellow, or blue, purple, and cyan. A combination of these colors in your images will appear harmonious and will therefore be correspondingly easy to compose, as the colors work together and can help bind together disparate elements within the scene. Broadly speaking, landscape photographers tend

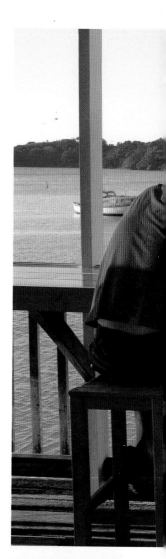

▶ Fashion parade
The saturated colors of the different T-shirts could lead to a chaotic composition. However, several other elements help to organize the image: the regular lines of the windows, chairs, and railing all cut the image into neat frames around the blocks of color. At the same time the blue of the sky and water form an even background against which the T-shirt colors can glow.

▼ Brilliance of pallor
Colors do not have to be highly saturated or intense to be effective. In many cases subtle contrast works best, such as the tiny area of red petal against the overall green balance of this image. The sharpness of the flower against the vague shadows also helps define the color regions.

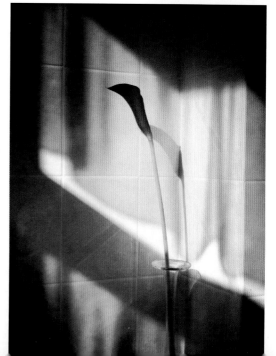

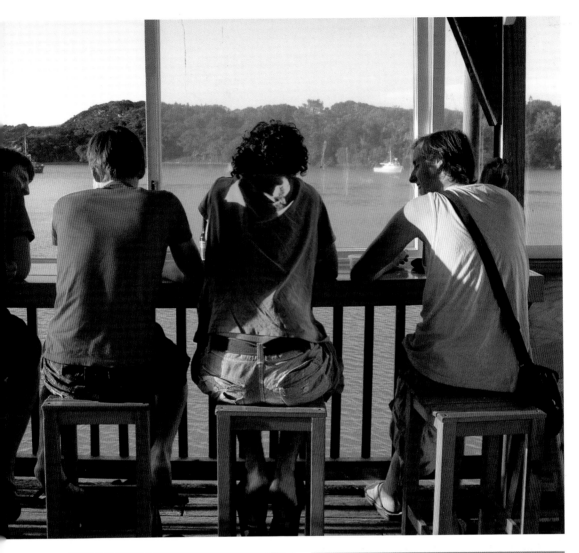

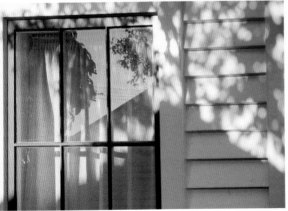

▲ Betting on white
Any color seen against white appears to be relatively stronger. The pale blue reflection of sky would be swamped by any other colors in the image, but with the large areas of neutral shades, even the very soft blues in the shadows become more apparent.

PERCEPTION OF COLOR
If a pale subject is seen against a background of a complementary color, its saturation seems to increase. Similarly, a neutral gray changes its appearance according to its background color, appearing slightly bluish green against red, and magenta against green. If you compare the gray patches in the two-colored panels below you can see this at work. If you were to cut small holes in a piece of white card, so that only the four patches are visible, you would see that the pale blues are, in fact, identical, as are the grays.

COLOR COMPOSITION CONTINUED

to prefer working with analogous colors, so the viewer concentrates on forms and texture, whereas garden photographers tend to seek out contrasting colors, for livelier results.

A version of the analogous scheme is the monochromatic, in which all colors are variants of the same hue. Such images—think of seascapes with their infinite varieties of blue—offer tonal subtlety instead of color contrasts. Close-ups of flowers are · often rewarding because they offer narrow, subtle color shifts.

Colors are said to clash where they lie opposite or far from each other on the color wheel. While compositions with strong contrasts are appealing when initially experienced, they are more tricky to organize into a successful image. Look for simplicity in structure and a clear arrangement of subject matter—too many elements jostling for attention can lead to a disjointed, chaotic image.

Pastel colors

Referring to pastel colors as the weak versions of a hue is accurate, but also does them a disservice: it suggests that they are of limited use. Pastels are certainly more pale and less saturated or vibrant than full-on colors. They are nonetheless vital tools for the photographer.

Pale colors suggest tranquillity and calm, and are gentle where strong colors are more vigorous. They evoke responses of peace and well-being—which is why they are so popular for home interiors—and, for a photographer, they are also important as counterbalances to strong colors. You can achieve striking results by simply concentrating on pastel colors in their own right. You will find them where there is a good deal of light—which tends to dilute colors—and where pastel shades have been used decoratively in architecture, interior design, or garden planting schemes.

The easiest way to create pastel-dominated images is to over-expose them: this can be very effective for creating unusual effects in nature and landscape photography. Such images are often associated with high-key lighting (*see also pp. 70–1*) as the presence of dark shadows tends to make even pale colors look richer. Alternatively, many digital cameras can be set to record all the colors in a scene as pastels.

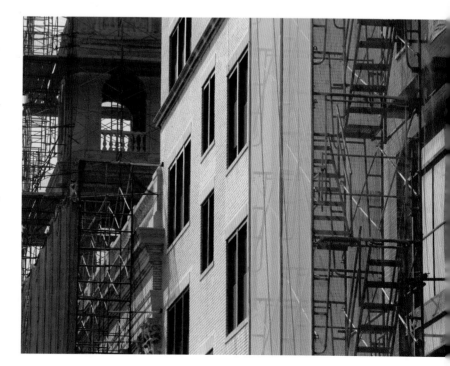

▶ **Strong structure**
The watered-down colors in this cityscape provide a canvas for the morass of steel structures that crawl up the buildings. It may be tempting to increase contrast and saturation, but that would over-dramatize the true nature of the view. In flat lighting, expose with care, as poor accuracy impacts on every tone in the image, and use the lens at its best aperture to ensure sharply defined details.

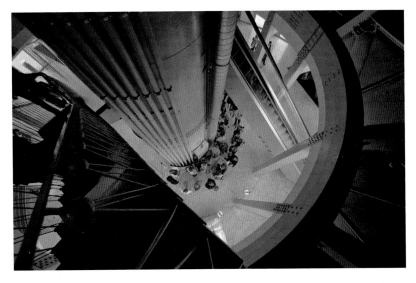

◄ Grounded color

The neutral block of gray in the center of the image provides a grounding for the opposing visual lures of the patches of deep blue and red. In addition, the structure imposed by strong lines and curves ensures this image, made in the Atomium in Brussels, presents a rich articulation of space and form.

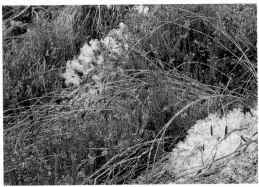

▲ Soft but strong

Flowers of a Scottish Highland spring make a striking image despite being made up of largely pastel colors, all seen under a dull light. Compose to overlap contrasting colors and try zooming to a long focal length setting to compress space and juxtapose different patches of color.

TRY THIS

One effective way to work with colors is to ensure the main colors in your pictures are complementary pairs—such as red–green, yellow–violet, orange–blue. Try to capture subject matter with complementary colors; it is not as easy as you might expect. But you will find that, with practice, complementary color pairs will catch your eye even if you are not consciously looking for them. As you refine your technique, see if you can use color complementaries to separate out elements in your image—use the language of color to express and communicate your response to a scene.

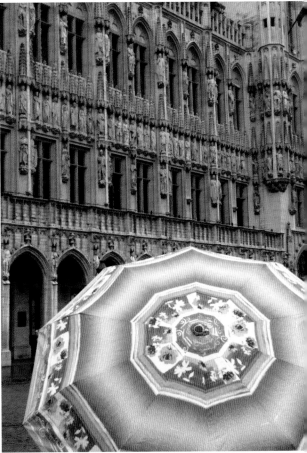

▲ Saturation contrast

The attention-grabbing colors of an umbrella appear to be even stronger than they are because of contrast with the gray tones of the buildings. This, together with the radial structure of the umbrella straining against the linear form of the building, creates a contrast that is almost too vigorous.

ADJACENT COLORS

Colors that lie immediately next to each other on the color wheel (see p. 54) are said to be analogous, or adjacent, colors. Examples of these include light green and yellow, dark green and blue, purple and cyan, and so on.

Color and harmony

Although it is difficult to generalize about what are essentially subjective reactions to the inclusion of particular colors, as a general rule if you include combinations of adjacent colors in an image you create more of a harmonious effect. This is especially true if the colors are approximately equivalent to each other in brightness and saturation. As well as being pleasing to the eye, color harmony also helps to bind together what could perhaps be disparate subject elements within a composition.

Color and mood

There is much to be said for learning to work with a carefully conceived and restrained palette of colors. A trick of landscape photographers at some times of the year, for example, is to select a camera viewpoint that creates a color scheme that is composed predominantly of browns and reds—the hues redolent of autumn. Thus, not only does a harmonious color composition result, all of the mood and atmosphere associated with the seasonal change from summer to winter are brought to bear within the image.

Depending on just how the photographer wants a picture to communicate with its intended audience, images that feature gardens as the principal subject might be dominated by colors such as various shades of green or blues and purples.

Monochromatic color

Another type of picture harmony results when the colors are all of a similar hue. The subtle tonal variations can impart a sense of quiet tranquillity or reinforce the drama of the scene. Duotone or sepia-toned effects (see pp. 238–41) are highly monochromatic, as are views of the sea and sky containing a range of different blues. Red and orange sunsets may be lively or serene, while flower close-ups are often beautiful because of their delicate shifts in color.

▶ Monochrome landscape

As the French painter Paul Cézanne taught us, every color of the rainbow can be seen in any scene if you look hard enough, especially in a landscape. However, the dominance of yellows and browns in this image encourages the viewer to admire the chiaroscuro and shape of the slopes without the distraction of color contrasts.

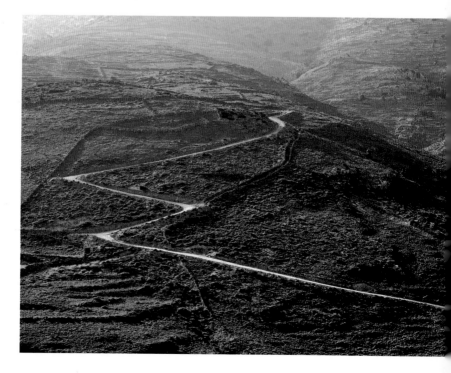

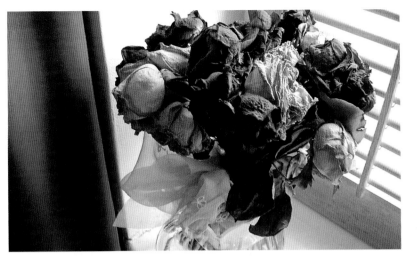

◀ Emotional content

Even though all the main colors in this photograph are tonally very close, the image lacks impact when it is rendered in black and white. The emotional content of the warm reds, pinks, and purples is essential to the success of the study.

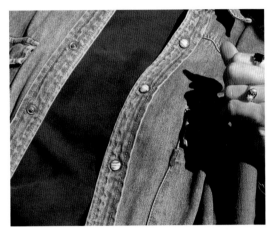

▲ Blue on blue

Although the strong and adjacent blues, which have been given extra depth by the bright sunlight illuminating them, are what this picture is all about, a total absence of some form of contrast—provided here by the small red label and the subject's flesh tones—would have left the picture unbalanced and overstated.

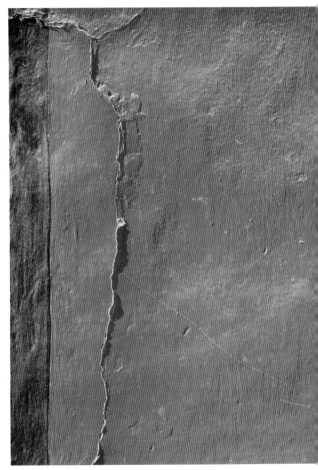

▲ Red and purple

When I first noticed this painted wall, it appeared to have promise, but it was not until it was strongly lit by oblique sunlight that the picture really came together—the dominance of the red and the strongly graphic crack both being powerful visual elements. A little post-processing work served to heighten the colors and strengthen the shadows.

TRY THIS

First, choose a color. It could be your favorite one—blue, yellow, orange—or any other. Next, set out to photograph anything that is largely or wholly composed of that particular hue. Allow only variations of that color within each picture. If any other colors are present, don't take the picture—unless you can get in close enough, or change your camera viewpoint, to exclude them. When you are done, put your collection of pictures together. The assembly of similar colors in different shades will have an impact that may surprise and delight you.

COLOR CONTRASTS

Color contrasts result when you include hues within an image that are well separated from each other on the color wheel (*see pp. 54–6*). While it is true that strongly colored picture elements may have initial visual impact, they are not all that easy to organize into successful images. Often, it is better to look for a simple color scheme as part of a clear compositional structure—too many subject elements can so easily lead to disjointed and chaotic pictures.

Digital results

Modern cameras are able to capture very vibrant colors that look compelling on your computer's monitor screen. Because of the way the screen displays color, these are, in fact, brighter and more saturated than those prints can produce. However, one of the advantages of using computer technology is that the apparent color range can be enhanced by the application of image-manipulation techniques, giving you the opportunity, first to create, and then to exploit, an enormous range of color palettes.

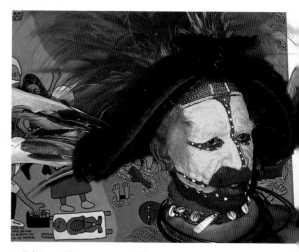

▲ **Distracting composition**
Combine strong colors with an unusual and an appealing subject, and you would think that you have all the elements needed for a striking photograph. In fact, there is far too much going on in this picture for it to be a successful composition. The painting in the background distracts attention from the man—himself an artist, from Papua New Guinea—while the white edge on the right disturbs the composition. A severe crop, to concentrate attention on the face alone, would be necessary to save the image.

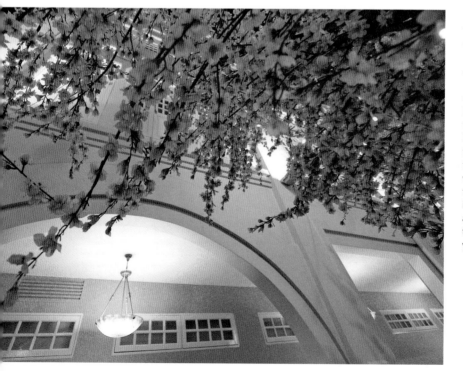

◀ **Strong contrasts**
This image, captured in China Town, Singapore, is simply a celebration of color contrast. But there is more than the color opposition between the blue-painted walls and the pinks of the cherry blossoms. The cool light from low-energy lamps in the arcade contrasts with warm light coming from the street lamps: the result is that whites in the arcade are neutral, but whites on the outside are distinctly yellow-red.

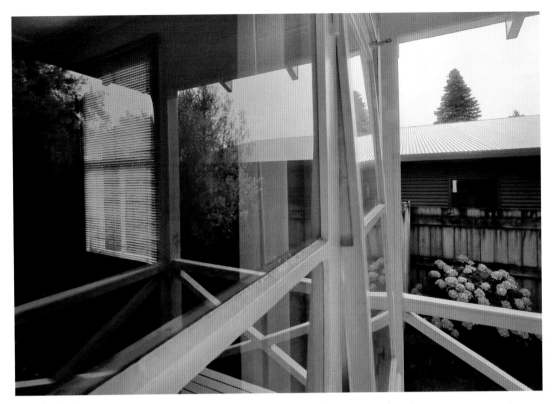

▲ Polar balance

This image is dominated by gray or near-neutral tones but is dynamically organized around the contrast between the reddish light of the wooden blinds and the bright blue of the hydrangea flowers. The strong patches of color appear even stronger because they are isolated in a neutral field (*see p. 55*), and they alternately demand a viewer's attention. This imparts energy to what would otherwise be a static composition.

COLOR GAMUT

The intensity of computer-enhanced colors gives them real appeal, but it is in this strength that problems lie. Strong colors on the page of a book or website will compete with any text that is included; they are also likely to conflict with any other softer image elements. In addition, you need to bear in mind that even if you can see intense, strong colors on the screen, you may not be able to reproduce them on paper. Purples, sky blue, oranges, and brilliant greens all reproduce poorly on paper, looking duller than they do on screen. This is because the color gamut, or range of reproducible colors, of print is smaller than that of the monitor.

Of the many ways to represent a range of colors, this diagram is the most widely accepted. The rounded triangle encloses all colors that can be perceived. Areas drawn within this, the visual gamut, represent the colors that can be accurately reproduced by specific devices. The triangle

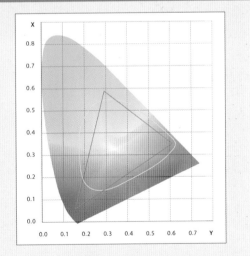

encloses the colors (the color gamut) of a typical RGB color monitor. The quadrilateral shows the colors reproduced by the four-color printing process. Notice how some printable colors cannot be reproduced on screen, and vice versa.

COLOR CONTRASTS CONTINUED

Rainy days are ideal for color photography because colors are more saturated, and there are no glaring patches of bright sunlight to deal with. As a result, you work with a spread of mostly mid-tones and darker tones—that is, colors that cover a narrow luminance range. This makes it easy to control lighting, contrasts, and exposure. It also enables you to work with contrasts of hue and soft gradations of tone without distractions from bright highlights, as in this image made in Kolkata, India.

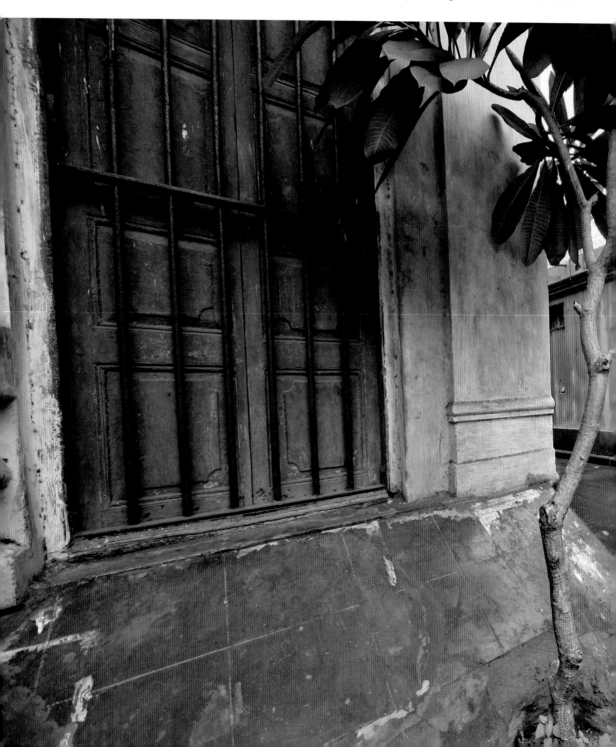

TECHNICAL INFO

CAMERA
Canon EOS 1Ds Mark II

LENS
Sigma 12–24 mm at 12 mm

SETTINGS
ISO 100 • f/4.5 • ¹⁄₆₀ sec

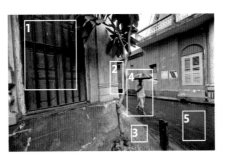

1 Green backing
A block of dark greens is a counterpoint to the warm colors elsewhere in the image. These colors tend to recede into the image space, allowing the brighter, warm colors to come forward to the viewer.

2 Image fulcrum
Strong vertical lines and the tree define the center of the image, around which all else is levered. The image was framed with this hard edge at the center while waiting for the passer-by to walk into view.

3 Ramp up
By a stroke of good luck, the corner of the building featured a ramp. Its sloping line exaggerates the converging lines toward the passer-by, giving the composition a subtle lift in energy.

4 Live element
Without movement from a living being, the image would be a dull study in colors and graphics. Almost anything would work: a passing sacred cow, a group of children, or even a car. But this passer-by sheltering under his umbrella is perfect, especially since he is caught in full, energetic stride.

5 Neutral ground
With so much going on in the rest of the image, it is helpful that the road is free of any significant activity, litter, or colors. Its neutrality provides a background against which the image can work.

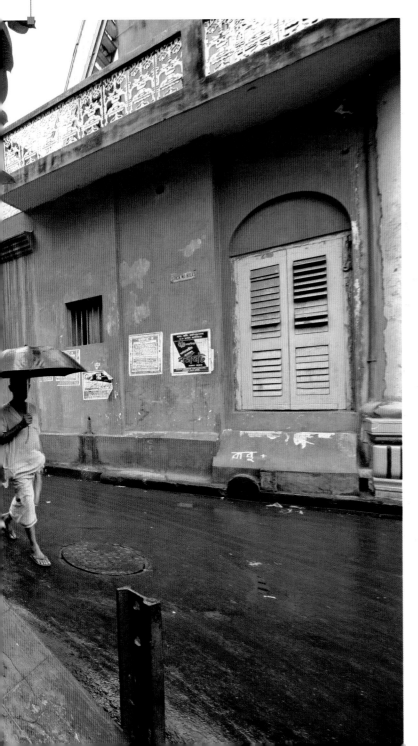

QUICK FIX WHITE BALANCE

White balance ensures that the color of illuminating light is as close as possible to that of normal daylight. This is the foundation for accurate color reproduction. If there is no adjustment for a tint, such as red, in the illumination, all colors in the scene will carry a reddish tint.

Problem: Images made indoors tend to appear unnaturally warm-toned. In other situations, pictures taken under fluorescent lamps appear greenish overall. A related problem occurs in outdoor shots: you see a blue cast in the shadows on a sunny day, or images appear unnaturally cold on cloudy days. Problems are compounded if you work in mixed lighting, such as daylight from a window and light from a table lamp. If you correct for the orange cast of the lamp, the window light looks too blue; if you correct for the window light, the lamp light looks too orange.

Analysis: All imaging systems assume that the light falling on a scene contains the full spectrum of colors. This produces the "white" light of daylight. If, however, the light is deficient in a specific band of colors or is dominated by certain colors, then everything illuminated by it will tend to take on the strongest color component. Our eyes and brain make automatic adjustments by balancing various color signals to reduce dominant colors. As a result, for example, we do not experience indoor light as being unduly orange. Likewise, we seldom notice the blue color cast that is often present in the shadows on sunny days.

Digital camera manufacturers have achieved a similar effect in their products' automatic white balance: the red, green, and blue signals are monitored, and the camera compensates for any dominant levels of a particular hue. But there are limits to the adjustment, and when these are exceeded, we see more or less strong tints in our images. The resulting "inaccurate" color reproduction may be important for establishing the mood of a scene; the red tones of a sunset or the cool tones of a snowfield, for example, are appropriate and integral to each situation.

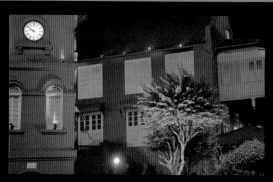

1 Orange street lamps
The lighting in this square in Malacca, Malaysia, was recorded as a lurid red in the image. Even the white windows look too red.

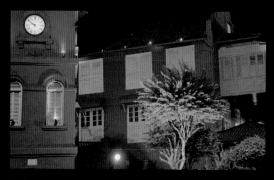

2 White balanced
A firm correction turns the white windows to a nearly neutral gray but at the cost of losing the atmosphere and mood of the scene. The tree now looks too blue.

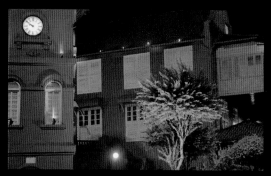

3 Half-correction
An incomplete correction gives an effective balance of realistic rendering with a retention of the mood and color contrasts of the original.

Solution: Image-manipulation software can make extensive corrections to white balance—use the White Balance tool, the dropper tools in Levels, or Curves controls. The dropper tool samples or measures a small area of the image to calculate the change. Choose carefully. If different parts of the image show different white balances, you may need to mask one area to limit corrections to that area (*see right*).

When capturing images in JPEG format, you may set Auto White Balance (AWB) for convenience. For better results, set a white balance appropriate to the scene—for example, "cloudy" for overcast days. For maximum flexibility, record in RAW format and decide on the white balance during post-processing.

White balance generally corrects the blue-yellow balance. Some images may need correction of the green-magenta balance, called "tint" control. These may be needed to correct skin tones and are available in some software.

HOW TO AVOID THE PROBLEM

- Avoid photographing in mixed-lighting conditions unless you specifically want the image to display unpredictable colors.
- Avoid making color-critical shots under fluorescent lamps: the color cast can prove very difficult to correct.
- For color-critical work, use a gray card to set custom color balance following your camera's instructions. Photograph the card or color chart to provide a standard for calibration.

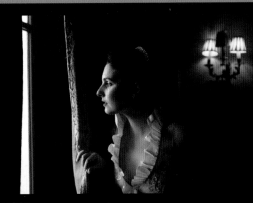

1 As captured
With white balance set to "cloudy," this model's skin tones are beautifully warm, but the lamps behind her are too yellow-red.

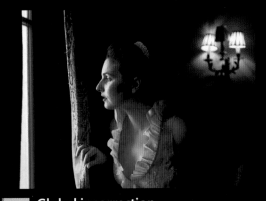

2 Global incorrection
A correction aimed at the lamps using the Highlight dropper—it sampled from the bright lamp area—leads to too much blue in the model.

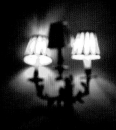

3 Masked correction
This result was achieved by selecting the area behind the model before sampling with the Highlight dropper, making sure to leave some yellow in the lamp.

EXPOSURE CONTROL

Exposure control is the process of making sure that you capture your image with the exactly the right amount of light needed to produce the effect you wish to obtain. You measure light levels with an exposure meter—usually one that is built into the camera or a separate handheld meter—and with the aid of meter readings, you adjust the shutter, aperture, and ISO settings.

It is important to control exposure accurately and carefully, as it not only ensures you obtain the best from whatever system you are using, but it also saves you the time and effort of manipulating the image unnecessarily at a later stage.

Measuring systems

To determine exposure, the camera measures the light entering the camera that is reflected from a scene. The simplest system measures light from the entire field of view, treating all of it equally.

Many cameras use a center-weighted system, in which light from the entire field of view is registered, but greater account is taken of that coming from the central portion of the image. This can be taken further, so that the light from most of the image is ignored, except that from a central part. This can vary from a central 25 percent of the whole area to less than 5 percent. For critical work, this selective area, or spot-metering, system is the most accurate.

A far more elaborate exposure system divides the entire image area into a patchwork of zones, each of which is separately evaluated. This system, commonly referred to as evaluative or matrix metering, is extremely successful at delivering consistently accurate exposures over a wide range of unusual or demanding lighting conditions. This is now widely used in modern cameras—from compacts and SLRs, to mirrorless cameras.

As good as they are, the exposure systems found in modern cameras are not perfect. There will be times when you have to give the automation a helping hand—usually when the lighting is most interesting or challenging. This is why it is so crucially important to understand what exactly constitutes "optimum exposure."

Optimized dynamics

Every photographic medium has a range over which it can make accurate records—beyond that, the representation is less precise. This range, or latitude, is represented by a scale of grays either side of the mid-tone—from dark tones with detail (for example, dark hair with some individual strands distinguishable), to light tones showing texture (for example, paper showing creases and wrinkles). If you locate your exposure so that the most important tone of your image falls in the

▶ What is "correct"?

To the eye, this scene was brighter and less colorful than seen here. A technically correct exposure would have produced a lighter image—thus failing to record the sunset colors. Although it looks like this might challenge a basic exposure-measuring system, by placing the sun center frame you guarantee underexposure, resulting, as in this example, in a visually better image than a "correct" exposure would produce.

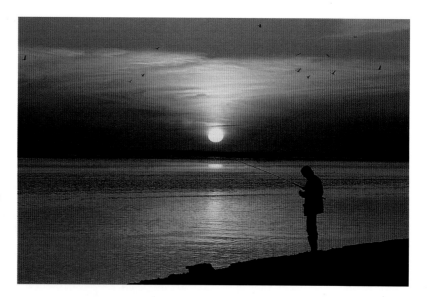

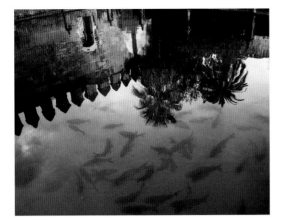

▲ Narrow luminance range

Scenes that contain a narrow range of luminance and large areas of fairly even, regular tone do not represent a great problem for exposure-measuring systems, but you still need to proceed with care for optimum results. The original of this image was correctly exposed yet appeared too light because, pictorially, the scene acquires more impact from being darker, almost low-key (*see pp. 70–71*). The adjustments that were made to darken the image also had the effect of increasing color saturation, which is another pictorial improvement.

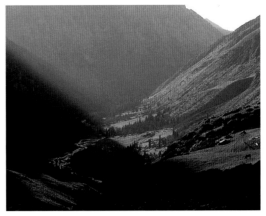

▲ Wide luminance range

The range of luminance in this scene is large—from the brilliant glare of the sky to deep foreground shadows. Exposure control must, therefore, be precise to make the most of the sensor's ability to record the scene. In these situations, the best exposure system is a spot meter, with the sensor positioned over a key tone—here, the brightly lit area of grass on the right of the frame. Evaluative metering may also produce the same result, but if you are using a film camera, you will not know until you develop the film.

middle of this range, the recording medium has the best chance of capturing a full range of tones.

In general, the aim of exposure control is to choose camera settings that ensure the middle tone of an image falls within the middle part of the sensor's recording range, to make the most of the available dynamic range while meeting the need to capture movement and adequate depth of field.

Spot metering

The most reliable method for achieving precision in exposure control is to use spot metering (see box below). Aim the measuring spot at the key tone to obtain a reading to ensure it is correctly exposed. The key tone could be a person's face or the sunlit portion of a valley wall. From this, the rest of the image's tones will fall into place (*see also p. 77*).

SENSITIVITY PATTERNS

Cameras use a variety of light-measuring systems, and the representations shown here illustrate two of the most common arrangements. With a center-weighted averaging system, most of the field of view is assessed by the meter, but preference is given to light coming from the middle of the frame. In the majority of situations, this arrangement gives predictable and reliable results. The metering on modern cameras can be arranged so that all of its sensitivity is concentrated in a small spot in the very middle of the field of view. Used in any auto-exposure mode with the reading held or memorized once made, this method gives reliable results quickly and easily.

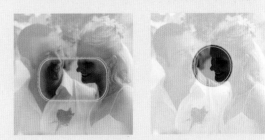

▲ Metering systems

Center-weighted metering (*above left*) takes in all of the view but gives more weight, or emphasis, to the light level around the center of the image, tailing off to little response at the edge. A spot-metering system (*above right*) reads solely from a clearly defined central area—usually just 2–3 percent of the total image area. So a bright light at the edge of the image will have no effect on the reading.

SILHOUETTES/BACKLIGHTING

Although the results may look different, silhouetted and backlit shots are variations on the same theme. In terms of exposure, they differ only in how much light is given to the main subject.

Silhouetted subjects

To create a silhouette, expose for the background alone—whether the sky or, say, a brightly lit wall—so that foreground objects are recorded as very dark, or even black. Make sure the exposure takes no account of the foreground. For this technique to be most effective, minimal light should fall on the subject, otherwise surface details start to record

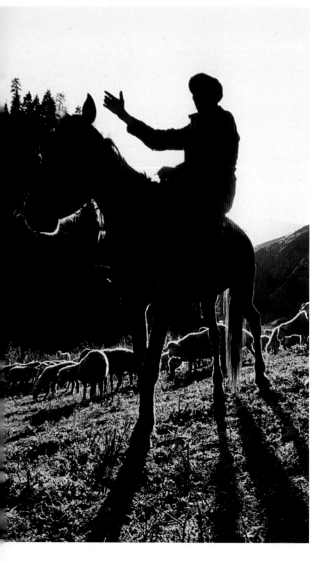

and the form loses impact. Your aim is to exploit outline and shape, and to help this a plain background is usually best.

When taking pictures into the light, you need to be aware of bright light flaring into the lens. As a rule, try to position yourself so that the subject itself obscures the light source, though it can be effective to allow the sun to peep around the subject to cause a little flare. Using a small aperture helps reduce unwanted reflections inside the lens.

Backlit subjects

The classic backlit subject is a portrait taken with a window or the sky filling the background, or figures on a bright, sandy beach or a ski slope.

The challenge in terms of exposure in these types of situation is to prevent the meter from being over-influenced by the high levels of background illumination. If you don't, you will end up with a silhouette. To prevent this, either override the automatics or manually set the controls to "overexpose" by some 1½–2 f/stops.

Another approach is to set your camera to take a selective meter reading (see pp. 66–7). Alternatively, with a center-weighted averaging meter reading, fill the viewfinder with the shadowy side of your subject, note the reading, or lock it in, move back, and recompose the image.

Backlit scenes are prone to veiling flare—nonimage-forming light—which is aggravated by the need to increase exposure for the subject. In strong backlighting, however, it is hard to prevent light spilling around the subject edges, blurring sharpness and reducing contrast.

◀ **Conflicting needs**
In this strongly backlit portrait of a Kyrgyz shepherd (which has been cropped from a wide-angle shot), I positioned myself so that the subject shielded the lens from the direct rays of a bright sun. It is very difficult to achieve the right balance of exposure—if the horse is fully exposed, the sheep will be too light. This is clearly the type of situation that would benefit from a little fill-in flash (see pp. 80–1). However, there was just enough light to pick out the color of the horse when the sheep were correctly exposed.

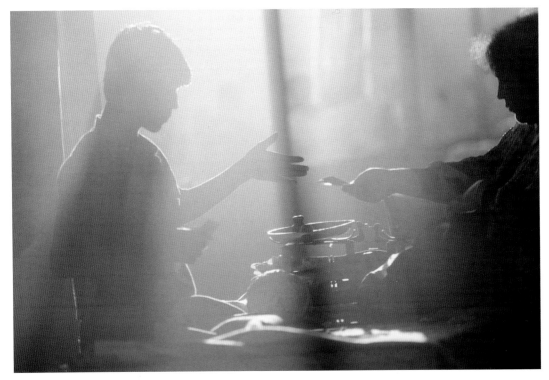

▲ Dealing with flare

As the sun sets on a market in Tashkent, Uzbekistan, the dust raised by street cleaners fills the air, catching and spreading the still bright sunlight. The lower the sun is in the sky, the more likely is it to become a feature in your composition. In the example here, the flare has been caused as much by the atmospheric dust as by any internal reflections within the lens itself. A normal averaging light reading taken in these conditions would be massively over-influenced by the general brightness of the scene, and so render the backlit subject as featureless silhouettes. Therefore, what may seem like a gross overexposure—an additional 2 f/stops—is needed to deal with this type of lighting situation.

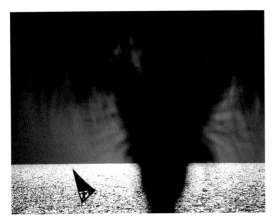

▲ Sky exposure

Strong light from the front and a symmetrical foreground shape immediately suggest the potential for a silhouette. A passing windsurfer, in the Penang Straits of Malaysia, completes the picture. Simply by exposing for the sky, all the other elements fall into their correct place—the black, shadowy palm tree, the sparkling water, and the surfer are transformed. Using a catadioptric (mirror) lens produces the characteristic "hollow" look of the out-of-focus palm.

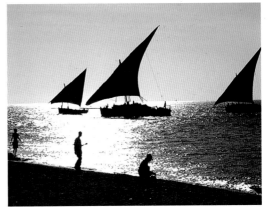

▲ Virtue of necessity

When shooting into a fierce, tropical sun, you may have no choice other than to produce a silhouette. If so, the strategy then becomes a search for the right type of subject. Here, on Zanzibar, dhows and beachcombers are complementary in terms of tone, yet contrasting in shape. Notice how the central figure seems diminished in size as his outline is blurred by the light flaring all around his body.

HIGH-KEY IMAGES

The key tone in the majority of images lies at or near the midpoint between the darkest or black tones and the brightest or white ones. This is what we see in average lighting and is what camera metering systems are designed to deliver. By deliberately shifting the key tone away from the average, we do not merely make an image appear lighter or darker overall, but we signal a mood or feeling to the viewer. By our control of the key tone we use the tonality of the image to convey meaning. We use high-key images most often to express a light and airy mood: this is ideal for modern interior shots and wedding photography, and is often used for fashion shoots and portraiture.

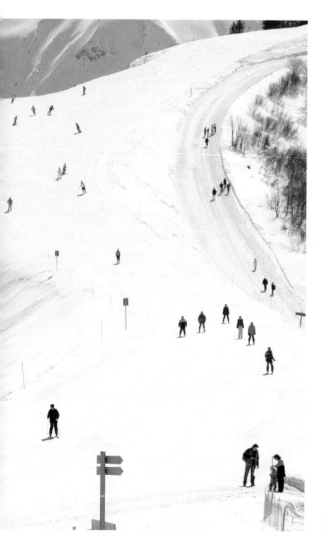

Bright and high

High-key images are those in which tones are all lighter than mid-tone, with a minimum of mid- and shadow tones. This is achieved in two ways. Primarily, high-key is a lighting effect that floods the subject with light to fill the mid-tones and shadows. High-key results can also be achieved by combining high levels of exposure with flat lighting conditions. The aim is to ensure all pixels are brighter than mid-tone. Image manipulation can also be used to reduce shadows and give an impression of high-key.

Filled with light

There are many ways, alone or in combination, to light your subject evenly. Place equal-power light sources aimed at your subject from both sides, use a fill-in or a ring flash, and supplement light sources with reflectors to reduce shadows. When metering, base your exposure on the shadow areas by ensuring that your meter reads light values in these areas alone. If your camera has a spot or selective-area meter, point it at a shadow that still retains some subject detail, lock the reading in, and recompose the shot. If you don't have this facility, you may need to move close enough to a suitable shadow so that it fills the sensor area. If you place the darker areas with detail as your mid-tone, all the other tones in the image will be shifted to be lighter, and there will be very little in the image that is darker than mid-tone.

Alternatively, you can record the image normally (in RAW format if possible) then create the high-key effect in post-processing using image-manipulation software. By recording in RAW, you will have some data in reserve for this extreme form of exposure manipulation (*see pp. 234–7*).

◄ **Snow seen**
Both snow and white sand seen in full sun reflect back a lot of light, which can, if not corrected, lead to dark, underexposed images. To retain the texture of snow or sand, you will need to set your exposure one or two stops higher than normal. The resulting deliberate overexposure lightens the snow to produce a high-key tonal rendering with minimal areas, such as the figures, darker than mid-tone.

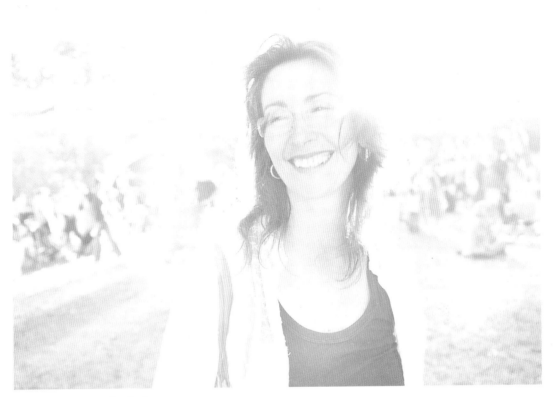

▲ High-key manipulation

High-key images result not only from lighting and exposure control, or the nature of a subject, but also from treatments given after the image has been captured. The original portrait showed dark tones in the black T-shirt. This area, along with some dark details in the background, were lightened using the dodge tools and levels in order to fill the image with light. The result is expressively perfect, even though the exposure is technically very incorrect.

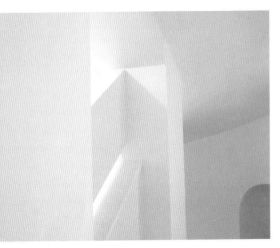

▲ Modernist interior

This corner of a minimalist hotel in Prague presented ideal surfaces for a high-key rendering. Originally a dimly lit scene, use of a generous overexposure softened the differences in color between the daylight and tungsten lighting and filled the surfaces with high-key tones.

TRY THIS

While high key is essentially a result of lighting that reduces shadows to a minimum, you can simulate the result by overexposing subjects that have a narrow range of luminances. Look for subjects with small differences between their brightest and darkest parts—such as flatly lit subjects on an overcast day. With portraits, use a reflector to bounce light into the shadow-side of the face. If accessory flash is available, use a ring-flash adaptor to even out the light and eliminate shadows.

Make a series of exposures, starting with the metered correct exposure, and steadily increase exposure. You will need an overexposure of at least one stop over the metered setting to fill the shadows with light. Choose the setting that gives you the results you prefer. Note that cameras with dynamic range correction or highlight preservation may need less overexposure.

LOW-KEY IMAGES

The mood of low-key images is in complete contrast to that of high-key: the dominant darkness casts a more somber and literally darker mood. More than with high-key, low-key images tend to simplify an image's content, as there is no room for detailed renditions.

Swing low

Technically, low-key images are easier to create than high-key ones, as less lighting, less exposure, and somewhat less control is required. Ideally you light a subject with a single weak light. For example, with a portrait a single source, such as a window, lights the face from an acute angle so that textures and features cast sharp shadows. You expose for the bright areas: this renders them as mid-tones or lower, which automatically forces all darker tones into deep shadows and blacks.

In a similar approach to high-key imaging, the most flexible technique for determining the exposure for low-key pictures is to concentrate your exposure reading on the light values that still retain subject detail. If you point your spot or selective-area meter at such a region of your subject, that tone will be rendered as a mid-tone gray. This means that everything darker than the light area (most of the image) will be darker than mid-tone gray. Shadows with detail will, therefore, become featureless black.

Note that underexposure with digital cameras can introduce unwanted visual noise, so it may be best to create a low-key effect from a normally exposed image via image-manipulation software. When it comes to printing out low-key images, beware—ink-jet prints with large areas of black can easily become overloaded with ink.

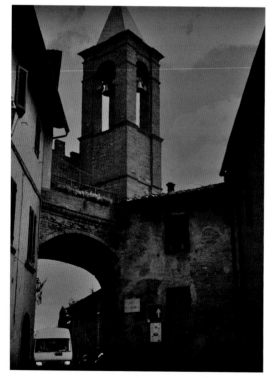

▲ By design
You can force mid-tones and highlights to be darker than usual through manipulation. Here, an image from Tuscany produced through the Hipstamatic app has been further darkened to emphasize the storm-laden atmosphere.

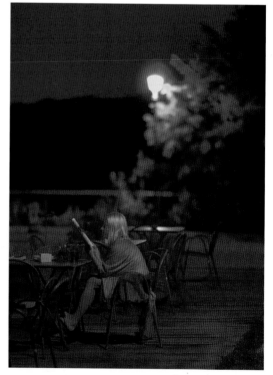

▲ Twilight
The natural time for capturing low-key images is the evening and night. Here a hotel guest reads by lamplight while the day darkens around her. Almost every tone is darker than mid-tone.

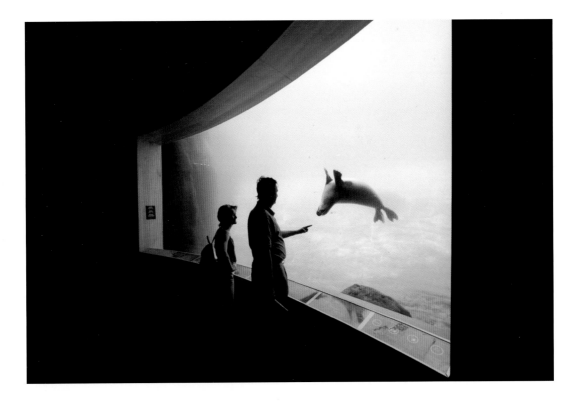

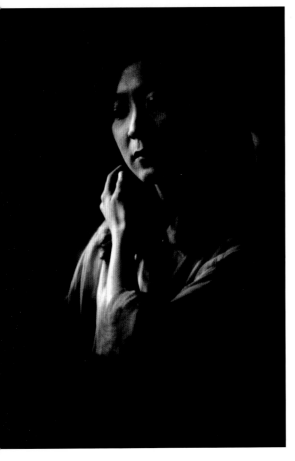

◄ Dramatic portrait

For a low-key portrait, all that is required is sidelighting from a low angle, as here, with enough underexposure to send the majority of tones into the shadow. The absence of really bright areas creates a moody feel. This type of portrait is much favored for older subjects, because it conceals imperfections and wrinkles.

▲ Two-toned

Silhouettes—in which the subject is seen only in dark outline against a relatively bright background—are a special kind of low-key imaging. By forcing mid-tones to be very dark, we lose all shadow detail and retain only shape.

TRY THIS

Seek out scenes with a broad subject-luminance range, such as a building with one side lit by sun leaving the other in deep shadow. Make a series of decreasing exposures, starting with the correct one. As the mid-tones progressively deepen to black, the bright areas simply shrink until the image consists of sharply drawn highlights. Notice that the image can work well at many stages.

Jewels on the floor

Canang sari—a type of offering made daily in Bali, Indonesia—often litter the ground there. In this image, the background needed to be as low-key as possible, though retaining detail, to show off the flower petals and leaves.

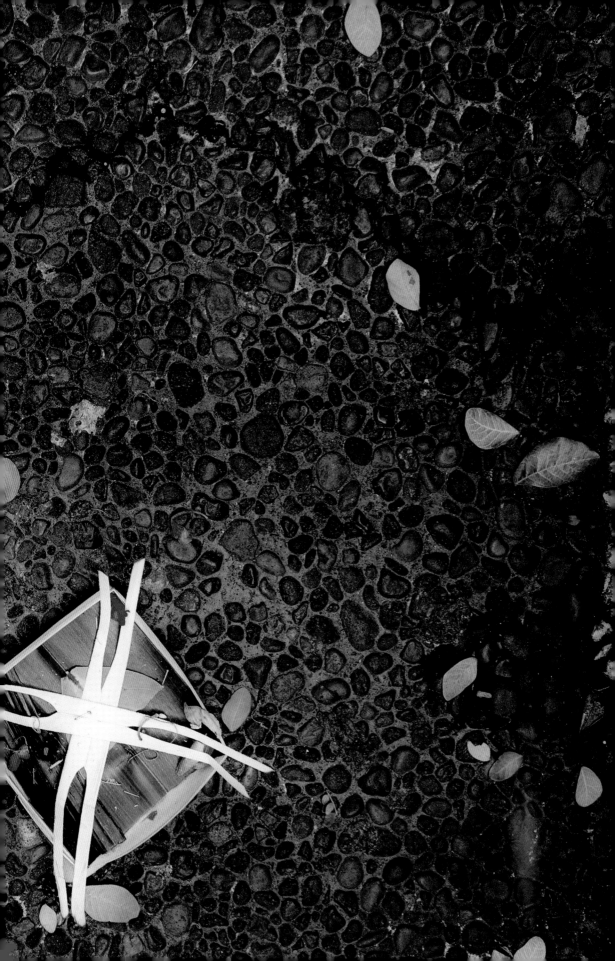

ADVANCED METERING

Determining correct exposure with precision is a challenge to any automated system. For experienced photographers, there is no substitute for taking more or less full control of the process. Unfortunately, this requires not only skill, but also time and careful attention to detail. However, not all work is hurried and, even with digital photography, precisely correct exposure always saves time and work later.

Incident-light metering

For much studio photography, taking an incident-light reading is a much-favored technique for determining exposure. The light-sensitive cell of a hand-held meter is covered with a translucent white hemisphere that collects light from a very large area. The meter is held at the subject position with the hemisphere pointing toward the camera. Thus, the meter integrates all light falling on the subject to arrive at a cumulative average.

The meter cannot distinguish between one side of the subject being in shadow while another is in bright light; it simply adds the two together. It also takes no account of the nature of the subject itself, which could be dark and absorbent or bright and reflective. In either case, the meter reading would be exactly the same.

The advantage that this method has over a reflected light reading is simplicity; and it always provides a good basis for bracketing exposures (see box below). However, you do need to move from the shooting position to the subject position, which may sometimes be difficult. In addition, small differences in the meter position can make a big difference to the reading, facing you with the problem of deciding which is the "correct" reading. Incident-light metering is, therefore, most useful where bright light is falling on the subject from the side or from behind the camera position; it is not advisable to use in backlit situations.

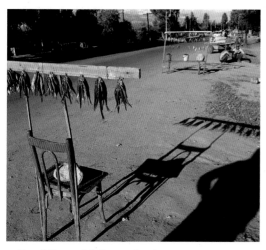

▲ **Deciding which method to use**
Bright, contrasty lighting from behind the camera or from the side, as in this scene, is ideally measured using an incident-light meter. The key tones in the image are the fish and chair, and if you get those correct then the rest of the scene falls into place. It would have been easy to underexpose this scene, as a normal reflected-light reading could be misled by the light-toned foreground and middle ground, and so set a smaller aperture or shorter shutter time.

BRACKETING EXPOSURES

Since correct exposure is central to good image and reproduction quality, many techniques have evolved to ensure that your pictures are properly exposed. The simplest is to take several bracketed exposures—that is, using steadily increasing, then decreasing exposure each time, so that the shots run from having more exposure than the metered "correct" setting through to having less. One of the images will have the qualities of exposure you want to see.

Some cameras offer an automatic bracketing mode to help you achieve this: they take several exposures in quick succession, all at different settings. Alternatively, you can take a series of exposures yourself, each time setting a different value on the exposure-compensation dial—for example, first the meter's recommended exposure, then exposures at +0.5, +1, +1.5, +2, over the metered exposure, then -0.5, -1, -1.5, -2 under. Steps of ½ stop are generally the most useful; smaller steps create too many images without a useful result, and larger steps may jump the correct exposure.

Spot metering

The majority of modern cameras offer a spot-metering mode, allowing you to make a reading from a very small area of the subject—typically around 5 percent of the total field of view. For work on location, spot metering has two major advantages: first, it allows you to be highly selective in choosing the key tone; and second, even when you cannot approach your subject, it allows you to take a reading as if you were close up.

To use a spot meter, decide which patch of color or tone in the subject should be exposed normally—in other words, which should be the mid-tone. Then you simply take a light reading from that area—typically it will be a skin tone or a key patch of color—and ignore the rest of the image (as far as exposure is concerned). The fastest way to make precise exposure readings is to use an auto-exposure mode such as aperture priority. Select your working aperture, point the spot meter, make the reading and hold it—usually with pressure on the shutter button—or lock the reading. Then, reframe your image and take the shot.

Some authorities suggest taking several readings—of highlight, shadow, and mid-tones—then using the readings to calculate the midpoint.

▼ Preset metering

With fast-moving clouds, Nelson's Column in London was bathed in changing light, while the blue sky behind remained relatively constant. I wanted to catch the sun just bursting through the rim of a cloud—too much sun created excessive flare, while too little lost the attractive burst of rays. If the meter had been left on automatic, the instant the sun appeared the exposure settings would compensate for the extra light and so render the sky almost black. In anticipation of this, I set the camera controls according to a manual meter reading of the sky, which included some bright cloud—thus ensuring the sky was a deep blue. The rest simply consisted of waiting for the sun to emerge, resisting the urge to respond when the meter reading shot up to indicate massive overexposure.

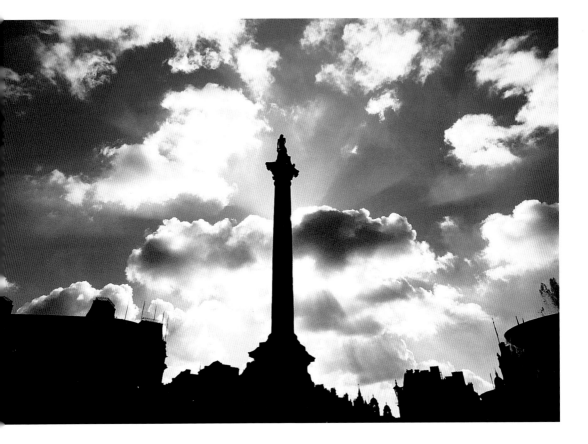

ADVANCED METERING CONTINUED

This procedure is useful for determining the luminance range of the scene—its span of brightness values. You can take a reading from a shadow area with detail and from a highlight area with detail, and see by how many stops they differ. If this difference is less than about 8 stops, you can comfortably record the entire scene. If, however, the subject luminance range is greater than about 10 stops, you may need to decide to sacrifice some subject details in the shadows or in the highlight values of the scene. The only other option is to adjust the lighting ratios (*see pp. 68–9 and 80–1*) to reduce the luminance range, if lighting is under your control. If you're working with subjects at close range, you may use flash to fill in shadows (*see pp. 80–1*).

Technical readings

One technique for dealing with unpredictable lighting conditions is to point your exposure meter at a standard target, such as a gray card. This target is printed in a neutral gray color with 18 percent reflectance—in other words, it reflects back 18 percent of the light falling on it, representing the mid-tone of paper. Instead of measuring the light reflecting from the subject or scene, you take your reading from the card instead. Not only is this a cumbersome method, but there are also variations in readings when the card is illuminated by directional light, depending on the angle at which the card is held (even though the card has a matte surface).

However, the gray card is an excellent control where image density or color accuracy is crucial, since it provides a standard patch whose density and color neutrality is a known quantity, and this enables an image to be calibrated to a standard. This degree of accuracy is important for technical imaging, such as copying artwork, clothing, or certain types of products for catalogues.

You can go further by including the gray card in the image itself. This provides a target when you make white-balance adjustments (*see also pp. 210–11*): when you click on the gray, you tell the software, "This bit is reliably neutral gray." When this is corrected to gray, every other color in the image should be accurate.

▶ **Full of light**
It may look like overexposure, but equally it could be said that the darkest corner under the veranda is correctly exposed. When you aim the spot metering into the darkest area of a scene to fully expose that area, you ensure that everything else is filled with light. For this shot, losing highlight detail is acceptable, as this helps convey the sense of brilliant airiness in this scene from Auckland, New Zealand.

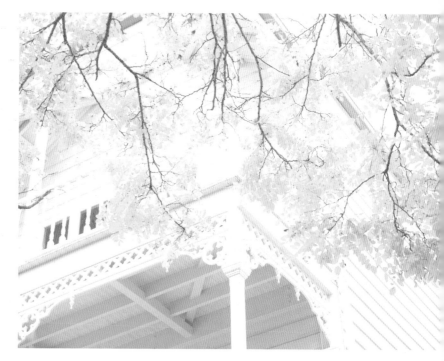

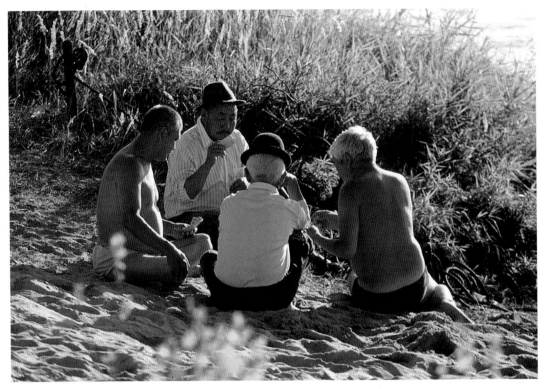

▲ Taking a spot reading

Light from in front of, or to one side of, the camera, as in this late afternoon scene in Kyrgyzstan, is best measured using the camera's spot-metering option (if available). You can then select the precise area of the scene that you want correctly exposed. In this shot, the reading was taken from the men's shadowy faces and bodies. The crucial goal is to ensure that the brighter areas of the scene are not rendered too light while retaining details in the shadows. Here, shadow detail has been helped by the reflective qualities of the sand.

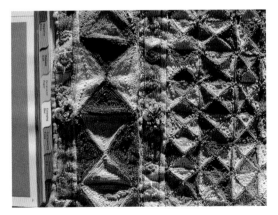

▲ Color accuracy

You can use a gray card—one printed with a mid-tone gray—as a standard target for the exposure meter when faced with subjects that are very dark or very light. However, gray cards are also useful when you need objective accuracy—as in this shot of a rare embroidery from Afghanistan. If you include the gray card, as you can see here, it provides a known standard for accurate color reproduction. The colored tabs also included with the object are useful for comparison with any paper print.

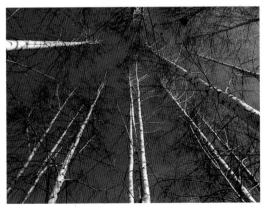

▲ Averaging metering

This view of silver birches is the ideal subject for meters that average light values throughout a scene. Indeed, it demonstrates how rare it is that this method of metering is applicable, as not many scenes have such a small dynamic range and even tone distribution. This scene is such that every method of metering should produce the same result—one that ensures the blues are rendered to mid-tone while the narrow tree trunks retain both highlights and shadows.

ACCESSORY FLASH

The modern flash is nearly universal because it is both highly miniaturized and "intelligent." Units may be small enough to fit in a camera phone, for example, yet deliver extremely accurate computer-controlled doses of light that balance the ambient light in the scene. Thanks to this versatility, flash units are found on virtually all camera phones, compact cameras, and many SLR and mirrorless cameras.

Making flash work for you

Whatever you might gain in terms of convenience by having a ready source of extra light built into the camera, you lose in terms of lighting subtlety. To make the best use of flash, you need to exploit the control facilities on your camera.

First, use the "slow-synch" or "synchro-sun" mode if your camera is equipped with it. In low-light conditions, this allows the ambient exposure to be relatively long, so that areas that are beyond the range of the flash can be recorded as well as possible, while the flash illuminates the foreground (*see below*). This not only softens the effect of the flash, but it can also mix white balance—the cool tint of the flash and the warmer color of the ambient light—which can be eye-catching.

Second, try using a reflector on the shadow side of the subject. If angled correctly, it will pick up some light from the flash and bounce it into the shadows. Any light-colored material can be used as a reflector—a piece of white paper or card or a white wall, for example. Flexible reflectors that are lightweight and opened out for use but can be collapsed to compact size are inexpensive and very effective. Some models offer two different surfaces—a gold side for warm-colored light and a matte or silvery white side for harder light.

Third, an advanced option is to use slave flash. These are separate flash units equipped with sensors that trigger the flash when the master flash (built into or cabled directly to the camera) is fired. If you have a flash unit, it is not expensive to add a slave unit. However, you will need to experiment with your camera to check if the synchronization of the multiple flash units is correct.

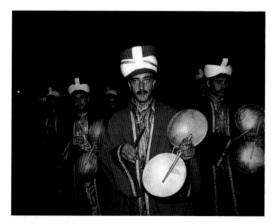

▲ Flash limitations

Dusk in Istanbul, Turkey, and traditional musicians gather. The standard flash exposure used for this image lights only the foreground subjects and the rapid light fall-off, characteristic of small light sources, fails to reach even a short distance behind the first musician. Adding to the problems, camera exposure is not long enough for the low ambient, or available, light levels prevailing at the time. As a consequence, the background has been rendered black. This type of result is seldom attractive, nor does it display any sound photographic technique.

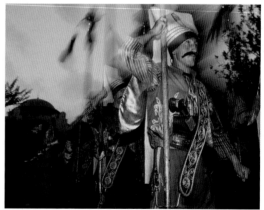

▲ Effective technique

When illumination is low, make the most of what light is available rather than relying on electronic flash. Here, exposure was set for the sky: this required a shutter of ¼ sec, giving rise to the blurred parts of the image. At the same time, the flash was brief enough to "freeze" the soldier in the foreground, so that he appears sharp. Utilizing all ambient light ensures that the distant part of the scene is not wholly underexposed—some color can even be seen in the background building. Compare this with the image in which flash provided all the illumination (*left*).

Using any setup with more than one flash means trying out different levels of flash output to discover the best results. Start by setting the slave to its lowest power output, bearing in mind that the task of this unit is to relieve subject shadows, not act as the main light. Some camera models are designed for multiple-flash photography.

Flash synchronization

Because the pulse of light from electronic flash is extremely brief, even when compared with the shortest shutter time, it is crucial that the shutter is fully open when the flash fires. Only then will the entire sensor area be exposed to the flash light reflected back from the subject. There is usually a limit to the shortest shutter time that synchronizes with the flash, often known as "x-synch." For most cameras with focal-plane shutters, this is between $\frac{1}{100}$ and $\frac{1}{250}$ sec. In some models, x-synch corresponds to the shortest available shutter time, which may be $\frac{1}{8,000}$ sec, but only when using flash units dedicated to that particular camera model.

FLASH EXPOSURE

All flash exposures consist of two separate illuminations occurring simultaneously. While the shutter is open, or the light sensor is receptive, light from the overall scene—the ambient light—creates one exposure. This ambient exposure takes on the color of the prevailing light, it exposes the background if sufficient, and it lasts longer than that of the flash itself.

The second exposure is in addition to the ambient one. The burst of light from a flash is extremely brief, possibly less than $\frac{1}{10,000}$ sec (though studio flash may be as long as $\frac{1}{200}$ sec), and its color is determined by the characteristics of the flash tube (which can be filtered for special effects).

The fact that there are two exposures means that it is necessary to control their balance for the best results. But it also allows you to make creative use of the process by, for example, allowing the flash to freeze movement, while the longer ambient exposure produces blurred results.

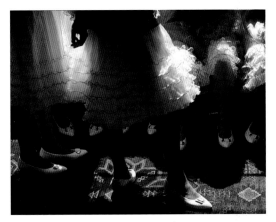

▲ Without flash

Bright, contrasty sunshine streaming in through large windows behind the subjects—a troupe of young singers dressed in traditional costume from Kyrgyzstan—produced a strongly backlit effect. Without the use of flash, the shadows would appear very dark, but in this case a wall behind the camera position reflected back some light from the windows into the shadows to relieve the contrast a little and so retain some subject details. Use of a fill-in flash would have spoiled the composition, which relies on the pattern of the shoes.

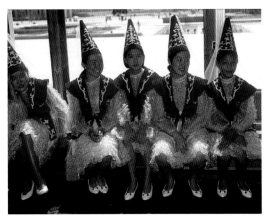

▲ With flash

In this alternative interpretation of the previous scene (*left*), flash has been used. This produced enough light to fill most of the shadows. Now we can clearly see the girls' costumes, but note the shadows that still remain on the carpet. The camera was set to expose the background correctly: here, an exposure time of $\frac{1}{250}$ sec was used. The f/number dictated by the exposure meter was then set on the lens, and the flash was set to underexpose by $1\frac{1}{3}$ stops. This ensured that the foreground was exposed by both the flash and the available window light.

QUICK FIX ELECTRONIC FLASH

Modern electronic flash units are versatile and convenient light sources, ideal for use when light levels are low (and the subject is relatively close) or when image contrast is high and you want to add a little fill-in illumination to the shadow areas. However, due to the intensity of their output, as well as their limited range and covering power, they can make it difficult to obtain naturalistic lighting effects and correct exposure.

Problem: Common types of problem that are encountered when using electronic flash include overexposed results—particularly of the foreground parts of the image—and underexposed results—particularly of the image background. In addition, general underexposure of long-distance subject matter is very common, as is uneven lighting, in which the corners or foreground are less bright than the centre of the image.

Analysis: Flash units are controlled with their own light-sensitive sensor or with sensors in the camera. These measure the light output from the flash or the amount of light reflecting back from the subject and reaching the sensor. As a result, they are just as prone to error as any camera exposure meter. Furthermore, the light produced by a flash unit falls off very rapidly with distance (*see above right and p. 80*).

Overexposed flash-illuminated pictures are usually caused by positioning the flash too close to the subject, or when the subject is the only element in an otherwise largely empty space.

Flash underexposure is caused by the unit having insufficient power to cover adequately the flash-to-subject distance. For example, no small flash unit can light an object that is more than about 30 ft (10 m) away, and even quite powerful flash units cannot adequately light an object that is more than about 100 ft (30 m) distant.

Uneven lighting is caused when the flash is unable to cover the angle of view of the lens—a problem most often experienced with wide angles. And another problem occurs when an attached lens or lens accessory blocks the light from a camera-mounted flash.

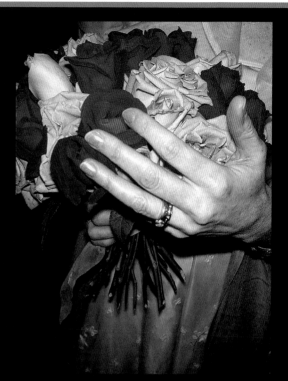

▲ Light fall-off

Light from a flash unit mounted on the camera falls off, or loses its effectiveness, very rapidly as distance increases. This is evident in this close-up image of a bride holding a posy of flowers. The subject's hands and the roses nearest the flash are brightly illuminated but even just a little bit further back, the image is visibly darker. This is evident if you look at the back edge of the wedding dress, for example. The effects of this light fall-off can be greatly minimized by using a light source that covers a larger area—hence the very different lighting effect you get when using bounced flash (*opposite*).

Solution: For close-up work, reduce the power of the flash if possible. When photographing distant subjects in the dark—landscapes, for example, or the stage at a concert—flash is usually a waste of time and is best turned off. A better option is to use a long exposure and support the camera on a tripod or rest it on something stable, such as a wall or fence. With accessory flash units—not built-in types—you can place a diffuser over the flash window to help spread the light and so prevent darkened corners when using a wide-angle lens.

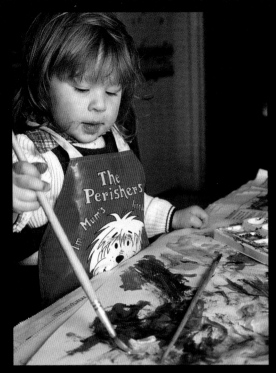

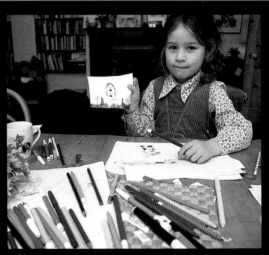

▲ Mixed lighting

The result of balancing flash with an exposure sufficient to register the ambient light indoors delivers results like this. The lighting is soft but the color balance is warmed by the ambient light. Also, the background is bright enough for it to appear quite natural. If a greater exposure had been given to the background, there would have been an increased risk of subject movement spoiling the image.

▲ Bounced flash

Direct flash used at this close distance would produce a harshly lit subject and a shadowy background. In this shot, the flash was aimed at the wall opposite the child. In effect, the light source then becomes the wall, which reflects back a wide spread of light. Not only does this soften the quality of the light, it also reduces the rapid light fall-off characteristic of a small-sized source of light. But bounced flash is possible only if you use an auxiliary flash unit. Note, however, that the background is rather darker than ideal—to overcome this, there must be sufficient ambient light to mix with the flash illumination to provide correct exposure overall (*above right*).

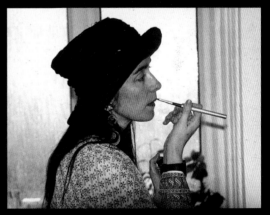

▲ Uneven light

On-camera flash typically delivers these unsatisfactory results. The lighting is uneven, the shapes the flash has illuminated look flat, and there are hard, harsh reflections on all shiny surfaces. In addition, the flash has created unpleasant shadows (note the shadow of the lip-brush on the background woodwork). Always be aware of any flat surfaces positioned behind your subject when using flash from the camera position.

HOW TO AVOID THE PROBLEM

The best way to obtain reliable results with flash is to experiment in different picture-taking situations. With a digital camera you can make exposures at different settings in a variety of situations to learn the effects of flash. Some flash units feature a modeling light, which flashes briefly to show you the effect of the light—this is a useful preview, but it can consume a good deal of power and is likely to disturb your subject.

ELECTRONIC FLASH

Today's battery-powered electronic flash units offer an impressive combination of high power, portability, flexibility, and convenience. Moreover, these units are easy to use, with many automatic features. In addition, lighting effects are repeatable and color temperature is constant (*see p. 212*). In fact, portable electronic flash units are the single most powerful accessory you can attach to your camera. They widen the range of situations you can photograph in while expanding the lighting effects available for many situations. It is also easy to match flash units to budget, as low-power units are very affordable. For greater expense, you are rewarded with higher power, more rapid recharging, and more automatic features such as wireless (infrared or radio) synchronization.

Digital advantages

Digital photographers are at a great advantage compared with their film-based counterparts in being able to assess the result of a flash exposure immediately after it is made—either by observing the image on the camera's review screen or on a computer monitor. Assessing images on the relatively small screen of a typical digital camera is more reliable than before, thanks to improved and larger screens. Nonetheless, if possible, it is always preferable to download the image onto a computer for assessment via a full-sized and calibrated monitor (*see pp. 356–7*).

Types of equipment

For a range of photographic tasks, from still life to portraiture, a single flash unit will suffice. The single most useful light-shaper—which changes the quality of the emitted light—is a large diffusing panel, also called a soft-box. A substitute for a soft-box is a reflector, but that incurs a big loss of light through the inefficiency of reflection.

A second synchronized lighting unit is useful for adding highlights—a halo of light from behind, for example, or controlling background lighting, or increasing overall light levels. The two units need to be synchronized with the camera. This can be done wirelessly with infrared or radio, which is available on the better-specified models. You can also attach a sensor to one of the units: when it picks up a sudden rise in light levels, it triggers the unit it is attached to. Using these methods you can synchronize several units.

For the greatest flexibility, you also need a camera with a lens offering a wide range of adjustable

BROAD LIGHTING

Young children can be demanding subjects if you have too fixed an end result in mind. Often, they are curious about all the equipment in a studio, they are very mobile, their concentration span is short, and they are difficult to direct. One approach is to position them against a plain background and set a broad lighting scheme—perhaps two soft-boxes, one either side of the set. The wide spread of soft light allows your subjects to move about without you worrying where shadows will fall.

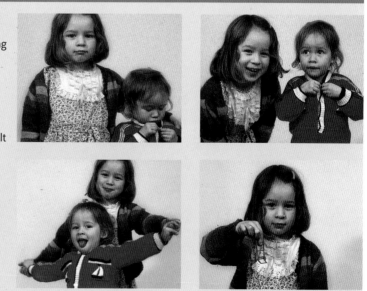

FILL-IN FLASH

Fill-in flash is used to light shadowy areas, particularly when the background is much brighter than the subject (*right*). The flash is set so that it lights the subject with between 0.5 stop to 1.5 stop less than a full exposure. For example, the aperture setting is f/5.6 but the flash level is set as if the aperture is f/4: this puts out 1 stop less than is needed as the actual set aperture is smaller by 1 stop. At its best, fill-in flash is invisible: the lighting simply looks gorgeous (*far right*).

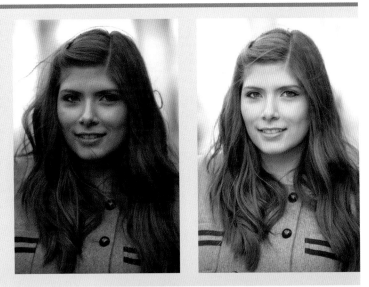

apertures. As adjusting the aperture is your principal means of controlling flash exposure reaching the camera sensors, cameras with just three or four aperture settings can limit your creativity.

Studio lighting

In mastering the basics of portable flash lighting you will also learn the fundamentals of studio flash lighting. The difference is that not only are studio units far more powerful and controllable, but also the range of light-shapers available is very wide, making it possible to create lighting effects that are all but impossible to reproduce outside the studio.

In the studio, you can have everything under control—from the color of the walls to whether you cover the windows. You may therefore light your subject with only the studio units, or you can balance existing, ambient light from the sky with flash light: the range of possibilities is infinitely rich.

Building a lighting scheme

The sequence on the following pages shows what differences you can achieve by working with the simplest lighting set-up: a single flash. Analyze the images for the quality of the light and shadows in order to learn how to obtain the same effects with your own equipment.

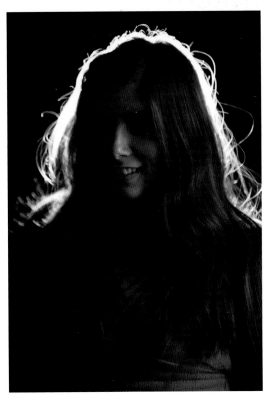

▲ Ring of bright light

One of the most delightful lighting effects in portraiture is the rim light or halo: place the flash pointing toward the camera but hidden behind the subject's head. This throws some of the hair into bright highlight while leaving the rest of the image in shadow and relatively flat light.

ELECTRONIC FLASH CONTINUED

INVERSE SQUARE LAW

If you double the distance between a light source and the surface that light falls on, brightness at the surface is not just halved. For a small, or "point," light source, without a reflector or lens for focusing output, doubling the distance reduces intensity by four times (by a factor of two squared). This is the inverse square law. Although commonly applied to studio and accessory flash lighting, the inverse square law gives inaccurate results since nearly all luminaires (sources of light) use reflectors or lenses, so light distribution is not even and equal in all directions.

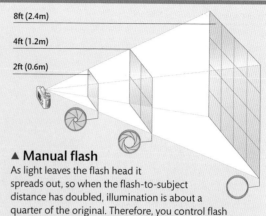

8ft (2.4m)

4ft (1.2m)

2ft (0.6m)

▲ Manual flash

As light leaves the flash head it spreads out, so when the flash-to-subject distance has doubled, illumination is about a quarter of the original. Therefore, you control flash exposure through both distance and lens aperture.

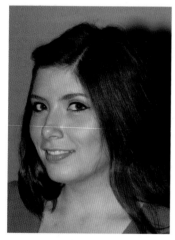

Direct on-camera with subject close to wall

The normal position for flash—mounted on the camera and pointed directly at the subject—is only for convenience. And it was necessary when flash units were weakly powered, as it makes the most efficient use of light. However, it is one of the worst possible ways to light a subject: shadows on the face are flattened, which smooths out form and texture, and any slightly reflective surface returns as a shiny bright patch. Furthermore, a strong shadow is thrown behind the subject, which is visible if there is a wall too close.

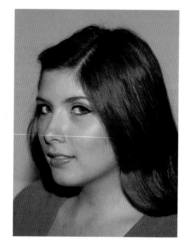

Direct on-camera with subject away from wall

The strong shadow from direct lighting can be reduced by moving the subject away from any wall or surface behind that would catch the shadow. By adjusting the distance from the wall, you may be able to balance the brightness of light on your subject's face with the background. However, the lighting is still harsh and unflattering.

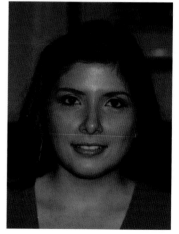

Direct on-camera with diffuser

You can soften the light from the flash by applying a diffuser: this can be as simple as a piece of white paper or tissue held in front of the flash-tube that emits the light. Or you can attach an accessory plastic dome onto the flash unit. The diffusing reduces the amount of light by spreading it over a wide area. This delivers soft shadows with just a hint of highlight concentration, giving a natural look.

HARSH SHADOWS

Using a single camera-mounted flash is by far the most convenient lighting arrangement. However, effects are often harsh and unattractive. Here, a flash on the left of the camera has provided adequate illumination but it has also cast hard shadows behind the subject and from the pen she is holding. At the same time, the modeling effect on the face is flat, while the background appears too dark due to the rapid fall-off of light. To avoid these problems, you will either have to bounce the flash off an intervening surface or, better, use more than one lighting unit.

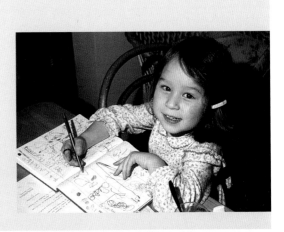

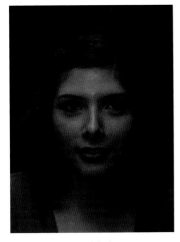

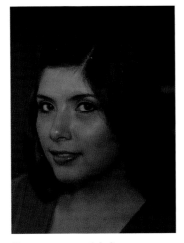

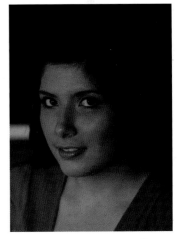

On-camera with bounce from above

Bouncing turns any nearby surface into a flash accessory: with your flash mounted on the camera, turn its head toward the ceiling. The flash travels from the flash unit to the ceiling which, in reflecting the light, becomes the main source of light. As the light has spread over a wide area on the ceiling before being reflected, the light is softened. However, because the light comes from above, it causes deep shadows over the eyes. A little light may leak from the flash to light the subject directly: this is useful for filling in shadows.

On-camera with bounce from side

There are two advantages to bouncing light from the flash against a nearby wall. As the light reaches the subject from the side, there is better modeling, with no heavy shadows around the eyes. Also, you can usually get closer to walls than to ceilings, which means you lose less light and can control its quality by varying your distance from the wall. Work close to the wall for a harder light; shoot from further away for a softer effect. Naturally, white walls (or ceilings) are the best to work with as they do not disturb color balance.

Detached with subject lit at 45°

Lighting becomes very interesting when the flash is freed from the camera. Some units use a cable to connect to the camera, others use infrared or radio to synchronize. At any rate, unless you have assistance, you can hold the flash only as far as you can reach. Fortunately, it is easy to hold the flash so that it lights a portrait subject from about 45 degrees. This oblique lighting brings out the form of the face or body; here giving shape to the nose, cheeks, and chin.

ELECTRONIC FLASH CONTINUED

HINTS AND TIPS

If you are new to working with studio flash and accessories (*see pp. 354–5*), you might find it useful to bear the following points in mind:

- As a general rule, always use as few units as possible to achieve the desired lighting effects. Start with one light only and use reflectors to control the quality of the illumination reaching your subject. Only if this is insufficient should you consider adding extra lighting units to the scheme.
- Remember that it is easier to remove light than to add light. Using accessories, such as barn doors or snoots, you can easily control the fall of light and any shadows that are created as a result.

However, an additional light immediately casts a set of new shadows.

- A reflector placed facing the main light, angled so that it bounces light into subject shadows, is usually a more effective solution than using another light source to reduce shadows.
- A large light source, such as an umbrella reflector or soft-box, produces softer light and more diffused shadows than a small light source.
- A small light source, such as a spotlight with a small bowl, produces harder light and sharper shadows than a large, diffuse light source.
- You can use colored gels to add tints to the background of your subject.

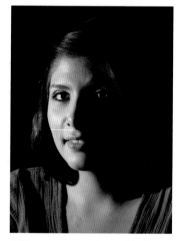

Off-camera at 90° with flash close to model

The closer a light-source is placed to the subject, the harsher the light appears to be. And if it is placed to the side, deep and long shadows result. The combination of hard light with deep shadows delivers dramatic effects thanks to the marked contrasts of tone and visible detail. At normal portrait distances, you will probably need to mount your flash on a small stand or ask an assistant to hold the flash to one side of the subject. For maximum contrast, ensure the subject is not close to a wall on the side opposite the flash.

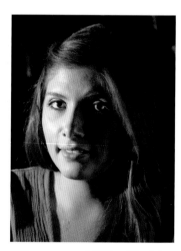

Off-camera at 90° with side reflector

If you light your subject from one side but place them so that they are near a wall facing the flash, some light bounces from the wall into the shadows. This lifts or fills the shadow side with soft light. This reduces the drama but creates a most attractive lighting. Alternatively, you can hold a card or sheet of paper on the shadow side to reflect light. By working with the color of the reflector and its surface texture—whether glossy or rough—you can alter the quality of the reflected light.

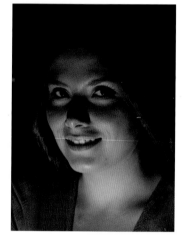

Off-camera from below pointing upward

Seldom flattering but always recognizable, lighting a portrait subject from below has the most specific uses of any lighting set-up. This is because it is the least likely to be found in the natural world. The light looks as if it comes from a fire or a flashlight held low down. By casting unusual shadows on the face and leaving everything else in the dark, this scheme conveys mystery and tension.

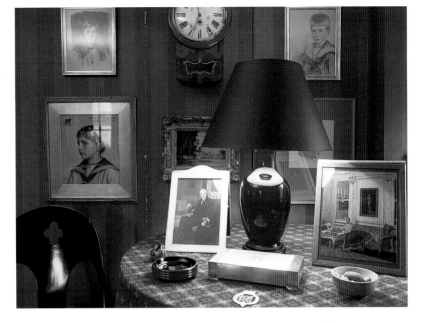

▶ Mixed light sources

An aim of studio lighting can be to mimic the quality of daylight. In this scene, it was important that the table light appeared to be the main light source. The levels of daylight were inadequate to illuminate the dark-colored interior of the room, so a flash was directed at the ceiling behind the table. The reflected light was just enough to bring out important details in the setting without creating tell-tale hot spots in the glass-fronted pictures.

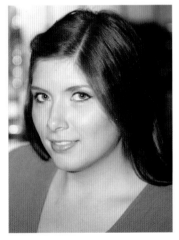

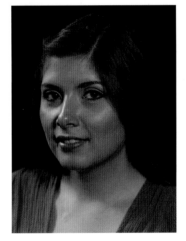

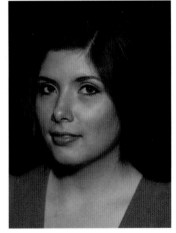

Ambient with full fill-in from flash

All flash exposures consist of two separate exposures: one using light from the flash, one using ambient or available light. When the levels of the two are equal, or the flash is brighter, the effect usually appears over-lit and unnatural. A full fill-in with flash is useful in situations where you do not wish to lose any details to shadows; where you need maximum clarity. If the ambient light is colored, as here, it will warm up the white balance of the image.

Reduced exposure overall with fill and ambient

Under-exposure softens the lighting by allowing shadows to differentiate from mid-tones. At the same time, colors become deeper and the contribution from the tinted ambient lighting from indoor lamps makes a significant shift in white balance.

On-camera flash with diffuser plus daylight

The white balance of many flash-units tends to be on the cool side of neutral, some giving a noticeably bluish color cast. You can correct this using a filter, in post-processing, or by working with ambient light. If you use indoor lighting, the resulting white balance will be distinctly warm. If you work with daylight, the balance is cooler. In this image, the brown walls of the room contributed their color to the final balance. This shows how each source of light and every reflecting surface in the scene contributes to the final result.

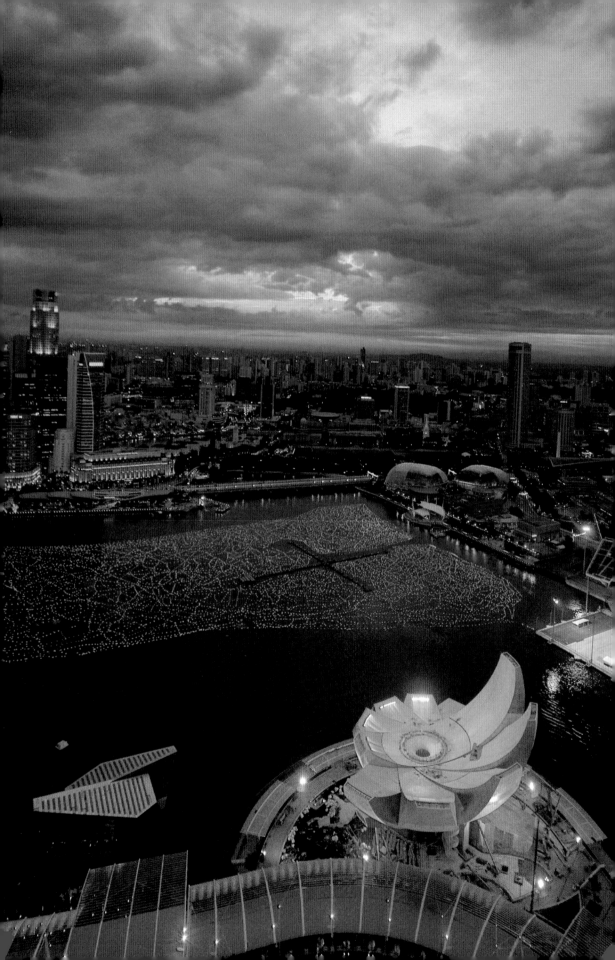

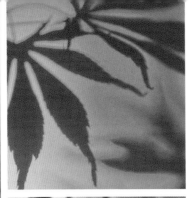

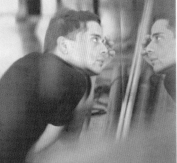

2 PHOTOGRAPHY
PROJECTS

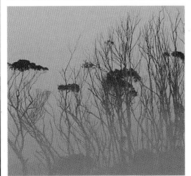

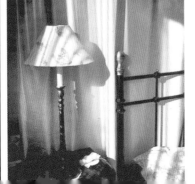

STARTING PROJECTS

A project gives you something to concentrate on, something on which you can focus your ideas or around which you can define a goal. Committing yourself to a specific project can give you a purpose and help you develop your observational and technical skills. In addition, a project provides you with a measure against which you can determine your progress as a photographer.

One of the most frequently asked questions is how you come up with project ideas—and a common mistake is to think that some concept of global interest is needed. In fact, the most mundane subjects can be just as rewarding and—even more important—achievable.

An action plan

■ It could be that your skills as a photographer could be put to use by some local community group. So, instead of giving money, you could provide photographs—perhaps with the idea of holding a local exhibition to raise funds.

■ If you try to do too much too quickly you are heading for disappointment. For example, you want to digitize all the pictures in your family albums. Fine; but don't try to complete the project in a month.

■ You have to be realistic about the money involved in carrying through a project, but preoccupation with cost can freeze your enthusiasm, kill the sense of fun, and become, in itself, the cause of the waste of money.

■ Nurturing a project idea is more about cooperation than coercion. You have to learn to work with the idiosyncrasies and character of the subject you have set your sights on. And doubts and misgivings are very common. If you find yourself inhibited or you are afraid to look silly, or if you think it has all been done before, then you may start to wonder what the point is. If so, then just bear in mind that you are doing this for yourself, for the fun of it. As long as you think it is worthwhile, why care what anyone else thinks?

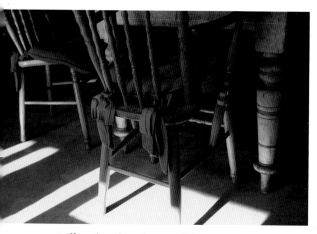

▲ Illuminating domesticity
This is the type of domestic scene that could easily pass unnoticed at home, unless your concentration is sharpened by having a project in mind. Yet, if you were to see the exact same scene on your travels, the simple fact that you were not in your familiar surroundings may make the light and balance of the complementary colors and the rhythm of the vertical or near-vertical lines immediately striking.

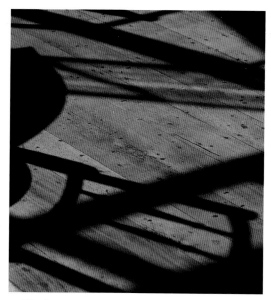

▲ Shadows
Strong light casting deep, well-defined shadows and the warm colors of the floor make for an abstract image. To ensure that the lit area was properly exposed, I took a spot reading from the bright area of floor, entirely ignoring the shadows.

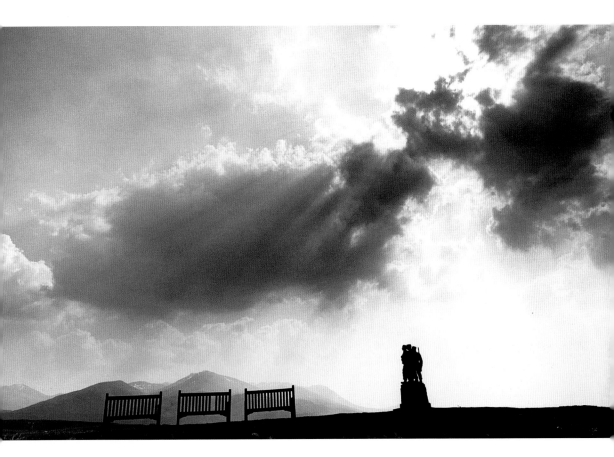

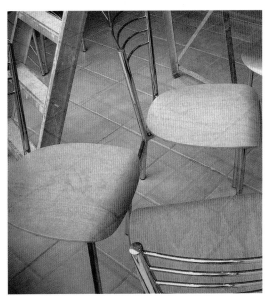

▲ Interior arrangements

The paraphernalia of a restaurant under construction produced a complex of lines and tones that caught my eye. The picture benefited from having the left-hand side slightly darkened to balance the darkness toward the top right of the image.

▲ Juxtaposition

A monument to three wartime commandos in Scotland reflects the three benches erected for visitors to sit and enjoy the view. A long wait in a bitingly cold wind was rewarded when a spectacular burst of sunlight broke through a gap in the cloud-laden sky.

TRY THIS

Make a list of objects you are familiar with. These can be as simple and ordinary as you like—dinner plates, for example, bus stops, drying clothes, or chairs. Do not prejudge the subject. If the idea comes to you, there is probably a good reason for it. Choose one subject and take some pictures on the theme: again, do not prejudge the results, just let the subject lead you. Be ready to be surprised. Don't think about what others will think of what you are doing. Don't worry about taking "great" pictures. Just respond to the subject—if it is not an obviously visual idea, then you might have to work that bit harder to make it work as an image. Don't abandon the subject just because it initially seems unpromising.

ABSTRACT IMAGERY

Photography has the power to isolate a fragment of a scene and turn it into art, or to freeze shapes that momentarily take on a meaning far removed from their original intention. Or chance juxtapositions can be given significance as a result of your perception and the way you decide to frame and photograph the scene.

Close-ups and lighting

The easiest approach to abstracts is the close-up, as it emphasizes the graphic and removes the context. To achieve this, it is usually best to shoot square-on to the subject, as this frees the content from such distractions as receding space or shape changes due to projection distortion.

Longer focal length settings help to concentrate the visual field, but take care not to remove too much. It is advisable to take a variety of shots with differing compositions and from slightly different distances, as images used on screen or in print often have different demands made on them. For example, fine detail and texture are engrossing but if the image is to be used small on a web page, then a broad sweep may work better. And since you will usually be shooting straight onto flat or two-dimensional subjects, you do not need great depth of field (*see pp. 24–7*). This is useful, as it is often crucial to keep images sharp throughout.

▶ Complicated abstract
Abstract images do not need to be simple in either execution or vision. Try working with reflections and differential focus (focusing through an object to something further away). Here, in Udaipur, India, a complex of mirrors, colored glass, and highlights from window shutters battle for attention—and bemuse the viewer. Control of depth of field is critical: if too much of the image is very sharp, the dreamy abstract effect may be lost.

▼ Found abstract
Here, the decaying roof surface at a busy railway station must have been glanced at by thousands of commuters every day but seldom seen. Perhaps it is a simple expression of the process of aging, the origins of which can only be guessed at.

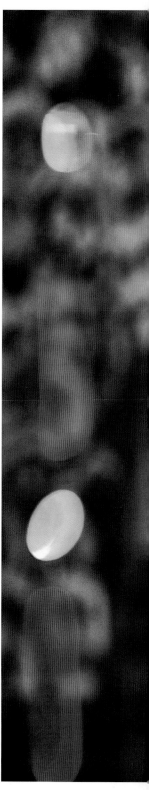

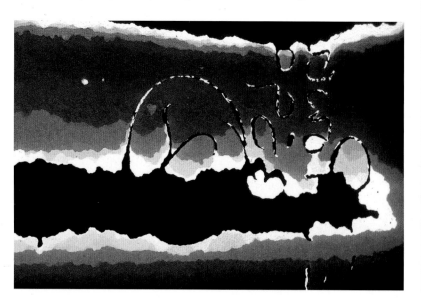

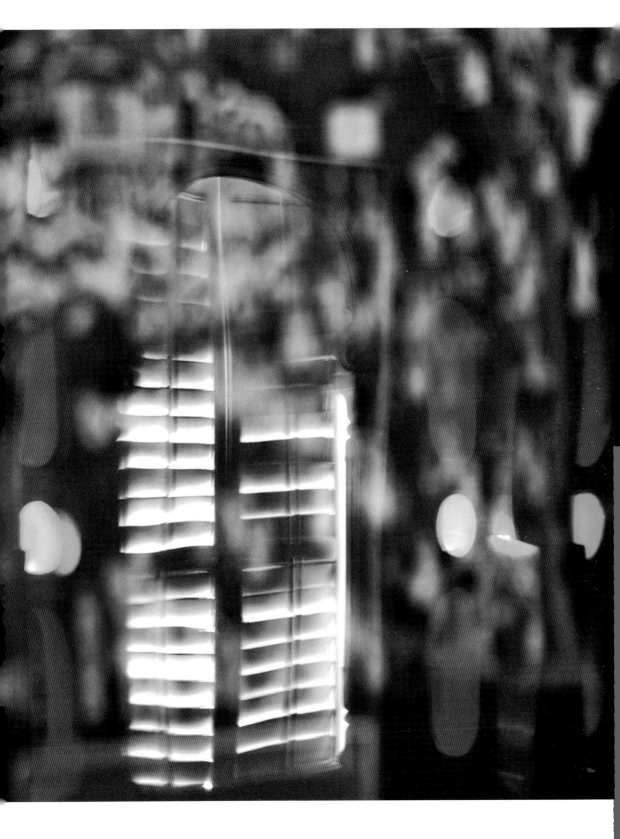

ABSTRACT IMAGERY CONTINUED

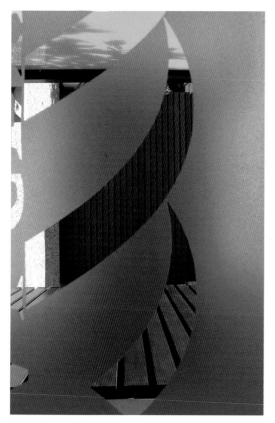

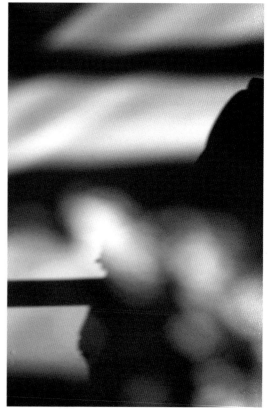

▲ Modern forms

Contemporary architectural details are rich sources of abstract imagery. Their strong graphic design invites you to take—and delight in—small elements and examine their interaction with other, equally graphic elements. Here, the frosted glass of an apartment building gives a partially obscured view of the courtyard beyond. To increase the abstract look of the image, I simply turned it on its side.

▲ Light play

Observe shadows closely and you will find a challenging and constantly changing source of images. Clear, clean light helps give well-defined shadows that contrast sharply with man-made textures and surfaces. Take care not to overexpose, because that will cause you to lose highlight textures. This type of image often benefits from increased contrast and saturation, as seen here.

COPYRIGHT CONCERNS

You may think that because a poster or other subject is on public view, you can photograph it with impunity. If you are taking the photograph for research or study, for example to illustrate a school essay on advertising, then this may be true. In other cases, however, you may be infringing someone's copyright. If you use a recognizable and sizeable portion of an image on public view as a significant part of another image that you go on to exhibit, publish, or sell, then in many countries you would be in breach of copyright. If you really want to use the image, then at least be aware of the potential legal situation. Note that sculptures, buildings, logos such as McDonald's arches, cars such as the Rolls-Royce, the French TGV train, certain toys, for example Disney characters—even landmarks such as the Lone Cypress tree at Pebble Beach, USA—all enjoy a measure of copyright protection. In reality you may never be taken to court for photographing them—but be aware that, theoretically, you could be.

ARCHITECTURE

The built environment can provide endless photographic opportunities—the problem is not in finding subject matter, but in reducing it to a manageable scale. At the same time, digital techniques make it easier than ever to create stunning images. For example, we can work with a wider range of lighting options than ever before, thanks to tone-mapping software, which blends different exposures into a tonally compressed image (*see pp. 266–7*).

Technical considerations

You can approach photography of buildings in broadly two ways—artistically, in which you treat the architecture as a subject for free interpretation; or you can attempt to be faithful to the architect's design intentions. For technical renderings, you need to ensure that straight lines appear straight and, where possible, that parallel lines are also recorded as parallel. This means using lenses with accurate drawing; that is, those that produce images with minimal distortion. A secondary requirement is that the illumination of the image is as even as possible, so that the corners of the image are not darkened. In practice this is achieved with medium-

KNOW YOUR RIGHTS

Areas open to the public such as shopping malls, or even landmarks such as London's Trafalgar Square, may be privately owned, so if you intend to publish pictures of a particular building, you may need to obtain permission first. Avoid using professional-looking equipment, and make your shots swiftly to avoid drawing attention.

Fears that photographs may be used for planning terrorist acts have caused some police and security forces to prevent pictures being taken in certain urban locations. In many countries you cannot be made to delete your images or to hand over your memory card without being charged with an offense, but it is always best to cooperate with the authorities when you are abroad.

▼ Dramatic highs

The architect may not thank you for this vertiginous view (of Singapore's first high-rise apartment building), but it effectively conveys the structure and its height. Wide-angle views looking directly upward or downward are usually quite disorienting, but added to the strongly converging lines, the result is visually powerful.

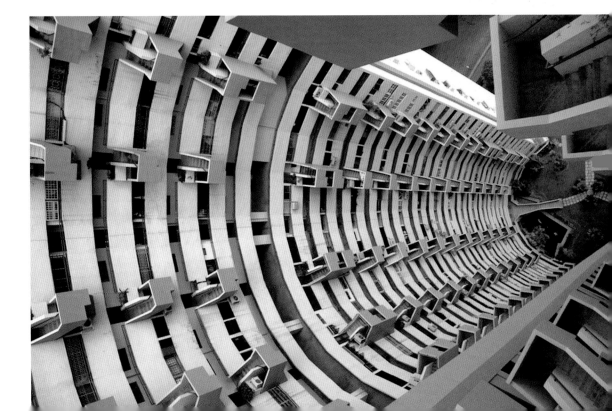

ARCHITECTURE CONTINUED

speed prime or single-focal length lenses such as 35mm, 28mm, or 24mm—all of around f/2.8 maximum aperture. Note that almost all zoom lenses cause unacceptable levels of distortion and uneven illumination, although some defects can be corrected in image manipulation software.

Foreground reduction

You can also use software to improve the shape of buildings—correcting converging parallel lines and turning distorted rectangles into a squared-off (orthogonal) shape (see pp. 208–9). But there are limits to how convincing image adjustments can be, compared to correct capture. Aim the camera level and square to any subject that you do not wish to distort. If you cannot capture the whole height of the building, photograph from further away, if possible, or use a lens with wider angle. Both options result in capturing a great deal of foreground, but this is easily cropped off. For professional architectural work, the shift lens (see p. 345) is indispensable: the lens slides upward to crop out foreground.

View variety

Extreme wide-angle views, that is, focal lengths less than 24mm or equivalent, are tempting, but objects near the edge of the frame appear distorted in small images when viewed close up. If you need really wide views, you can stitch several shots together to create a panorama (see pp. 298–9): this is best done with the aid of a panoramic head and tripod (see p. 346).

Although it is natural to reach for a wide-angle lens to photograph buildings or interiors, a wide view is not always best. A carefully chosen, narrower field of view can reveal more of a building and its surroundings, so remember to look for telling details, such as a high-up window or decorative elements. In fact, the best way to improve your architectural photography is not by buying a new lens, but by being painstaking about choosing perspective and framing.

Dynamic color

Photography of buildings needs perhaps greater flexibility with white balance than any other field of photography. This is because lights originating inside the building are usually of a different color temperature to the light coming from outside. A contrast of colors can be attractive, but too great a difference can distract from the building itself. For the greatest amount of flexibility in adjustment, capture in raw format (see pp. 234–7). You do not always have to correct color balance fully: improvements can often be made simply by reducing the saturation of reds, or increasing their lightness—or a bit of both (see pp. 214–15).

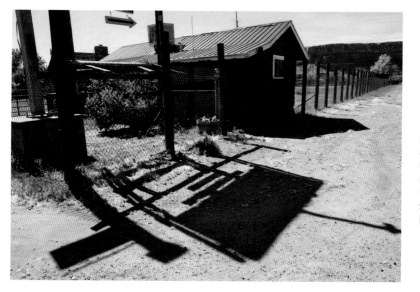

◀ **Vernacular**
Pictures of buildings usually focus on the grand and the monumental, but there are many more possibilities. Buildings locally made without design pretensions—ranging from animal shelters, barns, sheds, and farm houses to fishing huts—are all rich imagery sources. Use local signage and street furniture to enrich picture content.

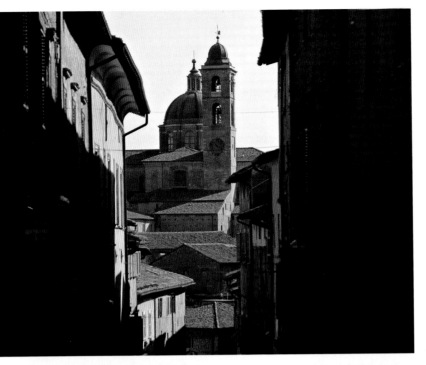

◀ Distant charms

When in search of the perfect Italian piazza and the grandest duomo, you can start shooting long before you arrive. Here, in Urbino, great towers dominate street views, guiding your exploration of the town and inspiring each step of the way. You can include the ephemera of street signs, hanging washing, and bunting or flags to provide context—or avoid them, to reinforce the atmosphere of timelessness.

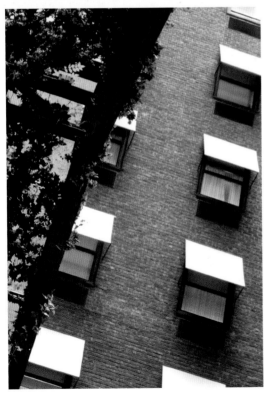

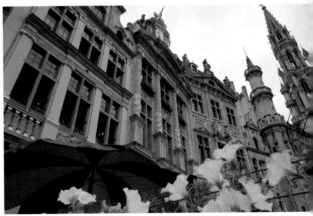

▲ Leaning back

Pointing a camera upward to capture a building seldom flatters it, but for specific pictorial effect, a steeply upward view can work well. Use contrasting foreground elements to help articulate the space in an engaging way.

TRY THIS

Photographing from one spot, using a zoom lens to vary framing, helps train the eye to find compositions. Choose a location to shoot from, then create the greatest variety of images you can by using only the zoom to change the framing. Return to the same spot at different times of the day and in different weather conditions to obtain an even greater variety of images.

▲ Opportunities

Even as you enter a hotel, you may spot a picture possibility. Take a second out to make the shot, for the light may change or you may lose the inspiration of the moment. If your lens does not take in a sufficiently wide-angle view, tilt the camera to use the diagonal of the frame.

INTERIORS

Essential for advertising property for sale or rental, interior views have long been a staple of the professional photographer. Produced with the aim of showing the space in as favorable a light as possible—spacious, tidy, airy, and attractive—the potential for creativity and experimentation is limited. But if you are not working for clients, there is no reason to restrict yourself.

Mania for mood

Interior views are most interesting when they convey a mood—the faded charm of a once luxurious hotel, the mysterious ruins of an abandoned house, the remains of a grand palace.

To capture atmosphere, work with light, compose to make the most of intriguing details, but do not feel that you have to get everything into one shot. The best way to use flash to light dark spaces is to aim the light into a specific area to create an atmospheric accent, but not to provide the main illumination. You might manipulate the image to introduce a vintage look, if that will help create a sense of times past and lost.

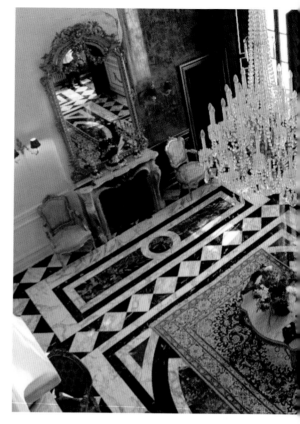

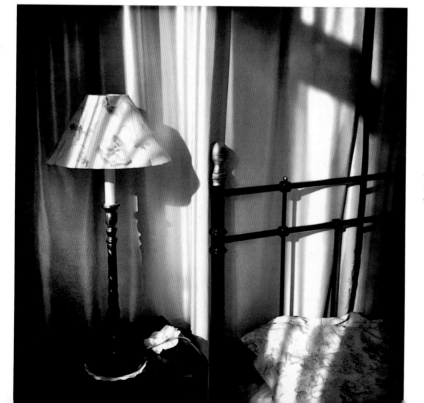

◄ Vintage interior
For a vintage hotel in Brussels, a faded look, as provided by the Hipstamatic app, was more appropriate than a straight shot. The app applies a filter that turns the overall tone to yellow-green, reduces contrast and desaturates the majority of colors. The result is similar to that obtained from out-of-date high-speed transparency film of the 1980s.

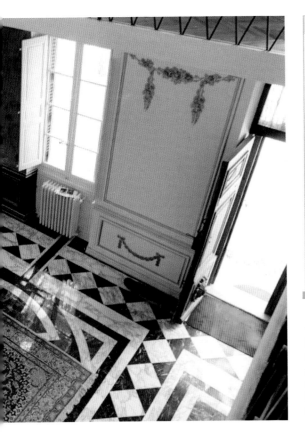

◄ Chateau grandeur

With grand spaces made to impress, it is easy to obtain an eye-catching image. You can shoot from any corner of the room—although it is best to have your back to the windows—and you can shoot from a high vantage point. From an atrium balcony you need only a moderately wide-angle lens to give good account of the space.

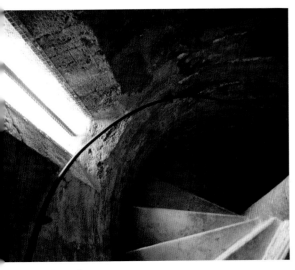

▲ Transit zones

Architects love transit zones or areas: they are often neglected by the average visitor, but of course no building can do without them. They are usually used more than the main rooms, and they structure the character and style of the spaces, so make room for them in your photography.

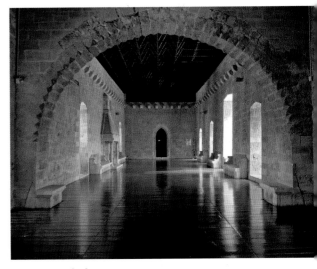

▲ Restored glory

The extensively restored throne-room of Frederick II, in Gioa del Colle, Italy, is seen here from the throne itself. This viewpoint was chosen to show that subjects entering the room are very well lit by large windows. In contrast, the throne itself is in darkness.

INTERIORS CONTINUED

An extreme-wide-angle view of the Britomart shopping center in Auckland would normally include much floor space. By using the reflections of a interior fitting, the usually empty lower area has been filled with the mirror image of the ceiling. Resting the camera on a store fixture supported it, removing the need for a tripod, which would have attracted unwanted attention. So, making opportunistic use of whatever was available solved two problems at once.

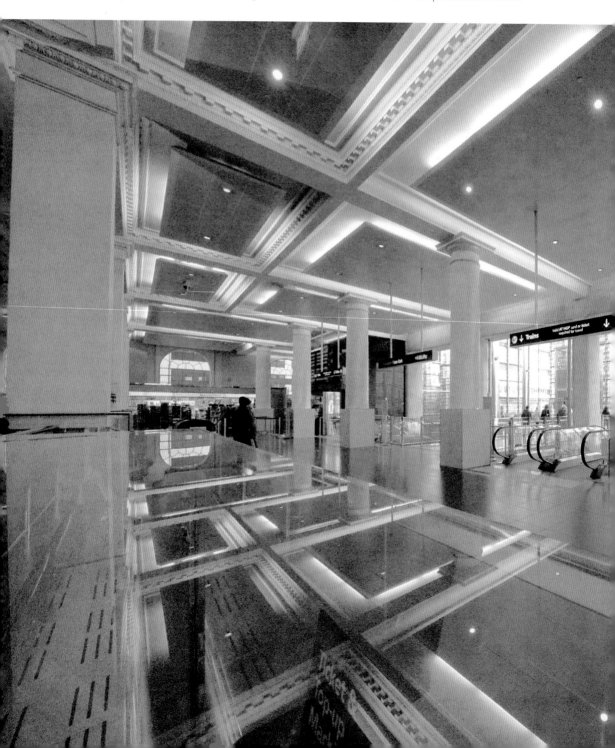

TECHNICAL INFO

CAMERA
Sony Alpha 7R

LENS
Canon 11–24 mm at 11 mm

SETTINGS
ISO 2000 • f/22 • 1/60 sec

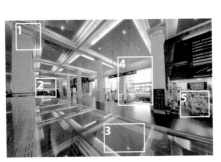

1 Acute angles

One of the costs of very wide-angle views is that normally square corners take on acute angles. This is caused by looking obliquely at features that point away from the camera at an angle. Lines that run through the center of the image, appear in their correct, non-distorted relationships with each other.

2 Vanishing point

Part of the wide-angle effect is to exaggerate the convergence of parallel lines, making the vanishing point appear very far away. When seen next to solidly vertical lines, the effect is to emphasize the dynamism of the lines.

3 Symmetrical mirror

Reflective surfaces introduce strong symmetry into an image automatically. This increases depth, as well as graphic impact and balance.

4 Reduced highlights

If the subject has uncontrollable highlights—as here, with the sky and the indoor lighting—it is extremely difficult to balance the necessary exposures. The best solution is to frame the scene in such a way as to reduce their impact on the image as much as possible.

5 Contrasting textures

After many hard, shiny, and angular lines in the rest of the image, it is a relief to encounter the softer textures of a flower store. Without its mollifying influence, the image would appear too cold, industrialized, and unwelcoming.

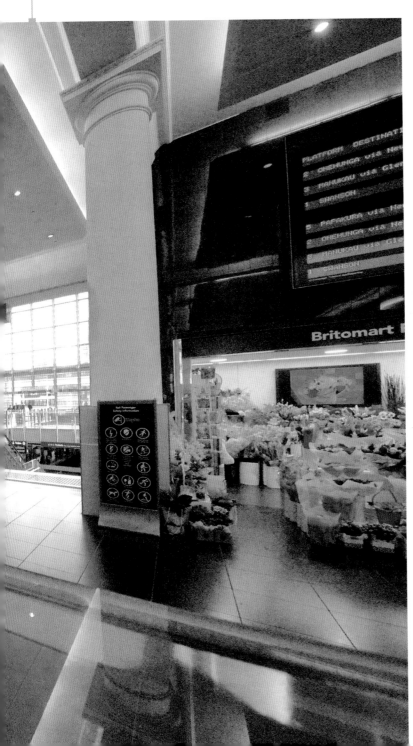

DOCUMENTARY PHOTOGRAPHY

The full spectrum of documentary photography covers prosaic recording, or the "soft" story, such as construction progress or family life, through to the "hard" stories, such as a civil war or drug trafficking. Whatever the subject, what matters is the approach: classic documentary is about recording with empathy the everyday existence of people, wherever they may live—if necessary revealing unpalatable truths, and recording for posterity events that some would prefer to be forgotten.

Preparation

In this, perhaps the most vocational of all genres of photography, subjects tend to choose you, the photographer. Injustices in an occupied territory may suddenly come to your attention, and you feel you must do something about it. Orphans in a city may break your heart, and you are moved to tell the world about them. While it is important to be motivated, it is also important to be a dispassionate observer. Study the subject area: read relevant legislation, speak to people affected, talk to local experts and charity workers: become expert yourself. This prepares you for the photography by informing your vision and directing your search for the telling image. It will also prepare you for the essential step of writing informative, accurate captions.

When it is clear to your subject that you are serious in your intentions, know what is going on, and can be trusted, you will find it easier to obtain cooperation. This is vital a step, if only to ensure your safety: do not be too eager, nor believe that you have to be pushy and determined. And never forget that your safety is more important than any images you could obtain.

Softly, softly

Technically, documentary photography is 90 percent being there, 10 percent pressing the button. Small, discreet cameras such as point-and-shoot or compact interchangeable lens (CIL) models attract less attention and are less intimidating than large SLR models with long zoom lenses. Cameras without mirrors are also quieter than SLRs—some are totally silent in operation. Point-and-shoot cameras are also much less expensive, so you can use two or three at the same time and you do not have to worry too much about damaging them in rough conditions.

When choosing a camera, look for good low-light operation—rapid autofocusing and images with low noise (*see pp. 194–5*)—so you do not have to use flash indoors or at night. Cameras with larger sensors—APS-C or larger—give the best performance at high ISO settings, and CIL cameras can be fitted with very fast (large maximum aperture) lenses, for example 24mm f/1.8. The ability of modern cameras to capture high-definition (HD) video can also be invaluable in documentary work—more and more documentary photographers are combining moving images and sound with still images.

Formal requisites

Reliable documentary work relies on the unaltered digital image in order to be a truthful, unvarnished record. It is acceptable to make tonal, exposure, and color balance corrections, and to convert to black-and-white. There should be no change of content such as the removal of distracting elements.

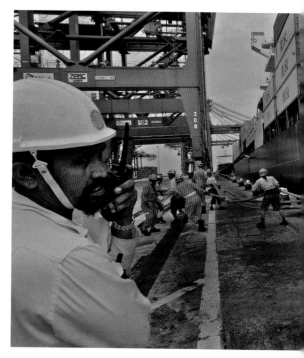

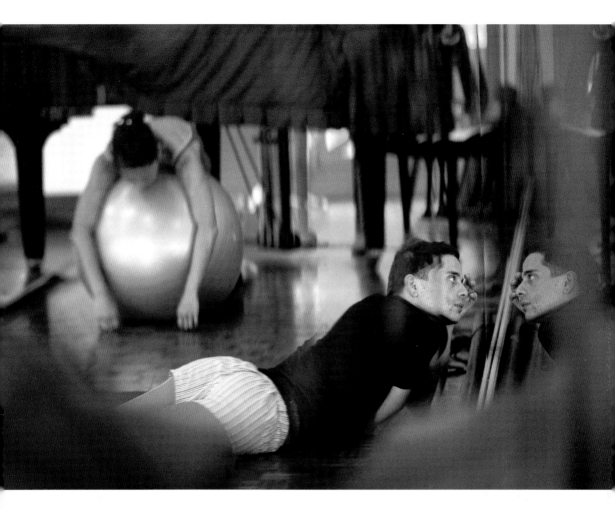

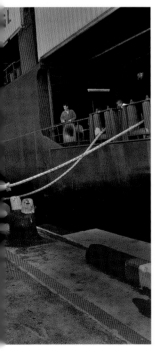

◄ Container movements

Even if circumstances—such as safety concerns—prevent you from being close to the action, there is always a way to pull the viewer into the shot. Here, by holding the camera with an ultra-wide-angle lens close to the operator's head, I made him appear large compared to the workers behind. Converging parallel lines draw attention into the "back" of the image.

▲ Intermezzo

Dancers of the Singapore Dance Theatre relax between rehearsals in an image that may not be first choice for publicity or promotion, but is an affectionately truthful portrayal of a moment in the lives of hard-working dancers.

CITIZEN REPORTING

With more than 3 billion cameras and camera phones in use around the world, there is sure to be a photographer near any newsworthy incident. Increasingly, ordinary people are recording news instead of being passive witnesses. It is essential that all of them accept the responsibility for accurate reporting, with truthful, non-manipulated images and no staging or reenactment of news events. Camera phones are ideal for posting images to media news desks and to social-network sites. Before submitting images, including to photo-sharing sites, ensure you do not lose your rights in the image.

DOCUMENTARY PHOTOGRAPHY CONTINUED

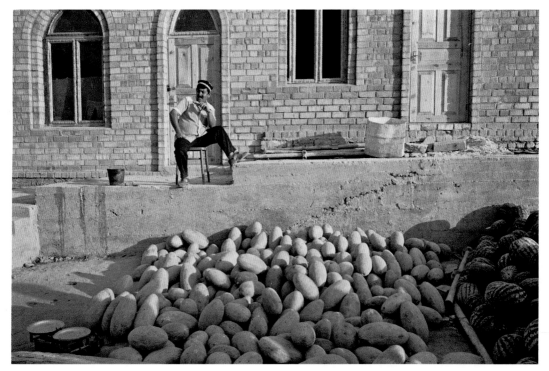

▲ Proud portraits

Some people can be too cooperative, sitting to attention with a broad smile when they see a camera pointing at them—as this melon-seller in Tajikistan did. Make the exposure anyway, thank them and expose again when they return to a relaxed, more natural pose.

▼ Wordless image

The ideal documentary photograph says it all in the image; there is no need for a caption to tell you what is going on. All you might need to identify it is location: in this case, Tashkent in Uzbekistan, where heavy rain in a desert-dominated country is unusual.

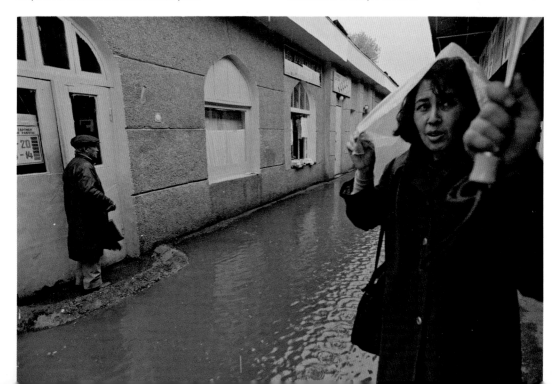

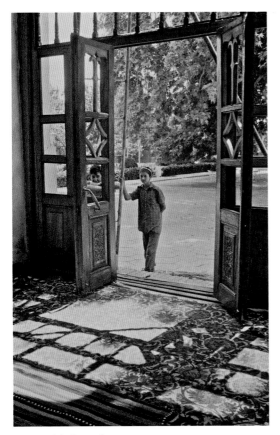

MODEL RELEASE FORM

If you take pictures of people and intend to use them in commercial ventures, a legally binding agreement between subject and photographer allows you to use the pictures without any further financial obligation or reference to the person depicted. For the personal use of a photograph, it is generally not necessary to obtain the model's release; however, if an image is intended for commercial use, it is advisable—sometimes mandatory—to obtain signed consent. A simple form of words is: "I permit the photos taken of me (subject's name) by (photographer's name) to be printed and published in any manner anywhere and at any time without limit." The release form should also note the date and location the pictures were taken and carry the signature and contact details for both the subject (or parent/guardian) and the photographer. Both parties should sign two copies—one is kept by the photographer, the other by the subject. The payment of money or giving of a gift—for example, a print of the image—may be required to make the contract binding.

▲ Combining elements

In documentary photographs everything counts: there is information in every corner of the image, and every portrait of a person is also a portrait of the place and the situation. Make it all count: a boy tailing me wears local clothes, the door casts shadows on carpets—all have stories to tell.

▼ Eloquent scenes

It is easy to capture pictures of buildings and living spaces, but it is always worth waiting for a little of ordinary life to pass by. You never know what will turn up and what it will tell you. Here neglect of a traditional district is brought into focus by a woman crossing the road.

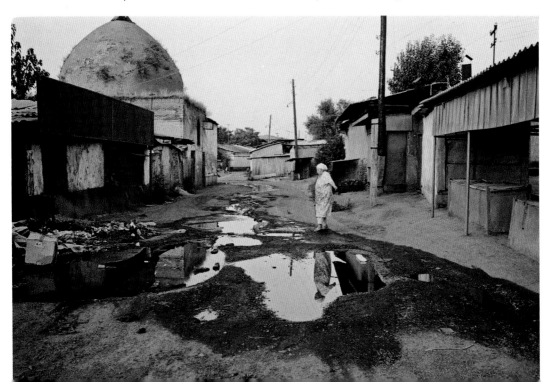

STREET PHOTOGRAPHY

The invention of 35mm miniature film and small cameras completely freed photographers from the studio to photograph the world at large. Since then the urban street, with its unending, bustling activity and unpredictability, has proved to be an inexhaustibly rich source of images. With your camera, you can explore any city's streets: the photographic rewards can be great, and you will also get to know your surroundings better.

Fortune telling

The core of street photography is the spontaneous juxtaposition of the different elements of a street scene—people, objects, and features of the urban landscape—in such a way that the composition gains a meaning or significance that is greater than the mere accident of its subjects being in the same place.

This means that composition and timing are crucial, but more importantly, street photography is driven by a keen, highly tuned awareness of movements and objects in the street. With practice this leads to what is almost an ability to read the future. This is essential because meaningful compositions or juxtapositions usually appear with only a faction of a second of lead-in time, and dissolve in even less time. Therefore street photographers must anticipate every shot: a little experience will show that if you merely try to respond to a situation that you are witnessing, you will already be too late.

Street wise

The great French photographer, Robert Doisneau, explained that the secret of his success at street photography was to "Walk, walk, and walk some more." Explore your city on foot, watching and experiencing the variety of scenes and subjects on offer. Take advantage of the fact that many cameras are extremely compact and lightweight, and can be easily carried all day—keep your camera in your hand, powered up and ready to use.

Use manual focus set, for example, to 13ft (4m), and ensure you capture action within that distance: this greatly speeds up your camera's responsiveness. Remember that an imperfect shot perfectly timed is preferable to a perfect shot badly timed. Be mindful of your own safety while you are shooting on the street, especially at night; conversely, if you sense that your presence is making someone uncomfortable, desist immediately.

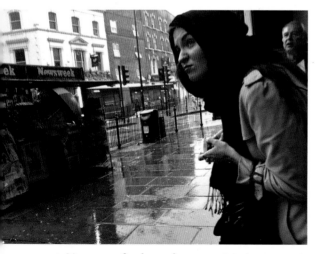

▲ **No room for boredom**
While waiting for your bus or train, or even for a thunderstorm to clear, you can help pass the time by being observant and taking an interest in how people behave. Here, a camera phone was the perfect tool for capturing reactions to a downpour in London.

PRIVACY AND SECURITY

In some countries, the legal view is that people have a right to private lives even in public. Therefore taking photographs of people in public spaces without their permission may be an offense. In other countries, photography of people may be offensive on cultural grounds. With increased awareness of photography worldwide, the safest and most polite course is always to obtain permission whenever you wish to photograph someone in such a way that they will become the main focus of the image. For an image to be used commercially, a model release will be mandatory (*see p. 107*). Street photography featuring large numbers of people is not usually problematic, but even so, you should be sensitive to people's feelings, which take precedence over your right to photograph.

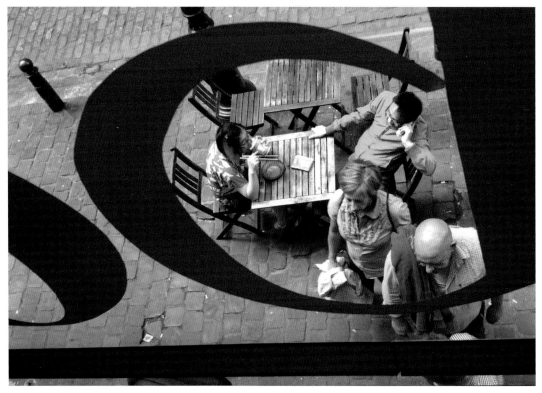

▲ Opportunistic juxtaposition

From a vantage point in a Brussels café, the signage on the window provided a stylish framing for the activity on the street below. By adjusting the camera's position, the curves fitted around the table below. All that remained was to pay attention to what was going on. A compact camera is ideal for such shots because it is easy to hold for long periods.

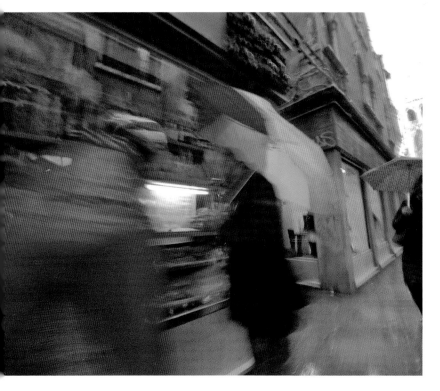

◄ Blur of life

There are no rules in photography: you do not have to frame or time your shots precisely, you do not have to capture expressions, and your images do not have to be sharp. Enjoy yourself by working with random occurences such as unexpected combinations of color and light—you can even capture them while on the move. In this shot, the varying degrees of blur add textural variety.

VACATIONS AND TRAVEL

Modern cameras make it a fun pursuit to capture pictures of your vacation that will remind you of the trip for years to come. But you will find it far more satisfying to create images that can stand on their own, and that have an appeal and interest that goes beyond your circle of friends and family. At the same time, if photography is not a priority for other members of the group, you need to be careful not to spoil their fun or keep them waiting around while you take pictures.

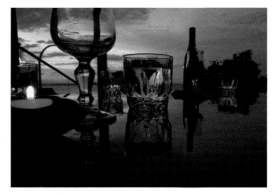

This is us

An effective way to get everyone used to you pointing the camera at them is to start shooting from the very beginning—for example, from the moment you meet up at the airport. Avoid arranging everyone into a formal group shot, but capture your friends as they chat to each other, consult maps, or send last-minute texts. Keep shooting as you move from one location to another. Before long, you will be creating a natural, sequential record of your trip, in which the more obvious shots of landmarks and monuments will have a fitting context.

Subjects and approaches

Looking to your broader surroundings, you can develop photography projects that tell the viewer

▲ Food and drink

Part of the fun of vacationing is experiencing different food in new locations. You can incorporate this into your photography: record not only the meals, but the place settings, the reflections of a sunset on the table and the refractions of candlelight in your wine glasses.

something about the location—for example, local street food, posters, transportation, or graffiti—whatever interests you. As you travel, your portfolio will grow in depth and extent in a most rewarding way. More importantly, you will find that as you become attuned to your subject matter—perhaps pursuing a particular theme and actively seeking out interesting or unusual examples—your eye for all kinds of other detail will be sharpened, with great benefit to your photography.

▶ Sunbed views

Even from a lazily prone position, you will see picture opportunities. Be prepared to grab your camera phone to snap the shot, and then you can get back to the serious business of relaxing.

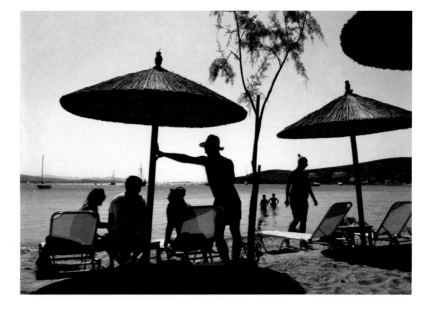

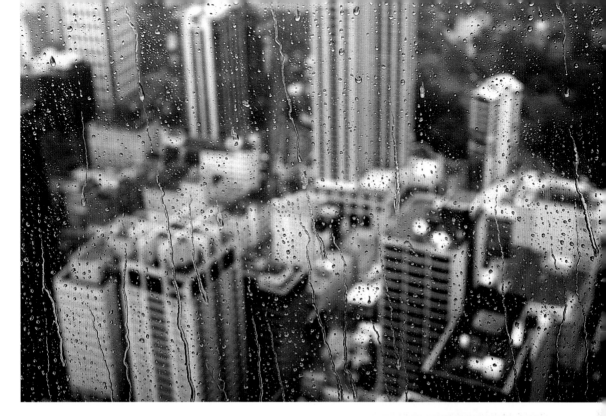

▲ Changing emphasis

Even when the weather is less than perfect, the observant photographer can always find picture opportunities. In this view of downtown Auckland, New Zealand, rain from a storm beats on the windows of an observation tower. It is usual to focus on the distant view, but by concentrating on the raindrops the scene shifts, and there is suddenly a picture to be made.

Looking beyond

However, your travel pictures do not have to be simply a record of a place, or of the day-to-day minutiae of your visit. If you can capture a human emotion, tell a story in which one picture entices the viewer to look forward to the next, and create images that inform as well as delight, you will make a breakthrough. This takes skill: you will need sharp reflexes to respond to changing circumstances—your subjects may move unpredictably, you will be in unfamiliar situations, and light conditions may change without warning. This calls for well-practiced camera technique, and it helps if you have equipment that can react quickly.

Even more important is acute sensitivity to the friendliness or antipathy of your subject, and to the cultural and social subtleties of your surroundings. You will also find it much easier if you are engaged and involved with your subject on a personal level that goes beyond simply photographing them in passing.

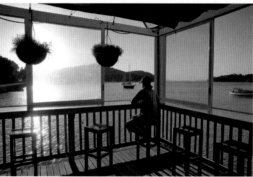

▲ Key components

Instead of posing them in front of the sunset, try incorporating your travel companions into the scene, so that their presence enhances the image.

SHARING MEMORIES

Of the many tasks to follow up after you return home, perhaps the most easily forgotten is the promise to send prints to people you have made friends with and photographed on your trip. However, digital photography makes this easier than ever before. You can make individual prints from files, or even travel with one of the very small, portable printers available. You can also post images onto social networking or picture-sharing websites, then contact people you have met and direct them to the sites.

VACATIONS AND TRAVEL CONTINUED

Recording relationships

A photograph of someone you meet on a trip is much more than a likeness: it is a record of your encounter, the meeting of two worlds. Pictures of people are perhaps the single most rewarding aspect of travel photography, particularly since developing genuine relationships with people opens doors that would otherwise remain closed to you.

A useful practice is to restrict your focal length (see box opposite). In order to fill the frame with your subject, you will have to move physically closer. This is easier if you have first formed a relationship with them—even if it is a fleeting one. Indeed, if you have created a rapport—often all that is needed is eye contact and a friendly smile—it is actually more comfortable to photograph from close up than from a distance.

The eyes have it

The most eloquent part of a portrait image is a person's eyes; that is what we instinctively look at first. Face to face, a glance at a person's eyes tells us their mood and intention, and likewise with images: we immediately gather information about the person from their eyes. The expression in your subject's eyes concisely conveys the nature of your relationship with them: if there is warmth and cordiality, we will be drawn to the image.

When you see someone you want to photograph, get your equipment ready. Set aperture depending on whether you want minimum depth of field with a blurred background, or if you want your image to be sharp throughout. If your subject is dark-skinned, set any exposure compensation to underexpose by around ⅔ stop. Anticipate the best angle, bearing in mind the direction of ambient lighting and the background, as well as what the subject is doing. Only when prepared should you reveal your intention to photograph. The rest involves simple life skills: approach honestly and openly, make eye contact, and say hello in the local language.

▼ Evocative imagery

The receding parallel lines of these railway tracks in Uzbekistan powerfully evoke a sense of space. In this image I balanced the need to show a long stretch of track with the size of the people on the line. If they were too far away, they would appear too small to have impact, and if they were too near, they might overpower the background.

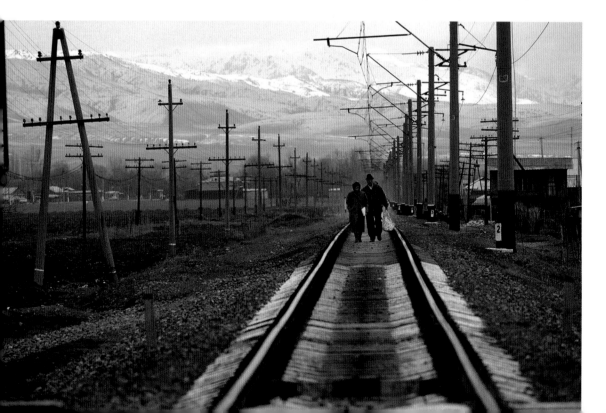

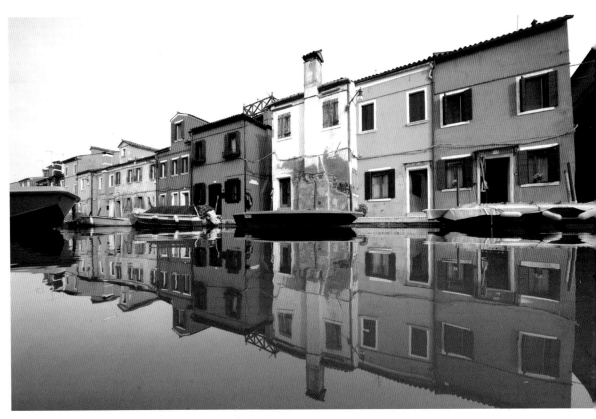

▲ Fresh views

Every corner of Burano, one of the prettiest settlements in the bay of Venice, cries out to be photographed. If you are not satisfied making the same old images, there is still room for innovation. You need a little more patience—here, to wait for water to settle to mirrorlike calm—and a bit of luck too. By seeking out the unexpected, the surprising shots will come to you: be ready for the unusual, and stay alert for you may get only one chance.

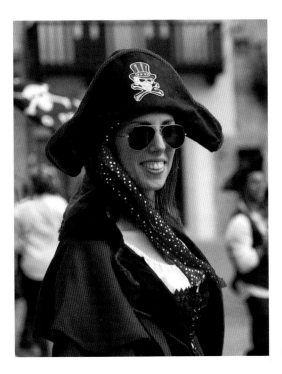

◄ Incongruities

A glamorous pirate in sunglasses is not something you encounter everyday. But if you are in Arezzo, Italy, you may see a band of "pirates" rampaging through its most perfect piazza regularly as an event put on for tourists. Treat such unexpected opportunities as a gift, and photograph freely.

TRY THIS

Restricting the focal lengths available to you helps improve agility, composition, and your ability to get close to subjects. Start with a maximum of 90mm or equivalent and compose your images by moving toward or away from your subject. Try to fill the height of a landscape format or width of a portrait format with a person's head and shoulders. Next, learn to use a 50mm setting. Then a 35mm setting: try to fill the frame with action and content. You can do this only by stepping inside the action. As you gain experience, try to use even shorter focal lengths; however, 24mm or less is widely considered very tricky for general use.

VACATIONS AND TRAVEL CONTINUED

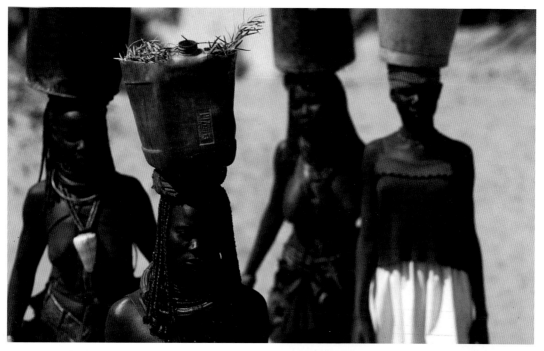

▲ An outsider's eye
There is no clear distinction between travel and documentary photography. A single shot of Himba and Herrero women collecting water makes an engaging travel shot. But they are walking in the heat of the day instead of the cool of evening: this tells us something is amiss. Indeed, there was a lion attack earlier, so it was safer to walk during broad daylight. Revealing aspects of a subject's life can lend a documentary element to your vacation photographs.

RESPECT YOUR HOSTS
You will find that when you dress and behave appropriately, you will receive a warmer, more cooperative reception when you want to photograph. Treat your hosts' country with the same respect you would expect of tourists in your homeland. Dress in a style that is appropriate to the cultural or social expectations of the country you are in: wear long sleeves and cover your legs if you expect to visit religious sites. By the same token, be respectful of the locals: don't insist on taking pictures of people if they wave you away or seem unhappy about it. And always keep in mind the sustainability principle that you should leave a country as you would wish to find it.

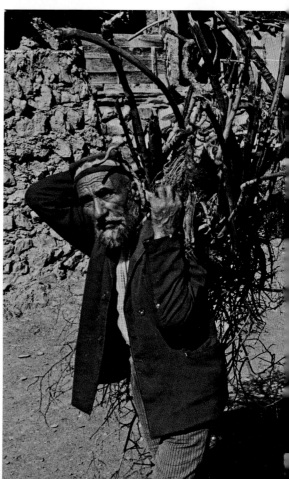

▶ Selective view

Ostensibly this is a study of contrasts—between the baby's hands and those of his grandmother; of colorful clothes against tanned skin—but this view also delicately draws the viewer's gaze from the subject's faces, making an unusual portrait.

▼ On the road

The advantages of staying awake while traveling cannot be stressed enough. After six hours on a bus it is easy to nod off, but you would miss telling moments such as this: the driver had to be paid from outside because the bus was so full.

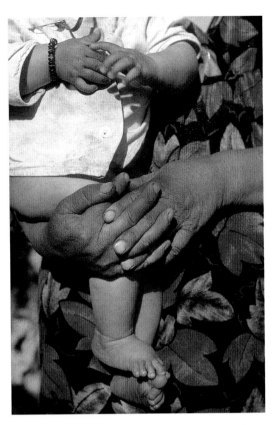

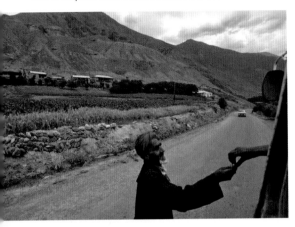

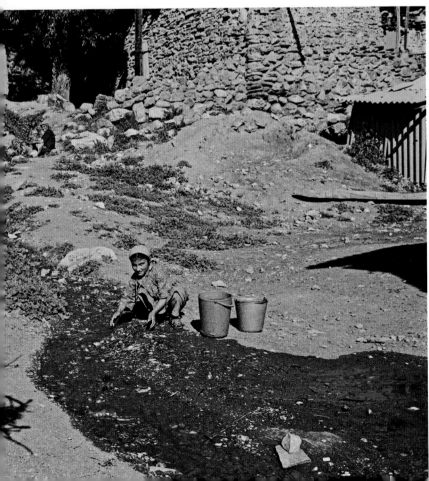

◀ Way of life

It is natural to concentrate on the exotic beauties of a country, its customs and way of life. While it may not be very beautiful, the realities of day-to-day existence in a foreign land are not only more true and useful for an understanding of the country, they are vastly more interesting. You do not need to seek out poverty or destruction—you are not working on a documentary story. All it takes is to keep your eyes open and camera at the ready: this scene in Tajikistan came and went in a second.

Winged chaos
The pigeons in Thimpu Dzong, Bhutan, bring a lively pattern of movement to the great palace. A 600mm focal length view compresses myriad separate elements into an abstract pattern.

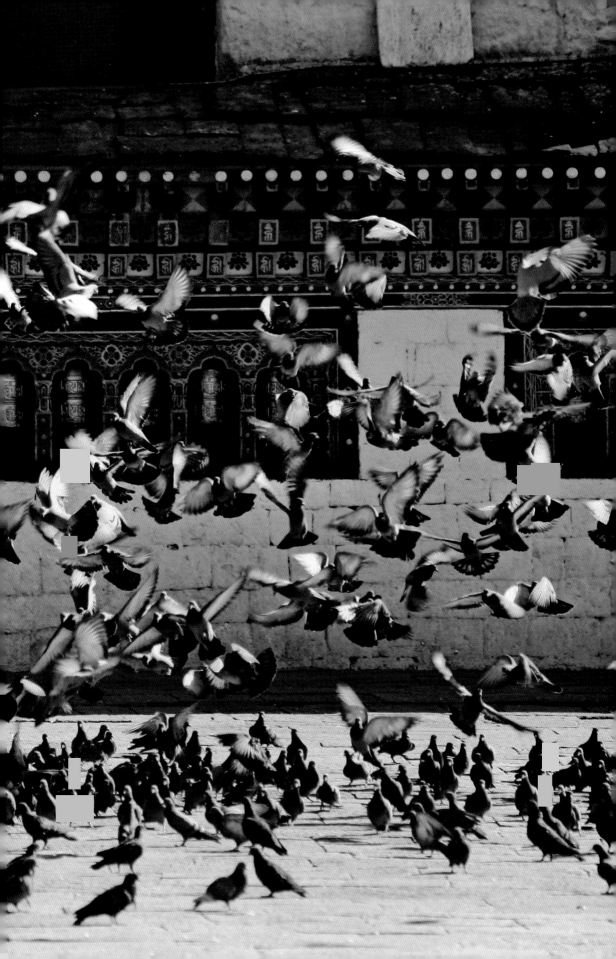

WEDDINGS

The documentary approach to weddings is as much a reaction against stiffly posed formal shots as it is a product of improved cameras. This enables every wedding guest—from grandmother to toddler—to capture pictures of the event. If you are not the official photographer, you can shoot freely without concerns for comprehensive coverage of all guests and ensuring all the formal groupings are captured.

Professional challenge

The role of the professional wedding photographer is to provide a set of unique images that will record and evoke the experience of one of the biggest days in a couple's lives. To do this they must search for angles and interpretations that, as well as being creative and inventive, raise their images well above the ordinary: a celebration of a special day should be matched with some very special pictures. A popular solution is to capture the couple in a fantasy setting. Use an off-camera flash to balance against twilight skies or shoot the couple against a plain screen (green is preferred but any plain or black background can work) ready to composite against a glorious sunset or woodland scene.

At the same time, you need to capture all the key moments too. Make sure you are familiar enough with the ceremony to position yourself ready to take the shot of the exchange of rings, the signing of the register, or the first married kiss. Take care not to interrupt delicate moments such as the exchange of vows or the blessing from the presiding person.

One straightforward way to distinguish professional work from others is to work with a very large-aperture lens—for example, a 85mm f/1.4 or 135mm f/2—which you can use exclusively at large aperture settings. The resulting shallow depth of field and softness is unlikely to be matched by people using compact point-and-shoot cameras. Besides, the soft focus also perfectly suits the romantic nature of the subject.

Another way to stand out from the crowd is to use available light instead of flash when working indoors or at night. Full illumination by flash is often necessary, but it easily destroys the atmosphere of dim or colored lights.

Rounded views

The inventive wedding photographer does not neglect to record those aspects which others may not think of capturing, but which create a rounded record of the event. Often the most charming and amusing moments occur in the run-up to the main

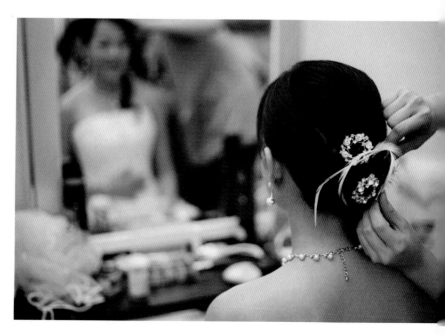

▶ **Bride showered**
The intimate moments of preparation may be barred to all but female photographers or close relatives, but it is worth capturing the process of adorning not only the bride but the bridesmaids, as well as best man. The images display the process of transformation—from the ordinary to the celebratory. Use limited depth of field to emphasize key elements such as the jewelry and accessories.

event: seek out fleeting moments in the frenetic activity of preparation. A lot of effort goes into the details, so make sure you look at the rows of champagne glasses, the furniture decorations, and the details of the costumes and flowers.

Follow on

Once you have captured all the happy moments, you have completed only half the work. Unlike many photography assignments, the choice of images is one in which the photographer may be expected to lead, as clients are usually not experienced in picture editing. In addition, some images are obligatory, whatever small technical defect they may have.

Remember to be clear to the couple about the images rights at all times, and when handing over the images remind them that the pictures should not be reproduced or posted on social networking sites without further fees.

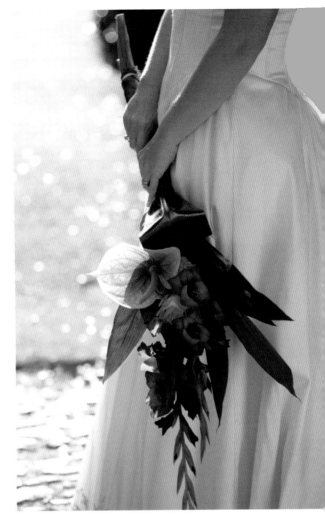

▶ Supporting cast
Everyone and everything is important on the big day: the bride's flowers will be seen in many pictures taken by the guests, so aim for a shot that is less obvious. Here, backlighting and graceful continuation of lines gives charm to the complementary beauty of bride and bouquet.

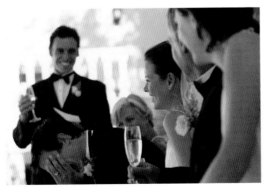

▲ Hilarity seriously shot
The funny moments of a wedding are essential for recreating happy memories of the event. However, you can shoot them with some sophistication. Wide-angle views lit with flash are commonplace. Try using a long focal length setting and exploit blur and overlap. In this shot, the blurred figures frame the beautiful profile of the bride, while the champagne glass helps anchor attention around the smiling faces.

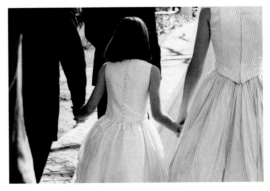

▲ Transitional states
While the key moments, such as the exchange of rings and the kiss, are must-have shots, the quiet moments also make up the event as a whole. These transitions often reveal touching moments and true relationships between family members and guests. Here, a bridesmaid walks happily between older family members, her head of dark hair framed by backlighting against the dark jacket of another guest in front of her.

CHILDREN

Children tend to be photographed in different ways according to whether they are known to us or not. The reason for this is that we tend to approach familiar subjects in a different way to unknown ones. For example, most people prefer to photograph their own children when they are looking their best in attractive, clean clothes, and smiling for the camera. However, the opposite approach may present itself when, for example, you are visiting another part of the world and you photograph a child as part of the local color of a street scene. This will naturally give your image a very different feel.

PUBLIC STANDARDS

Taking photographs of children may create unexpected risks for the photographer because of the—entirely understandable—desire to protect children's safety. Photography of children who are not your own should be approached with caution, particularly in public spaces such as parks and beaches, and near schools. Always seek the permission of parents or legal guardians (carers may not have sufficient authority) before starting to photograph. If you are at all in doubt, err on the side of caution.

A change of attitude

So the photographic challenge is clear: how to bring the two approaches together, being more honest when photographing our own children, while being respectful and considerate when our photographs feature other people's children, especially those from other cultures.

Informed photography is the key, as the more we know, the more perceptive our photography becomes. For example, try to learn about the games that children play, or take an interest in their pastimes. If you are photographing your own children, try to avoid obviously staged images, and instead concentrate on capturing some of the spontaneous moments that occur in everyday family life. Children tend to pose either too readily or not at all. The trick is to wait for them to get bored of you. Keep shooting, whatever they do: aim at them if they are acting up, or aim away if they are being shy. Sooner rather than later, young children will tire and let you get on with shooting. All you need is to have more patience than they do.

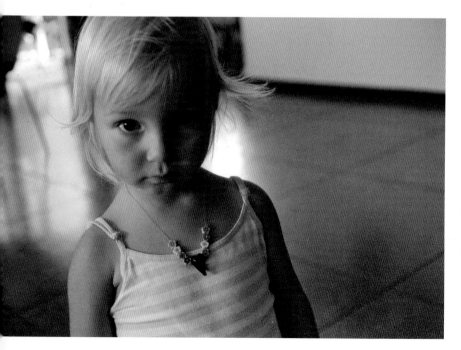

◄ Having a chat
Children often learn to pose for the camera from an early age. If you are looking for a more natural portrait, try engaging your subjects in conversation. When they become interested in what you are talking about, they will stop playing up to the camera. They also stop running about and become easier to keep in focus, giving you a chance to set maximum aperture to throw the background out of focus, and use a shorter exposure time.

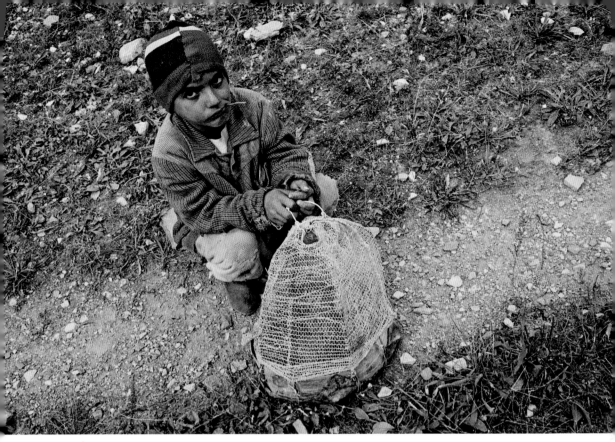

▲ The eyes of mistrust

A lad in the high mountains of Tajikistan looks decidedly cautious, as well he might. More important to him than how he looks on camera is whether he will have to fight to keep the birds he has captured in his makeshift cage. Once he overcame his mistrust, a very different image resulted, but it is this edgy image that is more interesting.

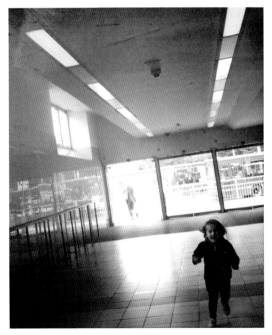

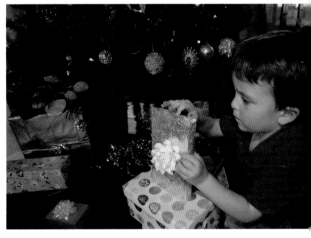

▲ Otherwise occupied

A distraction can be beneficial for the photographer: it not only takes the child's eye off the camera, it can show your subject lost in his or her world. Recording the best of these moments may call for many exposures, but do not be tempted to keep only "the best": these judgements vary over time, so hold on to everything you shoot. With cheap mass storage readily available, your only regret will be deleting an image.

▲ Child's world

Images of children are not only about them, but also about the space they inhabit. By zooming out, you can show the child in relation to the world at large.

CHILDREN CONTINUED

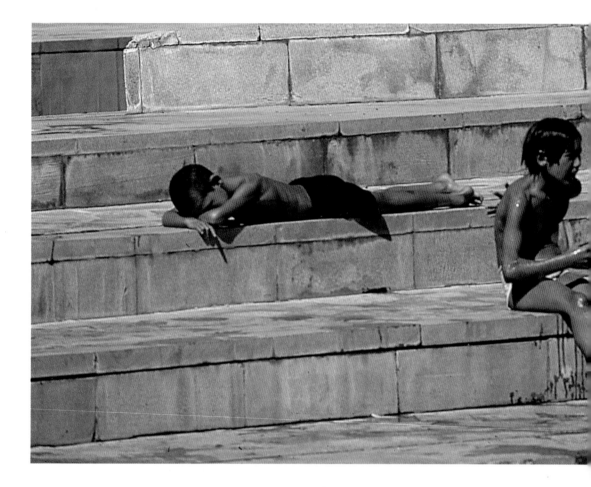

HINTS AND TIPS

Children can be a challenge in technical terms, as they are small, low down, and move quickly. They require stamina and fitness on the part of the photographer, as well as quick reflexes. You can help yourself by trying out these techniques:

- With very small children, work at a fixed distance: focus your lens manually to, say, 18in (0.5m) and keep your subjects in focus by leaning backward or forward as they move. Small children move very quickly but usually only over short distances. This method requires little effort and can be superior to relying on autofocus.
- When you first photograph a group of children, fire off a few shots in the first minute—they need to get used to the sound of the camera or light from the electronic flash, while you need to exploit their short attention span. Once they have heard the camera working, they will soon lose

interest and ignore you. If, however, you wait for them to settle before taking your first picture, they will be distracted by the noise.
- For professional photography of children, the best cameras to use are CXL (compact interchangeable lens) or SLR cameras, preferably equipped with a prime lens. These give you more flexibility than compact point-and-shoot cameras. You also need the shortest possible shutter lag (the time interval between pressing the shutter and actually recording the picture) if you are not to miss out on the really spontaneous images.
- In low light, increase the ISO setting in preference to setting the lens's maximum aperture when using nonprofessional lenses. If you have high-quality optics, use the widest aperture freely, but you will need to focus more carefully. Avoid using flash lighting except as a fill-in (see pp. 80–9).

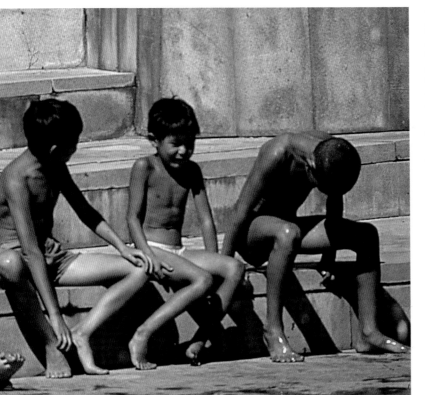

◄ A candid approach

A large fountain in hot weather is irresistible to children anywhere in the world. The problem here was trying to photograph the boys without them realizing—otherwise they would start playing to the camera. I mingled with the crowds, enjoying the sun, and waited for a suitable grouping and rare moment of repose.

▶ Sibling rivalry

A set of nothing but smiling, happy pictures of children quickly makes for predictable and dull viewing. Children also get angry, cry with frustration, exhaust themselves, and fight or play with siblings. With compact and responsive cameras and camera phones, you can be on hand to record all those telling moments.

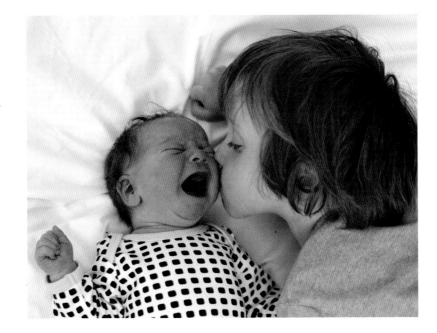

LANDSCAPES

The natural landscape—topographies of land and water decorated with plant forms and lit by sun and sky—is one of the most accommodating yet challenging areas of photography. A landscape may be photographed from any angle, at any time, and in any weather. But you have to do all the work. Stylistically, you also have decisions to make about how much of your own individual mark you wish to to make in your images.

Patience and perseverance

A vital but little-appreciated truth about landscapes is that anywhere can look wonderful at some point in time. A plowed field, the edge of a forest, or a grand sweeping vista is, photographically, a set of ingredients just waiting for the key elements of light, sky, and your personal vision to come together to concoct a stunning result. You just need to be sure to be there for the occasion. A glorious landscape photograph is seldom the product of a happy accident. While practice can prepare you to be in the right place at the right time, the truly great

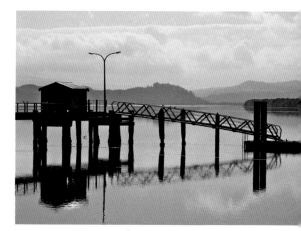

▲ Clarity and tranquility

Use man-made structures to contrast with topography: these sharply-defined silhouettes provide a foil to the soft clouds and distant hills of New Zealand's Northlands.

images are usually the result of a photographer returning to the same spot again and again, sometimes over a period of years. From time to time they may obtain a successful shot, but they know there will always be a better one—tomorrow, next month, perhaps next year. Over time, these photographers also explore and refine their viewpoint and composition, until, one quiet and perfect moment, everything comes together.

▼ Self inclusion

It is fun to include yourself in a view, but there are many ways to do it. Here, the long, late-afternoon shadows suggested a natural way to put ourselves into the shot.

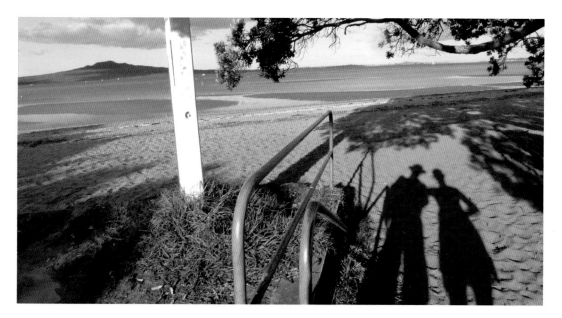

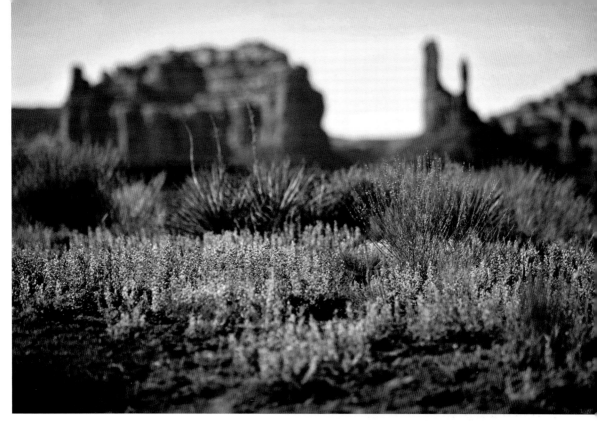

▲ Upstaging

As one's eye is drawn to the monumental landforms—here in Valley of the Gods, USA—it is natural to focus on the distant features. You could use extensive depth of field to keep the foreground in focus too, but a more inventive variation is to focus on the small elements at the front, using a large aperture to blur the giants further away.

Bare necessities

There are therefore three essentials of landscape photography—place, time, and means—but the most crucial of all is place. Once you see a view that is promising, it is best to slow down completely—even put your camera away. Then just walk and look, walk a little more and look a little harder. What you are seeking is a manipulation of the relative scale of elements in the scene, with which to create a powerful sense of space within the picture frame. For example, flowers in the foreground appear as tall as mountains in the distance, and pebbles in a river bed are the size of trees further upstream. Your viewers share your experience of the world and the distorting effects of perspective, so they understand the real relative sizes of objects. What they see in your image leads them to reconstruct the spirit of the landscape in their minds, but guided by you. You will find that miniscule changes in position or height can make the difference between a revealing image and one that is unsurprising and ordinary.

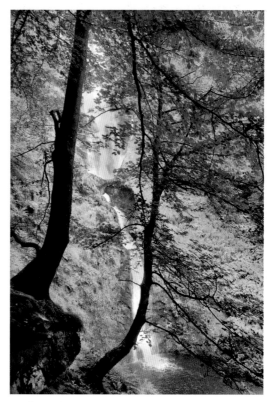

▲ Three in one

Tone compression is effective not only for scenes with extremely wide dynamic ranges, but also flatly lit scenes where you wish to extract shadow detail. Combining three different exposures of this subject, in the Welsh Marshes, provided great flexibility over tonal control.

LANDSCAPES CONTINUED

Once you find your position, you may need to wait for the light to add the finishing flourish. This might mean pausing while a cloud makes its way across the sky, or returning again and again until you catch the perfect moment. Light may be raking and dramatic in effect, or flat, bringing out subtleties of tone. On three different days you might obtain three very different images—and all from the same position.

Style and means

A tradition has developed that demands large, high-resolution cameras for "proper" landscape photography. This is an issue of style rather than technique. If you wish to make poster-sized prints and you prize extreme detail, by all means use the highest quality equipment you can afford. However, even a camera phone is perfectly acceptable, if you actively use the imperfections of the capture— such as light fall-off—as features of your images. Furthermore, any lens may be used, from ultra wide-angle through to the longest telephoto.

Working in black and white is another way to individualize your landscapes: the exact way you remove the variety of hues to translate a full-color facsimile of the view turns any black-and-white image into an artistic interpretation. You might also manipulate the image toward a vintage look, to make it appear to be the product of irregularities of processing. Other ways to build a personal style include consistent use of extremely shallow depth of field, by setting apertures not smaller than f/2, for example. Some photographers use long telephoto lenses, while others exploit motion blur through long exposure. Or your could try overexposure in flat lighting to obtain pale, bright results.

▼ Unconventional views
In a world saturated with beautiful travelogue-style landscape images, there is a place for the more dispassionate view, one that does not flinch from showing scarring from agriculture or the impact of industry. This image, from the Marche of Italy, was made with a long telephone zoom to pull far-separated elements onto the same plane.

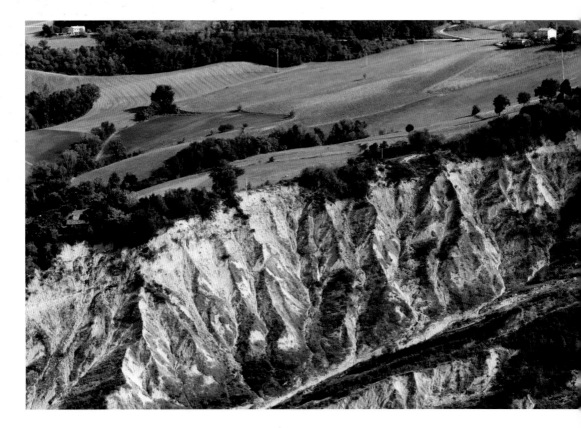

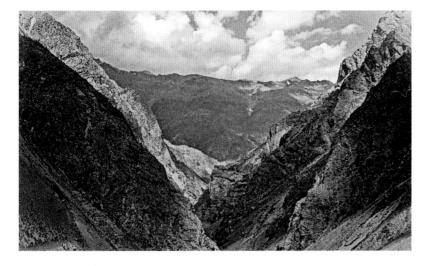

◄ Vintage views

While it always pays to capture the best image you can at the time, the demands of the enviroment may mean that you have to grab what you can when you can. This image of a snow-line walk in Tajikistan, was improved in post-processing by adding a layer of tone and vignetting to suggest it was captured by early processes.

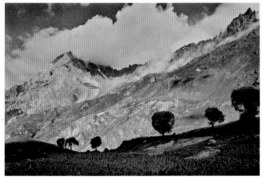

▲ Friendly shadows

Often treated as an enemy, shadows are in fact a landscape photographer's friend: they sculpt shapes, define textures, and delineate distance. Fully lit, this scene lacked depth, but when a cloud darkenened the foreground, it was visually separated from the valley sides that were still in sun. A duotone effect (*see pp. 238–9*) recompresses the tones.

HINTS AND TIPS

All landscape views respond well to being shot as black-and-white or converted from color. However, default conversions often deliver a lackluster result.

- Convert color using channel mixing or similar controls that allow different tones to be assigned to bands of color, for example, to make greens lighter, or to darken the blues (*see pp. 224–9*).
- After conversion, exposure and contrast may need improvement: use tonal controls such as Levels (*see pp. 188–9*) or Curves (*see pp. 218–21*) to effect this.
- Try applying unsharp masking (*see pp. 196–9*): this applies a micro-contrast adjustment to edges, which adds sparkle to an image.

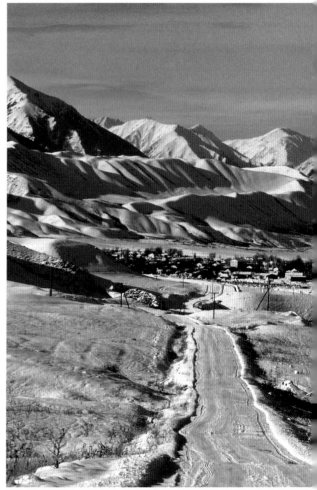

▲ Cold toning

Conversion from color darkened the blue shadow areas in this snowy scene in Kazakhstan, allowing sunlit areas to define the topography. Changing to Duotone mode, a blue tone was added to enhance the effect—with special care taken to keep the highlights white (*see pp. 238–9*).

LANDSCAPES CONTINUED

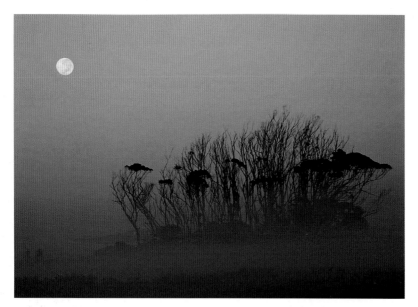

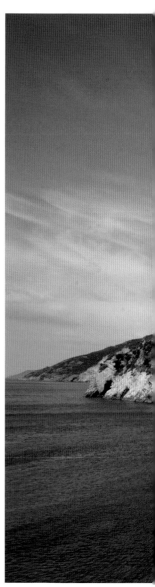

▲ Dawn mist
Landscape photography may seem leisurely, but often you have to act quickly. As I drove out of Auckland airport just after dawn, this mist-shrouded scene presented itself. I knew that it would disappear quickly, so I jumped out of the car and raced back down the road to record it. Just seconds later, the rising sun masked the delicate hues in the sky and the mist evaporated.

▶ Receding lines
It is unusual to find strong parallels running from side to side in a landscape. Here, in the Cinqueterre, Italy, the eroded strata of the rocks in the foreground inspired a composition that strongly converges to the point of land at the extreme right-hand edge of the picture. A gull helpfully defines the principal Golden Section of the image.

POLARIZING FILTERS

One of the most popular accessories for the landscape photographer is the polarizing filter. This is a neutrally dark filter in a rotating mount. When fixed on the front of a lens, pointing away from the sun, then rotated, it has the effect of making blue skies appear much darker at certain settings compared to others. This is because blue light from a clear sky vibrates in a small range of angles: as you turn the filter it passes some light at most positions but when it reaches the "crossed" position it maximally blocks the light from the sky, making it dark.

Note that maximum darkening may not be a good idea as the sky can appear almost black. The filter can also be used to reduce reflections on glass, leaves, or water. This makes it useful for controlling scenes with a large luminance range, as it reduces the specular shine on smooth surfaces. This filter is best used on an SLR, where you can monitor changes through the viewfinder. The circular type of polarizer should be used with SLRs, but linear polarizing filters may be useable with some cameras, such as compact interchangeable lens cameras (CILs); check your instructions to confirm.

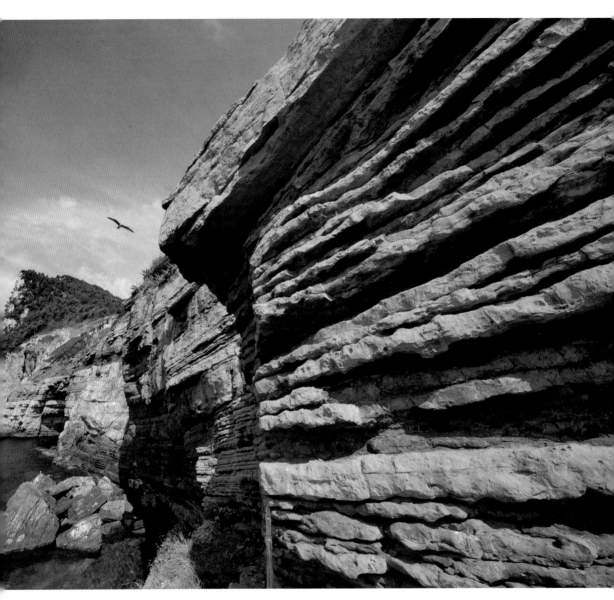

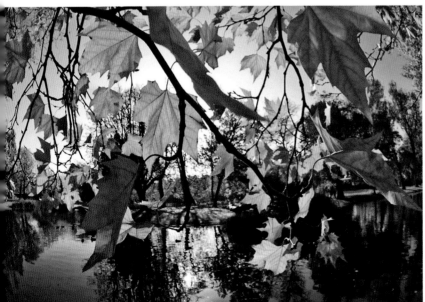

◄ Lowly views

With experience, you will find it helpful to work within the framework of a project, rather than searching for any kind of promising landscape. This image was taken with a fish-eye lens as part of a project that views the world as seen by local wildlife—from close to the ground, or partly obscured by foliage, or both.

LANDSCAPES CONTINUED

An early morning walk catches clouds rolling over sea cliffs before they are burned off by the summer sun, in Queen Charlotte Sound, South Island, New Zealand. A virtue was made of the foreground silhouetted trees to frame the landscape, rather than searching for an uninterrupted viewpoint. Since the trees were in the middle distance and a telephoto setting of around 150 mm was used, a moderately small aperture was sufficient to render them sharp against a well-defined background.

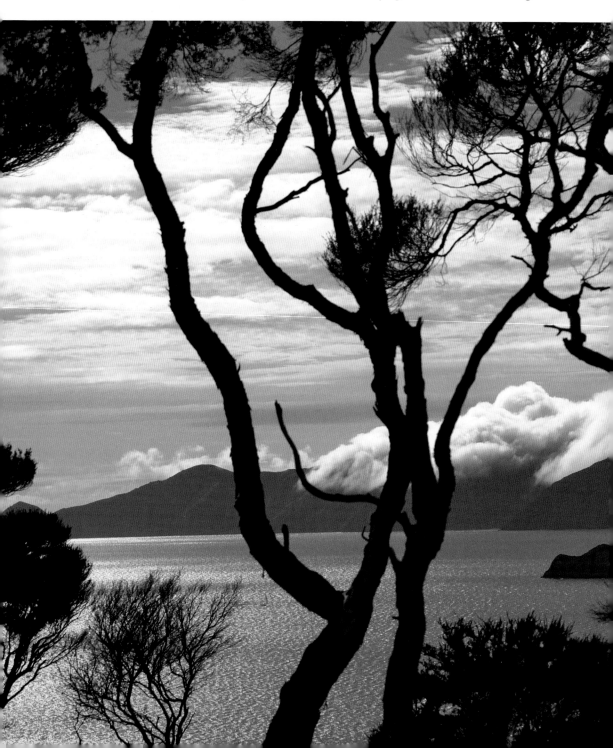

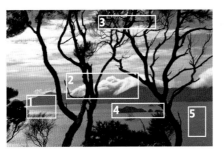

TECHNICAL INFO

CAMERA
Canon EOS-1Ds Mark II

LENS
Canon 70–200 mm f/2.8
at 150 mm

SETTINGS
ISO 100 • f/5.6 • ¹/₁₀₀ sec

1 Sunrise glint
The sparkle in the water informs the viewer of the direction of the sun and thus "motivates" the light in the sky and clouds. It also puts texture and energy into an otherwise quiet area of the image.

2 Long white cloud
Long, rolling clouds are characteristic of this region since strong winds are pushed up by mountain ranges. It is important for the exposure to render the clouds bright white. Other parts of the image can be allowed to fall to their tones as they will—from black shadows on trees, to light sky tones.

3 Framing branches
The exposure for the clouds renders the branches a solid black silhouette, since no detail is needed in the trees. There is no need to attempt to retrieve details in the shadows.

4 Central islands
The viewpoint for this image was adjusted to ensure the islands in the center of the frame fell between the trees and above the small branch leaning to the left in the middle distance. If this branch had intruded into the island, the sense of separation would have been damaged, leading to visual confusion.

5 Empty sea
With a picture that is busy in every part of the frame, this featureless area seems too quiet. It does not function as a restful spot in the image; instead, it seems to call for some movement, such as a yacht in full sail.

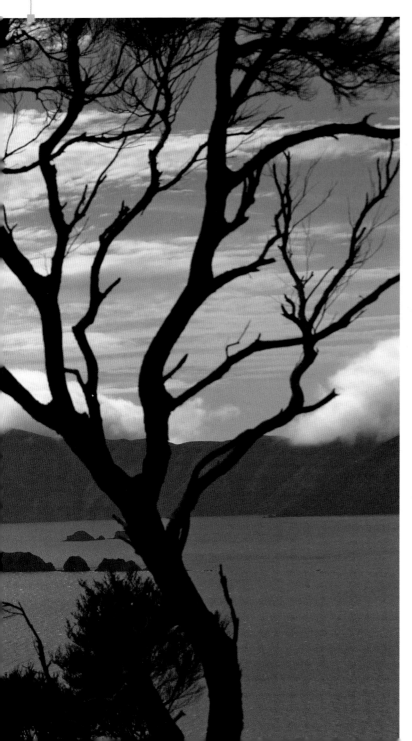

CITYSCAPES

As most of the world's population lives in cities, it is natural that the city is one of the richest sources of pictures. In any city in the world, whether drab or stunning, medieval or modern, you will find endless potential for photography. Indeed, entire careers in photography have been built on the photogenic qualities of cities as diverse as Prague, New York, Delhi, and Paris. Cityscapes concentrate on the architecture of the built environment and its layout, shapes, and structure. While it does not actively exclude people, cityscape photography largely ignores them, unlike street photography.

Finding inspiration

In choosing an approach, it is instructive to follow in the footsteps of great photographers who have portrayed their beloved cities, such as Alfred Stieglitz of New York, Josek Sudek of Prague, and Eugene Atget of Paris. Their achievement was to show the myriad aspects of their cities without any kind of artifice, and all in black-and-white. In fact, working in black-and-white can simplify your compositions, allowing the viewer to appreciate form, texture, and depth without the distraction of color.

However, you have important advantages over photographers of the past: you are highly mobile and can work in just about any lighting condition. Exploit the capabilities of your camera and work to capture images not only in bright sunshine, but on rainy days, in the fog, or at night.

Exploration

You can go further than the masters of the past: use color in an abstract way, capture the surprisingly deep and rich colors of the city at night, or zoom into the distance to find magnified views that are not visible to the naked eye.

The city is a rich source of reflections and unintended juxtapositions—of shapes, colors, and signs. Just as a landscape can be seen in overview as well as in detail, you will find cities yield different layers of meaning and possibility with each change of scale. You could also choose one prominent landmark and investigate the way it can be seen from different places all over the city.

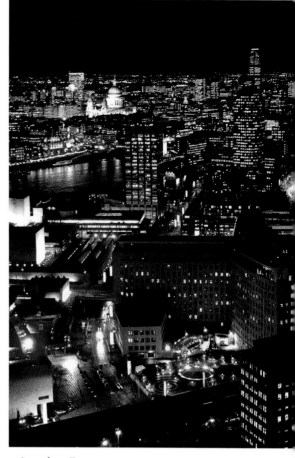

▲ London Eye

Capturing the colors of city lights at night is less of a challenge than it used to be. This shot was taken from London's giant ferris wheel at the top of its trajectory, using a high ISO and underexposing by 1.5 stops.

BUILDING RIGHTS

In the majority of cities you can photograph buildings freely. But exercise caution if any that are in view are flying a national flag or appear to be military in character. In some countries photography of bridges, airports, police stations, armed forces barracks, and government buildings is illegal. Beware that commercial use of images featuring certain iconic buildings such as Rockefeller Center, the Flatiron Building (New York), the Eiffel Tower, the Louvre, and the Pei Pyramid (Paris) may be subject to legal processes by various rights holders. Restrictions may also apply to commercial use of images that show works of art, such as installations or sculptures.

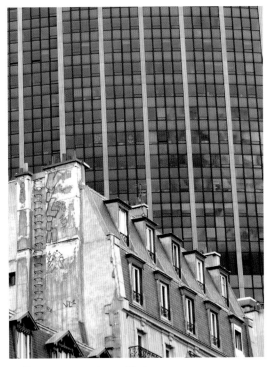

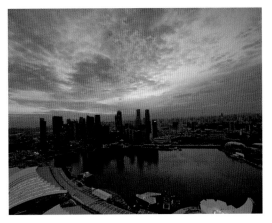

▲ City skies

The skyline of a city is defined as much by the sky above—the so-called "negative space"—as by the outlines of the buildings themselves. And if we are given a gloriously fluffy-clouded sunset, so much the better. This view of Singapore needs to give emphasis to the sky as the "hero" of the shot with the skyline taking a secondary role, so it can be allowed to go into deep tones.

▲ Contrasts and conflicts

Using a long-focal-length lens brings relatively distant objects together, emphasizing their differences—old apartments in Paris and the high-rise building appear to be right next to each other, but are in fact hundreds of feet apart. Frame from as far away as possible, using a zoom to adjust image size and composition.

▼ Working with the enemy

Cars rarely contribute to city scenes in a positive way, yet they are perennially present, and are therefore a common problem for photographers. Try to use them to your advantage, for example by making a feature of the red lights of a traffic jam at night, or by looking for interesting reflections in their windshields, and so on.

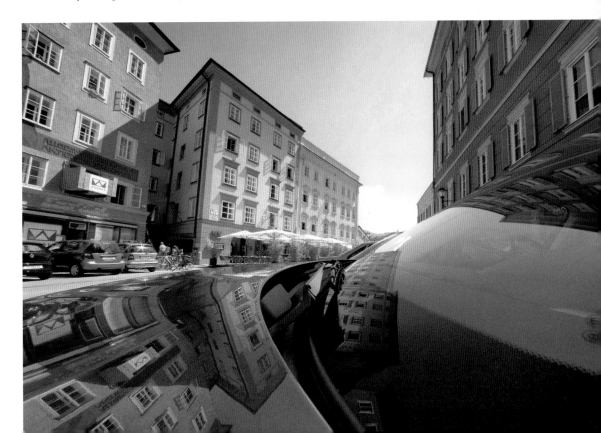

CITYSCAPES CONTINUED

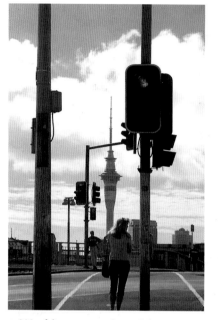

▲ Working around a subject

A simple exercise is to take an obvious landmark and then shoot as varied a set of views of it as possible. These images of the Sky Tower in Auckland, New Zealand, were all taken as I went about my business in that city. This shot, taken from a car, was very nearly missed—it is of such an ordinary scene, yet there is a rhythm in the multiple framing, a sense of a hidden story. In addition, its crisp colors make it a surprisingly rich picture. The passenger seat of a car makes a wonderful moving platform from which to work.

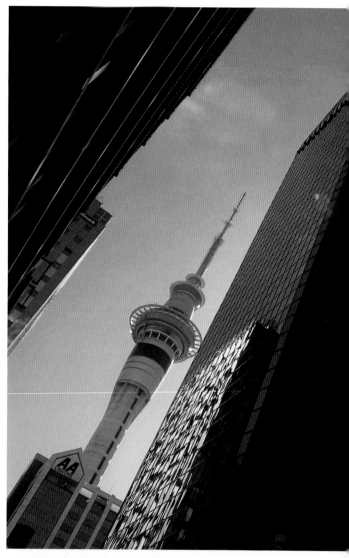

▶ Supplementary flash

Noticing these flowers first, I went over to photograph them only to find the tower unexpectedly in view. The flash on the camera illuminated the foreground flowers but not those a little further away. The shadow visible on the bottom edge of the image was caused by the lens obstructing the light from the flash.

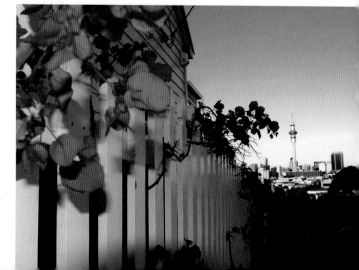

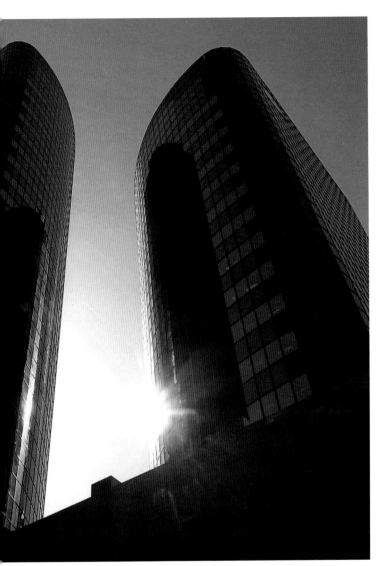

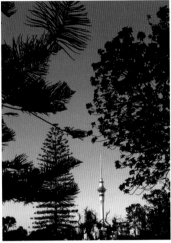

▲ Silhouette lighting

The silhouettes of a variety of trees serve to frame the sleek, industrial lines of the distant tower. As the trees are represented by shape alone, they look very sharp—although depth of field in such views appears extensive, it is, in reality, an illusion of perception.

◄ Converging lines

Generally you would want to avoid pointing the camera steeply upward at buildings, as the strong convergence of normally parallel lines causes distortion. However, this can be exploited to create the sense of disorientation or of being loomed over. Its effectiveness is increased in this view by avoiding any alignment between the picture frame and the sides of any buildings.

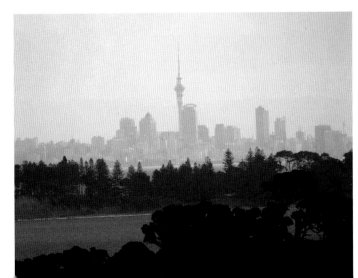

◄ Distant view

The Sky Tower is visible even an hour's ride away by hydrofoil. A strong telephoto perspective—produced by the 35efl of a 560mm lens—leaps over the distance and appears to compress the space between the intervening islands. The haze has desaturated colors to give a nearly neutral gray.

REFLECTIONS

Apart from light emitted directly from a lamp or the sun, every ray of captured light reaches your camera having been reflected from a surface. These rays literally write the image of the scene; in that sense every image is made of reflections. But it is when the light reflects off a smooth surface that the magic happens: the light rays bundle together to form a new image of the scene, yet one that lies within the scene.

Going deep

Working with reflections doubles the number of calculations you need to make when composing an image: every shift in position causes a different shift in the reflection. For reflections with the greatest depth or largest reflected image, you need to place the camera as close to the reflecting surface as possible. Compact cameras are best for this, as you can place their lenses almost at the same level as the surface. When working with reflections in water be very careful not to break the surface: you do not want to ruin the reflection (never mind the camera).

Virtual images

The illusion of a scene-within-a-scene imbues images of reflections with an ethereal quality; they seem other-worldly. Indeed, in physical terms, a reflection is known as a "virtual image": it cannot be reproduced on a screen, or projected, but instead it appears to exist in three-dimensional space, because of a fundamental property of light-paths.

Optically, there are two features that impact on how you capture images of reflections. The first concerns the fact that the reflection is located as far "inside" the reflecting surface as the actual scene that is reflected. This often delivers far more depth of field than usual in your image. The second is that the reflection may be much darker than the actual scene reflected, particularly when the reflecting surface is glass or water. This can create problems with balancing exposure between brighter and darker parts. This can be tackled using tone-mapping techniques (*see pp. 266–7*), provided there is no strong flare, as this can disrupt tone mapping at brightly lit edges.

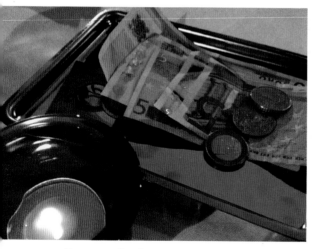

▲ Borrowed color

Working with reflections usually calls for precision positioning and careful observation. As I paid my bill at a restaurant, I noticed that the banknotes flashed bright blue as I placed them on the metal tray, because their metal strips reflected the color of the evening sky. In order to capture this image, I had to place the lens in a very particular position—near the table and close to the candlelight—cue the entry of a camera phone.

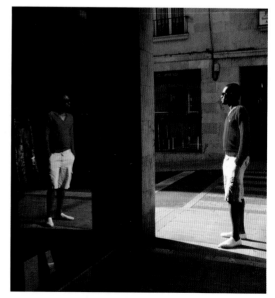

▲ Parallel worlds

In a town center, a dark store window suddenly comes to life when a bright reflection appears. The red sweater is so brilliant it appears to be at the same exposure in the reflection as in the original, helping to balance the image.

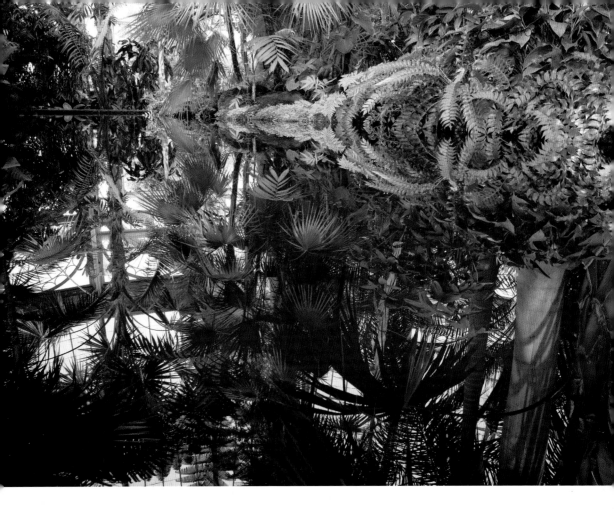

▲ Depth of feeling

Still water provides the best of reflecting surfaces, as long as it is dark; light reflected from the bottom of this pool would have diluted the intensity of color. By placing the camera very low—almost touching the surface of the water—at wide-angle, with minimum aperture set, I captured the greatest extent of reflection.

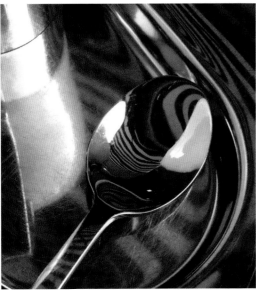

▲ Art in the mundane

The humblest subject can be turned into a tapestry of geometry through distorting reflections. Keep your eyes open for the potential in everyday objects. Here, a wait for service in a café was turned into a creative interlude.

PLAIN POLARIZATION

The polarization of light is a tricky subject—as is demonstrated by the fact that it took a number of great scientists, from Bartholin to Brewster, Young to Faraday, to pin it down. Today, the exploitation of polarization effects is commonplace, for example in Polaroid® sunglasses. Using the same technology, we can control reflections in photography: light reflected from certain surfaces such as glass, water, and leaves (but not metals) is strongly polarized, so if you fit a filter that cuts out polarized light, you can reduce the reflection to varying degrees. With an SLR camera lens, ensure that you use a circular polarizing filter (see also p.128) to avoid confusing the auto-focus system.

LOW-LIGHT PHOTOGRAPHY

Taking photographs in low light used to involve extra lighting, the use of ultra-large aperture lenses, or inevitable loss of image quality—or all of these things. No longer. The sensitivity of sensors has improved to the point that images can be captured by the light of the moon. The result is an extension of the world of available light photography. Simply set a high ISO setting, for example, ISO 1600 or greater, and a large aperture: you are then ready to concentrate on artistic issues, rather than struggle with technical limitations. If your camera produces noisy images at high ISO settings, you can deal with the problem in post-processing (*see pp. 194–5*).

Perception shift

The most thrilling aspect of low-light photography is that the camera sensor is not subject to the same limitations as the human eye when perceiving color in low light. In brief, sensors see almost as much color in low light as they do in bright light (there is a slight reduction due to increase in noise). This means that scenes that appear lacking in color, or where lights appear white, will record with much more color than you can see. This is particularly true of the evening sky: what appears gray to our eyes can be recorded as brilliant dark blues, while colorless city lights can be recorded as yellows, reds, or even greens. With a little experience, you will learn how to exploit these differences between our own visual experience of low light and the images that can be captured on camera.

Staying in the dark

One aspect of low light photography that poses problems for many photographers is how to allow dark subjects to stay dark. In general, you are aiming for low-key images (*see pp. 72–3*), that is, images in which the key tones are darker than mid-tones. The key tone should convey the sense of low light, while important details are distinguished and, at the same time, colored lights are not overexposed. This means that you override auto-exposure to -1 to -2 stops, in other words, you set the exposure as underexposed to the usual meter reading from -1 stop to -2 stops, or even more.

Remember to set any automatic flash to remain off. If the flash is effective at all, it is effective in destroying the character of the lighting. And at distances greater than about 10ft (3m), built-in flash has no effect whatsoever on the scene.

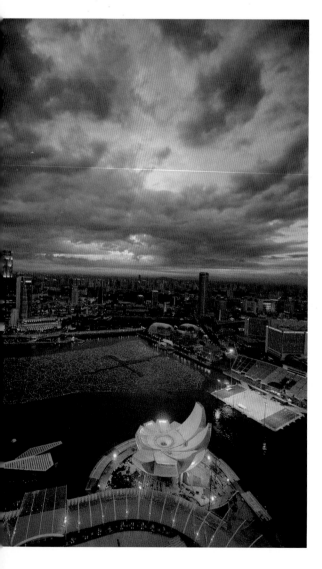

◀ Twilight zone
The half-light between the day and the onset of full nighttime darkness is a truly magical time as you can easily balance foreground and sky light. At the same time, colors seem much more intense than at any other time, with the sensors capturing all the perceived brilliance. Underexpose by at least 1 stop to obtain rich colors.

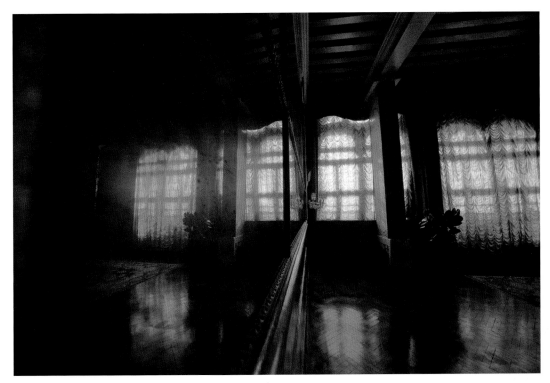

▲ Noisy interior

Even when there is dazzling sunshine outside, the interiors of buildings can be very dark—as was the case here in the hall of The Casino, Venice. Tripods were not permitted, so I pressed the camera against the mirror to keep it steady during the exposure, which I set at 1 stop less than metered. As noise is greatest in dark shadow areas and this image is almost all dark shadow, noise levels were judged to need

post-processing. For normal purposes, noise reduction filters in standard software such as Adobe Lightroom, Apple Aperture, and Adobe Photoshop produce acceptable results. For high and obtrusive levels of noise, use speciality software such as Topaz Denoise or Noise Ninja.

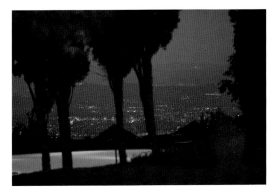

▲ Night blindness

To the eye, this scene appeared to be hopelessly dark, relieved only by the bright points of the city lights, and the pale blue glow of the pool's underwater illumination. Exposed at -1.3 stop to the metered reading, the image revealed blues and purples in the distant hills and the city. The image also made the light in the trees, which came from distant street lamps, more easily visible.

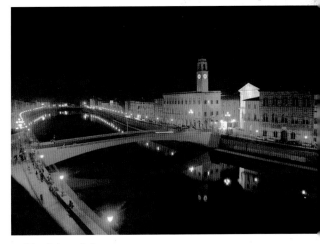

▲ Black as night

When there is very little light in the sky, any attempt to capture it will result in overexposure of lights on the ground. In this image of Pisa and the River Arno, the main concern is to expose the street lamps correctly: the better-lit buildings are overexposed and the sky is featureless. But what we really want is the lovely reflection in the river.

ANIMALS

When photographing a much-loved pet, it is easy to let your feelings influence the creation of the image. A more detached approach—in which you aim for visual interest in addition to the aesthetic qualities of the animal—is sure to result in more successful images, with appeal that extends beyond immediate family. Look for interesting compositions by focusing not only on the face; wait for moments of elegant gesture or expressive action.

Unusual approaches

You can broaden the scope of your images by including the relationships between people and their pets, or the contrasts between human and animal behavior. The challenge lies in finding original or illuminating approaches to the subject. One controversial technique is to use unusual props, or even clothes—take a look at the work of the artist William Wegman, who achieved worldwide acclaim for his portraits of Weimaraner dogs. Or you could experiment with abstract images. The isolated details of just about any animal can be rendered with beautiful results, for example using dramatic lighting to highlight sculptural detail on the body of a horse. Consider shooting in black and white (with or without tinting) or sepia instead of full color. Basic manipulations such as cross-processing (*see pp. 250-1*) can lift animal portraits out of the ordinary.

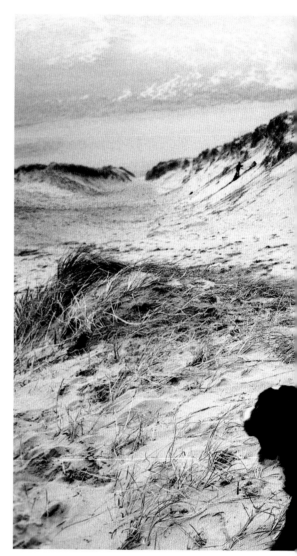

▶ All shapes
All kinds of animals are kept as pets. Pursuing the idea that owners look like the animals they adore, you could track down people who keep different kinds of animals, and photograph animal and owner together. This image of a golden eagle with his falconer in Kyrgyzstan provides a rich testament to relationships between man and animal.

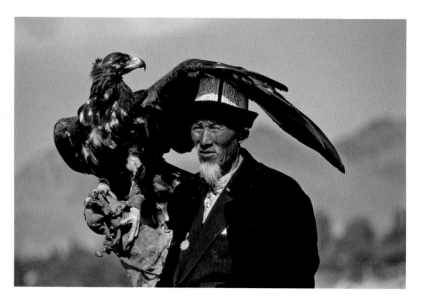

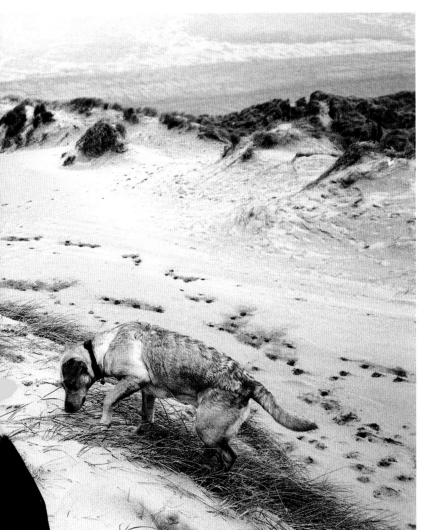

◀ Quick reflexes

A cold, windswept beach makes an unusual setting for pet photography, but it also presents many opportunities. For a split second a picture may present itself—you need to stay alert to record it. Here, the dogs not only appear to blend with the tones of the beach, they also seem to be responding to the contours of the landscape. The original color image was converted to black and white, then tints were added to hint at the natural colors.

▼ Laying low

This puppy makes a wonderful subject, but you can raise the bar by looking for an angle that is unusual, yet natural and intimate. As with people, work with your subject to gain their trust so you can catch them looking happy and relaxed.

PROFESSIONAL SERVICE

Proud pet owners seeking professional portraits of their animals can provide a good source of work for a photographer. Although potentially unpredictable, pets can also be most rewarding subjects, and the immediacy of digital photography means that you should easily be able to make a varied range of images for your clients to choose from. You can display the images immediately on a monitor, or even simply on the camera's preview screen—this spontaneity can be a great asset, especially if the owners have seen you capturing their pets' charming antics. It also saves time and enables you to fulfill the order with the bare minimum of delays.

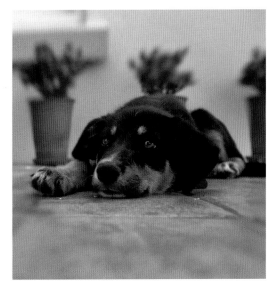

ANIMALS CONTINUED

Know your subject

Animals can be notoriously tricky subjects. They do not respect your wishes—in fact, it often seems that they know precisely what you do not want them to do, and then do it. In these circumstances, knowledge of the animal's behavior can be as important as photographic skill.

Having an appropriate lens for the kind of image you want to make will also save you a great deal of time and trouble. Normal to medium-long focal lengths are the most useful for portraits, and wide-angle lenses are good for shooting in aquaria, and for scene-setting shots. The smaller the animal, the longer the focal length needed to fill the frame. Very long focal length lenses are best for following highly mobile animals, as you only need to pan the lens a little to follow them as they move about. Animals with very long heads such as horses are also much easier to photograph from a distance: set a medium-small aperture to ensure depth of field covers the whole length of the head.

Animals in captivity

Modern zoos in major cities are taking on the role as centers for the study and preservation of wildlife; they are often models of animal care. You can see well-fed animals in something that resembles their natural habitat, and for many people, zoos offer the only chance to get up close to wild or exotic animals. Of course, this offers many opportunities for photographing animals you would not normally come into contact with.

Zoos are ideal places to practice elements of wildlife photography before venturing into the field. You will learn that if you set up at the right place at the right time, your wait for the right shot can be greatly shortened—and from this you learn the importance of knowing your animal and its habits. Try to pick a time for your visit when the zoo will not be too busy, for example midweek mornings. It may be possible to gain privileged access to some of the animals by approaching the relevant keepers or the zoo director, and offering free photographs for use in the zoo's publicity material or on its website.

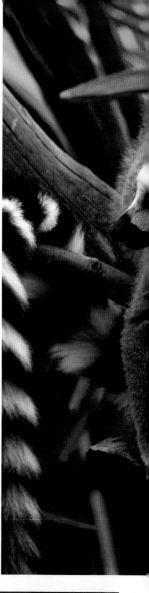

▶ The right moment
When taking pictures of animals in zoos, you can take your time to wait for a perfect expression or composition—family groups are especially interesting to watch. Keep shooting and pick the best shots later: try not to review your images while on location because you are bound to miss something.

▼ Eye to eye
It is thrilling to be close to a normally elusive animal, such as this giant otter. Even if you know it is tame, it is wise to keep your distance: use the long end of a zoom with a high ISO setting to enable you to set a combination of relatively small aperture and short exposure time.

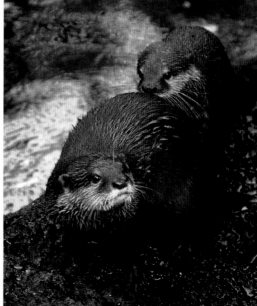

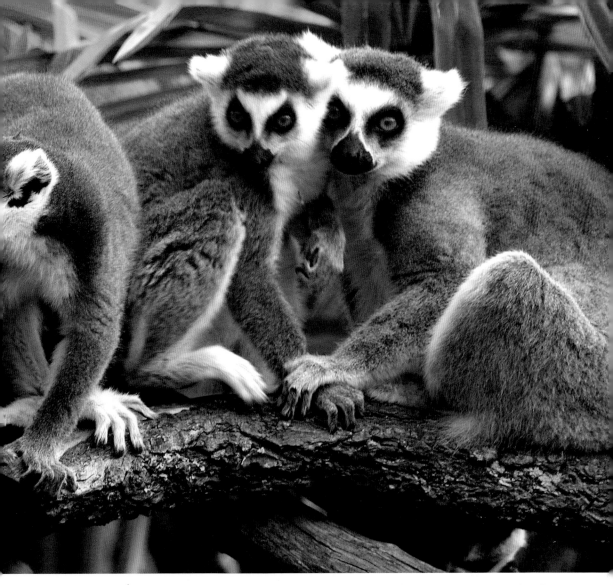

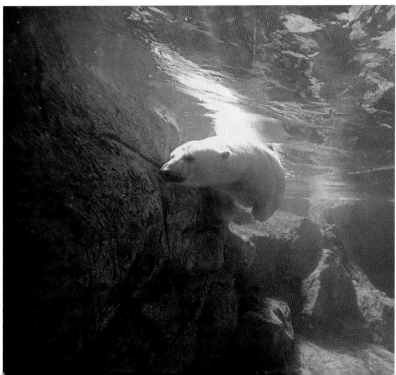

◀ **In their element**
In modern zoos it is possible to photograph animals in their element, such as a polar bear underwater, which only a very few specialists ever see in the wild. Make full use of the unusual level of access provided by the artificial environment.

PLANTS AND GARDENS

Digital photography might almost have been designed for the study of plants and natural history. Of the many features that make this technology ideal for record-keeping, chief among them must be its automatic indexing of all images. At the very least, all digital cameras give a unique file name to every image captured, thus allowing pictures of plant types to be linked to notes taken in the field. Many cameras record far more information—date, time, shutter and aperture setting, zoom lens setting, exposure compensation used—allowing you to review both the plant specimen and the way in which it was captured. Some systems are even able to link in with Global Positioning System (GPS) instruments, so that picture coordinates are automatically recorded—useful if you are doing fieldwork in various different locations.

A creative approach

Of course, plant photography is not purely scientific. Plants and gardens are enormously varied and aesthetically pleasing subjects, and they offer excellent opportunities to both hone your camera skills and develop your photographic eye. You could, for example, set a camera to take images at relatively long intervals—say, once every hour—to reveal the different stages of the opening of a flower (for this you would need a continual power source, and would probably need to set up a flash to ensure adequate and consistent lighting).

Alternatively, you can explore the freedom made available to you by the scope of the subject matter—there are few areas in which you have such a wide choice of composition and approach. You can shoot anything from close-up details of a plant's anatomy to wide-angle views that encompass a whole garden—and everything in between.

▶ **Contextual advantages**
Your photograph of a flowering cactus could concentrate solely on its enchanting red flowers. But then it could have been shot in a living room or a botanical garden—there are no clues to help place it. A shot such as this sets the specimen in its environment, giving a sense of other plant life around it, in the deserts of New Mexico, USA.

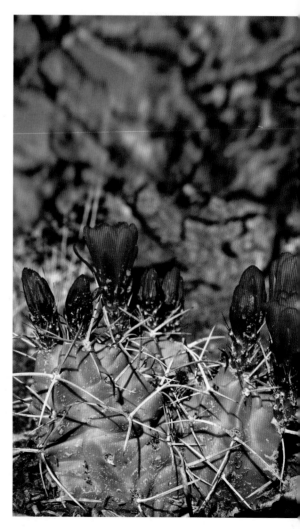

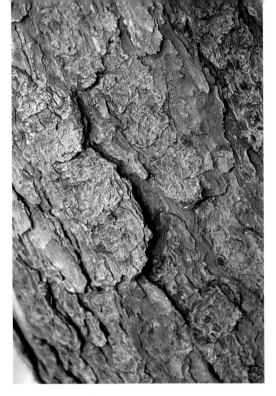

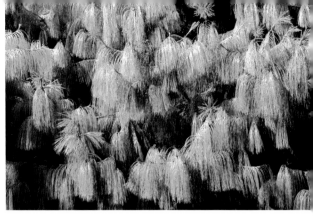

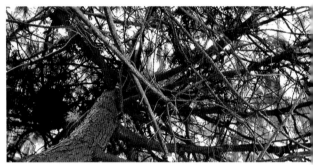

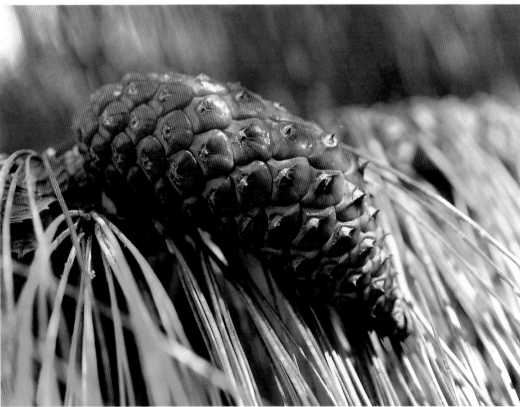

▲ A subject in detail

For many, one of the most satisfying areas of photographic interest is the natural world, and one of the easiest subjects is plant life. Discipline and a systematic approach can bring you great satisfaction, deepening your pleasure both in photography and the world around you. Here, a beautiful fir tree has been studied and recorded so that any expert could readily identify it—the cone, the organization of its branches, its bark, and its leaves are all unmissable clues. You could also add its habit (spreading, weeping, and so on) by photographing the entire tree. For more rigorous work, it is good practice to include some indication of scale by, for example, including a ruler in close-up shots.

PLANTS AND GARDENS CONTINUED

Organized wilderness

Whatever the style or level of organization, a garden is essentially an attempt to bring order to wild things. Whether it is a Japanese *karesansui* of exquisitely natural forms, or simply an untidy urban patch, gardens offer limitless photo opportunities. You can work at many different levels, both conceptually and physically: from the ground looking upward, for a worm's eye perspective. Or you could concentrate on bird's-eye views, such as from the upper floors of a house.

Because the subject is almost static, you can experiment freely, focusing at different points, and zooming from one extreme to the other. You might work with variations in depth of field and vary lighting by using flash for some shots. You can try different color settings, and set very high ISO settings too—all with the aim of finding a visual "voice" or a personal style that corresponds with the way you see, and feel about, the subject.

But, of course, a garden is not quite static: it is in constant, if understated, motion. And a garden can be radically transformed over the course of a day thanks to the movement of the sun. Plants and gardens also undergo dramatic changes with the seasons, so a view that is unpromising one month could be a treasure-trove the next.

Problems may occur due to the extended dynamic range arising from shiny leaves and the combination of bright sky and deep shadow. Use reflectors or supplementary flash to fill shadows; record in RAW to capture a broad enough range of data to make extensive changes, or use tone-mapping techniques (*see p. 266*) to compress tones.

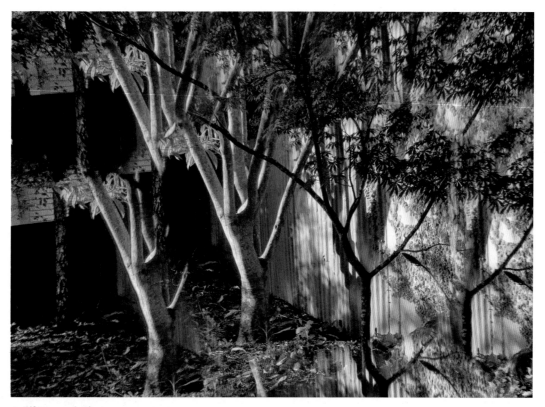

▲ Filter variation

Image post-processing can reproduce the majority, but not all, the effects of plastic or glass filters placed over a lens. Using a multiple prism over a 135mm lens helps to disguise an unattractive steel fence in an urban garden by overlaying it with a partial triple repeat of the scene. These small, random effects and variations in focus and depth of field would take hours of work to re-create using post-processing.

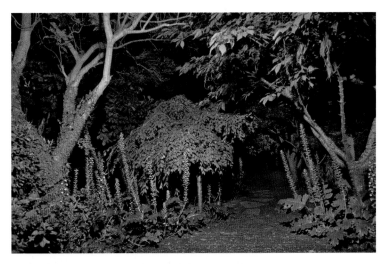

◀ Change of emphasis

The security light is usually entirely functional. But on this occasion—with the tall, spikey flower heads in evidence, and a tapestry of petals scattered over the decking—the lights revealed a very different garden to the one that could be seen during the day. The darkness beyond the reach of the lights hides distractions and flattens the perspective, making the image appear somewhat painterly.

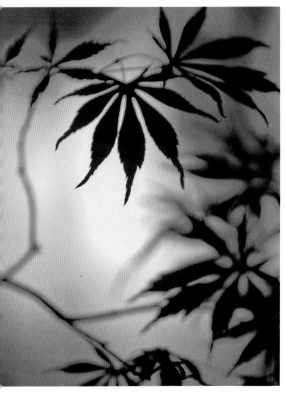

◀ Depth in shallowness

By minimizing depth of field—produced here by a 135mm lens set to f/1.8—almost nothing is sharp in this image. But what we lose in sharpness we actually gain in clarity—a Japanese maple seen by the light of a weak evening sun.

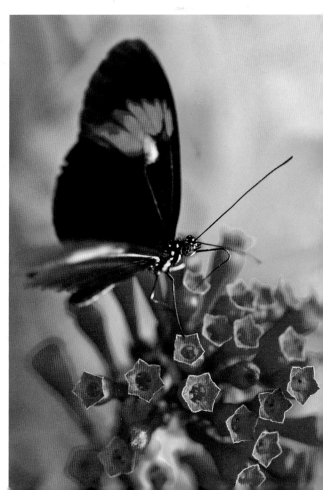

▶ Just passing

Although it is easy to think of plants as stationary, unchanging subjects, insects and other creatures can add an extra dimension to your shots, if you can catch them in passing. If you are shooting hand-held, an image-stabilized lens or camera helps ensure sharp images, but when you are shooting this close up and with a limited depth of field, you will need to focus critically to create the right emphasis within the image.

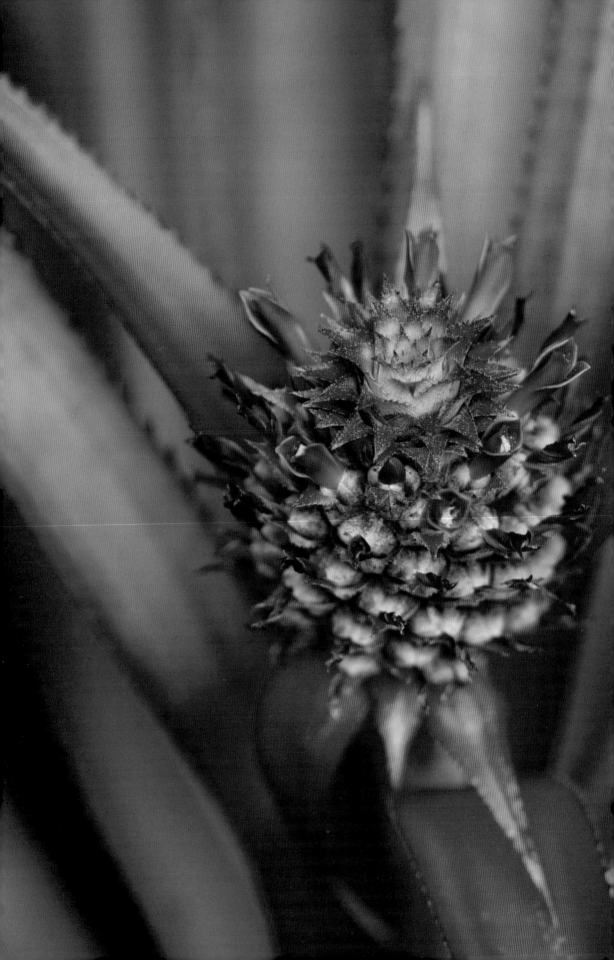

Structured colors
Limited depth of field from using a 100mm f/2.8 lens at full aperture keeps the leaves blurred, allowing the reds full freedom to "project" out of the image, giving a three-dimensional effect.

PANORAMAS

A panorama is an image that encompasses more of a scene than you could see at the time without having to turn your head from one side to the other. In fact, to obtain a true panoramic view, the camera's lens itself must scan the view from one side to the other.

Visual clues

The give-away visual clue to a panorama is that there is necessarily some distortion—if the panorama is taken with the camera pointing slightly upward or downward, then the horizon, or any other horizontal line, appears curved. If the camera is held parallel to the ground, any objects near the camera—usually those at the middle of the image—will appear significantly larger than any objects that are farther away from the camera.

▼ Landscape view

The landscape is the natural subject area for the panorama, and it also presents the fewest technical problems. In addition, it can transform a dull day's photography into a breathtaking expanse of quiet tones and subtle shifts of color. Here, a still day in Scotland creates a mirrorlike expanse of water to reflect the fringing mountain, thus adding interest to an otherwise blank part of the scene. This image consists of six overlapping shots, and it was created using Photoshop Elements.

Digital options

In recent times, the concept of panoramas has been broadened (confusingly) to include wide-angle shots that have had their top and bottom portions trimmed or cropped into a letterbox shape. As a result, the images have a very long aspect ratio—that is, the width is much greater than the height of the image. These pseudo-panoramas are popular because they do not suffer the curvature of horizon or exaggerated distortion of image scale of true panoramas. They can be created simply by cropping any wide-angle image.

True panoramas are almost as easy to create. For best quality, set the camera on a panoramic head on a tripod, ensure the camera is pointed horizontally, and adjust for the lens in use. (Handheld capture can also give acceptable results.) Next, capture a number of overlapping images of the scene from side to side or from top to bottom. Once you are back at your computer, stitch or join all these individual views together using readily available software (*see 298–9*). Many cameras offer a panorama mode, which stitches images in camera: you turn on the mode, then swing the camera steadily across the scene as it takes either a single exposure or several, depending on the technology used.

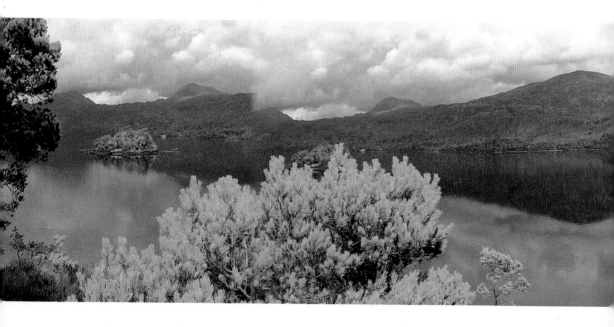

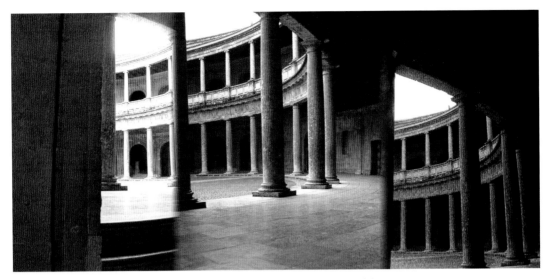

▲ Unlikely subjects

You can experiment with component images (*left*) that deliberately do not match, in order to create a view of a scene with a contradicting or puzzling perspective. The software may produce results you could not predict (*above*), since it is designed to make the best matches of subject detail on either side of the join. You can crop the result to form a normal panoramic shape or leave it with an irregular shape. While the final picture is by no means an accurate record of the building, in Granada, Spain, it may give the viewer more of the sense of the architecture—of the never-ending curves and columns.

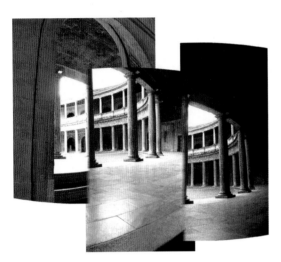

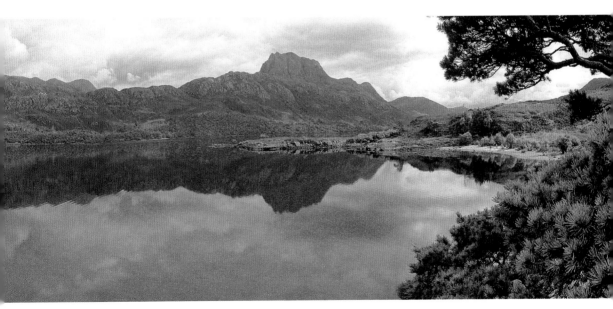

PANORAMAS CONTINUED

▶ Canal scene

The distortions in scale that are caused by swinging the view from one side to another, so that near objects are reproduced as being much larger than distant ones, can produce spectacular results. In this view, taken under a railway bridge crossing a canal in Leeds, England, one end is reproduced as if it is the entire width of the image, while the other end takes up only a small portion of the center. The mirror calm of the canal water helps to produce a strong sense of symmetry, which is in opposition to the powerful shape of the wildly distorted bridge.

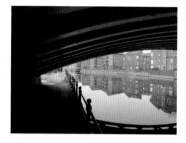
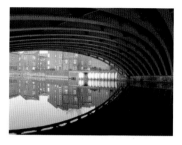
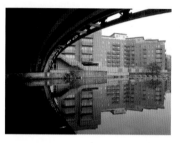
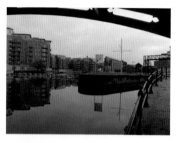

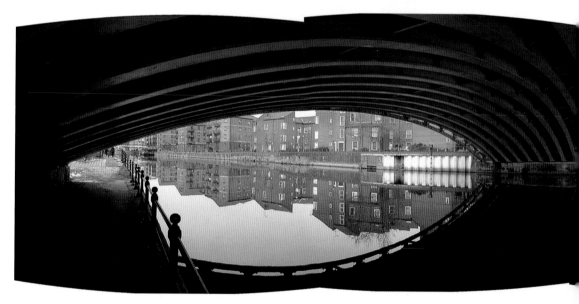

PERFECT OVERLAPS

The image projected by a lens appears to come from a point in space that is usually defined by the position of the aperture. If you rotate a lens horizontally about an axis through this point, you will notice little or no parallax. A panorama head allows you to set the axis of rotation so that the camera rotates without objects moving relative to each other to give perfect overlaps.

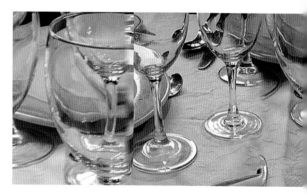

HINTS AND TIPS

The following suggestions will help you to obtain the best-quality panoramic images.

- Secure the camera on a tripod, and level it carefully.
- Use a so-called virtual-reality, or panorama, head: this allows you to adjust the center of rotation of the camera so that the image does not move when you turn the camera. If you simply turn the camera for each shot, the edges of the images will not match properly.
- Set the camera to manual exposure, and expose all of the images using the same aperture and exposure-time settings. As far as you can, select an average exposure—one that will be suitable for the complete scene.

- Allow for an ample overlap between frames— at least a quarter of the image width to be safe.
- Set your lens's zoom to the middle of its range, between wide-angle and telephoto. This setting is likely to produce the most even illumination of the whole image field and also the least distortion.
- If possible, set the lens to a small (but not the smallest) aperture—say, f/11. Larger apertures result in unevenness of illumination, in which the image is fractionally darker away from the middle.
- Make sure that important detail—a distinctive building, for example—is in the middle of a shot, not on an overlap.

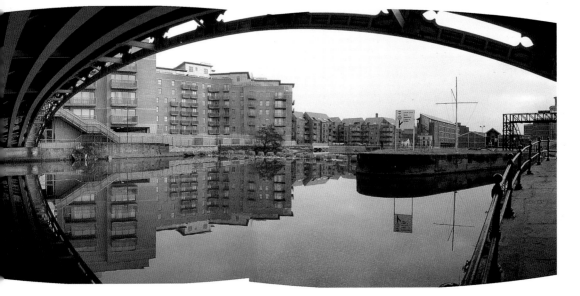

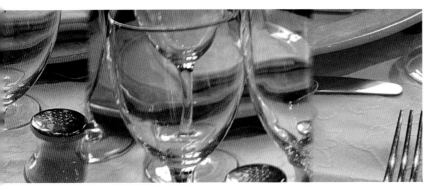

◀ **Table setting**
It can be fun to create panoramas of close-up views: here, a collection of views were blended together, playing with the pastel colors and repeated elliptical shapes.

LIVE EVENTS

Photographing live events such as parades, street parties, or concerts presents many challenges: fast-moving subjects, unpredictable lighting, and action that may be over in seconds. This is also true of weddings, family gatherings, or school sports days. Fortunately, with today's marvelous cameras, you do not need to worry too much about camera settings: "sports" mode should cover most of your needs. However, if you want more control, set a medium ISO of around 400 in good lighting. Using SLR and mirrorless cameras, you can set ISO 8000 or more indoors, with shutter priority and an exposure time of $\frac{1}{250}$ sec or shorter.

Right place, right time

The most important question here has little to do with equipment: where exactly should you stand to be sure to get the shots you want? The answer relies on one part instinct, one part planning, and a big dose of luck.

Instinct is what might prompt you to walk that bit further than you intended, or to look around a corner. It is what tells you to wait a little longer to capture an unexpected moment. The vital element to improving your photography at events is taking the time to go this extra distance.

Combine your instinct with careful planning, and luck will favor you. Once you have explored the location thoroughly, choose the best vantage points, and have your camera ready at all times. Then, when the bride unexpectedly turns around to flash a gorgeous smile, for example, you have your picture, not only because you were lucky but also because you were prepared.

Golden rules

Begin covering the event before it starts: images of preparations, such as set-building or make-up artists at work, produce a well-balanced view. During the height of the event, keep the camera switched on and close to your face, or hold it at arm's length above your head to shoot over the crowd. You need to be quick, so do not record at the highest resolution or in RAW format if this slows down your camera's operations.

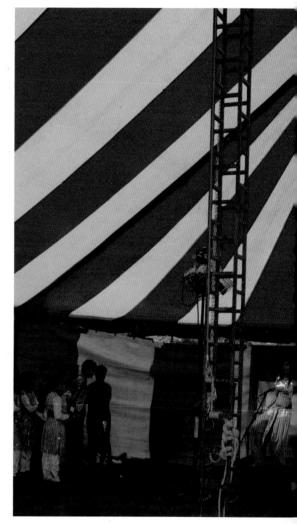

STAYING SAFE

There are no medals for bravery in photography. Do not put yourself or others at risk in pursuit of your photograph. Ask for advice from the staff in attendance, obey all safety notices, and wear appropriate and high-visibility clothing. Have your identification pass easily visible so you aren't asked to prove identity at inconvenient times. When photographing high-speed vehicles, do not shoot from corners unless there is adequate protection. Keep your wits about you at all times, and pay attention to your surroundings, as well as to the viewfinder.

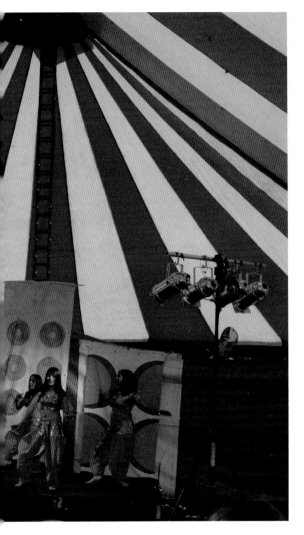

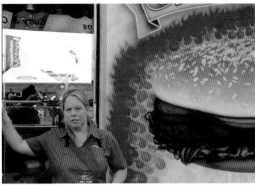

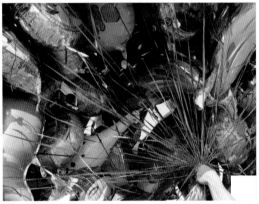

◄ All aspects, great and small

Use the full capabilities of your equipment to cover the different aspects of live events—the main event, the supporting activities, and the action on the periphery. Use wide-angle settings and get into the thick of things whenever possible. Use normal or wide-angle settings when shooting people to ensure a good level of involvement. Look out for colorful details, such as souvenirs and merchandising (above).

► Character study

The reputations of live events lie not only in the central attractions but also in their environments. A full account of an event records its context—whether it is a theater festival in a Greek amphitheater, a car rally in the desert; or, as here, at Glastonbury, in England, where the music festival famously turns into a sea of mud when it rains, as it usually does.

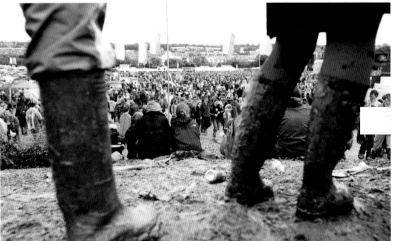

LIVE EVENTS CONTINUED

Sports coverage

While many professional sports events are now inaccessible to amateurs, there are still a vast number of other sporting events open to photography. Outdoor events such as marathons and triathlons often welcome photographers, as do sailing events and gymkhanas. It is worth renting a long lens such as 300mm or even 400mm, used with a monopod or tripod to enable you to "reach" right into the action. Amateur sportsmen like to have good images of their exertions, so you might find a market for your work.

When using a zoom lens, choose a loose, wide setting for the event, and avoid changing it while framing shots, since this slows you down. It is very inadvisable to check the image preview during action: wait for a break before reviewing your shots. Remember: the event is not over until you are off-site. Even when the action is over, you can shoot the clean-up, the exhausted players, and more.

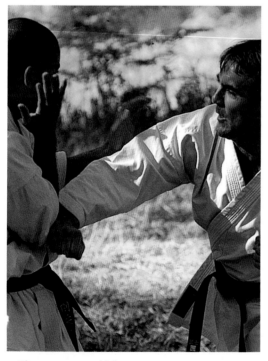

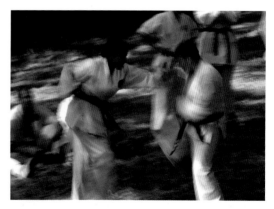

▲ **Sharpness and blur**
It takes the reflexes of a martial artist to photograph sports well, and the better you know a sport, the greater your chance of catching the moment of truth. But remember that sports are about movement, so sometimes it is appropriate to use long exposures to capture action as a blur—this is certainly true of fast-moving full-contact sparring.

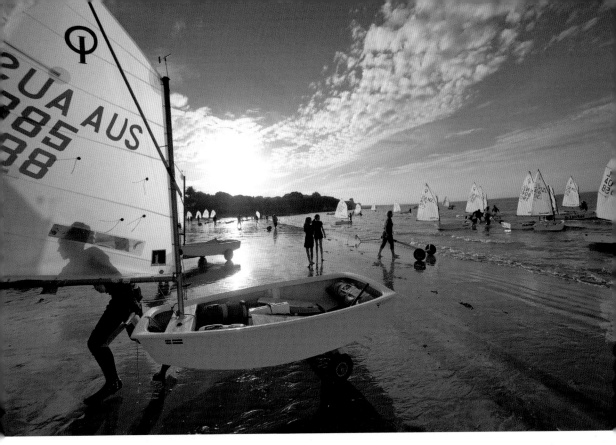

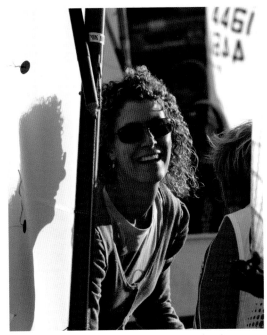

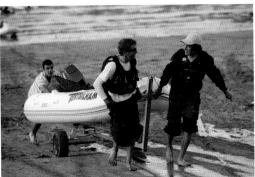

▲ Keeping up

Where you want to photograph a lot of activity concentrated into a short period of time, the best chance of covering it all is to work with two cameras. Use your compact point-and-shoot in addition to your SLR, or supplement your compact with a camera phone. The cameras can be set at different focal lengths—one to capture wide-angle views (*top*), the other to zoom in on the action (*above*). And if one slows down, you can give it a rest and use the other.

THE ART OF PASSES

Many public events around the world are tightly controlled, both for security and to limit recordings and photography of the event. From school sports days to concerts with top artists, you may need to obtain a pass before taking pictures. Apply to the organizers for permission, explain your interest, and give them a reason why they should welcome you. With commercial events, you may have to sign a contract limiting the use you make of photographs. But before you sign away your rights, remember: you never know what might happen to make your photography extremely valuable to you.

PORTRAITS

The possibility of easily making lifelike representations of family and friends was what most excited everyone about the invention of photography, and portraiture remains the most cited reason for making photographs today. With changes in society, a portrait now means any image that shows an aspect of a person's personality. This means the face may not even be visible or clear. In short, stylistically, there are no limits.

Anything goes

It is a very exciting time to take up portraiture: while you cannot rest on formulaic solutions, you are also no longer limited by them. In fact, anything goes. Faces can be hidden in the dark with only a sliver of hair visible, or distorted by blur from movement or lack of focus. You can photograph from behind, above, or below; you can have your subject pose naturally or with exaggerated artifice; and props, clothes, and makeup offer endless possibilities.

Relationship matters

Central to portraiture is your relationship with the sitter. How well you know them, and how much they trust you, may dictate the kinds of poses and expressions your sitter can give you. Even with paid models, a session will go more smoothly once they understand what you are trying to achieve and are able to work with you on it.

A great variety of portraits is possible when photographing a willing sitter. Once you have covered the basic, straight-on shots, it is time to explore other approaches. Have fun, be inventive and, above all, work at a creative partnership with your sitter. The following tips will help you get the best results from your portrait session:
■ Agree with your sitter the kind of image you wish to create, or that they wish to see.
■ Review the first few shots with the sitter to show them what you are trying to achieve.
■ After the first shots, do not show the model any images until the end of the session unless you wish to try some other pose or effect. Constant reviewing interrupts the flow of photography.

Technical pointers

We humans retain extremely clear ideas about the normal range of facial features: departures from the norm are obvious. As a result, it is best to avoid approaching within touching distance of your subject when using short focal length lenses or a zoom set to the short end of the range, unless you

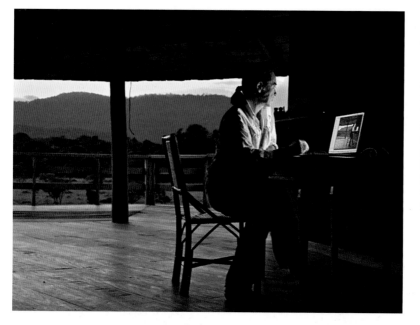

◀ At work
To photograph someone at work, it is best to let them do what they normally do: if they move quickly, watch out for moments of quiet, or learn when it is safe to ask them to hold a position. Use all local props such as tools, desks, and computers. In this shot, the light from a laptop perfectly balances the dim evening light in rural Guyana.

BOKEH

In portraiture more than in any other genre of photography, the quality of the blur in the out-of-focus parts of the image—the bokeh—is vital to the picture's success. Whether you expose with maximum depth of field or not, it is usual for the majority of the image to be rendered blurred. If the lens creates blurs that do not blend smoothly with each other, but instead create distinct disk-shaped blobs of color, the result is very distracting. Good bokeh produces a fuzzy or feathered blur, even at high-contrast junctions. At full aperture, virtually the entire image is composed of blur, so if you intend to use a portrait lens at full aperture it is vital that its bokeh is good, and that is usually a product of top-class design and construction—in other words, an expensive lens.

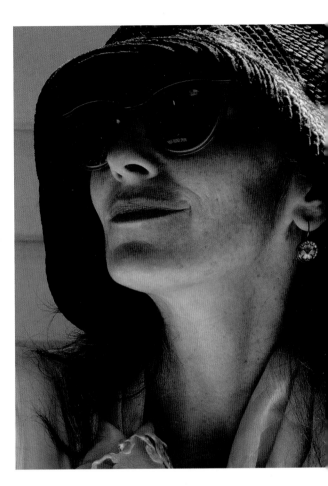

▶ Breaking rules
Less than half the face is visible here, the eyes can't be seen, and the hair is obscured. Yet the strong character and beauty of the subject is apparent. That is thanks to the inclusion of the accessories: the chic hat, fashionista shades, and expensive clothes. An image may break the rules yet still deliver an effective portrait.

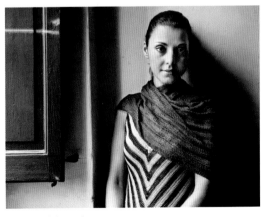

▲ Transitional mystery
Portraits are most interesting when they do not tell the whole story, and when they raise more questions than they answer. In this image, the contrasts between the refined clothing and the prosaic background, the strong shadow, and the cool color tones all intrigue, yet the whole is visually appealing.

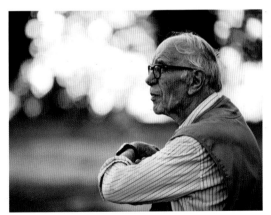

▲ Editorial accuracy
Newspaper and magazine markets are the hungriest for good portraits. There is a constant demand for images that depict personalities in an attractive but accurate way in an atmosphere or context that is appropriate to the feature article or interview. Here the out-of-focus highlights frame the profile effectively and sympathetically.

PORTRAITS CONTINUED

intend to distort your subject comically. On the other hand, being able to get so close to someone suggests trust and intimacy, so that can be a useful signifier to exploit.

It is hard to go wrong if you focus on the eye nearest the camera, particularly if you are using a large aperture (f/2 or greater). This forces attention on the all-important eye, while painting the rest of the scene with broad, blurred brush strokes. If your camera uses multiple focusing points, it is easiest if you set it to use the focusing point over or nearest to the eye. It always helps to ensure there are no highlights or specular reflections in the background, unless it is an important part of the scene—a desk lamp or the setting sun, for instance.

Environmental impact

By making portraits outside the studio, you can take full advantage of your sitter's environment—their living or working space—as part of the observation about the person. Remember that the size of the person in the image relative to the space shown is intuitively proportionate to the importance of the context to the person's life. For example, if you make someone appear small in their work space

you are commenting on their relative power in that context: you could have shown them dominant in the same space. The environment and person reciprocally contribute significance to a portrait. The following points are also worth bearing in mind:

- Locating the sitter in the center of the image signifies that they truly are intended to be the center of attention, even if they are small in relation to the background.
- Locating the sitter to one side suggests that atmosphere, mood, or the environment is just as important as the person, particularly if they are small relative to the background.
- If you are working in color, pay particular attention to colors of objects in the background: they can contribute information and visual interest, or they can tear the image apart. Intense, hot colors are distracting, as are bright highlights and shiny objects with strong, geometrical shapes. Movement blur in the background is also distracting.
- Compositional techniques such as converging lines and framing devices, such as doorways or tree branches, help direct attention to your sitter.
- Shallow depth of field with a varied background works well to bring the sitter forward visually.

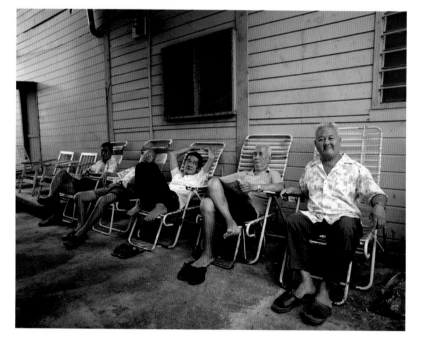

◄ Team work
Group photographs may concentrate on the team, in which everyone is equally important: the photograph is really about the team as a whole and is best composed as such. Or groups may be made up of individuals: it is part of accuracy in visual language that the composition reflects the dynamics of the group of people. Here, each person is shown relaxing in different ways, paying varying levels of attention to the photographer, all held by the receding lines and repeated chairs.

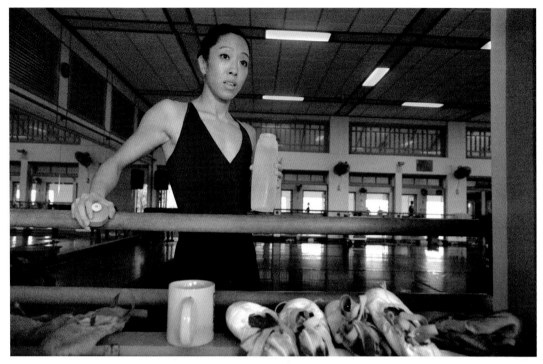

▲ Grace under fire

Even when exhausted from hard training in stifling hot conditions, this dancer holds herself with peerless elegance, surrounded by the paraphernalia of her studio. Greens, browns, and pinks in the scene were too distracting, but rendered in black-and-white, we can concentrate on the dancer who is framed by the geometric shapes around her. Unfortunately, the light behind her head is too bright to be welcome, but this can be easily removed digitally.

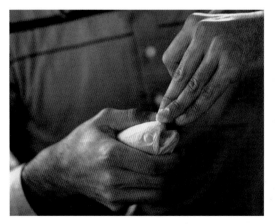

▲ Handyman

While the face is the most emotional and evocative part of the body, telling much of the story, it does not tell the whole story. Hands, feet, hair, and arms can all contribute. In the case of working hands, they may be able to tell the story by themselves. You usually have to work in low light, so prepare your settings—high ISO and large aperture for short exposure time—then approach closely and observe.

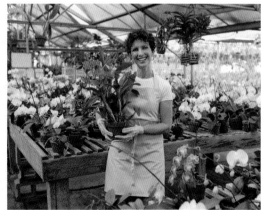

▲ Keep it simple

For many purposes, such as small business websites, pamphlets, and picture albums, the straight-forward posed shot remains the best option. A smile and an example of the product in the context of the business is the kind of image that is equal to a thousand words. Shoot such images in flat lighting, with centered composition with a normal or moderately wide-angle lens.

PORTRAITS CONTINUED

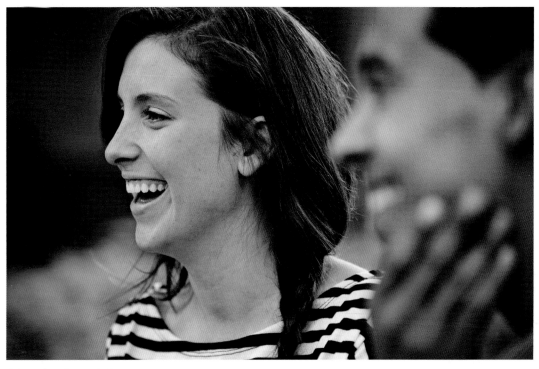

▲ Involved spectator

Informal, candid portraiture is only an eye contact away from more formal approaches. You can ask a third party to talk to your subjects, particularly if they are nervous about being photographed. The result can be more lively and relaxed: they are relating to a person and no longer trying to keep up appearances for the camera, which then becomes a spectator to their exchanges. Although you may be photographing a couple, you do not have to render both equally sharp. It may be more important to reveal the differences in the character: one open and relaxed, the other a little more reserved and shy. Try varying the depth of field until you get the desired effect.

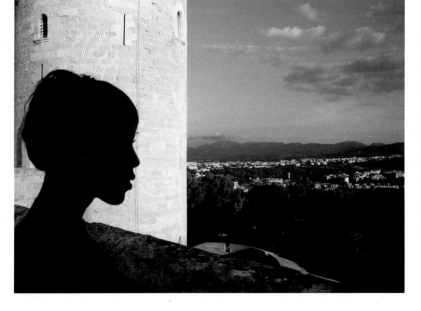

◀ In profile

In difficult lighting conditions, try working with the profiles of your subject's face. Allow the face to be in shadow while the background is bright. This technique is particularly effective when photographing people with dark skin tones, as dark-skinned faces are notoriously difficult to render correctly. Here, sudden and clear differences in distance have been exploited to create space in the composition.

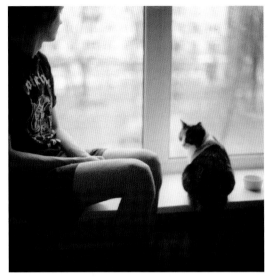

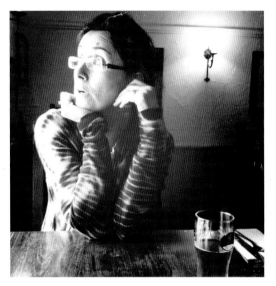

▲ Room for the view

Leaving lots of room for the subject to breathe can be as effective as filling the image with the subject. Here, space is used actively to contain the subjects, while coloration is very subtle: essentially monochrome with browns and flesh tones against blacks and near-whites.

▲ App expression

As they are almost constantly on hand these days, camera phones have become the most-used kind of camera for portraits. For unusual or imitation vintage effects, you can use built-in apps to apply tones and tints, to give a change from the norm.

▶ Close-ups

The 105mm or equivalent focal length is ideal for revealing close-ups of faces without the change of proportions that results from working with too short a focal length at close distances. When working at close quarters, set medium to small apertures, as depth of field is very limited, and failure to capture sharp highlights in the eye becomes obvious.

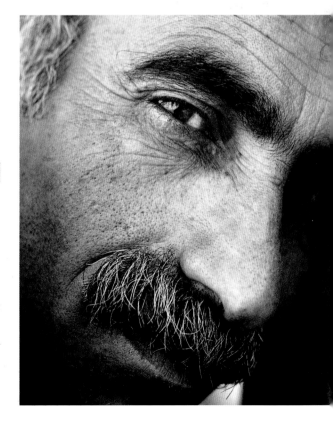

TRY THIS

A common question is "what is the best way to photograph strangers?" The answer is that the key lies in eye contact. If you can make and hold eye contact, you are half-way across the bridge to creating a relationship. And it is not until you have a relationship of trust—however fleeting, however shallow—that you can make a portrait. Next time you travel or have your camera with you, try looking into people's eyes if you wish to photograph them. If they are not comfortable with you, move on. If they respond positively, develop the relationship before lifting your camera. Never approach children without their parents' permission.

CAMERA PHONE PHOTOGRAPHY

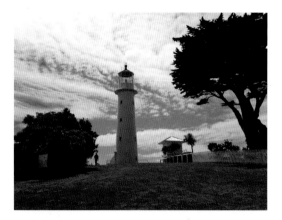

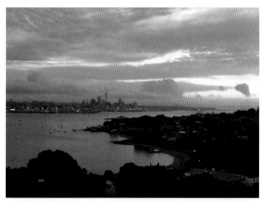

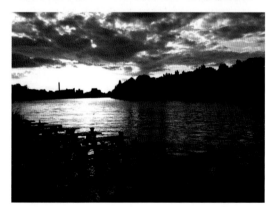

▲ Project compilation
As image quality is more than acceptable in many camera phones, there is no reason not to use them for photography projects. They are especially useful for ongoing projects, where you need to keep a camera with you at all times, such as capturing a variety of weather conditions, collecting interesting cloud formations, or cataloging landforms.
If you need to make wide-angle views, you can take overlapping shots that you then stitch together as if making a panorama (*see pp. 298–9*).

The cameras built into modern cell phones comfortably surpass the quality and capability of early digital cameras. By combining utmost convenience—you always have a camera with you because you always carry your phone with you—with fair- to good-quality imaging, camera phones have become the most widely used type of camera. It is worth noting that the companies making the most cameras (by a very large margin) are, in fact, in the business of making phones.

Bare necessities

One of the main attractions of camera phone photography is that you are forced back to the very basics: with minimal controls, you have no choice but to concentrate simply on picture-making. Some camera phones allow digital zooming, some offer touch-screen choice of focus point and exposure, and many allow images to be shot in various modes such as vintage (usually sepia), or with filter effects applied, either after normal capture or as part of image processing (*see pp. 232–3*). But simplicity is the overriding virtue.

Bare technique

For all its simplicity, you can help your camera phone to produce superior results. The Achilles heel of the camera is the tiny lens: because it is so small, even the smallest smudge or smear will reduce the quality of the image. Use a microfiber cloth to keep the lens scrupulously clean.
■ Hold the phone steadily during exposure: squeeze or tap gently for the shot.
■ Give the sensor plenty of light to work with: low light produces noisy images.
■ Give the camera time to focus: camera phones cannot focus as quickly as larger cameras.
■ Use features that give more accurate focus or exposure control; for example, on touch-screen camera phones such as the iPhone, touching on the image shifts the focus and exposure determination to that part of the scene.
■ The flash on camera phones is very weak and is effective only to about 6ft (2m). Turn it off for more distant objects.

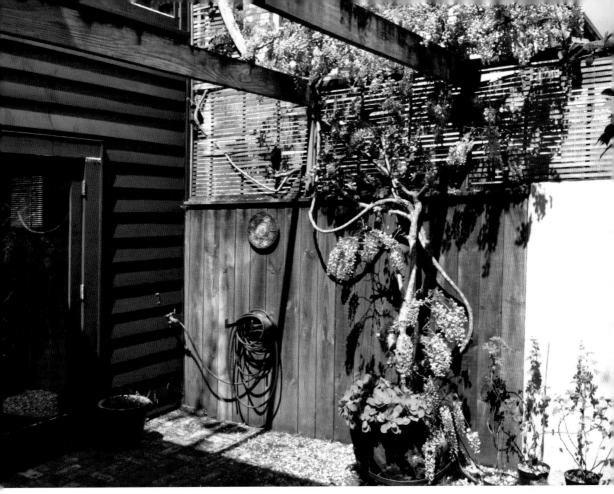

▲ Visual notebook

Camera phones are the ultimate visual notebook: you can use them to snap images of captions in exhibitions, make visual notes of items of furniture or objects for interior design, or to help document a house-hunt. The ability to attach GPS and other data to images increases their value for documentation. And, despite everyone being familiar with phones being used as cameras, a camera phone attracts much less attention than even a compact camera.

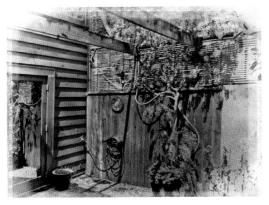

▲ App effects

There are a number of applications available that allow you to apply effects to your camera phone images. Some, such as Instagram, apply the effect to a normally captured image. Others, such as Hipstamatic, apply the effects as part of the capture process. This commits you to the effect and is a challenging and refreshing way to work.

DIGITAL HUB

The modern cell phone is also a camera that can make calls and connect to the world. Images captured on a camera phone are eager to be sent around the world to social-network sites such as Facebook to be viewed by friends, uploaded to picture-sharing sites such as Instagram or Flickr, or attached to an email or text message.

- Ensure the orientation of your images is correct for its intended use before sending them out.

- Resize the images to no larger than 640 pixels on the longer side for quick transmission (if that facility is available).

- If you are not in your home country, sending images can be expensive. Check with your service provider to ensure that you do not exceed your data limit.

RECORD-KEEPING

Digital cameras have revolutionized record-keeping. Not only are they unencumbered by the need to process film, the amount of equipment required can be minimal and little or no physical materials are consumed. And once the information is recorded, you can send it around the world in an instant.

Applications

The everyday applications of digital technology are numerous. If you want to sell your car, just take a picture and upload it to a website with your details. For insurance, take images of your valuables and possessions, room by room, but keep the computer image files separate from the computer in case it is destroyed or stolen.

Digital photography is also useful if you need to transfer information. You may, for example, want an expert on the other side of the country to identify a document or object—emailing an image of it is quicker and easier than making the journey yourself or mailing it. And sometimes a quick response can save lives—a doctor can email or phone through advice after seeing images sent in from the field via camera phone, for example. And in some circumstances it is crucial to record the time, date, and a sequential number along with each digital image. This is invaluable for many types of scientific work, such as an archaeological excavation.

The combination of digital photography for making straightforward records and software for managing images makes it very easy to print out lists and notes to accompany images.

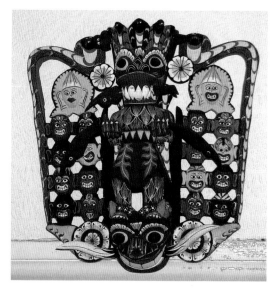

▲ **Reassembly**
This fine sculpture from Sri Lanka is designed to protect a home from illness, but for transportation it needs to be disassembled into numerous small parts. A series of photos quickly records the positions and orientations of every piece so that eventual reassembly is both easy and accurate.

Color accuracy

If you have to produce an image of an object and maintaining color accuracy is crucial, you should include a color bar along with the subject. Such a bar need be visible only on the edge of the image and does not have to be an expensive, standard type. At its most basic, the colored subject divider tabs of a loose-leaf folder will do. The crucial factor is that you have the color bar to hand to compare with the printed image.

GOOD WORKING PRACTICES

- Carefully preserve your back-up copies, and always keep them separate from your working files.
- Lock your archive files to prevent accidental or malicious tampering, especially if the contents are crucial to your work. Non-rewritable optical disks, such as CD-R, DVD-R, DVD+R, or BD-R, are most secure and are also archival. Keep more vulnerable disks physically secure, in different premises from the computer.

- Once your images number more than a few hundred, regularly print out a list of file names with notes about image content. You cannot hope to remember details of them all, and these notes will help.
- Use cataloging software (*see pp. 178–9*) to keep track of pictures. This software makes it easy to print out indexes of pictures, which are easier to search through than scrolling down long lists of names on a monitor.

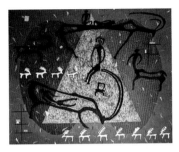

▲ Art preview
Digital photography proved to be incredibly useful for the Russian artist of this picture. Being rather isolated in Kazakhstan, he photographed it and emailed the picture file to an expert gallery owner for an opinion on its value before committing to a sale. In this instance, it is not of crucial importance that the flash has lit the painting unevenly.

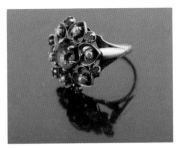

▲ Identification
Even if jewelry is not very valuable, it may still be precious. One problem police encounter when they recover stolen goods is matching items with their rightful owners. If you have ink-jet prints of your possessions, it will be a great help to everybody concerned. But take care to keep the prints separate from the items they depict to prevent them being stolen along with the items they are recording.

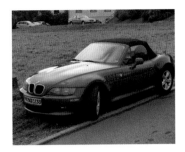

▲ Car for sale
If you are offering an item such as a car for sale, it is a matter of just a few seconds to take a picture of the item and email it to the newspaper or website, along with a full written description and your details.

FLAT COPYING

The purpose of flat copying is to make a record of a print, map, or drawing. The easiest method is to scan the original, provided you have a scanner of sufficient size. If, however, the original is too large, you will have to take a photograph of it instead. There are three main considerations:

- The image must be geometrically undistorted and at a known reproduction ratio.
- Lighting must be even and exposure accurate.
- The color reproduction should match the colors of the original as closely as possible.

For accurate alignment of camera and original, a speciality copystand is ideal, but a tripod can be used if you can ensure that the camera is exactly parallel to the original being copied. For the best results, use an SLR camera with a 35efl of a 50 or 55mm macro lens. If using the zoom, set it to the middle of its range, as this is where distortion is likely to be minimal. The lighting should be arranged as shown in the diagram (*see right*), and to ensure color fidelity, reproduce a color bar or step wedge with the original. It is not necessary to use an expensive type—any set of standard colors is more useful than none.

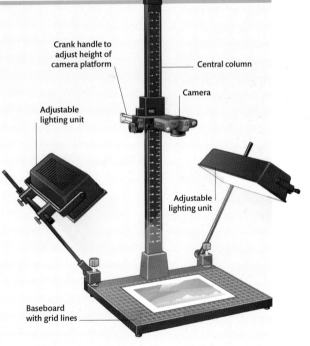

Crank handle to adjust height of camera platform

Central column

Camera

Adjustable lighting unit

Adjustable lighting unit

Baseboard with grid lines

▲ Copying set-up
The copying of flat documents, such as maps, artwork, drawings, and printed material, requires even lighting at a constant level, consistent color temperature, as well as a steady support for the camera, as shown in the copying set-up here.

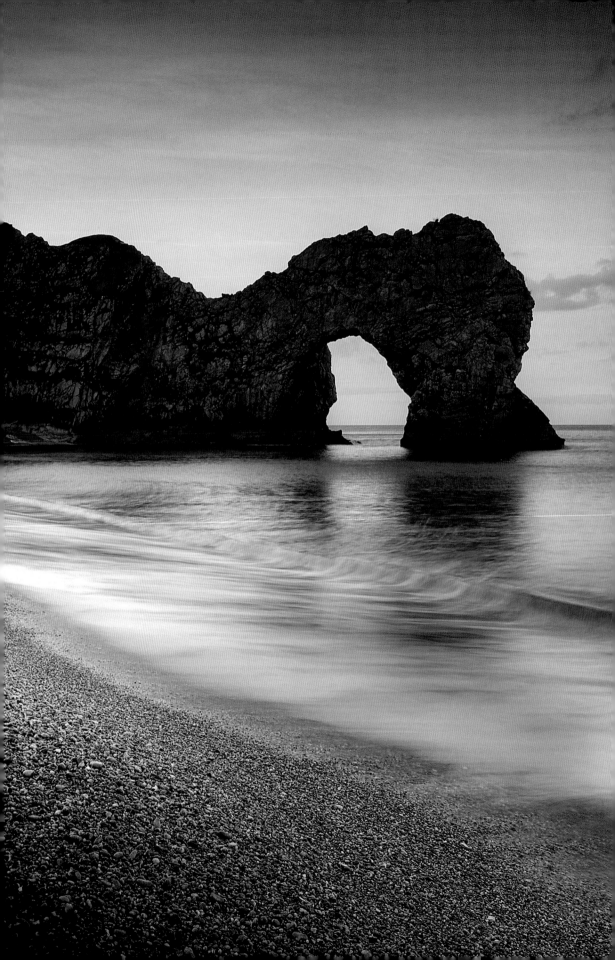

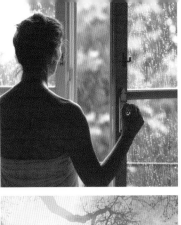

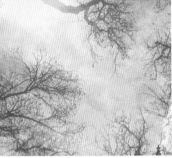

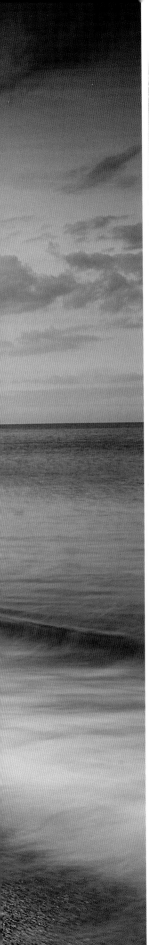

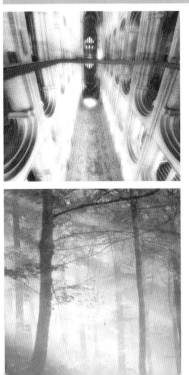

3 IMAGE DEVELOPMENT

SCANNING BASICS

Scanning is the bridge that takes film-based negatives and transparencies or printed images into the digital world. The process converts all color, brightness, and contrast information into digital data for your software to use. The quality of the scanner and the skill with which it is used are the key factors that determine the quality of the digital information and, hence, the quality of the image you have to work with.

Scanning steps

You can think of scanning as a three-stage process:
■ Gather together originals for the job in hand. You may wish to make prints of family portraits, say, or collect archive images for your club's website.
■ Next is the actual scanning. To do this, the scanner makes a prescan to allow you to check that the original is correctly oriented, or to set the scanner so that it scans only as much of the original as you want, or to set the final image size and resolution. You then make the real scan and save the result onto the computer's hard-disk.
■ The final stage is basic "housekeeping"—put your originals somewhere safe, somewhere you can readily find them again, and, if the work is critical, create a back-up copy of the scans.

Basic procedures

To get the most from scanning, it is a good idea to follow some commonsense procedures designed to help streamline your working methods.
■ Plan ahead—collect all your originals together.
■ If you have a lot of scans to make from a variety of different types of original, sort them out first. If, for example, you scan all black and white originals and then all color transparencies you will save a huge amount of time by not having to alter the scanner settings continually.
■ Scan landscape-oriented images separately from portrait-oriented ones. This saves you having to rotate the scans. And you will minimize visits to dialog boxes if you classify originals by the final file size or resolution you want.
■ If you are using a flat-bed scanner, clean your scanner's glass plate, or platen, before starting.
■ Make sure originals are clean. Blow dust off with compressed air or a rubber puffer. Wipe prints carefully to remove fingerprints, dust, and fibers.
■ Align originals on the scanner as carefully as you can: realigning afterward may blur fine detail.
■ Scan images to the lowest resolution you need. This gives you the smallest practicable file size,

---

SETTING UP A SCANNER

Many scanners give excellent results with practically no adjustment at all. However, it pays to calibrate your scanner carefully right from the outset. Follow the procedure set out below to ensure best results.
■ Obtain a standard target. The IT 8.7/1 is intended for use with color transparency film, and the IT 8.7/2 is for color prints. These targets may be supplied with your scanner; if not, a camera store may be able to order them. Alternatively, choose an original for scanning that is correctly exposed and contains a good range of colors and subject detail.
■ Make an initial scan using the machine's default settings—those set at the factory.
■ Check the image produced by the scan against the original. If necessary, make adjustments using the scanner driver's controls so that the scan matches the original. Some scanners require you to make these changes in the preview window. However, be aware that on some scanners the preview image is not really an accurate representation of the final scan. It is always best to open the image in your image manipulation software, and view it on a calibrated and profiled monitor (see pp. 182–3)
■ Once you have a scan you are happy with, save or note down the settings. Call it by the name of the film used—such as "Kodak Elite 100" or "Fuji Provia."
■ Repeat these steps with all the various types of film you scan—color negatives and transparencies use different scanner settings.
■ Then, for all subsequent scans, load the relevant saved settings as your starting point.

which, in turn, makes image manipulation faster, takes up less space on the hard-disk or other storage media, and gives quicker screen handling.

■ Use file names that are readily understood. A file name you choose today may seem obscure in a few months' time.

■ When scanning, crop as much extraneous image detail as is sensible in order to keep file sizes small, but allow yourself room to maneuver in case you decide to crop further at some later stage.

■ You may need to make your output image very slightly larger (say, an extra 5 percent all around) than the final size. This may be essential if, for example, you want your image to "bleed," or extend to the very edge of the paper so that no white border is visible.

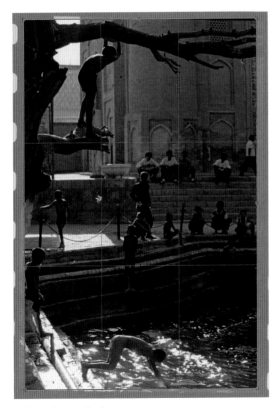
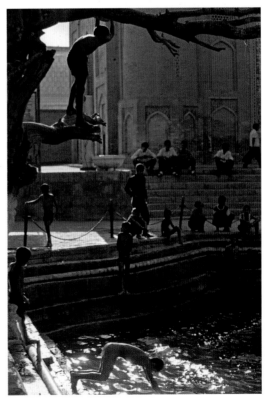

▲ Preview window

All scanners show a representation of the image in a preview window (*above*) prior to the final scan (*right*). This gives you a chance to make improvements before committing to a final scan. While it will save you time and effort later if you make the preview image as good as you can, bear in mind that it is only a general indication of the final scan. With some scanners, the preview may actually be rather inaccurate: if yours is one of these, you may need to experiment in order to learn how to compensate for its quirks.

WORKFLOW ESSENTIALS

Digital workflow is similar to processing black-and-white film in that there are efficient ways and less efficient ways of working. And just like film processing, an error can reduce the quality of your images, or even ruin them. The big difference is in the numbers of images you can work with: now you could have thousands of images after only a wedding. It is important to avoid having to spend hours in front of the computer wading through them. A little time planning a workflow will save days over the course of a year.

Horses for courses

It makes sense to match the flow of images to suit the project. If you shoot for yourself, a plan that fine-tunes one image at a time is fine: this is how it was done in the early days of digital photography. One simple plan is to set up your camera so that you can use the images immediately—on photo-sharing and social networking sites, or for printing out—without any post-processing. This workflow is almost effortless and all that is needed for many users. It is only when you want higher quality and more control that the extra effort is justified.

Soft options

One of the key decisions you need to make is whether to use the same software application—such as Google Picasa, Adobe Photoshop or Lightroom, ACDSee, or Apple Aperture—to manage and correct your images throughout. Lightroom, ACDSee, and Aperture treat all images nondestructively, operating only on proxy files. Alternatively you can use a different software package for each task—for example, Photo Mechanic for managing files, then Adobe Photoshop Elements for manipulation. Match the type of software and its cost with your needs. (*See also pp. 360–1.*)

Basic steps

The principle of workflow is to minimize time at the computer by never duplicating work unnecessarily and ensuring that at any time in the future, it will be easy to find an image. At the time you upload your

images is when all the details of the shoot are fresh in your mind and you know where, when, how, and why you made the images. This is when crucial tagging data and notes should be appended to the image. Following the sequence below will give you an efficient and time-saving workflow:

■ **Ingest:** on your computer, create a new folder named by subject, date, or location, and upload your images into this. Add metadata such as subject, date, location, and copyright to each image. If necessary, you can rename the images with sequential numbering. Finally, you should back-up the images to a secondary disk.

■ **Inspect:** check the technical quality of a sample of your images. Ensure that they are sharp, well-exposed, and have accurate white balance. If your camera does not turn images that you have shot in portrait format to the upright orientation, you

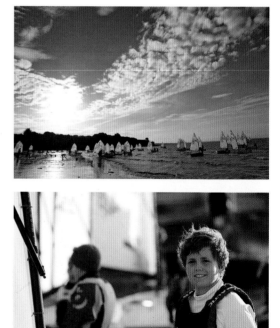

▲ **Plain sailing**
In the early stages of editing images, you may have wildly differing images to choose from. Leave the final selection until you have become very familiar with the shoot. Making tonal and color adjustments is easiest with proxy-working software such as Lightroom, Aperture, and ACDSee.

should do that now. If any of the images appear corrupted, upload them again.

- **Evaluate:** locate the first choices, second choices, and reject images, and apply ratings to rank them.
- **Apply metadata:** write information-rich captions. Make sure that you add identifying tags and other descriptive keywords.
- **Set up:** create a new folder for work in progress. Save images with new filenames if you are making changes to the original files. Use a storage device different from that holding the original image. Straighten, crop, or resize images as required.
- **Enhance:** normalize the blacks and highlights with exposure and curve correction.
- **Soft proof:** check how the image will look when outputted by reviewing proof colors. Adjust the image settings as required.
- **Clean up:** remove any flaws such as dust spots.

- **Final effects:** apply any drastic changes, such as conversion to black and white or sepia. Leave noise reduction to this step; apply sharpening, if required.
- **Prepare:** if you used layers, use Save As to keep the layered image in case you wish to modify the corrections you applied. Prior to export, flatten the image, resize it, and save it in the required format.
- **Use:** export directly to the target destination; for example, from Lightroom straight into your Facebook page. If you cannot export directly, create a transit folder for exports.
- **Archive and tidy up:** Make back-up copies of new files on hard disks. If you have created any folders for temporary files or files for download, remove them from your main machine. Double-check that you have two copies of images from your memory cards, then reformat the cards in your camera so they are empty and ready to use.

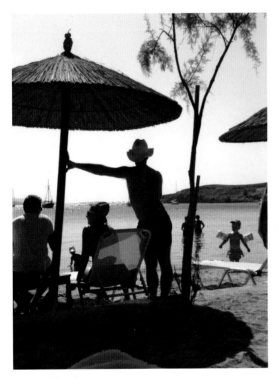

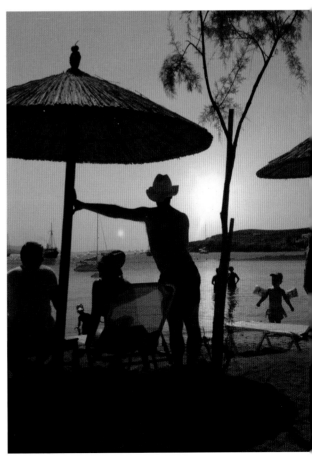

▲ Drastic changes

Substantial image changes, such as layering a sunset with a mid-afternoon scene, should be made on a copy of the original file. Work at full resolution even if you need only a small final image: perhaps one day someone will want to use the image large, having seen it on your website.

DOWNLOADING

Like it or not, the center of your photographic work is the computer. It is crucial to download images captured on your camera to hard disks under the control of the computer, as you can then back-up and work on the images. Then, when images are ready to be used, you will upload them from your computer to picture sites or into emails.

Computer by-pass

However, there are ways to avoid using the computer. You can download images from a memory card directly to a portable storage device that combines a hard disk drive with a card reader. Also, you can send images from camera phones directly to social networking sites. Cameras equipped with WI-FI can connect to the internet and upload images to distributed networks—this is popularly known as Cloud computing. Having logged-on to your cloud account using, for example, Google Docs, Dropbox, or Box.net you can upload your images to the storage space in your account. Sooner or later, however, the images will need to pass through your computer. One reason for this is security: your digital images are safe as long as you keep copies in different places at the same time.

Quick download

The fastest way to download images is to remove your camera's memory card and use a card reader connected to your computer via USB 3.0, Firewire 800, or Thunderbolt—whichever is your fastest connector. You can connect your camera directly but if you have multiple cards, it saves wear and tear on the camera to use a dedicated card reader.

The key to keeping your images safe is to download the pictures—as soon as possible—to your computer's hard drive or a mounted drive, leaving the images on the memory card. When you can, copy the images to another hard disk, or DVD or Blu-Ray disk; then they will be in three different places and pretty safe from loss. If you are working wirelessly and subscribe to services such as Apple iCloud or Adobe Carousel, then upload to these services. Only when you are sure your images are backed-up should you reformat the memory card.

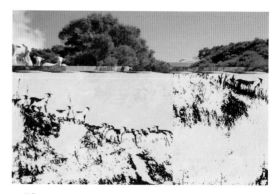

▲ **Bit error**
Errors in the memory card or occurring during download cause a break in the sequence of data, so part of the image looks fine but the rest is corrupted. Download it again to isolate the error: if it recurs, the memory card is at fault.

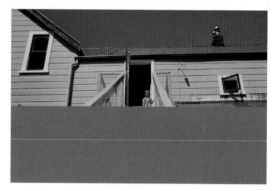

▲ **Incomplete scan**
If data recording or downloading was interrupted for some reason, this results in a blank area. The preview may be visible but the full file may not open at all. The memory card may be faulty or the download might need repeating.

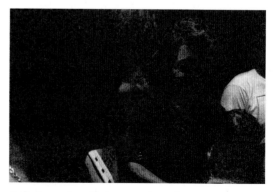

▲ **Auto correction**
Images may be corrected automatically by the camera when they are saved or downloaded. If there was a serious error at the time of capture, the image may appear but be seriously degraded, but the file itself is not faulty.

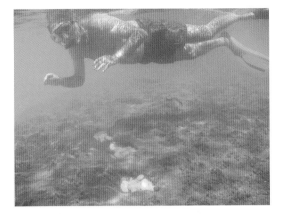 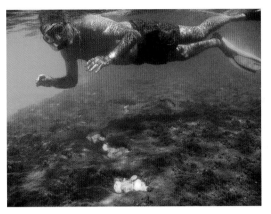

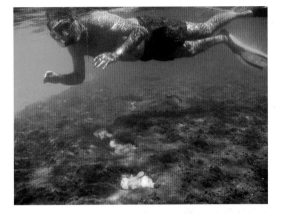

▲ Choosing color mode

An image's color mode is crucial to the success and quality of manipulation. RGB is useful for most image enhancements, but it is not the only mode. LAB is less intuitive to understand, but it is most flexible and versatile when preserving color data to maintain image quality is a high priority. Here, the initial RGB capture underwater (above) was low in contrast and carried an overall green cast. If left in RGB, Auto Levels correction gives it a bright, colorful, but not accurate result (above right). In LAB mode, Auto Levels correction produces true-to-life colors with accurate tonality (right).

CHECKING THE IMAGE

- Check the color mode and bit depth. Files from scanners may be saved as LAB files. Most image-manipulation software works in 24-bit RGB color, and if the image is not in the correct mode, many adjustments are unavailable or give odd results.
- Check that the image is clean—that there are no dust spots or, if a scan, scratches or other marks. Increasing the contrast of the image and making it darker usually helps to reveal faint dust spots.
- Ensure that the image has not had too much noise or grain removed.
- Assess the image sharpness. If the image has been overly sharpened, further manipulation may cause visible edge artifacts.
- Is the exposure of your pictures accurate? If not, corrections may cause posterization or stepped tonal changes.

- Is the white balance accurate? If the file is not in RAW format, corrections may cause inaccurate colors and tones.
- Are the colors clear and accurate? If not, corrections may cause posterization, stepped tonal changes, or less accurate hues.
- Check that there is no excess border to the image. It may upset calculations for Auto Levels or other corrections.
- Check the file size. It should be adequate for your purposes but not much larger. If it is too small, you could work on it for hours only to find it is not suitable for the output size desired. If it is too large, you will waste time as all manipulations take longer than necessary.
- Check the color profile for the image: for general purposes, use sRGB; for demanding uses, set Adobe RGB (1998).

FILE FORMATS

File formats define different ways of organizing information. While the bulk of an image file is the image data itself, in order for software to know how to read the data, it needs to know how it has been organized—just like headings on instruction sheets tell you where to find the Chinese, French, or English language versions. Fortunately, digital photography has a universal "language," JPEG, which is used for all common purposes, from emails and web sites, to printing and sharing.

JPEG

JPEG is a way to compress data. We trade small file size against lower image quality by compressing files. Generally, high compression gives lower quality, and vice versa. However, the data that is discarded cannot be recovered, so it is best to err on the side of caution. When capturing images, save them at high quality (low compression) to allow for later manipulation. When working with large images (with a high pixel count) you can use a lower quality setting than if you capture very small images.

FILE SIZE

For the internet and basic printing, small, compressed files, such as JPEGs, are adequate. For books and magazines, larger, uncompressed images, such as TIFFs, are commonly used.

Ink-jet print	3 x 5in (7.5 x 12.5cm)	1.9 MB
	4 x 6in (10 x 15cm)	2.7 MB
	8 x 10in (20 x 25.5cm)	5 MB
	Letter (A4)	6.9 MB
	Tabloid (A3)	12.6 MB
Image for webpage	480 x 320 pixels	0.45 MB
	600 x 400 pixels	0.7 MB
	768 x 512 pixels	1.12 MB
	960 x 640 pixels	1.75 MB
Book/ magazine printing	Letter (A4)	18.6 MB
	8 x 10in (20 x 25.5cm)	13.6 MB
	5.8 x 8.3in (A5)	9.3 MB
	5 x 7in (12.5 X 17.5cm)	6.7 MB

It is often recommended that you do not save and re-save files in JPEG because each save loses more data. In practice, numerous re-saves at mid- to high-quality settings make little difference to quality. See the panel opposite on JPEG compression.

TIFF

TIFF is popular with publishing professionals as the format can hold more color information than JPEG, but at the cost of much larger files. The LZW compression of TIFF comes without any data loss.

RAW format

RAW files comprise the image data that comes directly from the camera sensor, with minimal processing, such as pixel-based balancing. In contrast, JPEG files pass through several image processing stages and also drop data during compression. Therefore the promise of working in RAW is that the data is unadulterated, therefore promising the best potential image quality. (*See also pp. 234–7.*)

If you process the RAW files yourself, you obtain maximum flexibility with the images' tonal range and white balance (although that is not a licence to be careless about exposure control). Performing your own processing also removes the limitations of fixed in-camera processing such as sharpening, color space, noise reduction, and even the basic extraction of color data. Most importantly, RAW processing does not alter the original file at all; you always save a new image file. This means that, as RAW conversion methods evolve, you can return to the old RAW files to extract even better images.

Other formats

Many other formats are in use, such as BMP, PNG, GIF, and PICT. Some store data in a specifically efficient way, such as GIF for graphics, but other formats were created for manufacturers' convenience—for example, to evade patents—rather than that of consumers. Modern imaging software easily converts images from one format to another. For most practical photographic purposes, JPEG is all that you need to output or deliver.

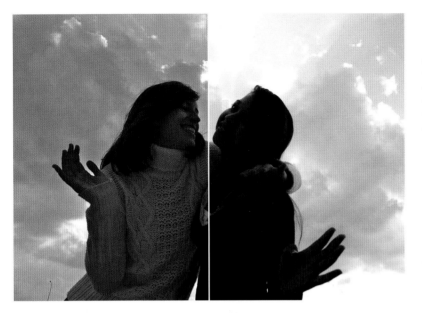

◀ RAW

By not committing to full image development when saved, RAW formats give you plenty of scope for adjustment. This is clearly demonstrated in this shot deliberately captured against the light without reflectors or fill-in. The improvement in both highlight and shadow detail, as well as the recovery of colors from the shadows is remarkable (left side). With low-noise cameras, a little under-exposure is permissible. Avoid over-exposure of bright areas.

JPEGs IN DETAIL

JPEG compression is efficient due to the fact that several distinct techniques are all brought to bear on the image file at the same time. Although it sounds complicated, thankfully modern computers and digital cameras have no problem handling the calculations. The technique, known as "jay-pegging," consists of three steps.

1 The Discrete Cosine Transform (DCT) orders data in blocks measuring 8 x 8 pixels, which creates the characteristic "blocky" structure you can see in close-up (*see right*). Blocks are converted from the "spatial domain" to the "frequency domain," which is analogous to presenting a graph of, say, a continuous curve as histograms that plot the frequency of occurrence of each value. This step compresses data, loses no detail, and identifies data that may be removed.

2 Matrix multiplication reorders the data for "quantization." It is here that you choose the quality setting of an image, balancing, on the one hand, your desire for small-sized files against, on the other, the loss of image quality.

3 In the final stage of jay-pegging, the results of the last manipulation are finally coded, using yet more lossless compression techniques.

The effect of these compressions is that JPEG files

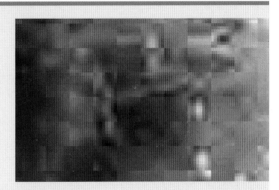

▲ JPEG artifacts

This close-up view of a JPEG-compressed image shows the blocks of 64 pixels that are created by the compression feature. This can create false textures and obscure detail, but on areas of even tone, or where image detail is small and patterned, such artifacts are not normally visible—even with very high levels of compression. Note how the pixels within a block are more similar to each other than to those of an adjacent block.

can be reduced by 70 percent (or, reduced to just 30 percent of their original size) with nearly invisible image degradation; you still have a usable image even with a reduction of 90 percent. However, this is not enough for some applications, and so a new technology, known as JPEG2000, based on another way of coding data, offers greater file compression with even less loss of detail.

IMAGE MANAGEMENT

Whether you are a casual, amateur, or professional photographer, your photographs represent a considerable investment. It is not just the cost of the camera and the computer equipment, but also the time spent learning how to use the equipment and software, not forgetting the time spent on chasing photos. And, no false modesty here, there is also the valuable input of your artistry and skill.

There are two sides to managing your photographic assets. One is ensuring that you do not lose any, and that they last forever. The other is to make them easily available—at least to yourself and, at best, to anyone who wishes to use them.

Safety in numbers

In the current state of technology, no digital medium can match film-based images for archival safety— the ability to survive unchanged and easily used for more than a hundred years. Those who would like their legacy to stretch into the next century or two may be best advised to return to shooting on film. For the more modest, the best strategy is to keep digital image files in multiple storage systems and in multiple places. For small numbers of images, use DVD or Blu-Ray disks to archive your images, even though these are slow to write and access. Hard disk systems are much better for working with, but are less reliable (*see p. 358*).

Hard disk systems called RAID (redundant array of independent disks), which allow for the failure of one or more disks without any loss of data, are now affordable to anyone who takes photography seriously. They may cost as much as an SLR, but they are arguably more important than an extra camera if you value your photos. The RAID's contents can be backed up on inexpensive desktop drives that are kept in different locations—for example, at a relative's house.

Soft gold

The total number of pictures on the internet is climbing well beyond a trillion, thanks to your contribution, among several hundred million other photographers. Locating a particular image, for example, to illustrate a magazine feature or use on a leaflet, must be text-based. Metadata or tags (also called soft data) are descriptive words, names, and other data added to or embedded in an image.

We find an image of Cape Town, for instance, not by examining millions of images on the lookout for features belonging to South Africa's great city, but by first looking for images carrying the name tag "Cape Town." What is more, you might have no idea what Cape Town looks like, yet you can collect dozens of excellent shots merely by searching for the tag. In fact, any image failing to carry the tag is very unlikely to be found, even if it is the best possible shot of the city.

The addition of metadata is an essential skill. Minimally, metadata should identify the subject or event, the date, the location, the copyright holder, and the photographer. The information should be enough for anyone to know for sure what the picture is about and to be able to contact you, so it should carry a caption and your details. In addition, keywords that refer to key elements of the image and a unique identifier, such as a serial number, can help anyone to locate your image.

Caption marvel

The rule for an effective caption is simple: answer the what, when, where, and who questions. Many agencies have a limit to the number of characters you can use, so it takes some skill and planning to get down all the information in the space available. While keywords are essential in helping a potential user to locate your photograph, the caption may clinch the deal as it can confirm the exact details and timing needed.

Start today

It may seem unnecessary to organize a collection of a few hundred images, but it is an easy task, and you will learn through the process. If you start when you really need to—with a collection of thousands of images—the task could be discouragingly onerous. So your most important decision is to decide to start right now, before you lose any precious images in a hard disk crash and long before it is really necessary.

CALLING NAMES

- There are two main ways you can name your images. You can use the names given by the camera, usually a generic DSC1234 or _IMG1234. (The underscore prefix means that the embedded profile is Adobe RGB.) Alternatively, you can name files more specifically. Professional users will benefit most from using specific image names.

- File names are most easily changed at download time or renamed in a batch.
- If you create specific names, keep a running catalog to ensure that each is unique—for example, by job number or date.
- Camera-generated names usually repeat after 9,999 images.

◄ File lists

Image files can be shown in lists that display a thumbnail of the image together with all its associated metadata. Selecting one of the images allows the metadata to be edited. In software such as Apple Aperture (shown here) or Adobe Lightroom, image-enhancement controls are available alongside tools for organizing material for slide shows, web pages, or books.

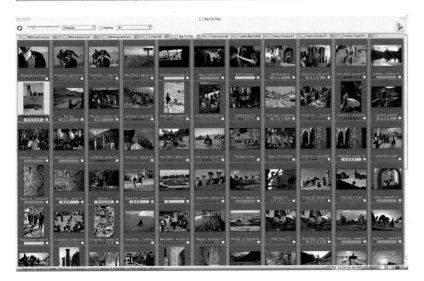

◄ Management software

One of the best ways to organize your images is to use management software. Applications worth considering include Adobe Lightroom, Apple Aperture, Extensis Portfolio, ACDSee, and Camera Bits Photo Mechanic (shown here). Not only do all these programs help you to keep picture files organized, they can also create "contact prints" and slide shows, as well as publishing picture collections to the web.

CAPTURE DEFECTS

There is a story about a group of great photographers who decided to make a list of what could go wrong in photography. They gave up when they reached 200 items. The defects highlighted here are only the common errors that are easy to miss—some even for the experienced photographer—leaving out the obvious such as poor focus or camera shake.

Original sins

There are two kinds of image defect: those arising from inadequacies of equipment such as poor image quality, flare, noise, and problems with color. The other defects result from inadequacies in technique, such as poor focus or exposure, camera shake, and unwanted distractions—such as an object sticking out of a subject's head, or telephone wires across the sky.

To varying degrees, all defects can be corrected or hidden: this is one of the glories of digital photography. However, you will find that you save yourself a great deal of time and frustration at the computer by taking utmost care when capturing the image. Your ultimate aim is never to have to manipulate an image to make it usable.

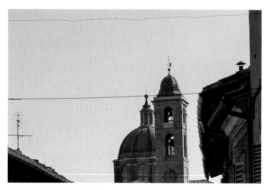

▲ Distractions
Some distractions may be avoided altogether through careful choice of position and framing, but wires and cables that stretch between buildings, spoiling the view of the sky, are notoriously difficult to avoid. Treat them as an image defect, whose removal is part of post-processing.

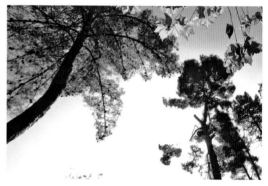

▲ Highlight clipping
When overexposure causes highlights to lose all color and detail they are said to be clipped. It is impossible to recover these areas, so they are best avoided altogether. Recording in RAW format and bracketing exposures for tone compression (*see pp. 266–7*) may help.

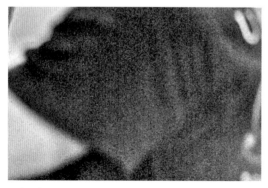

▲ Noise
When visible, irregular spots of color or large "clumps" of light or dark pixels disrupt image detail and color. Noise is commonly blamed on sensor performance, but can also be made apparent by post-processing; it is the price you pay for rescuing underexposed images.

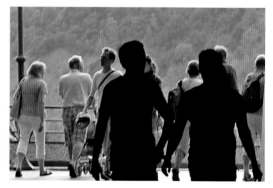

▲ Shadow clipping
The opposite of highlight clipping (*above*) is loss of detail and color in shadows due to underexposure. It is usually easier to extract some detail and color from clipped shadows than from clipped highlights. Recording in RAW (*see pp. 234–7*) increases the chance of a successful fill.

Avoid if possible

Certain defects are impossible to correct fully. If a lens hood for a wide-angle lense is misaligned it will cause shadowing or vignetting in the corners: the only way to remove them is to crop the image. The same applies to tilted horizons. Flare caused by pointing the camera at the sun can be extremely troublesome to remove or disguise. And, of course, poor focus leads to loss of details that cannot be recaptured. However, some unsharpness or blur resulting from movement can be reduced using modern algorithms.

WORSHIPPING QUALITY

Image quality is usually overrated. While the combination of a stunning image with technical perfection is a very fine thing, it is a common mistake to focus on quality alone. Remember that many of the greatest pictures in the history of photography were made on equipment and film far inferior to even today's amateur cameras. But no-one complains about their grain or poor color. Concentrate on making a wonderful image; quality comes a long way behind.

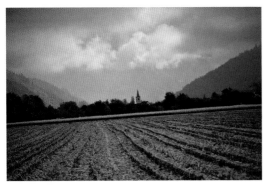

▲ Tilted horizon

This problem is commonly caused by cameras that are heavier on one side than the other, also by using small live image screens. A tiny tilt looks like an error, but very obvious tilts look deliberate and can be acceptable. Correcting the tilt is easy but always involves cropping (*see pp. 208–9*).

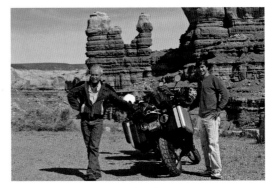

▲ Excessive depth of field

A common problem arising from the widespread use of small sensors, too great a depth of field gives too much prominence to the background, distracting the viewer from the main subject. Use post-processing to blur the background selectively (*see pp. 200–3*).

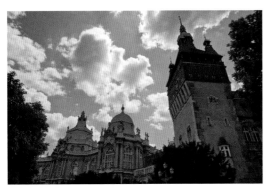

▲ Leaning verticals

Tilting the camera up to take in the full height of a building usually causes the building to look as if it is leaning back awkwardly. This often looks like poor technique. But tilting up strongly is often accepted as a deliberate visual effect. Small amounts of lean can be corrected (*see pp. 208–9*).

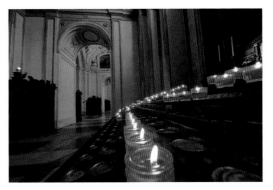

▲ Unbalanced color

Until more cameras use intelligent white balancing, a common defect is the inaccurate capture of neutrals in the presence of a strong illuminating color, such as here, where the red candles cause the white walls to look blue. This may need careful, hue-specific correction (*see pp. 210–13*).

COLOR MANAGEMENT

The aim of color management is to control the imaging chain so that between the subject, its captured image, the image displayed on a monitor, and any of its printed forms, there is the least possible variation in appearance. The key strategy is to define the behavior of each component in terms of a common standard, known as the profile connection space.

Digital color management

The central problem is that the color gamut or range of reproducible colors of different devices vary considerably. It is easy to make a set of adjustments that ensure our images appear on our monitor as they print out: this was what the old Adobe Gamma control was used for. But we might change our printer or update our camera: each time we make a change—even of paper type—we need to make new adjustments.

The solution is to use a common color space—essentially that which can be seen by the eye—to describe how the color reproduction of a correctly set up device differs from the standard. This generates the device's profile. Note that the device must be correctly set up: this is the task of calibration. Cameras and printers are essentially self-calibrating, but monitors need to be set up manually because a number of variables (gamma, white point) need to be set by the operator.

Monitor calibration

There are software-based methods for calibrating monitors and hardware-based methods. The former is free but less accurate than the latter, which you have to purchase, but prices are now a fraction of what they used to be. CRT (cathode ray tube) monitors should be warmed up for 30 minutes before calibration, and should be recalibrated at least once a month. LCD monitors need less warm-up time, but should also be recalibrated regularly.

After calibration, a profile for the monitor is created. This should be used as the monitor profile. In addition, you need to ensure that your work takes color management into account—for details see pp. 222–3 for color settings. This profile can be set as the output space or applied to the viewed image directly. Applying an output profile usually makes the image look duller, but it should be a close match to the print.

Viewing conditions

It is useful to consider the features of ideal viewing conditions, if only to make you realize how far your own conditions fail to reach them. Walls should be

CALIBRATION

Using the most accurate monitor calibrators or using on-screen targets will be of little help if the basic settings for gamma and white point are not carefully chosen to suit the end use of your images. If you supply to third parties such as stock agencies, magazines, or printers, consult them to find out their preferred monitor settings.

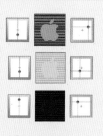

▲ On-screen calibration

On-screen calibration offers prompts such as the above, showing steps for setting luminance response curves and the balance between the three colors. Settings are altered to match targets.

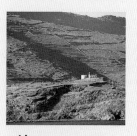

▲ Linear gamma

With the screen set to Linear Gamma, the overall result is very bright, blacks are gray, and colors look washed out. Images adjusted on this screen would look too dark, saturated, and contrasty on normally adjusted screens.

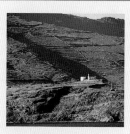

▲ 1.8 gamma

The 1.8 gamma was formerly the default setting in Apple Macs and the print industry. It is now regarded as too bright compared to the 2.2 gamma standard on Windows machines. A gamma of 2.0 may be set as a compromise.

painted white or a mid-tone neutral gray. Curtains should not be colored, that is, they should block out the light without filtering it—neutral colored blinds are best. Light levels in the room should be constant, and preferably only bright enough to allow you to find your way around the room—around 4 lux is ideal—and those parts of the image that are black should look black on screen.

The monitor should be hooded against local light sources such as desk-lamps.

Ideally, prints should be viewed in standard daylight viewing booths and transparencies should be viewed on standard light-boxes, placed as close to the screen as possible. Booths should comply with ISO 3664:2000, that is, they should use the CIE reference illuminant D50.

PROFILE RELATIONSHIPS

This diagram demonstrates how color characteristics of different devices can be translated to each other, using color profiles and a common color space.

Source profiles are seldom used because the majority of files are processed visually and are only of value with digital images in highly controlled environments, such as studios.

An image file may be embedded with a color profile so that it can be accurately reproduced when it enters a different working color space.

Working color space is your starting point. The sRGB color space is widely used for digital cameras and gives acceptable results. Another standard is Adobe RGB (1998), which gives better results for professional use.

Ink-jet profiles are perhaps the most troublesome for keen photographers. But produced accurately and used correctly, they can help maintain reliable, consistent results.

Monitor profiles are important because they help the computer system control the monitor, ensuring that colors are produced accurately.

CMYK output profiles are important for professional users and publishers of magazines and books, but they need not concern the majority of photographers.

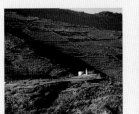

▲ **2.2 gamma**
The standard on Windows machines, indicating a high level of correction to the monitor's output. Colors are rich, and blacks appear solid while retaining shadow detail but the image quality is a poor match for print quality.

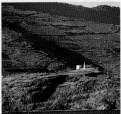

▲ **D50 target white**
Formerly widely accepted as the standard target white point for a monitor—that is, the monitor attempted to display white according to the definition for D50. The result appears to modern eyes to be creamy or yellowish.

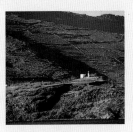

▲ **D65 target white**
As incadescent lights are used less and more prints are made on bright white paper, the D65 target white has become more widely adopted. It gives a cooler, bluer result than D50 and is a good choice for general digital photography.

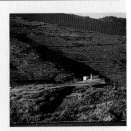

▲ **9300 target white**
Suitable for domestic TV and video, where the final viewing is on TV sets, this white point is generally too blue for digital photography. Using 9300 will result in images that look too red or yellow, and with flattened contrast.

CROPPING AND ROTATION

The creative importance of cropping, to remove extraneous subject detail, is crucial in digital photography—it can even be used as a compositional tool in its own right. A single image can have many different interpretations according to how it is cropped, although you should not let this affect your decisions when composing and framing your images.

Not only does digital cropping reduce picture content, it also reduces file size. Bear in mind that you should not crop to a specific resolution until the final stages of image processing, as resizing by interpolation will then be required (*see pp. 206–7*). This reduces picture quality, usually by causing a slight softening of detail. Image cropping without a change of resolution does not require interpolation.

Image rotation

The horizon in an image is normally expected to run parallel with the top and bottom edges of the image. Similarly, you may want to make sure that vertical lines in your image are correctly aligned, particularly when photographing buildings (*see pp. 97–9*) or other subjects with strong geometry. Slight mistakes in aiming the camera—not an uncommon error when you are working quickly or your concentration slips—can be corrected by rotating the image before printing.

With film-based photography, this correction was carried out in the darkroom during the printing stage. In digital photography, however, rotation is a straightforward transformation, and in some software applications you can carry out the correction as part of the image-cropping process.

Note that any rotation that is not 90°, or a multiple of 90°, will need interpolation. Repeated rotation may cause image detail to blur, so it is best to decide exactly how much rotation is required, and then perform it all in a single step.

Correcting scans

Cropping and rotation are also useful tools if you are scanning old film images from your archive. For example, you may want to remove the border caused by inaccurate scanning. This area of white or black not only takes up valuable machine memory, it can also greatly distort tonal calculations, such as Levels (*see pp. 188–9*). If a border to the image is needed, you can always add it at a later stage using a range of different applications (*see p. 209*).

Rotation can also be used to correct any innacuracies in placement on the scanner. However, always check that scanned negatives are correctly oriented—that left-to-right in the original is still left-to-right in the digital image.

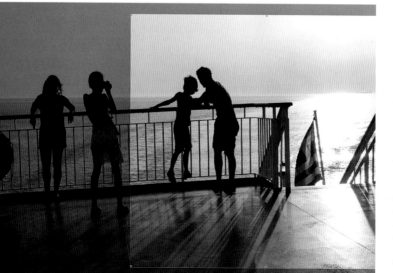

◄ Creative cropping
Cropping can help rescue an image that was not correctly framed or composed. By removing elements that are not required or are extraneous to what you intended, you can create a more visually coherent final image. Beware that crops to one side of a wide-angle image may appear to distort perspective, since the center of the image will not correspond to the center of perspective. Cropping decreases the size of the image file and calls on the image's data reserves to maintain image quality.

SAVING AS YOU GO

When working on image manipulations, make sure you adopt good working practices: always work on a copy of the original file, and get into the habit of saving your working file as you proceed: press Command + S (Mac) or Control + S (PC) at regular intervals. It is easy to forget in the heat of the creative moment that the image on the monitor is only virtual—it exists just as long as the computer is on and functioning properly. If your file is large and what you are doing is complicated, then the risks of the computer crashing are increased (and the resulting loss of the work more grievous). A good rule to remember is that if your file is so large that making frequent saves is an inconvenient interruption, then you definitely should be doing it, inconvenient or not.

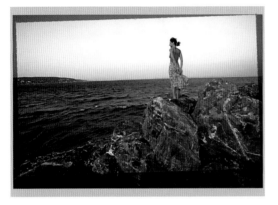

◄ Sloping horizon

A snatched shot taken with a wide-angle lens left the horizon with a slight but noticeable tilt, disturbing the serenity of the image. But by rotating a crop it is possible to correct the horizon (*below*), although, as you can see from the masked-off area (*left*), you do have to sacrifice the marginal areas of the image. Some software allows you to give a precise figure for the rotation; others require you to do it by eye.

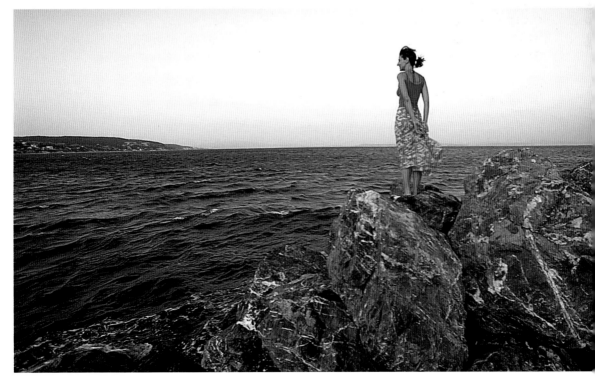

QUICK FIX POOR SUBJECT DETAIL

Producing the sharpest possible image in most situations provides the most flexibility later. You can easily blur a sharp image, but it is very difficult to rebuild detail that is lost to blur.

Problem: Images lack overall "bite," and sharpness and subject detail is soft or low in contrast overall.

Analysis: Unsharp detail rendered with low contrast can be caused by any of the following: use of a poor-quality lens; inaccurate focusing; dust or scratches on the lens; or an intervening surface, such as a window. Movement of the camera or subject during exposure may also cause loss of detail.

Solution: The core technique for improving detail is digital sharpening, or increasing clarity, using a variety of techniques such as unsharp masking (USM). Some cameras also apply USM as they record so that images appear sharper when viewed on screen. However, too much in-camera sharpening effectively reduces the final image quality, so it is best to apply manually controlled sharpening, viewing the effects on a large computer screen. Monitor sharpening effects with your image at 100 percent or larger while you apply them. For print use, sharpen until the improvement is just visible. For screen use, sharpen until the effect is apparent but no more than that (*see also pp. 196–9*).

A boost of image mid-tone contrast and color saturation also improves the appearance of image sharpness. Sharpening filters cannot retrieve details lost by movement during exposure, but new algorithms can help reduce motion blur.

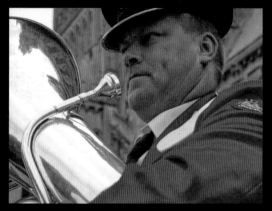

▲ Lacking bite
This snap of a bandsman lacks clean definition of detail, in particular in the face. The shiny metal gives the impression of sharpness, but that is just an illusion as a result of the reflections and high-contrast lines.

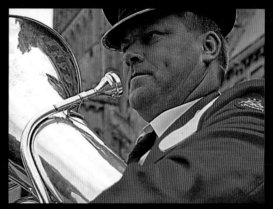

▲ Clarity of detail
By applying strong unsharp masking to the image, its impact is greatly improved. In particular, the musician's eye reveals an intense concentration, probably focused on the band leader.

HOW TO AVOID THE PROBLEM

- Keep the front and back surfaces of your lens and any lens filters clean. Replace filters as soon as they are scratched.
- Focus as precisely and carefully as possible.
- Release the shutter smoothly, in a single action. For longer handheld exposures, make the exposure as you breathe out, just before you start to breathe in.

- For long exposures, use a tripod or rest the camera on some sort of stable support—such as a table, window ledge, wall, or a pile of books—to prevent camera movement.
- Experiment with your lens—some produce unsharp results when they are used very close up or at the extreme telephoto end of their zoom range.

QUICK FIX POOR SUBJECT COLOR

If subject color is disappointing, despite your best efforts, the key to effective improvement is to be selective.

Problem: Your images are underwhelming, with lackluster color vibrancy and dull tones overall. These problems most often occur in pictures captured on overcast days.

Analysis: Your camera may make conservative adjustments to a captured image. In addition, light that is lacking a full range of colors—for example, on overcast days—is weak in warm colors, resulting in a bluish color cast that gives dull, cold images.

Solution: A sound first step is to correct the white balance if it is too blue or yellow. Then the simplest solution is to apply increased saturation to the whole image. But this often overemphasizes some colors in the effort to make others more lifelike. It is better to analyze the image and decide which colors—the yellows, say—would most benefit from improving, then limit the increased saturation to yellows (*see pp. 210–15*).

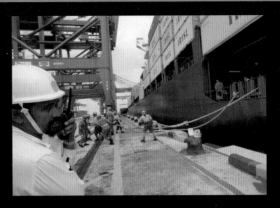
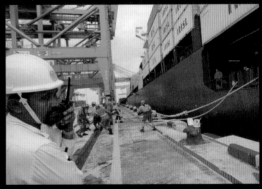
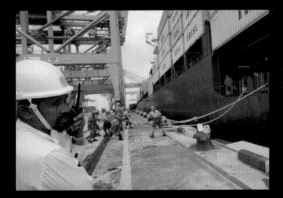

▶ Selective saturation
The original image (*top*) suffers from dull colors. An overall increase in saturation brings the green of the cranes back to the remembered color, but the face of the supervisor is too red (*middle*). We increase saturation limited to greens - for the cranes, yellows—for the markings on the wharf, and cyans—for the sky, by amounts to match needs. This allows the skin tones to remain natural-looking (*bottom*).

HOW TO AVOID THE PROBLEM

- In bright, contrasty lighting conditions, it may help to underexpose by a small amount: set the camera override to -½ of a stop or -⅓ of a stop, depending on what the controls permit.
- To avoid computer-based image manipulation, try using camera modes that boost image saturation. These are typically called something like Landscape, Brilliant, or Vivid.

- Set your camera's white balance to a setting that is appropriate to the prevailing conditions—for example, "cloudy" on an overcast day.
- Avoid setting the camera to very high sensitivities, such as ISO 800 or above. And if you still work with a film camera, you should not use high-speed color film of any type if color accuracy is crucial.

LEVELS

The Levels control shows a representation, in the form of a histogram, of the distribution of tone values of an image. Levels offers several powerful options for changing global tone distribution. The easiest thing to do is to click on the Auto Level button. This, however, works effectively in very few cases. What it does is take the darkest pixel to maximum black and the brightest pixel to maximum white, and spreads everything else evenly between them. This, however, may change the overall density of the image.

Another control that may be available is Output Level. This sets the maximum black or white points that can be produced by, say, a printer. Generally, by setting the white point to at least 5 less than the maximum (in other words, to about 250) you prevent the highlight areas in your output image appearing totally blank. Setting the black point to at least 5 more than the minimum (in other words, to about 5) you will help to avoid the shadow areas looking overly heavy in your output image.

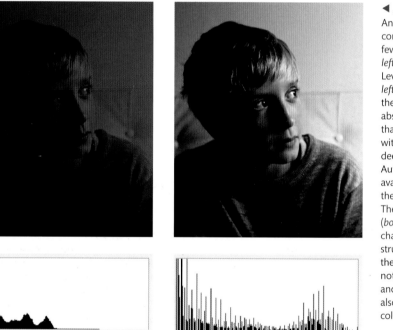

◀ Auto Level
An underexposed image contains dark tones with few high-value ones (*far left*), confirmed in the Levels display (*bottom far left*). The gap on the right of the histogram indicates an absence of values lighter than three-quarter tone, with peak values falling in deep shadow. Applying Auto Level (*left*) spreads all available pixel values across the whole dynamic range. The new Levels display (*bottom left*) has a characteristic comblike structure, showing gaps in the color data. Auto Level not only brightens colors and increases contrast, it also causes a slight overall color shift.

HOW TO READ LEVELS

The Levels histogram gives an instant check on image quality—perhaps warning of a need to rescan.
- If all values across the range are filled with gentle peaks, the image is well exposed or well scanned.
- If the histogram shows mostly low values (weighted to the left), the image is overall low-key or dark; if values are mostly high (weighted to the right), the image is high-key or bright. These results are not necessarily undesirable.
- If you have a sharp peak toward one or other

extreme, with few other values, you probably have an image that is over- or underexposed.
- If the histogram has several narrow vertical bars, the image is very deficient in color data or it is an indexed color file. Corrections may lead to unpredictable results.
- A comblike histogram indicates a poor image with many missing values and too many pixels of the same value. Such an image looks posterized (*see pp. 216–7*).

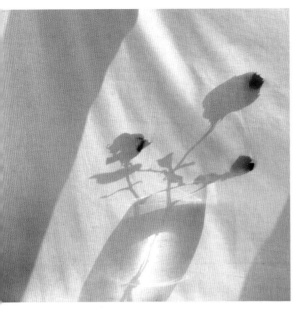

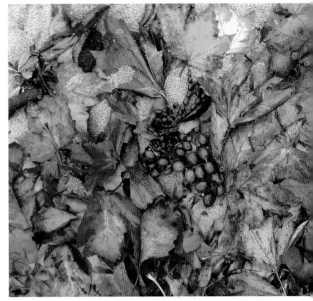

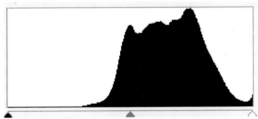

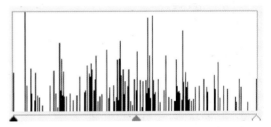

▲ Well-distributed tones

As you can see from this Levels histogram, a bright, well-exposed image fills all the available range of pixels, with no gaps. Since the image contains many light tones, there are more pixels lighter than mid-tone, so the peak of the histogram lies to the right of center. This image would tolerate a lot of manipulation thanks to the richness of color data it contains.

▲ Deficient color data

An image with only a limited color range, such as this still-life composition, can be turned into a very small file by saving it as an indexed color file (*see p. 222*). In fact, just 55 colors were sufficient to represent this scene with hardly any loss of subject information. However, the comblike Levels histogram associated with it indicates just how sparse the available color data was. Any work on the image to alter its colors or tonality, or the application of filter effects that alter its color data, would certainly show up artifacts and produce unpredictable results.

HISTOGRAM DISPLAY

The histogram for this image shows the mid-tones dominated by green and red, consistent with the strong yellows and browns of this warm, wood-dominated interior. Applications can be set to display histograms for each RGB channel or combined, usually as luminance for an accurate view of brightness.

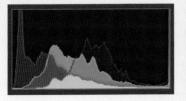

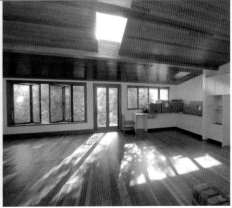

BURNING-IN AND DODGING

The two key techniques for manipulating the local density of an image in digital post-processing are known as burning-in and dodging.

Controlling density

Burning-in increases the density in the area of the image being worked on (it becomes darker), while dodging reduces it (a dodged area becomes brighter). Both techniques change the tonal reproduction of the original to correct either errors or imbalance, or for visual effect. For example, the highlights and shadows in any image are low in contrast, and to counteract this you can burn-in

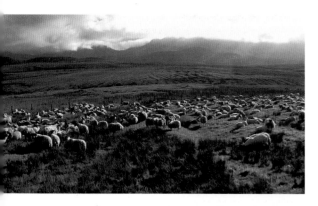

and dodge to bring out what shadow and highlight detail does exist by increasing local image contrast.

The same techniques can be used in order to reduce contrast—to darken highlight areas, for example—to bring them tonally closer to image mid-tones. An often-used application of this is burning-in areas of sky to darken them while dodging the foreground. This helps match the sky tones to those of the foreground.

Precision work

Using the brushes available in all image-manipulation software, you can apply effects over as broad an area or with as much precision as you like—down to the individual pixel, if necessary. You can adjust brush size—the area over which an effect is applied—how cleanly the edge of the brush is defined, and also its "pressure," or strength of effect. Some software programs allow you to set "flow," or how quickly the effect is applied. The tools should also allow you to set the tool to limit its effect to the shadows, mid-tones, or highlights alone.

The Burn and Dodge tools in classic image-manipulation applications are relatively crude compared to new tools. Some new brushes can

▶ Correcting tonal balance

Looking at the original image (*above*), the temptation to burn-in the foreground and some of the background in order to "bring out" the sheep is irresistible. Brief applications of the Burn tool on the foreground (set to mid-tone at 10 percent) and background hills, plus the Dodge tool on the sheep (set to highlight at 5 percent) produced an image (*left*) that was very similar to the scene as it appeared at the actual time of shooting.

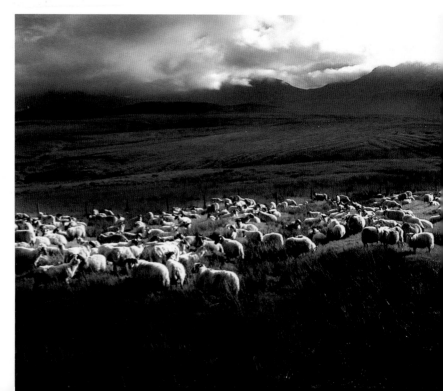

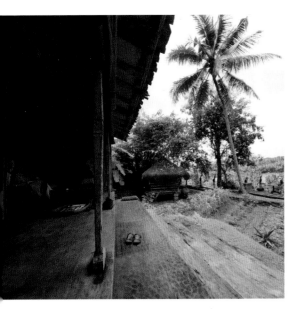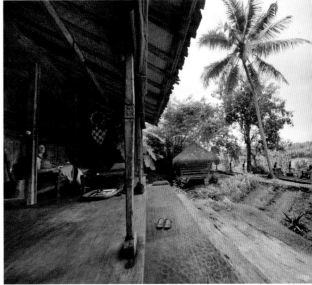

recognize edges and not apply an effect beyond the edge. Others can be set to adjust contrast as well as brightness when applied. Each tool is perfect for a different task, but you may need more than one software application to find the right tool.

You may also experiment with stronger effects by exploiting layer modes such as Color Dodge or Color Burn (*see pp. 278–83*). You create a new layer over your image, then apply tints: your choice of layer mode and layer opacity will control the density and contrast of whatever you apply.

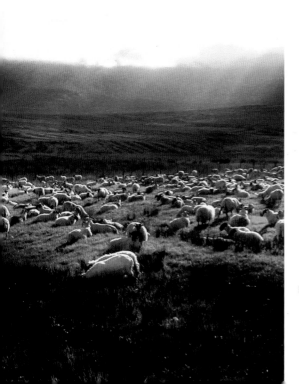

▲ Correcting exposure

An exposure biased for a tropical afternoon in Bali, Indonesia, rendered the shadows too dark (*above left*). By applying to the shadows a Dodging brush set to dodge mid-tones, a great deal of formerly hidden detail has been revealed (*above right*). Notice that colors emerge richer and brighter. Details in the open area were also burned in to extract more color from the dull light of the rainy day.

HINTS AND TIPS

- Apply dodging and burning-in techniques with a light touch. Start off by using a light pressure or a low strength of effect—say, 10 percent or less—and then build up to the strength the image requires.
- When burning-in image highlights or bright areas, set the tool to burn-in the shadows or mid-tones. Do not set it to burn-in the highlights.
- When burning-in mid-tones or shadows, set the tool at a very light pressure to burn-in the highlights or mid-tones. Do not set it to burn-in the shadows.
- When dodging mid-tones, set the tool at very light pressure to dodge the highlights or mid-tones. Do not set it to dodge the shadows.
- When dodging shadows, set the tool to dodge the highlights. Do not set it to dodge the shadows.
- Use soft-edged or feathered Brush tools to achieve more realistic tonal results.

BURNING-IN AND DODGING CONTINUED

Prayer flags in Bhutan are always a visual treat. With their mountain setting and colorful arrays, it is hard to make a dull image. A photo that fully takes in the flags and the scenery works best with a physical approach. The wide-angle lens was almost touching the closest flag in order to see the landscape through and past it. This combines many effects: extreme perspective, depth perception through changing focus, and interweaving lines all serve to bind the elements together.

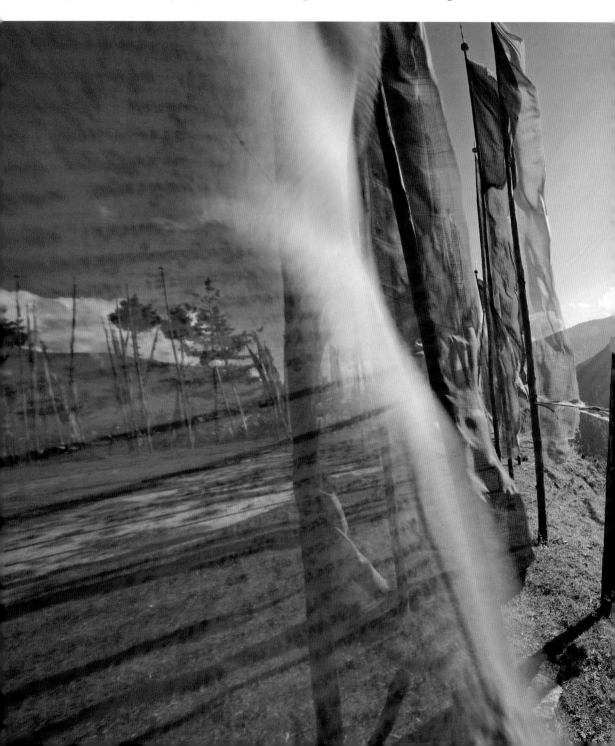

TECHNICAL INFO

CAMERA
Canon EOS-1Ds Mark II

LENS
Sigma 12–24 mm at 12 mm

SETTINGS
ISO 100 • f/11 • ¹⁄₁₂₅ sec

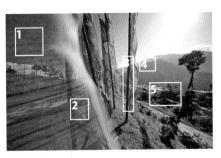

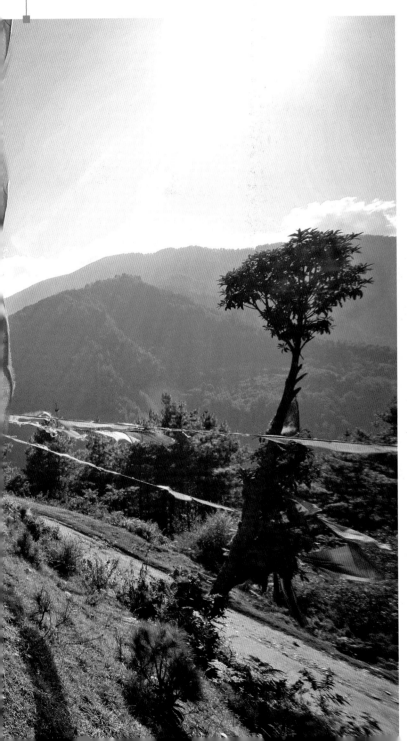

1 Gossamer texture

Looking at the scenery through a prayer flag brings the viewer close to the flag—and closer to the experience—than a conventional view that would separate the flags and scenery. This approach also serves to disguise ground that has been eroded by numerous tourists visiting the site.

2 Lettering hints

Thanks to the extensive depth of field resulting from using a small aperture with an ultra-wide-angle lens, the lettering is visible despite it almost touching the lens. The flag is blurred because it was flapping in the wind, but the lack of sharpness does not detract from the image.

3 The golden pole

This flagpole visually anchors the whole image: it lies just on the golden mean—that is, it divides image at about 0.618 of the total width, giving classically harmonious proportions.

4 Compositioal lines

By luck and fair wind, the lines of the distant mountains continue to the left into the double line in the yellow flag. This helps subtly hold the composition of the image together, without being too obvious or imposing.

5 Converging paths

While the flags occupy the foreground, the space around them is defined by elements including the distant skyline and converging lines, such as the strings of flags and the path below. All work to create a sense of large, airy spaces rapidly receding from the flags.

DUST AND NOISE

Two factors are the "forever enemies" of image quality: dust and noise. Dust spots on the image result when material lands on the photosensor of a camera or on film to be scanned. It is a serious problem with SLRs as the debris is recorded on every image. Noise—usually seen as pixels markedly different to neighboring pixels and not caused by subject features—arises from the electronic properties of the photosensor of a camera or scanner.

Noise control

You can reduce noise where the noise has a higher frequency than the image detail itself—in other words, if the specks are much smaller than the detail in the image. This is one advantage of increasing the pixel count of images. In low-resolution images, applying a noise filter smudges image information along with the noise signals. Digital filters such as Noise Ninja are effective at reducing noise only where required, and all raw converters can reduce noise. DxO Optics stands out by reducing noise before applying color interpolation.

Dust-removal options

Some scanners provide features to mask dust damage, replacing the resulting gaps in the image with pixels similar to those adjacent to the problem areas. These can work well, although some may disturb the film's grain structure, while others work only on color film.

Many cameras incorporate mechanisms to reduce dust, using, for example, rapid vibration to shake off particles or antistatic coatings to avoid attracting particles. Certain SLRs offer dust-removal software: you photograph a plain surface, have the result analyzed by the software, which then creates a "mask" that can be applied to images to remove the dust. You can also help the camera directly by cleaning the sensor using ultrasoft microporous swabs or ultrafine brushes that sweep up the dust and reduce static charges.

Manual removal

The key image-repair technique is to replace the dust with pixels that blend in with neighboring pixels. Depending on your tool of choice, you either

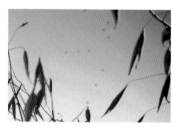

▲ Dust on sensor
A 300 percent enlargement of the corner of an image shows a few faint specks of dust. They are blurred because they lie some distance above the sensor, which "sees" only their shadows. However, with manipulation, the pale spots will become more visible.

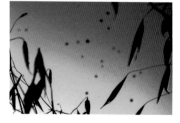

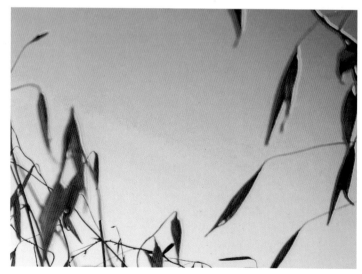

◄ Dust revealed
The full extent of the dust spots is revealed when we apply an adjustment layer to increase contrast and decrease exposure of the image. This presents the worst-case scenario and makes it easy to identify and eliminate the spots.

▲ Dust removed
Use the Spot Healing Brush, Healing Brush or Clone Stamp tool to remove the dust spots. Set the brush to just slightly larger than the average spot, with a sharply defined brush edge, and sweep systematically in one direction.

manually select the source for the pixels to cover the dust—this is Cloning—or you let the software sample from around the dust and apply an algorithm that blends local pixels with the dust to hide the spots—in Photoshop, this is called Healing. Where the spots are too numerous, a blurring filter may help, but this will also blur image detail that is the same size as the spots.

HINTS AND TIPS

- Clone with the tool set to maximum pressure, as lighter pressure produces a smudged clone.
- In even-toned areas, use a soft-edged or feathered Brush as the cloning tool. In areas with fine detail, use a sharp-edge Brush instead.
- You do not always have to eliminate dust specks; reducing their size or contrast may be sufficient.
- Work systematically from a cleaned area into areas with specks, or you may find yourself cloning dust.
- If cloning looks overly smoothed, introduce some noise to make it look more realistic. Select the area for treatment and then apply the Noise filter.

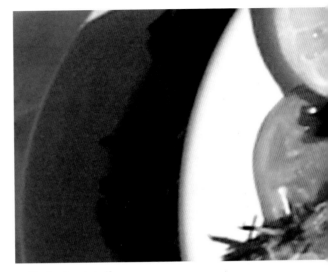

▲ Noise in detail

In this close-up view of an image, it is clear there is more noise, or random pixels (seen as specks and unevenness of tone), in the darker areas than in the brighter ones. Compare the blue shadow area, for example, with the white plate. This is because noise in the photosensor is normally drowned out by higher signals, such as those generated by strong light.

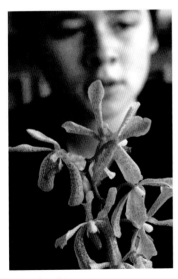

▲ Noisy image

Poor noise-suppression circuitry and an exposure of ⅛ sec gave rise to this "noisy" image. Long exposures increase the chance of stray signals, which increase noise in an image.

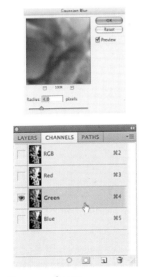

▲ Screen shots

Examining the different channels (*above*) showed that the noisiest was the green one. This was selected and Gaussian Blur applied (*top*). The radius setting was adjusted to balance blurring of the specks while retaining overall sharpness.

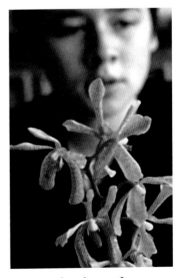

▲ Smoother but softer

The resulting image offers smoother tones—especially skin tones—but the cost is visible in reduced sharpness of the orchids. You could select the red and blue channels to apply Unsharp Masking to improve the appearance of the flowers.

HARPENING

The ease with which modern image-manipulation software can make a soft image appear sharp is almost magical. Although software cannot add to the amount of information contained in an image, it can put whatever information is there to the best possible use. Edges, for example, can be given more clarity and definition by improving local contrast.

Digitally, sharpen effects are true filters, as they hold back some components and selectively let others through. A Sharpen filter is, in reality, a "high-pass" filter—it allows high-frequency image information to pass while holding back low-frequency information.

Unsharp Masking

The most versatile method of image sharpening is Unsharp Masking (USM). This takes a grid of pixels and increases edge definition without introducing too many artifacts. Unsharp Mask has three settings. In Photoshop, they are called Amount, Radius, and Threshold. Amount defines how much sharpening to apply; Radius defines the distance around each pixel to evaluate for a change; Threshold dictates how much change must occur to be acceptable and not be masked.

It is possible to overdo sharpening. In general, assess image sharpness at the actual pixel level, so that each pixel corresponds to a pixel on the monitor. Any other view is interpolated (*see pp. 206–7*) and edges are softened, or anti-aliased, making sharpness impossible to assess properly.

As a guide, for images intended for print, the screen image should look very slightly over-sharpened, so artifacts (such as halos or bright fringes) are just visible. For on-screen use, sharpen images only until they look right on the screen.

Sharpening makes deep image changes that cannot easily be undone, so it is generally best to leave sharpening to last in any sequence of image manipulations, except for combining different layers. However, if you are working on a scan with many dust specks and other similar types of fault, you should expect the final sharpening to reveal more fine defects, so be prepared for another round of dust removal using cloning (*see pp. 194–5*).

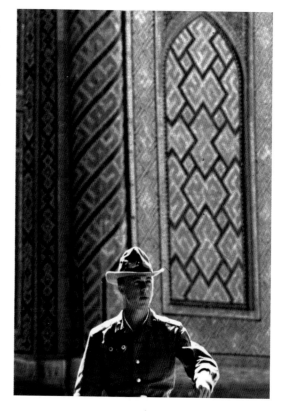

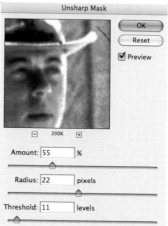

▲ Under-sharpening

In images containing large amounts of fine detail, such as this scene taken in Uzbekistan, applying a modest strength of USM filtering (55) and a large radius (22), with a threshold set at 11 does little for the image. There is a modest uplift in sharpness, but this is due more to an overall increase in contrast rather than any other effect.

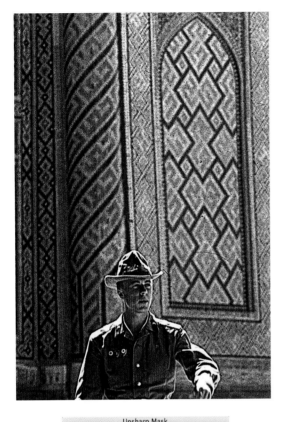

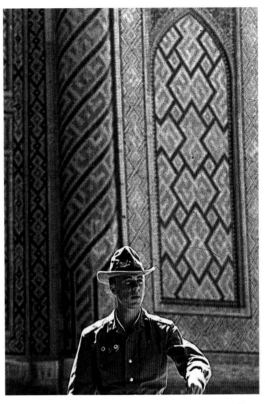

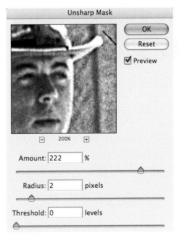

▲ Over-sharpening

The maximum strength setting used for this version results in over-sharpening—it is still usable and is arguably a good setting if you intend to print on poor-quality paper. The same setting applied to the Kashgar image (*pp. 198-9*) would simply bring out all the film grain—a technique for increasing noise in the image.

▲ Ideal setting

The best settings for images with fine detail is high strength with a small radius and a very low threshold: here, strength was 222, the radius was 2, and the threshold was kept at 0. Details are all well defined and if large-size prints are wanted, details are crisper than those obtained with sharpening using a larger radius setting.

SHARPENING CONTINUED

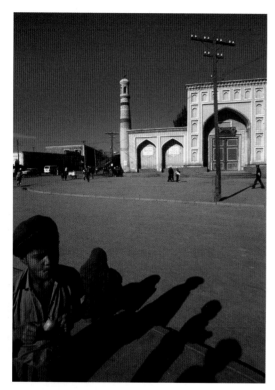

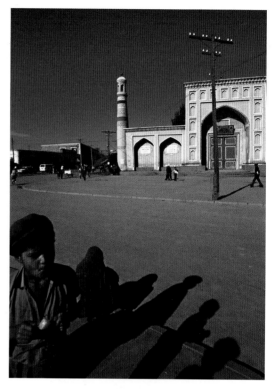

▲ Original image

This photograph of the main town square in Kashgar, Xinjiang, China, has large areas of smooth tone with little fine detail, and it would clearly benefit from the effects of image sharpening.

HINTS AND TIPS

Using an advanced Photoshop technique for image sharpening, first mask off areas (such as a face) to be protected from oversharpening and any associated increase in defects. Next, produce a duplicate layer of the background and set it to Soft Light mode. This increases contrast overall. Then apply the High-Pass filter (found under the Filter menu in Other > High Pass). Increasing the radius strengthens the effect (passes higher frequencies, or more detail). You can now enter Quick Mask mode or add a layer mask to control which areas of the image will be sharpened by the High-Pass filter. This method is also effective for sharpening an image overall and can be controlled by direct settings and by opacity. However, the preview window in the dialogue box does not give an accurate view because it samples only the top layer.

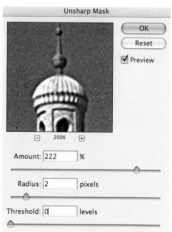

▲ Over-sharpening

If you increase the sharpening effect (222 in this version) and reduce the threshold (0), but reduce the radius to 2, virtually everything in the image increases in sharpness. The result is that film grain and fine detail are sharpened to an undesirable extent. Compare the result of these settings with that of an image that contains a mass of fine detail (*see p. 196*).

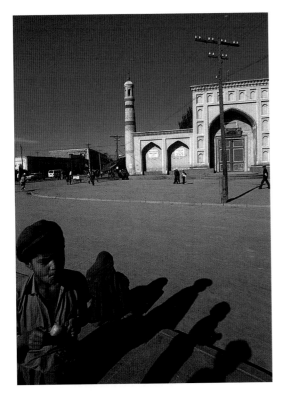

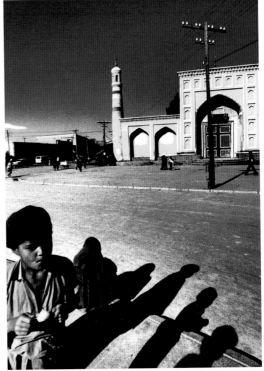

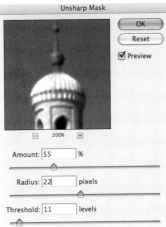

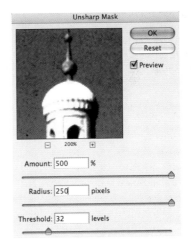

▲ Sharpening areas of tone

A moderate amount of sharpening (55) and a relatively wide radius for the filter to act on (22) improves sharpness where there is subject detail, without bringing out film grain or unwanted information, such as in the subject's skin-tones. A threshold setting of 11 prevents the filter from breaking up smooth tonal transitions, as the sharpening effect operates only on pixels differing in brightness by more than 11 units.

▲ Extreme settings

This version results from maximum amount and radius settings. The effect is extreme, but a threshold of 32 controls coloration. Even so, the image has highly saturated colors and brilliant contrast. In addition, film grain is emphasized. The random appearance of film grain gives more attractive results than the regular structure of a digital image, so if you want to use this effect introduce image noise first.

BLURRING

Blur can be introduced by lowering contrast to give boundaries a less-distinct outline. This is the opposite of sharpening (*see pp. 196–9*). Paradoxically, blurring can make images look sharper, for if you throw a background out of focus, then any detail in front looks sharper in comparison.

Blur options

Blur effects are seldom effective if applied to the whole image, since they often fail to respond to the picture's content and character. The Median and Dust & Scratches filters produce an effect like looking through clear, moving water. For some subjects this is appropriate, but for blur with some clarity, other methods are better. One approach depends on the data-loss caused by interpolation (*see pp. 206–7*) when reducing file sizes. First, increase the image size by, say, 300 percent, using Resampling, and then reduce it to its original size. Check its appearance and repeat if necessary. This does take time, but it can give well-detailed, softly blurred results. A quicker, though less-adaptive, method is to reduce the file size, and then increase it, repeating this step as necessary.

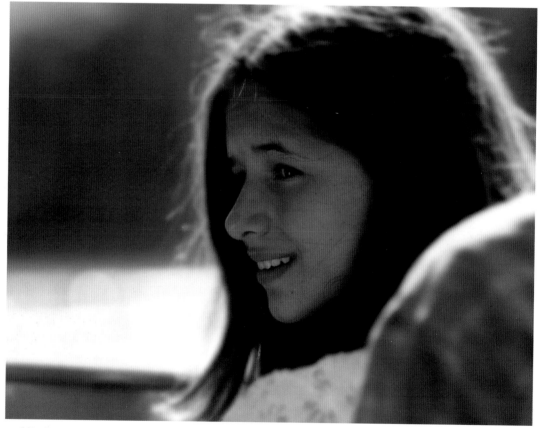

▲ Selective blur

Although you will not often want to blur an image in its entirety, selective blurring, and thus the softening of subject detail, can be extremely useful on occasion. To take one example, the blurred areas of an image could become the perfect background for typography—perhaps on a web page—as the wording would then be easier to read. Another example could be to introduce digital selective blur to simulate the appearance of using a special effects, soft-focus lens filter. This type of glass filter is designed to soften all but a central region of the image in order to help concentrate the viewer's attention on a particular feature. In the example shown here—an informal portrait of a traveler on a ferry on the River Danube, Hungary—the high-contrast sunlight and the sharpness of background detail was softened to emphasize the girl's features.

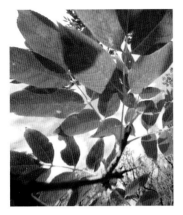
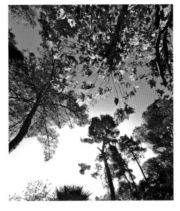
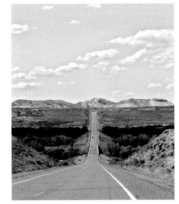

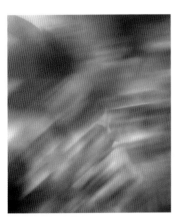
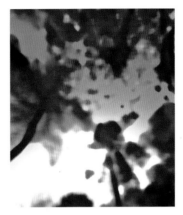
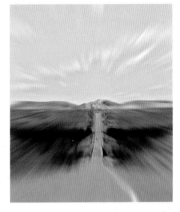

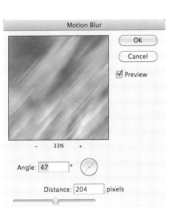
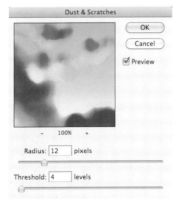
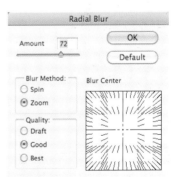

▲ Motion blur

This filter simulates the effect of rapid movement across the field of vision. Usual controls for this filter include altering the angle of the "smear" as well as its length: greater lengths suggest higher speed motion. For unusual results apply different angles to different parts of the image.

▲ Dust and scratches

While it is not strictly a blurring filter, at large radius settings the Dust & Scratches filter does an excellent job of blurring details while retaining outlines to give a watery effect. Setting the Threshold to higher values retains more details. Reduce saturation to create a watercolor look.

▲ Radial blur

Use this filter to apply the blur along lines radiating out from the center of the image. This can simulate the effect of speeding into the distance. For best results, apply in steps to selectively smaller areas. In Adobe Photoshop, the filter also offers an option for simulating a zoom blur (see p. 33).

BLURRING CONTINUED

Having spent a fortune on lenses that deliver super-sharp images, it seems madness to introduce blur into your images. But targeted blur is an essential part of the visual language: it can depict movement, it can be used to indicate centers of interest, and it can imitate effects created by articulated lens movements. The key to targeted blur is combining masks with blur filters.

Motion parallax

Blur is the result of an image moving a visible distance across the sensor. As nearby objects appear to move much more than distant objects, even if they are actually traveling at the same speed, they always appear more blurred. You see this when traveling on a train: the trees nearby are always blurred, but the mountains in the distance are

CREATING MOVEMENT BLUR

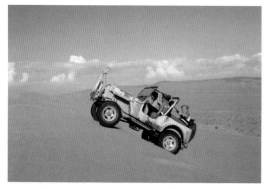

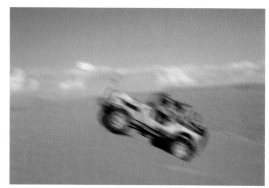

1 Original image
This travel shot is clearly taken in an exotic location, but lacks energy and a sense of movement. The four-wheel-drive vehicle looks as though it is stuck in the sand or about to roll backward. We need a sense of forward movement.

2 Motion blur
On a duplicate layer, we apply a Motion Blur filter: we line up the motion blur with the long axis of the vehicle, adjusting its strength to avoid losing too much detail.

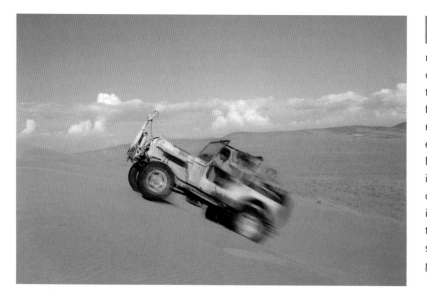

3 Mask
We now apply a mask over the majority of the image—the sky, the landscape, and the front of the vehicle. It now appears that the exposure time was too long to capture a sharp image. But a reality check will show that this is a manipulated image: the difference in sharpness in the vehicle gives the game away.

sharp. You can simulate this effect by applying blur to the objects close to the camera while keeping distant parts of the scene relatively sharp.

Lens movements

A blur effect that is completely different from motion is created by movement of the lens: this means that the lens is articulated so it can rotate at right-angles to its optical axis. A forward tilt can increase apparent depth of field, while a reverse tilt strongly reduces depth of field, making a scene resemble a small scale model. The strength of the effect depends on the angle of tilt and the working aperture set. You can simulate this effect by using graduated masks to control a blur applied to the whole image.

REVERSE TILT EFFECT

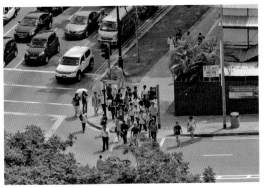

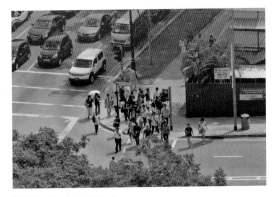

1 **High-angle original**
Tilt shift gives the impression of a model, so it works best on shots taken from a high angle, and is effective with objects such as people and cars. This street scene taken from a hotel window is perfect for this effect.

2 **Quick Mask**
In Quick Mask mode, select the gradient tool, draw a gradient from the center of the part you want to be in focus to the edges of the image. A few attempts may be needed to get the right area. The Quick Mask mode allows you to see clearly what will be blurred.

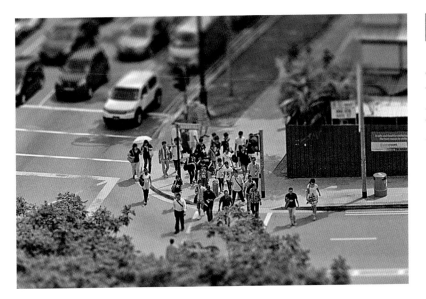

3 **Apply blur**
Back in standard mode, the lens blur filter can be applied; again this may take a few attempts to get it right. You are able to preview the amount of blur before you actually apply it. Although the effect will look finished now, using the unsharp mask filter makes the people more clearly defined and adds to the toy model effect.

QUICK FIX IMAGE DISTRACTIONS

Unless there is a fundamental problem with your image, most minor distractions can be removed, or at least have their pictorial impact reduced, in image-manipulation software.

Problem: While concentrating on your subject, it is easy not to notice distracting objects or colors in the picture area. This could be anything from a passer-by or street litter, to patches of strong color.

Analysis: The small viewfinders or screens of many cameras make it difficult to see much subject detail. Furthermore, although something is distant and looks out of focus, it may still be within the depth of field of your set aperture (*see pp. 24–7*). At other times, you simply cannot avoid including, say, telephone wires in the background of a scene.

Solution: You may not need to remove a distraction completely; simply reducing the difference between it and adjacent areas may be enough. The usual way to achieve this is with cloning—duplicating part of an image and placing it into another part (*see pp. 288–91*). For example, blue sky can be easily cloned onto wires crossing it, as long as you are careful to use areas that match in brightness and hue. Clone from as close to the distraction as possible (*see also pp. 288–9*).

You could also try desaturating the color: select the area of strong color, and lower it using Color Saturation to reduce its impact. You can also paint over the color by using the Saturation or Sponge tool set to desaturate.

Another method is to blur the background to render details less visible. This helps push the details in the main subject into visual prominence. Select the background directly, or if the main subject is easier to select, make your selection and invert it. Then apply a Blur filter (*see pp. 200–1*) that is appropriate to the detail you wish to blur; try different types of blur to evaluate their effect. Select a narrow feather edge to retain sharpness in the subject's outline. Use caution with strong Blur effects, because the selected region could be left with a distinct margin.

HOW TO AVOID THE PROBLEM

Check the viewfinder image carefully before shooting. This is easier with SLR cameras and those with large viewfinders. Long focal length lenses (or zoom settings) reduce depth of field and tend to blur backgrounds. And, if appropriate to the subject, use a lower viewpoint and look upward to increase the amount of non-distracting sky.

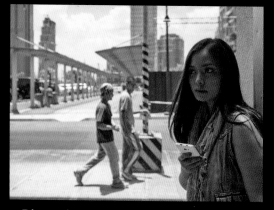

▲ Distracting movement
During a shoot in Manila, in the Philippines, the model's best expression coincided with passers-by in the background. Fortunately, there were many alternatives with a clean background that could be cloned.

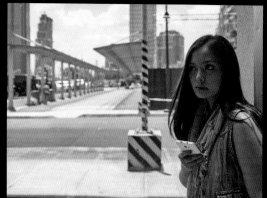

▲ Cloning
The clean background of one image was first made the source for the clone. The Clone tool was then very carefully aligned with the destination image and the cloned pixels applied, making the passers-by disappear.

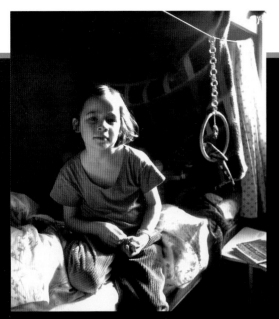

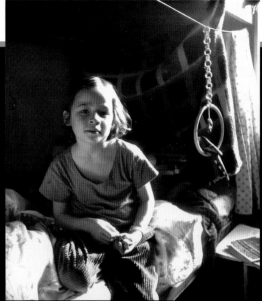

▲ Background distractions

In the chaos of a young child's room, it is neither possible nor desirable to remove all the distractions, but toning them down selectively can help center the viewer's attention on the main subject.

▲ Desaturated elements

A large, soft-edged Brush tool was chosen, and pressure was set to desaturation at 100 percent and applied to the background. With a lighter setting of 50 percent, the desaturation was also brushed over the clothes.

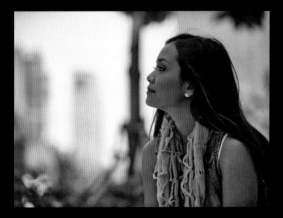

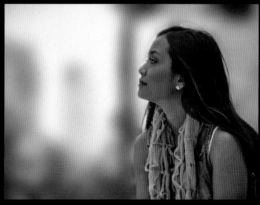

▲ Selective blur

Despite using a large aperture, the high-contrast blur of a tree is still obtrusive. By selecting the background and applying a large blur setting (*see right*), the impact of the tree can be reduced. Care needs to be taken to ensure the model's face is not blurred and that the fringe around the model is not left too sharp. You may need to experiment with different feathering settings (*see pp. 270–2*) until you get the best results.

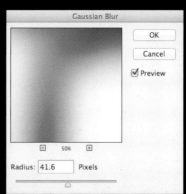

IMAGE SIZE AND DISTORTION

One of the most common manipulations is to change the image size. It is important to distinguish the three kinds of change possible. The first two methods change size uniformly across the entire image, so they do not change picture shape. In the first, you can change the output size of the image but keep its file size the same—that is, resizing without changing the number of pixels or resampling the pixels. You might do this to match image size to paper or to a picture box on a layout.

Alternatively, you may need to resize to change the number of pixels in the image, thereby altering the file size; this is to resize with resampling, because new pixel data are calculated from existing pixels. You might do this to reduce file sizes for sending in an email, for example. Or you may wish to increase the file size to make large prints. In general, you can increase the output size of your image by around 200 percent, but special techniques such as spline-based or fractal interpolation can give enlargements of up to 1,000 percent of acceptable quality. Note that as print size increases, the assumption is that the intended viewing distance also increases. Files of higher resolution will support greater proportional enlargement than those of lower resolution.

The third way

Finally, the size changes you make may be non-uniform—that is, when one axis is changed more than another, thereby altering the shape of the image. You may distort an image to make it fit a specific area or to correct distortions caused by camera position or lens projection. A common photographic problem is keystoning distortion that occurs when the camera is not held square to a building or other regular subject.

Modern software offers a range of corrections such as keystone, or perspective distortion. Before applying these corrections, make your tonal and color adjustments, but do not sharpen. Be prepared for sides of the image to be cut in by the corrections. Use the highest-quality images or work in RAW format, because substantial distortions can cause banding in areas with delicate tones.

WHAT IS INTERPOLATION?

Interpolation is a mathematical discipline vital to processes ranging from satellite surveys to machine vision—the recognition of number plates on speeding cars, for example. In digital photography, a number of methods of interpolation are used to alter image size. Three popular methods are explained here.

- **"Nearest neighbor"** copies adjacent values into new pixels. This gives poor results with color images but is best for bit-map line graphics (those with only black or white pixels).

- **"Bilinear interpolation"** looks at the four pixels to the top, bottom, and sides of the central pixel and calculates new values by averaging the four. This method gives fairly smooth results.

- **"Bicubic interpolation"** looks at all eight contiguous pixels and computes a weighted average to give the best results.

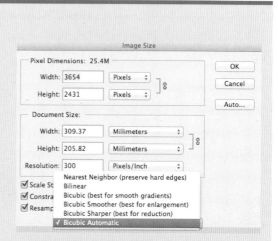

▲ **Image Size screen shot**
Modern image-manipulation software packages such as DxO and Photoshop offer interpolation options for each resizing operation. Choose carefully to suit the image you are working on, or allow the software to make the choice.

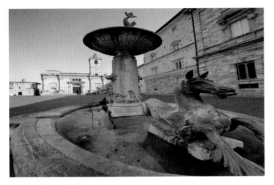

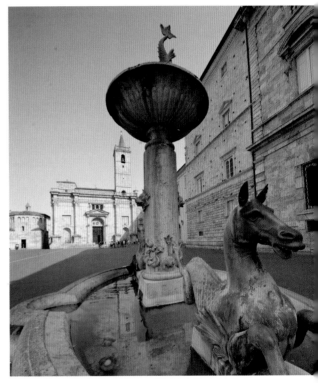

▲ Unbundling

Distortion is a natural part of the photographic process: whenever any surface is not captured square-on and the resulting image is not viewed at the correct magnification, the shape of the subject is not accurate and appears distorted. By changing the proportions of an image, you can either make some corrections by changing magnification on one axis, or you can use it to cause deliberate exaggerations of shape. Each of the images shown here is representative, if not an accurate depiction, of the principal piazza in Ascoli Piceno, Italy.

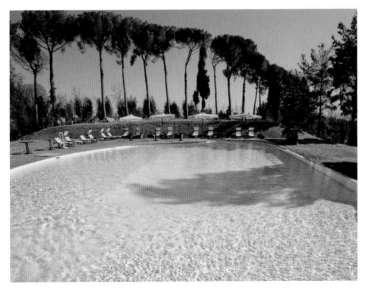

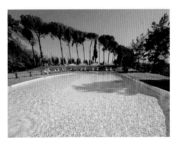

▲ Keystone correction

The original image (*above right*) was made with the camera pointing down to the pool to increase the area of water in the image. But this had the effect of causing the distant pines to tilt away from each other. Keystone correction reduces the upper part of the image to straighten the trees, while a stretch in the vertical axis also lengthens them to improve their scale in the image.

QUICK FIX CONVERGING PARALLELS

While the brain largely compensates for visual distortions—so, in effect, you see what you expect to see—the camera faithfully records them all.

Problem: Images showing subjects with prominent straight lines, such as the sides of a building, appear uncomfortable when printed or viewed on screen because the lines appear to converge. Regular shapes may also appear sheared or squashed (*see also p. 52*).

Analysis: The change in size of different parts of the image is due to changes of magnification—different parts of the recorded scene are being reproduced at different scales. This occurs because of changes in distance between the camera and various parts of the subject. For example, when you look through the viewfinder at a building from street level, its top is further away than its base—a fact that is emphasized by pointing the camera upward to include the whole structure. As a result, the more distant parts appear to be smaller than the closer parts.

Solution: Select the whole image and, using the Distortion or Transformation tool, pull the image into shape. Modern software offers Perspective Correction and other tools: try them all to establish which works best in each case.

HOW TO AVOID THE PROBLEM

- Choose your shooting position with care and try to compose the image in order to keep any lines that are centrally positioned as vertical as possible. In addition, look to maintain symmetry either side of the middle of the picture.
- Rather than pointing the camera upward, to include the upper parts of a building or some other tall structure, look for an elevated shooting position. This way, you may be able to keep the camera parallel with the subject and so minimize differences in scale between various parts of the subject as they are recorded by the camera.

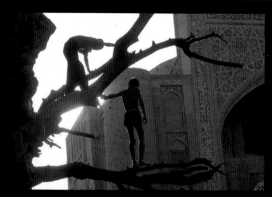

1 Verticals converge
Shooting from ground level with the camera angled upward caused the scene to appear to tilt backward.

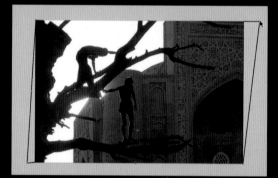

2 Image manipulation
Stretching the lower left-hand corner of the image using the Distortion tool is the solution to this problem.

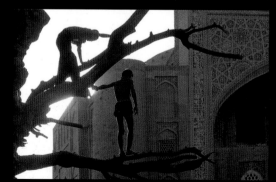

3 Verticals corrected
The corrected image looks better and corresponds more closely to the way the scene looked in reality.

QUICK FIX IMAGE FRAMING

Don't allow your images to become unnecessarily constrained by the sides of the camera viewfinder or the regular borders of your printing paper. There are creative options available to you.

Problem: The precise and clear-cut rectangular outlines around images can not only become boring, sometimes they are simply not appropriate—for example, on a web page where the rest of the design is informal. What is needed is some sort of controlled way of introducing some variety to the way you frame your images.

Analysis: In the majority of situations, producing images with clean borders is the most appropriate method of presentation. But with the less-formal space of a web page, a looser, vignetted frame might be a better option. On occasion, a picture frame can also be used to crop an image without actually losing any crucial subject matter.

Solution: Take pictures of textures and shapes that you would like to use as frames, remove the centers, and drop them onto the margins of your images. Many software applications offer simple frame types, which you can easily apply to any image and at any size. Specialized plug-ins simplify the process of applying frames and provide you with numerous, customizable framing options.

HOW TO AVOID THE PROBLEM

The need to create picture frames usually arises from the desire to improve an image that has not been ideally composed. Nobody thinks about picture frames when looking at a truly arresting photograph. Inspect your pictures carefully, checking the image right to the edges. Tilting the camera when shooting creates a different style of framing, or simply crop off image elements you don't need.

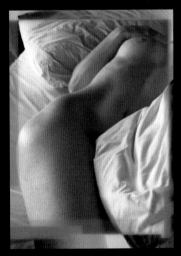

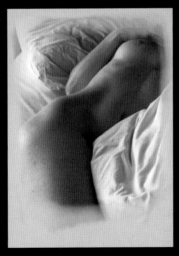

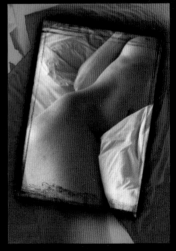

▲ Framing option 1
The first option applies a geometric frame in which it partially reverses the underlying tones of the image. It is effective in hiding unwanted details in the top left of the image, but its outline is perhaps too hard in contrast with the soft lines of the subject's body.

▲ Framing option 2
The simplest frame is often the best—here it is like looking through a cleared area of fogged glass. The color of the frame should be chosen to tone in with the image. However, you should also consider the background color: on this black page, the contrast is too high whereas against a white page or an on-screen background, the nude figure would appear to float.

▲ Framing option 3
Here a painterly effect is combined with a frame that reverses both hue and tone (a Difference mode). By carefully adjusting the opacity of the frame, the colors were toned down to match that of the main image. Finally, the frame was rotated so that the main axis nude figure runs across the diagonal.

WHITE BALANCE

The basis of accurate color reproduction is neutrality in the whites, grays, and blacks in the image. When you ensure these tones are not tinted with colors, you establish the accuracy of the hues you record. The white balance control on digital cameras helps neutralize tints in whites and grays. When you open the image, you may take the process further and adjust other dimensions of color, such as the lightness and saturation.

What balance?

An image that is color balanced is one in which the illuminating light offers all hues in equal proportion—in other words, the illumination is white and not tinted with color. Color balance is not to be confused with color harmony (*see p. 58*). Thus, a scene can be full of blues or greens yet still be color balanced, while another scene that features a well-judged combination of secondary colors may appear harmonious, but may not be color balanced at all.

The aim of color balancing is to produce an image that appears as if it were illuminated by white light; this is achieved by adjusting the white point. However, there are different standards for white light, and so there are different white points. For example, it would not look natural to correct an indoor scene lit by domestic lamps in order to make it look like daylight, so a warm-toned white point is called for instead.

Color Balance control

This control makes global changes to the standard primary or secondary hues in an image. In some software, you can restrict the changes to shadows, highlights, or mid-tones. This is useful for making quick changes to an image that has, for example, been affected by an overall color cast.

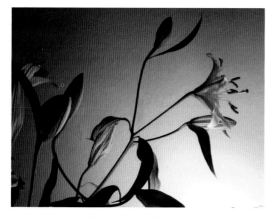

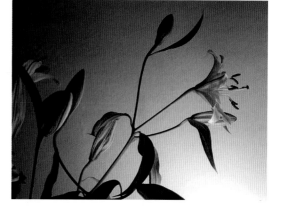

▲ **Warm white point**
The original picture of a simple still life (*above left*) has reproduced with the strong orange cast that is characteristic of images lit by domestic incandescent lamps. The corrected image (*above right*), was produced using Color Balance. It is still warm in tone because a fully corrected image would look cold and unnatural.

DROPPER TOOLS

A quick method of working when you wish to color-correct an image is to decide which part of the picture you want to be neutral—that part you want to be seen as without any tint. Then find the mid-tone dropper, usually offered in the Color, Levels, or Curves controls in image-manipulation software. Select the dropper, then click on a point in your image that you know should be neutral. This process is made easier if you used a gray card in one of your images—all images shot under the same lighting as the gray card will require the same correction. Clicking on the point samples the color data and adjusts the whole image so that the sampled point is neutral: the dropper maps the color data of all the image pixels around the sampled point.

When working with raw files, the choice of color temperature (blue to red) and of tint (green to magenta) is yours. Usually, you choose color temperature and tint to ensure neutral (achromatic or colorless) colors are truly neutral.

Balancing channels

While the Curves control is most often used to adjust image tonality, by altering the Curves or Levels of the individual color channels, you apply a color balance to the high tones that is different from that of the shadows. This is helpful, for example,

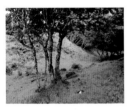

◀ Original image
This original image has not been corrected in any way, and it accurately reproduces the flat illumination of a solidly cloudy sky.

when shadows on a cloudless day are bluish but bright areas are yellowish from the sun. It is easiest to work by eye, adjusting until you see the result you wish for, but for best control you can analyze the color in neutrals and manually put in corrections to the curve. Working in CMYK, using Curves gives a great deal of control and the best results for print. The Color Balance control is essentially a simplified version of using the component RGB channels in Curves.

Channel mixing is effective where a small imbalance in the strengths of the component channels is the cause of color imbalance, due to, for example, using a colored filter or shooting through tinted glass.

The Hue/Saturation control can also be used, as it shifts the entire range of colors en masse. This can be useful when the color imbalance is due to strong coloring of the illuminating light.

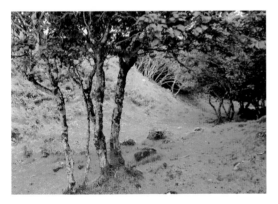

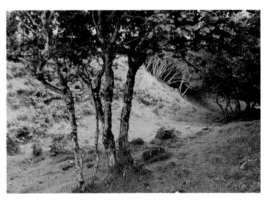

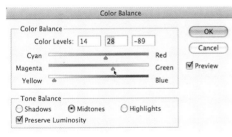

▲ Color Balance control
Strong changes brought about via the Color Balance control, mainly by increasing yellow in the mid-tones—which is the lowest slider in the dialog box here—make the scene look as if it has been lit by an early evening sun.

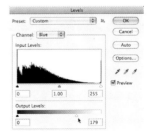

▲ Levels control
A golden tone has been introduced to the image here by forcefully lowering the blue channel in the Levels control—the middle slider beneath the histogram—thus allowing red and green to figure more strongly. Red and green additively produce yellow, and this color now dominates the highlights of the image.

COLOR ADJUSTMENTS

One of the most liberating effects of digital photography is its total control over color: you can control effects from the most subtle tints to the most outrageous color combinations.

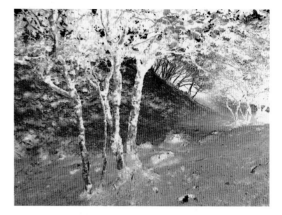

Curves

Manipulating Curves, either all at once or as separate channels, is a potent way to make radical changes in color and tone. For best results, work in 16-bit color, as steep curve shapes demand the highest quality and quantity of image data.

Hue/Saturation

This control globally adjusts hues, as well as color saturation, and brightness. You may also select narrow ranges of colors to change, thus altering the overall color balance. Beware of oversaturating colors, as they may not print out (*see pp. 61 and 304*).

Replace Color

This replaces one hue, within a "fuzziness" setting or wave-band, with another. Select the colors you wish to change by sampling the image with the Dropper tool, and then transform that part via the Hue/Saturation dialogue box (*see opposite*). By setting a small fuzziness factor, you select only those pixels very similar in color to the original; a large fuzziness setting selects relatively dissimilar pixels. It is best to accumulate small changes by repeatedly applying this control. Replace Color is good for strengthening colors that printers have trouble with (yellows and purples), or toning down colors they overdo (reds, for example).

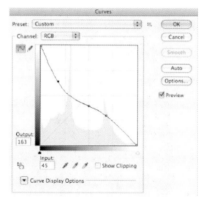

▲ **Curves control**

A simple inversion of color and tone leaves dark shadows looking empty and blank. Manipulating tonal reproduction via the Curves dialog box, however, gives you more control, allowing you to put color into these otherwise empty deep shadows (the bright areas after inversion). In the dialog box here you can see how the curve runs top left to bottom right—the reverse of usual—and the other adjustments that were made to improve density in the image's mid-tones.

COLOR TEMPERATURE

The color temperature of light has, in fact, nothing to do with temperature as we traditionally think of it; rather, color temperature is measured by correlating it to the color changes undergone by an object as it is heated. Experience tells us that cooler objects, such as candles or domestic lights, produce a reddish light, whereas hotter objects, such as tungsten lamps, produce more of a blue/white light.

The color temperature of light is measured in degrees Kelvin, and a white that is relatively yellow in coloration might be around 6,000 K, while a white that is more blue in content might be, say, 9,500 K.

While color slide film must be balanced to a specific white point, digital cameras can vary their white point dynamically, according to changing needs of the situation.

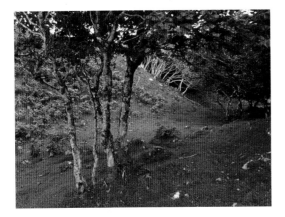

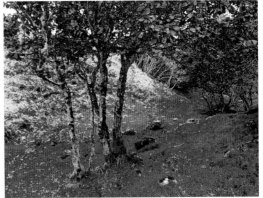

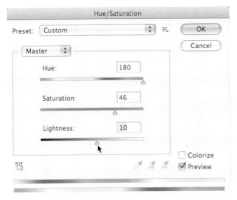

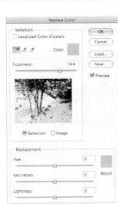

▲ Hue/Saturation control

In this dialog box you can see that image hue has been changed to an extreme value, and this change has been supported by improvements in saturation and lightness in order to produce good tonal balance. Smaller changes in image hue may be effective for adjusting color balance. Bear in mind that colors such as purples look brighter and deeper on a monitor than in print because of limitations in the printer's color gamut (*pp. 61 and 302–5*).

▲ Replace Color control

Four passes of the Replace Color control were made to create an image that is now very different from that originally captured (*p. 211*). The dialog box here shows the location of the colors selected in the small preview window, and the controls are the same as those found in the Hue and Saturation dialog box (*above left*), which allow you to bring about powerful changes of color. However, for Hue and Saturation to have an effect, the selected values must indeed have color. If they are gray, then only the lightness control makes any difference.

WORKING IN RGB

The most intuitive color mode to work in is RGB. It is easy to understand that any color is a mixture of different amounts of red, green, or blue, and that areas of an image where full amounts of all three colors are present give you white. The other modes, such as LAB and CMYK, have their uses, but it is best to avoid using them unless you have a specific effect in mind you want to achieve. When you are producing image files to be printed out onto paper, you may think you should supply your images as CMYK, since this is how they will be printed. However, unless you have the specific data or separation tables supplied by the processors, it is preferable to allow the printers to make the conversions themselves. In addition, CMYK files are larger than their RGB equivalents and so are far less convenient to handle.

SATURATION AND VIBRANCE

Technically, saturation is the colorfulness of something judged in relation to brightness. Light, low-saturated colors become darker as they increase in saturation, while well-saturated colors look brighter and livelier when their saturation is raised. This change in quality helps explain why we love to make highly saturated images: they look gorgeous on the screen. In image manipulation, Vibrance, rather than meaning "full of energy," is a saturation control that adapts to certain colors.

Saturation

One of the most common enhancements made to images is an increase in saturation: colors look richer, images look brilliant and, indeed, greatly enhanced. Camera manufacturers deliberately process images conservatively because oversaturation is hard to recover: variations of hue take on the same values, so any differences in hue are lost forever. However, global increases in saturation rarely lead to better images. The most

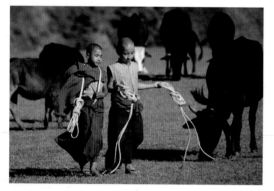

1 **Original**
Young monks in Bhutan chat as they run an errand on a sunny day—a delightfully photogenic scene. But overexposure in the capture leads to poor saturation after adjusting Levels. The yellows and reds are acceptable, but the greens are too dull.

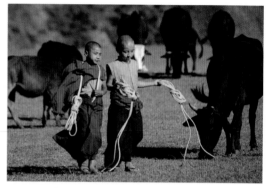

2 **High saturation**
Increasing saturation globally renders the grass rich and lively, and the robes and ropes stand out in brilliance. But the flesh tones look too tanned, and notice how the cattle have become more prominent in the image.

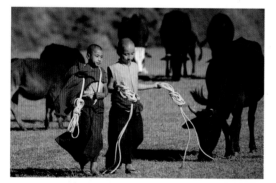

3 **High vibrance**
Returning to the Levels-adjusted original, the vibrance setting is increased: the result is a marked improvement over both the original and the high-saturation version, with rich colors in the robes and grass and natural skin tones.

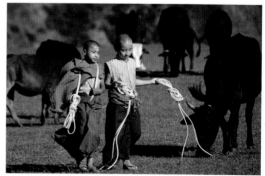

4 **Minimum vibrance**
If we set minimum vibrance we see that colors around flesh tones are reduced to almost grayscale: different applications vary in how strongly they reduce saturation of non-flesh tone colors and the effect also varies with white balance.

effective way is to be selective: identify the colors that appear weakest. If you would like a bluer sky, for example, instead of increasing saturation over the whole image, select Blues in your software's saturation control and increase saturation only for blues. The result is powerful, yet subtle.

Vibrance

The Vibrance control adjusts saturation to minimize clipping, that is, loss of definition at high values. Less-saturated colors increase their saturation more than the colors that are already saturated. Most importantly, Vibrance produces a flatter response with skin tones, which prevents them from becoming oversaturated. Vibrance is very useful for reducing the saturation of other colors while leaving flesh tones relatively unaltered. The cool pallor that results can be effective in a wide range of people-based photography—from fashion to photojournalism.

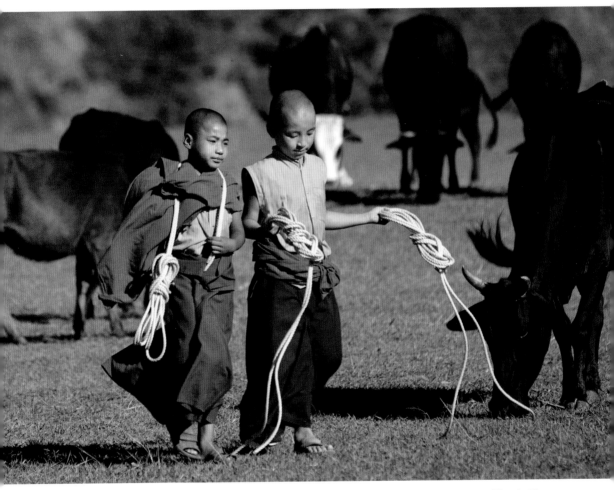

5 Low saturation, high vibrance

Combining the two controls can produce highly effective results, that balance delicate coloration with a strong sense of realism. If we set a low saturation, all colors are globally made grayer. Adding a high vibrance setting restores red-yellow colors closer to their natural levels. The difference in saturation helps the flesh tones to stand out against the naturally tinted background. Notice too how the cattle now "recede" into the background.

MANIPULATION DEFECTS

Post-processing techniques are brilliantly powerful. But it is good practice to avoid creating unintended defects while making corrections in some other part or aspect of the image.

Working methods

Like many other craft skills, post-processing proceeds most smoothly when you work methodically and steadily. Plan what you want to do with an image before you start working on it: you will make white balance, exposure, and tonal adjustments before tackling deeper changes to the image, such as cloning or working with layers. If you are using direct-working software such as Photoshop, make adjustments on Adjustment Layers where possible, to help preserve quality.

The majority of images will need only subtle or soft changes to make a vast improvement to their appearance: these types of change are unlikely to cause unwanted side effects. It is the application of strong changes that gives rise to the most problems. One useful trick that may help to reduce side effects is to make a series of smaller changes to achieve the same result.

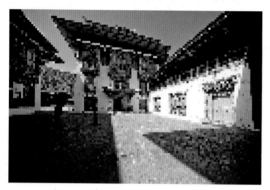

▲ Pixellation

The disruption of image detail caused by using too few pixels to create the image is relatively rare, now that cameras use high-resolution sensors. However, it is possible to use an icon or low-resolution version of the image by mistake. Reopen with a larger file.

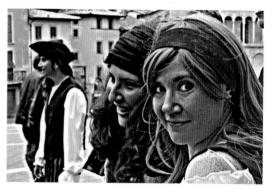

▲ Over-sharpening

Sharpening filters such as USM (UnSharp Mask) improve the appearance of sharpness but cannot make up for poor focusing or blur from movement. High levels of sharpening may improve blurred images but at the cost of creating haloes and unnatural tones.

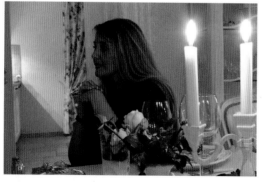

▲ Poor white balance

Scenes lit by colored lights such as candles or nightclub spots gain a strong color cast. Even if the overall color cast can be removed to create neutral whites, other colors—such as flesh tones—may be inaccurate. Record in RAW (*see pp. 234-7*) for the best chance of full correction.

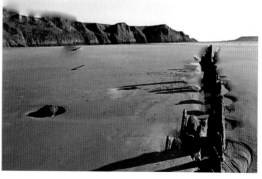

▲ Cloning or healing defects

While cloning and healing tools for removing defects are very powerful, they can introduce defects of their own, such as the blurring of neighboring boundaries and multiplying detail. Work at high magnification—at least 100 per cent—and use brushes just larger than the defects.

Principle of loss

A basic principle of digital photography is that loss of data from an image can never be recovered. Many manipulations, from adjusting levels and increasing sharpness or blur, to cloning—all destroy data. In recognition of this, if you are using applications such as Photoshop, Photo Painter, or Paint Shop Pro, always work with a copy of the image, never the sole image file. If you wish to create a completely new version of an image, open up a new copy of the original; do not reuse one that has already been heavily manipulated.

DEEP POCKETS

A class of image defects, including highlight clipping, shadow clipping, and banding, can be avoided by working with the data reserve of RAW format. The data in RAW may be extended by outputting the image in high bits per channel. Instead of the usual 8 bits per channel, RAW converters allow images to be coded with 10 bits, 12 bits, even 32 bits per channel. This results in large files that are capable of being very extensively processed.

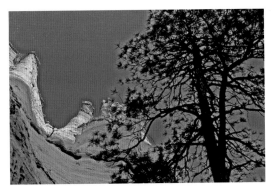

▲ Boundaries with haloes

Sharpening filters such as USM (UnSharp Mask) and adjustments such as Shadows/Highlights can cause contrasting bands, or haloes, to appear around edges when used with too high a setting (USM), or too small a radius combined with high settings (Shadow/Highlights).

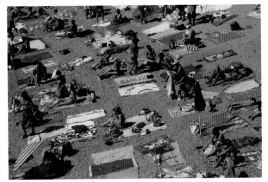

▲ Out-of-gamut colors

Brilliant colors can be made even more brilliant on the monitor screen. The result is eye-catching, but some colors may be impossible to print out, and some may lead to solid blocks of color that look unnatural. Use the saturation control conservatively (*see pp. 214–5*).

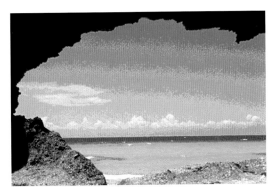

▲ Banding

Caused by having insufficient data to define smooth transitions, banding is seen as stepped changes as the result of applying strong tonal change via, for example, Curves, Levels, or Shadow/Highlights controls. It is less of a problem than it used to be, thanks to improved sensor processing.

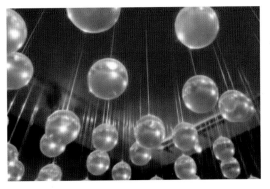

▲ Noiseless

In the eagerness to eliminate all signs of noise from the image, you can cause the image to look too smooth, with silky textures that blur details. Where detail is near the size of the noise, for example, the fine wires in this image, noise reduction also smears the details.

CURVES

The Curves control found in image-manipulation software may remind older photographers of the characteristic curves published for films. This is a graph that shows the density of sensitized material that will result from being exposed to specific intensities of light. In fact, there are similarities, but equally important are the differences. Both are effectively transfer functions: they describe how one variable (the input either of color value or of the amount of light) produces another variable (the output or brightness of the image).

The principal difference is that when it comes to image-manipulation software the curve is always a 45° line at the beginning. This shows that the output is exactly the same as the input. However, unlike the film curve, you can manipulate this directly by clicking on and dragging the curve or by redrawing the curve yourself. In this way, you force light tones to become dark, mid-tones to become light, and with all the other variations in between. In addition, you may change the curve of each color channel separately.

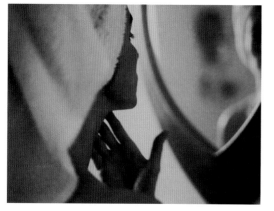

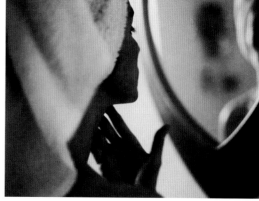

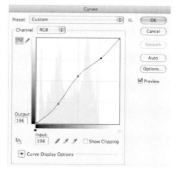

▲ Original image and curve

Since the original negative was slightly underexposed, the image from the scan is tonally rather lifeless. You cannot tell anything about exposure by looking at the curve in the screen shot (*above*) because it describes how one tone is output as another. As nothing has been changed, when it first appears the line is a straight 45°, mapping black to black, mid-tone to mid-tone, and white to white. It is not like a film characteristic curve, which actually describes how film is responding to light and its processing.

▲ Boosting the mid-tones

The bow-shaped curve displayed here subtly boosts the mid-tone range of the image, as you can see in the resulting image (*top*). But the price paid is evident in the quarter-tones, where details in the shadows and the details in the highlights are both slightly darkened. The result is an image with, overall, more tonal liveliness—note, too, that the outline of the subject's face has been clarified. With some image-manipulation software, you have the option of nudging the position of the curve by clicking on the section you want to move and then pressing the arrow keys up or down to alter its shape.

What the Curves control does

The Curves control is a very powerful tool indeed and can produce visual results that are impossible to achieve in any other way. By employing less extreme curves you can improve tones in, for example, the shadow areas of an image while leaving the mid-tones and highlights as they were originally recorded.

And by altering curves separately by color channel, you have unprecedented control over an image's color balance. More importantly, the color changes brought about via the Curves control can be so smooth that the new colors blend seamlessly with those of the original.

Explore the image by running your cursor over the image: the majority of manipulation software gives a "running commentary" of color values and will also show the position of the point under the cursor as a point on the curve. Click on the curve when you hit a tone you wish to alter, then use the arrow up/down keys to adjust the position of this curve. Make small changes progressively: this helps

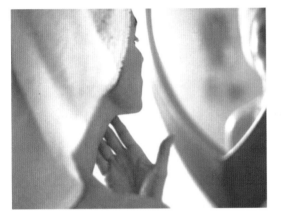

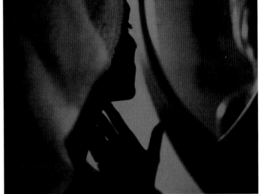

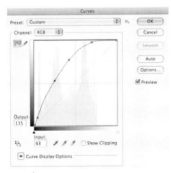

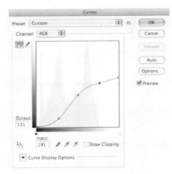

▲ Emphasizing the highlights

The scan's flat, dynamic range suggests that it could make an effective high-key image by changing the curve to remove the black tones (the left-hand end of the curve in the screen shot is not on black but is raised to dark gray) and mapping many highlight tones to white (the top of the curve is level with the maximum for nearly a third of the tonal range). The result is that the input mid-tone is set to give highlights with detail. Very small changes to the curve can have a large effect on the image, so if you want to adjust overall brightness, it is easier to commit to the curve and then use Levels to adjust brightness (*see pp. 188–9*).

▲ Emphasizing the shadows

The versatility of the original image is evident here, as now it can be seen working as an effective low-key picture. The mood of the picture is heavier and a little brooding, and it has lost its fashion-conscious atmosphere in favor of more filmic overtones. The curve shown in the screen shot has been adjusted not simply to darken the image overall (the right-hand end has been lowered to the mid-tone so that the brightest part of the picture is no brighter than normal mid-tone). In addition, the slight increase in the slope of the curve improves contrast at the lower mid-tone level to preserve some shadow detail. This is crucial, as too many blank areas would look unattractive.

CURVES CONTINUED

ensure you do not make dramatic changes which look impressive but usually lead to loss of quality.

Extreme curves

Curves are also a powerful and simple way to obtain extreme tonal effects, such as reversal of tones to imitate Sabattier effect (see p. 242). In general, the subjects that react best to the application of extreme Curve settings are those with simple outlines and large, obvious features. You can try endless experiments with Curves, particularly if you start using different curve shapes in each channel. The following examples show the scope of applying simpler modifications to the master curve, thereby

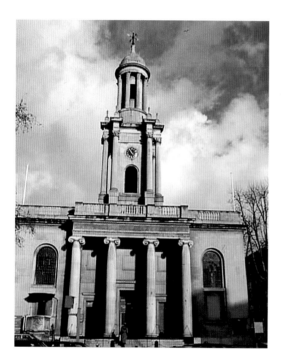

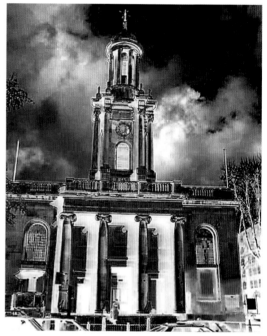

▲ Original image

The image you select for manipulating Curves does not have to be of the highest quality, but it should offer a simple shape or outline, such as this church. In addition, the range of colors can be limited—as you can see below, dramatic colors will be created when you apply Curves with unusual or extreme shapes.

▲ Reversing dark tones

A U-shaped curve reverses all tones darker than mid-tone and forces rapid changes to occur—an increase in image contrast, for example. The deep shadows in the church become light areas, giving a negative type of effect, but the clouds have darkened and greatly increased in color content. The effect of using this shape curve is similar to the darkroom Sabattier effect, when exposed film or paper is briefly reexposed to white light during development.

changing all channels at the same time. Note how seemingly even areas of tone can break up into uneven patches when an extremely steep curve is applied: this is due to a lack of data, which leads to aliasing or posterization.

The turning point of a curve also makes a great of demand on image data. If you wish to maintain smooth tonal transitions, you need access to as much image data as possible. Where extreme adjustments are anticipated, record your images in RAW format, then convert to RGB applying 16 bits per channel, or even more. With modern high resolution cameras and image processing, high-bit images are very resistant to break-up of the image.

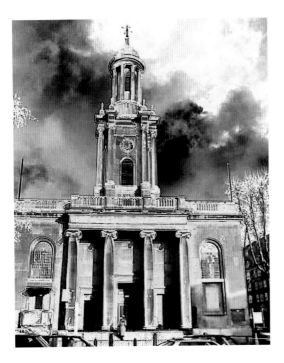

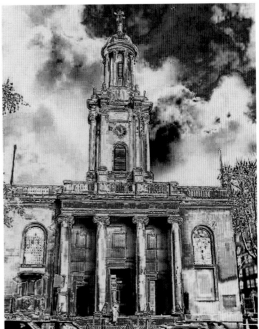

▲ Reversing light tones

An arc-shaped curve reverses the original's lighter tones, giving the effect shown here. Although it looks unusual, it is not as strange as reversing dark tones (*left*). Note that the curve's peak does not reach the top of the range—the height of the arc was reduced to avoid creating overbright white areas. The color of the building changes as the red-green color in the normal image was removed by the reversal, allowing the blue range to make its mark.

▲ Tone/color reversal

Applying an M-shaped curve plays havoc with our normal understanding of what a color image should look like. Not only are the tones reversed as a result, but areas with dominant color whose tones have been reversed will also take on a color that is complementary to their own. And since parts of the tonal range are reversed and others are not, the result is a variegated spread of colors.

BIT-DEPTH AND COLOR

The bit-depth of an image file tells you its tonal resolution—that is, how finely it can distinguish or reproduce tones or shades. A bit-depth of 1 identifies just two tones—black or white; a bit depth of 2 can record four tones; and so on. The number of tones that can be recorded is 2 to the power of the bit-depth, so a typical bit-depth of 8 records 256 tones. When these are applied across the color channels, bit-depth measures the resolution of colors. Thus, 8 bits over three color channels—8 bits x 3 channels—gives 24 bits, the usual bit-depth of digital cameras. This means, in theory, that each color channel is divided into 256 equally spaced steps, which is the minimum requirement for good-quality reproduction.

Number of hues

The total number of hues available to a 24-bit RGB color space, if all combinations could be realized, is in the region of 16.8 million. In practice this is never fully realized, nor is it necessary. A typical high-quality monitor displays around 6 million hues, while a color print can manage fewer than 2 million, and the best digital prints reach a paltry 20,000 different hues at the most. However, the extra capacity is needed at the extreme ends of the tonal and color scale, where small changes require much coding to define, and data is also needed to ensure that subtle tonal transitions such as skin tones and gradations across a sky are smooth and not rendered aliased (also described as stepped, or posterized).

Higher resolution

Increasingly, 24-bit is not measuring up to our expectations: tones are not smooth enough and there is insufficient data for dramatic changes in tone or color. This is why, when applying curves with very steep slopes, the image breaks up. Better-quality cameras can record images to a depth of 36 bits or more, but images may be down-sampled to 24-bit for processing. Even so, such images are better than if the images had been recorded in 24-bit. When working in raw format, you may be working in 16-bit space: if you wish to maintain the quality inherent, though not guaranteed, of 16-bit, process and save the file as 16-bit (48 bits RGB).

File size

Once the image is ready for use, you may find that surprisingly few colors are needed to reproduce it. A picture of a lion among sun-dried grass stems on a dusty plain, for example, uses only a few yellows and desaturated reds. Therefore, you may be able to use a small palette of colors and greatly reduce file size. This is particularly useful to remember when optimizing files for the web.

Some software allows images to be stored as "index color." This enables image colors to be mapped onto a limited palette of colors, the advantage being that the change from full 24-bit RGB to an index can reduce the file size by two-thirds or more. Reducing the color palette or bit-depth should be the last change to the image as the information you lose is irrecoverable.

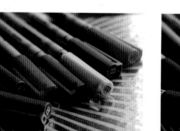 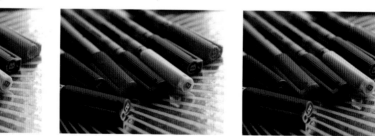

▲ Color bit-depth and image quality
When seen in full color (*left*), this image is vibrant and rich, but the next image (*middle*), containing a mere 100 colors, is not significantly poorer in quality. Yet this index color image is only a third of the size of the full-color original.

With the color palette reduced to just 20 colors (*right*), the image is dramatically inferior. However, since this change does not reduce file size any further, there is no point in limiting the color palette beyond what is necessary.

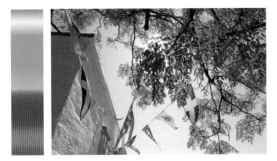

▲ Original full depth

This image of a church in Greece was recorded as a 12-bit (36-bit RGB) raw image, then processed into an 8-bit file (24-bit RGB). It retains full subtlety of the skies and the transparency and colors of the bunting.

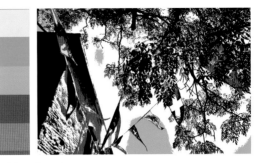

▲ Two levels

With only two levels per color channel, a surprising amount of the original image is retained, with many shapes still well defined. But note the wall in shadow is completely black, and many of the sky tones are blank.

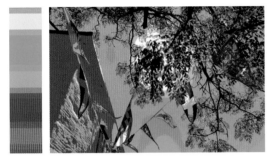

▲ Four levels

With four levels, the sky tones are filled in but they are very patchy and with large jumps in tone and no accuracy of color, simply because the nearest available hue is used. Generally, colors are more saturated than in the original image.

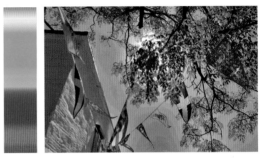

▲ 24 levels

With 24 levels, the original image is almost fully reproduced, but the failures are in the sky: note that it remains much darker than in the original, and what was a light area in the lower part of the original is darker than the rest of the sky here.

▶ Limited palette, numerous colors

This image appears to use very few colors. However, the tonal variations of deep cyans, blues, and magentas are so subtle that at least 200 different hues are needed to describe the image without loss of quality. Nonetheless, an indexed color version of the file is a quarter of the size of the RGB version.

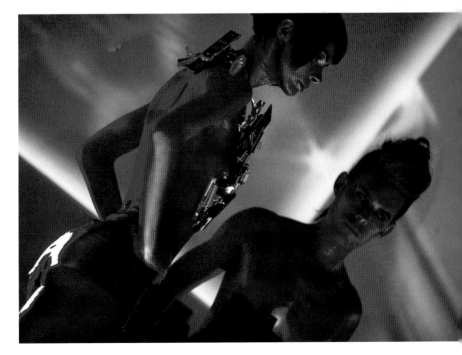

COLOR TO BLACK AND WHITE

Creating a black and white picture from a color original allows you to change the shot's emphasis. For example, a portrait may be marred by strongly colored objects in view, or your subjects may be wearing clashing colored clothing. Seen in black and white, the emphasis in these pictures is skewed more toward shape and form.

The translation process

A black-and-white image is not a direct translation of colors into grayscale (a range of neutral tones ranging from white to black) in which all colors are accurately represented—many cameras favor blues, for example, and record them as being lighter than greens.

When a digital camera or image-manipulation software translates a color image, it refers to a built-in table for the conversion. Professional software assumes you want to print the result and so makes the conversion according to a regime appropriate for certain types of printing press and paper. Other software simply turns the three color channels into gray values before combining them—usually giving dull, murky results.

There are, however, better ways of converting to black and white, depending on the software you have. But before you start experimenting, make sure you make a copy of your file and work on that rather than the original. Bear in mind that conversions to black and white loses color data that is impossible to reconstruct.

Before you print

After you have desaturated the image (*see box below*), and despite its gray appearance, it is still a color picture. So, unless it is to be printed on a four-color press, you should now convert it to grayscale to reduce its file size. If, however, the image is to be printed in a magazine or book, remember to reconvert it to color—either RGB or CMYK. Otherwise it will be printed solely with black ink, giving very poor reproduction.

Four-color black

In color reproduction, if all four inks (cyan, magenta, yellow, and black) are used, the result is a rich, deep black. It is not necessary to lay down full amounts of each ink to achieve this, but a mixture of all four inks (called four-color black) gives excellent results when reproducing photographs on the printed page. Varying the ratio of colors enables subtle shifts of image tone.

DESATURATION

All image-manipulation software has a command that increases or decreases color saturation, or intensity. If you completely desaturate a color image, you remove the color data to give just a grayscale. However, despite appearances, it is still a color image and looks gray only because every pixel has its red, green, and blue information in balance. Because of this, the information is self-canceling and the color disappears. If, though, you select different colors to desaturate, you can change the balance of tones. Converting the image to grayscale at this point gives you a different result from a straight conversion, since the colors that you first desaturate become lighter than they otherwise would have been.

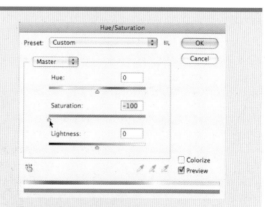

▲ **Saturation screen shot**
With the color image open you can access the Saturation control and drag the slider to minimum color. This gives a gray image with full color information. In some software you can desaturate the image using keystrokes instead (such as Shift+ Option+U in Photoshop, for example).

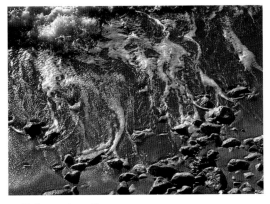

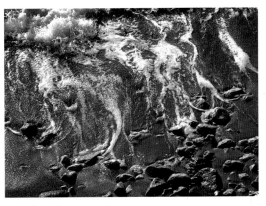

▲ Color saturation

While the original color image is full of light and life, the colors could be seen as detracting from the core of the image—the contrasts of the textures of the water, sand, and stones. This is purely a subjective interpretation, as is often the case when making judgments about images.

▲ Color desaturation

By removing all the colors using the Saturation control to give an image composed of grays, the essentials of the image emerge. The Burn and Dodge tools (*pp. 190–1*) were used to bring out tonal contrasts—darkening the lower portion of the picture with the Burn tool, while bringing out the sparkling water with the Dodge tool.

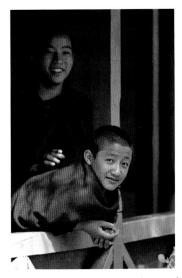

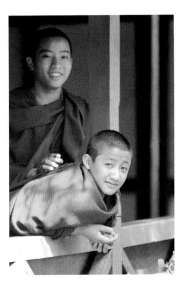

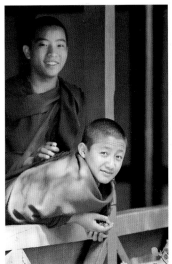

▲ Overcoming distracting color

The strong reds and blues (*above left*) distract from the friendly faces of these young monks in Gangtok, Sikkim. However, a straight desaturation of the image gives us a tonally unbalanced result. Attempts to desaturate selectively by hue will founder because the faces are a pale version of the red habits. We need to compensate for the tonally unattractive product of desaturation

(*middle*) by redistributing the tones to bring attention to the boys' faces. This involves reducing the white point to control the sunlit area in the foreground, plus a little burning-in

to darken the light areas of the habit and the hand of the monk behind. Then, to bring some light into the faces (*right*), we use the Dodging tool set to Highlights.

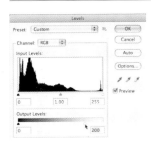

◄ Levels screen shot

With the desaturated image open, move the white point slider in the Levels dialog box to force the brightest pixels to be about a fifth less bright: in other words, to have a value no greater than 200.

COLOR TO BLACK AND WHITE CONTINUED

Channel extraction

Since a color image consists of three grayscale channels, the easiest way to convert the color to grayscale is to choose, or extract, one of these and abandon the others. This process is known as "channel extraction," but it is available only as part of more professional software packages.

When you view the image on the monitor normally, all three color channels are superimposed on each other. However, if you look at them one channel at a time, your software may display the image as being all one color—perhaps as reds of different brightnesses, for example, or as a range of gray tones, according to the software preferences you have set. If your software gives you the option, choose to view the channels as gray (by selecting this from the preferences or options menu). Then, simply by viewing each channel, you can choose

the one you like best. Now when you convert to grayscale, the software should act on the selected channel alone, converting it to gray.

Some software may allow you to select two channels to convert to gray, thus allowing you a great deal of experimention with the image's appearance. In general, the channels that convert best are the green, especially from digital cameras, because the green channel is effectively the luminance channel, and the red, which often gives bright, eye-catching results.

Another method, available in Photoshop, is to use Split Channels to produce three separate images. With this, you save the image you like and abandon the others. Note, however, that this operation cannot be undone—the extracted file is a true grayscale, and is just a third the size of the original file.

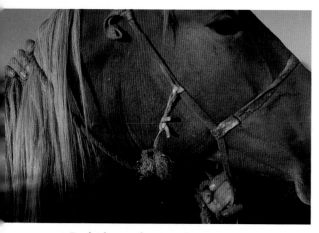

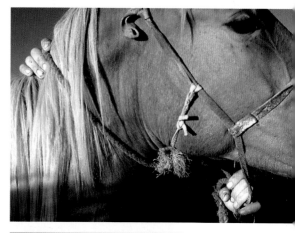

▲ Red-channel extraction

While the colors of the original image are sumptuous (*above left*), black and white seemed to offer more promise (*above right*). It is clear that the sky should be dark against the mane and cradling hand, so the green and blue channels (*right*) were of no help. Neither was the lightness channel (*opposite*), as it distributes tonal information too evenly. The red channel, however, presented the blues as dark and the brown of the horse as light. So, with the red channel extracted, no extra work was needed.

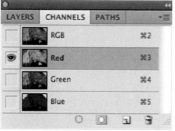

▲ Channels screen shot

If your software allows, select color channels one at a time to preview the effects of extraction. Turn off the color if the software shows channels in their corresponding colors.

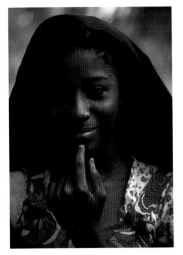

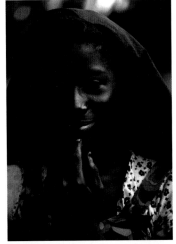

Blue channel

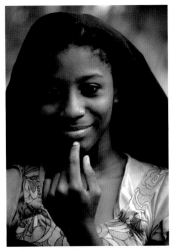

Red channel

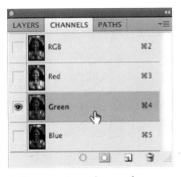

▲ Comparing channels

RGB color images comprise three grayscale images. Here, the B channel is dark while the R is too light, but the green is well balanced, as it carries the detail. This is confirmed by the L channel in LAB mode (far right).

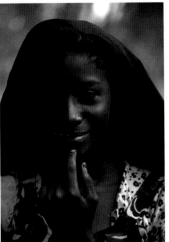

Green channel

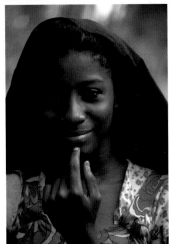

LAB (with Lightness channel extracted)

LAB MODE

When you convert an RGB color image to LAB, or Lab, mode (a shortened form of L*a*b*), the L channel carries the lightness information that contains the main tonal details about the image. The a* channel values represent green when negative and magenta when positive; the b* represents blue when negative, yellow when positive. Using software, such as Photoshop, that displays channels, you can select the L channel individually and manipulate it with Levels or Curves without affecting color balance. With the L channel selected, you can now convert to grayscale and the software will use only the data in that channel. If your software gives you this option, you will come to appreciate the control you have over an image's final appearance, and results are also likely to be sharper and more free of noise than if you had extracted another of the channels to work on. The extracted file is a true grayscale, and so it is only a third of the size of the original color file.

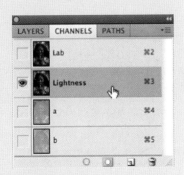

▲ LAB channels

In the Channels palette of Photoshop, you can select individual channels, as shown above. In this example, the screen will display a black-and-white image of the girl (*as above, right*).

COLOR TO BLACK AND WHITE CONTINUED

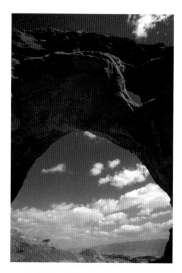

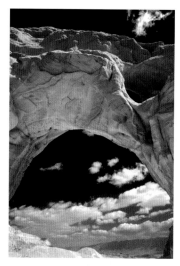

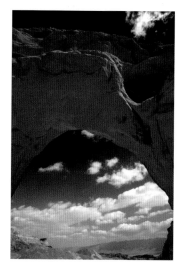

▲ **Original image**
A simple conversion of this image could make colors look lifeless— a problem avoided by using the Channel Mixer control (*below*).

▲ **Working in RGB mode**
In RGB, the blue channel was reduced, making the sky dark, and the red was increased to compensate. Results of using these settings are contrasty and dramatic, but the foreground is too bright.

▲ **Working in CMYK mode**
With the original image translated into CMYK mode, results are noticeably softer than those achieved via the Channel Mixer in RGB mode.

BLACK-AND-WHITE CONTROL

This conversion method offers the greatest control by separating the additive and subtractive primaries so that each can be individually adjusted. This means that, for example, the band of magenta colors in an image can be made dark while the red band can be made lighter. This gives a fine degree of control that enables you to separate tonalities of different colors with more accuracy than using Channel Mixer, and is more convenient than methods based on using layers. Adjacent bands should not be adjusted to be very different, however, as this can cause posterization or break-up of the image.

The work-flow is to capture in full color. Optimize the image for exposure and tone, then adjust the Black and White settings to obtain the results you like. Ensure that you save the settings as a preset that can be applied to other images: this will save you a great deal of time. You may need to make final tweaks with curves and levels.

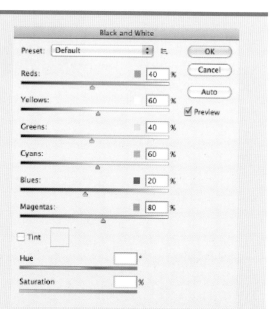

▲ **Black and white control**
The default setting renders a natural-looking black-and-white version of a color scene. In this control, from Photoshop, you can easily add a tint by ticking the box, and adjusting the hue and saturation sliders.

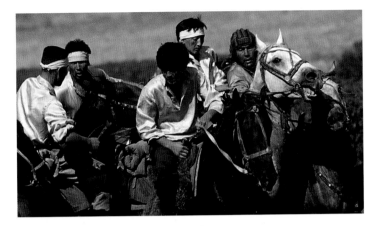

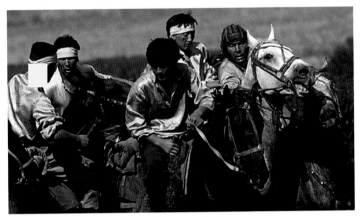

Channel Mixer
Preset: Custom
Output Channel: Gray
Source Channels
Red: 100 %
Green: 0 %
Blue: 0 %
Total: +100%
Constant: 0 %
☑ Monochrome

▲ Separating tones

Starting with this color image (*top left*), a standard grayscale conversion gives acceptable results (*middle left*), but channel mixing separates out the tones more effectively, particular in shadow areas (*bottom left*). The settings required were complicated, and arrived at by trial and error (*screen shot above*). The work done reduces the need for further processing of the image, but if you wish to refine the results further, a channel-mixed image makes such techniques as burning-in and dodging (*see pp. 190–1*) easier to apply, since, as you can see, the shadows on the shirts are far more open and susceptible to local density control.

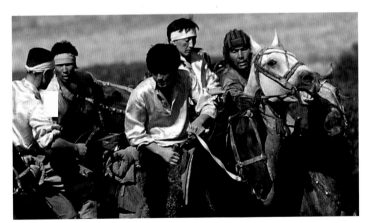

TRY THIS

To help learn how to isolate colors using the tools available in your software, start by selecting a bright, multicolored image—perhaps a collection of fruit, a flower stall, or something similar. Working on a copy of the image, now decide which color you wish to emphasize by making it light after conversion to grayscale. Use Color Balance, Replace Color, Hue and Saturation, or Channel Mixer tools to obtain the required result. If your first try does not work, return to the image and try a series of new settings. When you have a result you are happy with, note the settings. Use this information to replace another color in the image, and see if you can get to the desired result more quickly than the first time.

When less is more
This scene, near Samarkand, Uzbekistan, was full of bright and dusty colors. A conversion to black and white pares the image back to the essentials: the relationships between people.

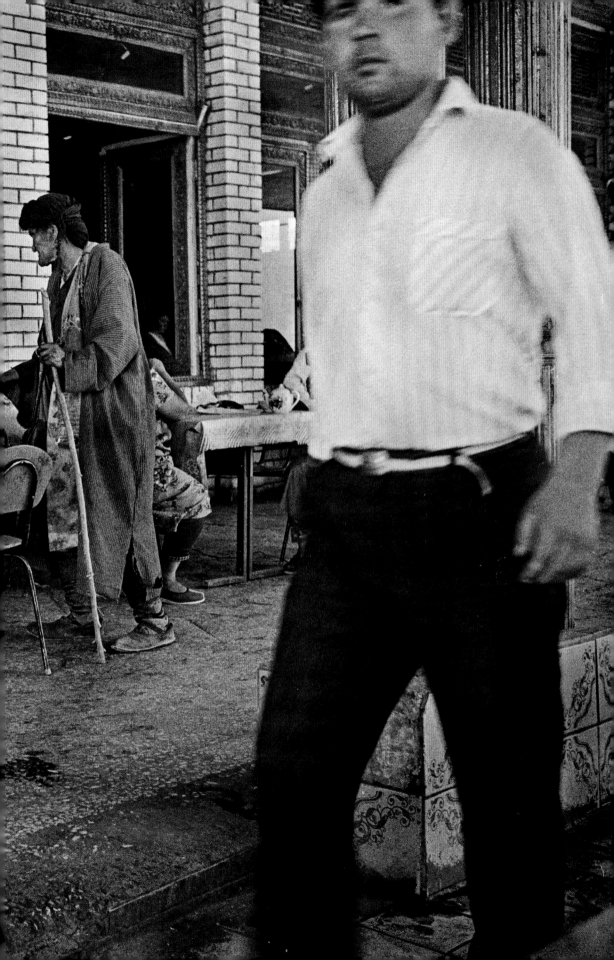

VINTAGE EFFECTS

The popularity of vintage effects, such as the look of distressed film, irregular blurs and flare, darkened corners, and distorted colors is, perhaps, a natural reaction against the modern, clinically-clean color image. These effects have found huge favor with casual snappers, particularly those using camera phones or Holga film-using cameras. For them, part of the appeal is in the way that the effects help to "fill in" empty areas in the image, immediately "improving" snapshots. At the same time vignetting serves to tighten picture composition, a effect that has been recognized since the dawn of photography.

Filters or apps

The traditional way to create vintage effects is to capture an image normally, then apply filter effects using image manipulation software. This allows you to apply different effects to the same image and to undo any effects you do not like. You can create your own vintage looks from scratch or use presets

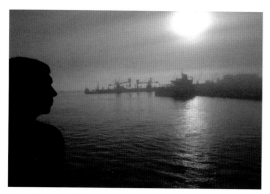

1 Original image
A passenger on a ferry sliding slowly into the port of Brindisi, Italy looks full of wistful thoughts. It is an image that suggests itself for a nostalgic treatment to convey the timelessness of the mixed feelings experienced when arriving at a new port.

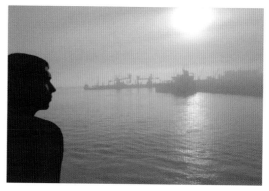

2 Lower contrast
Open the image and lower contrast with the Levels or Curves control, then reduce the black and white points. Vary the balance of color channels in Levels or use a color balance control to produce an overall tone.

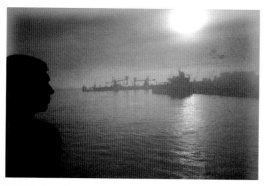

3 Apply irregular overlay
Open another image that has tones you like, select the portion that you want to use, and copy and paste it onto your original image. Resize to fit, then choose a layer mode (here it is Overlay) that gives your image the tone that suits your purpose.

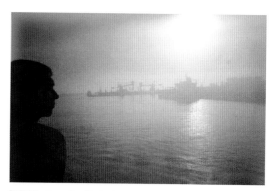

4 Apply lighting effects
Using a lighting filter in your image manipulation applications, apply a lens flare or vignette effect on the top layer. Or use a Brush set with an irregular head, such as rough bristles—loaded with a light color to paint on lighting effects.

for software such as Adobe Lightroom and Apple Aperture, or plug-ins such as Topaz Adjust or Alien Skin Exposure. Apps for iPhone such as Instagram apply a limited set of effects but are very easy to use. A more recent approach is to make the image through an application such as Hipstamatic, which applies the effects during image processing, saving the image in its final "vintage" form. This is more challenging as you need to be able to pre-visualize the results, but it is fun and saves on post-processing.

Suppose you would like an image with a vintage sepia look: a low-contrast brownish tone with some lens flare, vignetting, and a "hand-crafted" appearance. By adding effects systematically you will understand how the image is created and can refine the process, for example, by adding an irregular border that mimics brushed-on emulsion. If you use an application that can record the steps as a script or "action," do so, so that you can apply them to another image.

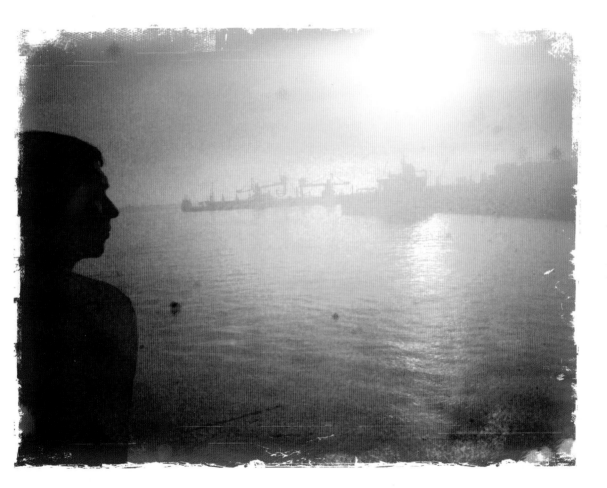

5 Create an irregular border

Select the Eraser tool with irregular "bristles," and set to a wide diameter with a low Flow setting. Run the eraser along the edge of the image. If you wish to have repeatable results create a layer mask using the Paint tool. An alternative option is to copy an image that has an irregular border and use this as the new border. For this image, I pasted one of my Hipstamatic shots on top, adjusted its shape, inverted its tone, then set the layer to Divide mode. A little extra erasing refined the final effect.

WORKING WITH RAW

It is a popular notion that RAW files offer the best possible image quality. However, some in-camera processing can produce results that are unobtainable with RAW. The real advantage of recording in RAW is that it provides the largest reserve of data for image manipulation.

Extracting color

Before opting for a RAW workflow, it is sobering to consider the JPEG alternative. All sensors produce raw image data. When a camera saves the image as a JPEG (or, rarely, as a TIFF—see p. 176) it first extracts the full color information from the sensor, then applies adjustments regarding contrast, color saturation, sharpness, and so on. These parameters have been designed by experts in color science and sensor technology. If you think you can do better than them, by all means work with RAW files. But a common complaint is of RAW processing producing images inferior to camera JPEGs.

Advantages of RAW

Nonetheless, while working with RAW requires a great deal more time and effort than with JPEG files, the rewards are there for those who truly require the quality—because they need to enlarge images to their limits, or publish them in top-class print media.

RAW processing preserves the maximum amount of original image data—particularly in shadow and highlights—which helps to ensure the highest possible image quality from each file. It offers you maximum flexibility with image brightness, white balance, and color space. However, remember that if you make prints smaller than the maximum recommended your files, many of the advantages of RAW processing will be lost in the print.

Batch conversion

The job of a RAW file converter, then, is to apply all the processing that the camera would normally do to deliver vibrant, sharp, and well-exposed images. All RAW conversion software allows you to save settings then apply the same setting to entire folders full of images: this is known as batch processing, and clearly it can save a great deal of manual effort and time-consuming supervision. However processing large numbers of images will take some time, even on fast computers, because of the large files involved.

You can go further than any camera by tailoring the presets to different conditions. With landscapes, for example, you may aim for higher sharpness and saturation than you would when making portraits. You can create presets to suit different subjects and styles: high saturation, contrast, and sharpness for landscapes and urban views; low vibrance for documentary photography; sepia tone and soft contrast for portraits, and so on. This workflow is flexible yet it saves a great deal of time.

RAW styles

Not all RAW conversion software is created equal. Indeed, not only do the interface design, ease and speed of operation, support for your camera, and cost vary, but each application applies subtly different philosophies to image processing; for example, noise reduction being preferred over detail preservation. Nonetheless, where output has been expertly processed, it is very hard to identify any significant differences. With modern solutions, it is safe to select an application based on what you find easiest to use, but first ensure that your camera's specific RAW format is supported.

DNG

Adobe Digital Negative (DNG) is an attempt to bring order to the proliferation of RAW formats by creating a common "wrapper," or structure, for the data. Introduced in 2004, it is based on a standard format known as TIFF-EP. It is designed to accommodate metadata (such as MakerNotes for the camera) in order to allow for any DNG-compliant RAW converter to work on raw data irrespective of its source. As of 2010, DNG was supported by over 300 non-Adobe products and software—but is by no means universally adopted, particularly among the larger camera manufacturers. Suffixes for files are .dng or .DNG.

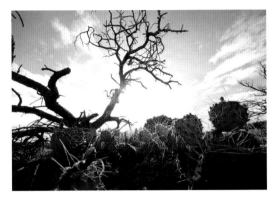

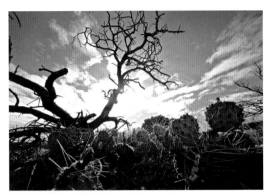

▲ Bright and dark

A hot desert sun burns through the clouds over Utah, while shadows in the foreground are rich in detail. Faced with such a subject, the best course is to record in RAW in the expectation of needing much remedial post-processing.

▲ Top and bottom

Strong recovery in the high values as well as darkening of blues brings the sky under control without banding (aliasing) artifacts. At the same time a great deal of digital "fill light" recovers lots of detail from the shadows.

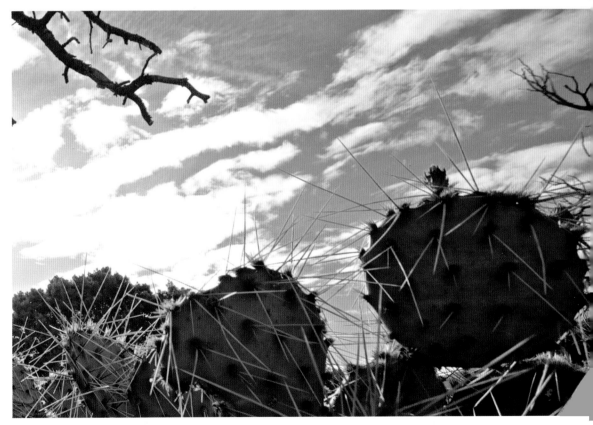

▲ Detailed promise

In addition to tonal recovery and repair, the other reason for working with RAW is to capture as much detail as possible. This means we need to do more than resolve the fine, spikey cactus needles convincingly. We also need the resolving power for accurate tone reproduction—here, to render with accuracy the extremely soft tonal transitions within the clouds and in the sky. In this enlargement—equivalent to a print about 33in (84cm) wide—there smoothness as well as fair micro-contrast that should satisfy all but the most critical viewer.

WORKING WITH RAW CONTINUED

When you first open a RAW file in a converter, the image will have been processed using the default conversion settings. The software will have identified the camera used, looked up its database of RAW formats and applied the appropriate settings.

RAW flow

If you use proxy-working, nondestructive software such as Adobe Lightroom or Apple Aperture, the work-flow is very simple. After downloading the images through the software, you work on the images and export only as you need: the applications provide an accurate preview of the output image. In addition, all the enhancements you make to images are automatically saved (*see also p.172*).

If you use stand-alone RAW converters, such as Adobe Camera Raw, DXO Optics, Phase One or Nikon Capture NX, open your RAW image from the back-up copy, then:

- Make settings—exposure, contrast, white balance,

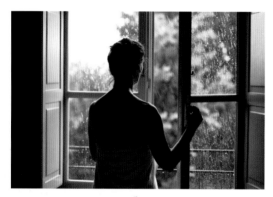

1 Tough conditions
An overcast, stormy day produces dull lighting, but the luminance range—between the sky and the shadows behind the window—is nonetheless very wide. At the same time, there are subtle skin tones that we will wish to preserve.

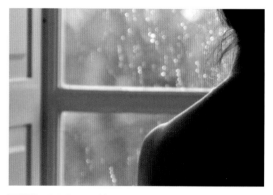

2 JPEG roughness
The importance of working in RAW is most evident in transitions from dark mid-tones with detail to the deepest shadows. Manipulation of this JPEG version results in unattractive, sudden changes of tone and color, due to poverty of data.

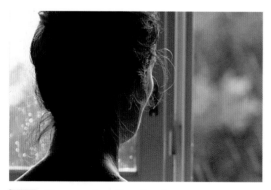

3 Conversion fine tuning
Assess the image in detail: you may need only small changes in brightness, hue, or sharpness, to perfect it. Some converters have a moiré control that applies a filter to reduce artifacts resulting from a clash between regular patterns and the sensor.

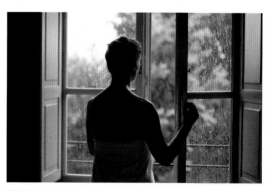

4 Color temperature
The potential of the image emerges when we decrease color temperature, that is, warm the white balance. This also brings out shadow detail because it is largely composed of dark reds. But it has the effect of making the greens dull, which we need to correct.

and color adjustments; correction for chromatic aberration; and sharpening—or load and apply saved settings to the image.

■ Set pixel dimensions, bit-depth, output resolution, and color profile for the output.

■ If you made a new set of settings, save it to use on other images made in similar conditions.

■ Output or export the image in a standard TIFF or JPEG file, with a new name, to a new or work-in-progress folder.

TRY THIS

Get familiar with the different RAW converters before you purchase. Modern software allows you a trial—some give a generous 30 days full function, others are less generous—so take full advantage of it. Download and install the converters, collect some of your RAW images, then convert them with each trial version. Allow yourself at least four hours using the software before making any judgments about its suitability and quality of conversion.

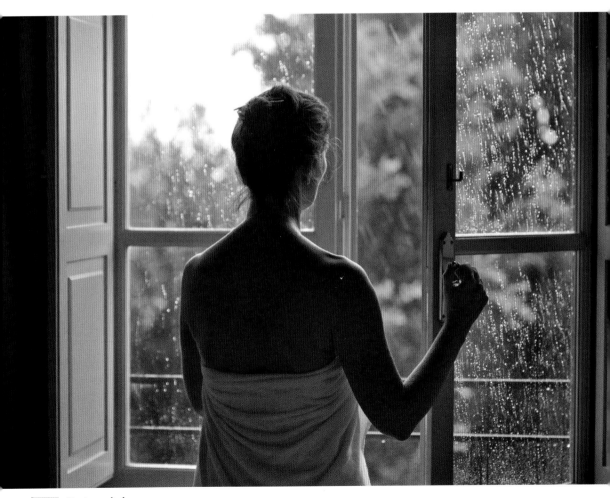

5 Data mining

The image resulting from the RAW conversion is entirely usable, but we can do better. The warming of the white balance improved the skin tones but compromised the greens and also reduced the brilliance of the raindrops. So we need to top up vibrance to improve the greens, leaving the skin tones alone. Burning-in set to Shadow darkens the shadows around the raindrops, which has the effect of accentuating them. A final touch is to use the Clone tool to remove the window catch by the model's face.

DUOTONES

Much of the art of traditional black and white printing lay in making the most of the limited tonal range inherent in the printing paper. A common tactic was to imply a wider tonal range than really existed by making the print contrasty. This suggested that shadows were really deep while highlights were truly bright. The success of this depended on the subtleties of tonal gradation between these extremes. A further technique was to tone the print, adding color to the neutral gray image areas.

Modern digital printers have opened up the possibilities for toning well beyond that possible in the darkroom. The range of hues is virtually unlimited as you can simulate all those that can be created with the four-color (or more) process.

Creating a duotone

Starting with an image, even a color one, first turn the file into a grayscale (*see pp. 224–9*) using, in Photoshop, the Image > Mode menu. This permanently deletes color information, so you need to work on a copy file. Similar results can be obtained in the Sepia Tone effect, a menu option in almost all image-manipulation applications.

Now that you have a grayscale image you can enter the Duotone mode, where you have a choice of going it alone or loading one of the preset duotones. If you are not familiar with the process, use the Duotone Presets (usually found in the "Presets" folder of Photoshop). Double-click on any one to see the result.

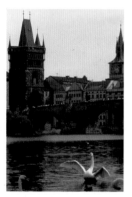

◄ Simple duotones
This view of Prague (*left*) has been rendered in tones reminiscent of a bygone era. After turning the image to grayscale, two inks were used for the duotone, neither of them black. This gave a light, low-contrast image characteristic of an old postcard.

▲ Duotone Options screen shot
The curve for the blue ink (*above*) was lifted in the highlights in order to put a light bluish tone into the bright parts of the image and also to help increase the density of the shadow areas.

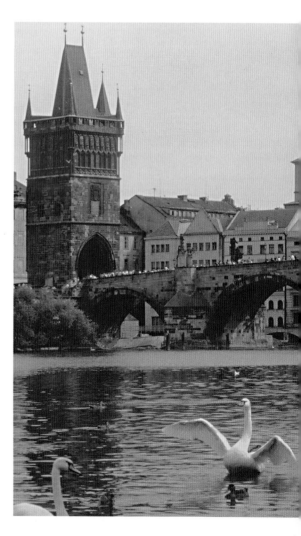

Clicking on the colored square in the dialog box (*see opposite*) changes the color of the second "ink." Bright red could give an effect of gold toning; dark brown, a sepia tone. This is a powerful feature—in an instant you can vary the toning effects on any image without any of the mess and expense of mixing chemicals associated with the darkroom equivalent.

If you click on the lower of the graph symbols, a curve appears that tells you how the second ink is being used, and by manipulating the curve you can change its effect. You could, for example, choose to place a lot of second ink in the highlights, in which case all the upper tones will be tinted. Or you may decide to create a wavy curve, in which case the result will be an image that looks somewhat posterized.

In Photoshop, you are able to choose to see Previews. This updates the image without changing the file, thereby allowing you to see and evaluate the effects in advance.

You need to bear in mind that a duotone is likely to be saved in the native file format (the software's own format). This means that to print it you may first have to convert it into a standard RGB or CMYK TIFF file, so that the combination of black and colored inks you specified for the duotone can be simulated by the colored inks of the printer. This is the case whether you output on an ink-jet printer or on a four-color press.

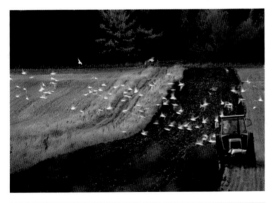

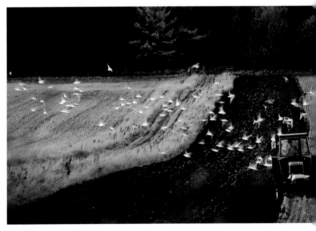

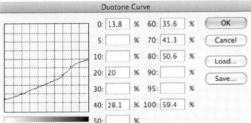

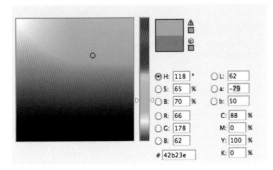

▲ Retaining subject detail

In the original image (*above left*), there was so much atmosphere it was a pity to lose the color. But the resulting duotone, with a green second ink, offers its own charms (*above right*). To reduce overall contrast and allow the green ink (chosen via the Color Picker dialog box, *bottom left*) to come through, it was necessary to reduce the black ink considerably—as shown by the Duotone Curve dialog box (*center left*). The low position of the end of the curve in the dialog box (*center left*) indicates a low density of black, but the kinks in the curve were introduced to increase shadow contrast and retain subject detail. The lifted end of the curve shows that there are no real whites: the lightest part still retains 13.8 percent of ink, as shown in the top box labeled "0:" in the Duotone Curve dialog box.

TRITONES AND QUADTONES

The addition of one or more inks to a duotone (*see pp. 238–9*) adds extra layers of subtlety to an image. Using most image-manipulation software, you will have tritone or quadtone boxes offering additional inks and curves for you to apply.

Bear in mind that with the extra inks on offer you can produce tinted highlights or you can hint at colors in the shadows that are not present in the mid-tones, and in this way create more tonal separation. However, there is no substitute for experimenting by applying different curves and colors, as this is the best way to learn how to use this powerful control. As a starting point, try using color contrasts by applying third and fourth inks in small amounts. Or, if you want a graphic-art effect, try curves that have sharp peaks.

One technical reason for using a quadtone is to help ensure accurate color reproduction. While not guaranteeing results, the chances of an accurate four-color black are greatly increased by specifying a quadtone in which the colors used are the standard cyan, magenta, yellow, and black of the printing process.

You can save curves and sets of colors and apply them to other grayscale images. When you find a combination that appeals to you, save it for future use in a library of your favorite settings.

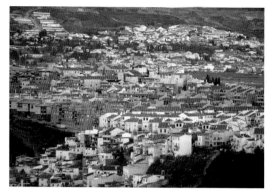

▲ **Original image**
Starting with this view of the city of Granada, in southern Spain, I first made a copy file of the original to work on. Then, using the copy file, I removed all the color information to make a grayscale, before deciding on which inks to apply.

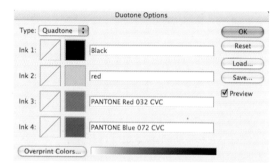

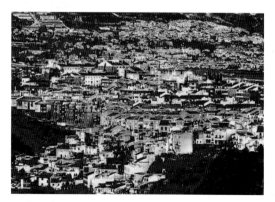

▲ **Quadtone**
For this image, black has been assigned to the dark featureless shadows, green to those shadows that still retain details, and blue to the lower and mid-tones. This is shown by the peaks in the graphs next to each color ink in the Duotone Options dialog box (*above right*). Adjusting the heights of the peaks changes the strength of the colors.

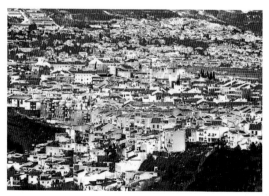

▲ **Tritone**
Assigning different-colored inks to specific tonal densities in the image produces visual effects that are very difficult to achieve in any other way. In this tritone version of the scene, the fourth (blue) color has been switched off, and the result is a brighter, lighter image compared with the quadtone (*left*).

SEPIA TONES

With digital technology you can bring about image changes with more control than was ever possible in a traditional darkroom. A prime example of this is the digital equivalent of sepia toning—the low-contrast, nineteenth-century technique that gives warm, brown tones with no blacks or whites.

Old prints lack contrast due to the film's recording properties and the makeup of the print's emulsion. The softness is likely due to the lens, while the brown tone is down to the print being treated with a thiocarbamide compound.

Many digital cameras will produce "sepia-toning," if they are correctly set, and most image-manipulation applications will also give these effects with just a single command, though with little control.

For greater control, first convert your grayscale image to RGB color mode. Once in RGB, desaturate the image. Use the Levels command (*see pp. 188–9*) to make the image lighter and grayer, and then remove the blacks and whites.

Now you can add color. The easiest way to do this is by using Color Balance (*see p. 210*) to increase the red and yellow. Or use the Variations command (if available) to add red, yellow, and possibly a little blue to produce a brown that you find suits the content of your image.

Another option is to work with a grayscale image in Duotone mode to add a brown or dark orange as the second ink. Using Photoshop, this provides the most subtle effects.

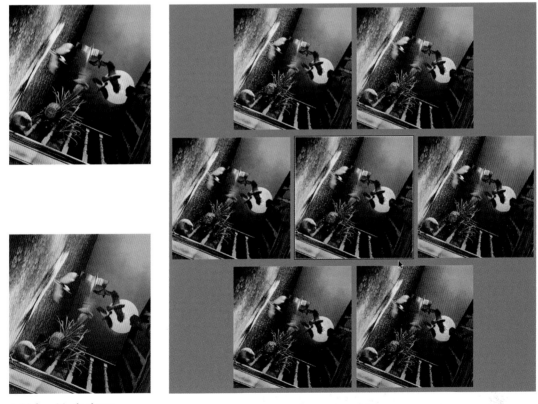

▲ Using Variations
There are several ways to add overall color to the type of interior view shown here. Although subject content is strong, the black and white version (*top left*) lacks atmosphere. The multi-image Variations dialog box (*right*), an option available in most image-manipulation software packages, presents several versions of the toned original from which to choose. By clicking on one (*shown outlined in the dialog box above*), you turn it into the image of choice, and you can then compare it against the original. To arrive at the final sepia-toned image (*bottom far left*), the Levels control was used to reduce shadow density and so produce a flatter contrast.

SABATTIER EFFECT

When a partially developed print is briefly reexposed to white light, some of the tone values are reversed. Although developed areas of the print are desensitized to light, partially undeveloped areas are still capable of being fogged. If these are then allowed to develop normally, they will darken. As the doctor and scientist who discovered this effect, Frenchman Armand Sabattier (1834–1910), described this process as "pseudo-solarization," it has become incorrectly known as "solarization"—which is, in fact, the reversal of image tones due to extreme overexposure.

Digital advantages

For the traditional darkroom worker, the Sabattier effect is notoriously time-consuming and difficult to control—it is all too easy to spend an entire morning making a dozen or more prints, none of which looks remotely like the one you are trying to create. Using digital image-manipulation techniques, however, this type of uncertainty is a thing of the past.

The first step is to make a copy of your original image to work on and convert that file to a grayscale (*see pp. 224–9*). Choose an image that has fairly simple outlines and bold shapes—images with fine or intricate details are not really suitable as the tone reversal tends to confuse their appearance. You can also work with a desaturated color image if you wish (*see pp. 214–15*).

There are several ways of simulating the Sabattier effect using Curves and Color Balance. Another method, if you have software that offers Layers and Modes (*see pp. 278–83*), is to duplicate the lower, original layer into a second layer. You then apply the Exclusion Layer mode, and adjust the tone of the image by altering the Curves or Levels for either layer.

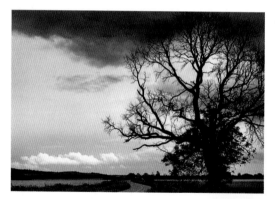

◀ Working in color

Working digitally, you can take the Sabattier effect further than is possible in the darkroom. By starting with a slightly colored image, you will end up with results displaying partially reversed hues. In this landscape, the grayscale was warmed using the Color Balance control to add yellow and red. On applying a U-shaped curve to this image, the highlights to mid-tones remained as they were, but the darker tones reversed—not only in tone but also in color, as you can see here (*below*). An arch-shaped curve would produce the opposite effects.

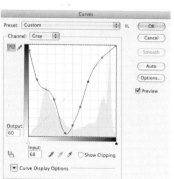

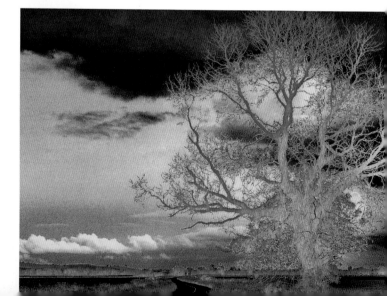

GUM DICHROMATES

A gum dichromate is a flat colorization of a grayscale image with compressed tonal range. The darkroom technique is a bit messy but once you know the look of a typical gum dichromate, you can easily reproduce it digitally without handling dyes and sticky substances.

Clean working

Images with clean outlines and subjects without strong "memory colors" (colors that everyone recognizes, such as flesh tones) are suitable. Start by selecting the areas you want to color. Next, fill your selection with a color using the Bucket or Fill tool set to Color mode. Working in this way ensures that you add colors to the existing pixels, rather than replace them. Keep colors muted by choosing light,

pastel shades rather than deep, saturated hues—it is easy to create too many brilliant colors.

Another approach is to work in Layers, with a top layer filled with color and the mode set to Color or Colorize. This colors the entire image, so you will need to apply some masking (*see pp. 274–5*) to remove colors from certain areas. Another layer filled with a different color and different masks will apply colors to other parts of the image. If you want to lower the color effect overall, use the opacity setting. In fact, this method is the exact digital counterpart of the traditional darkroom process.

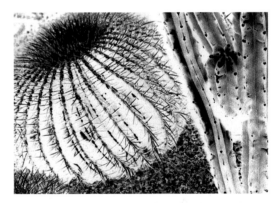

▶ Color and opacity

For this image (*below*), a scan of an old negative print (*left*) was made. Working in RGB and a new layer, an area was selected with the Lasso tool with feathering set to a high level, to ensure a soft-edged coloration. Color was added to the selection, using the Fill Layer mode set to Color. This tints the underlying layer. Different selections on new layers were filled with color and their opacities adjusted so that they balanced well to give the final image.

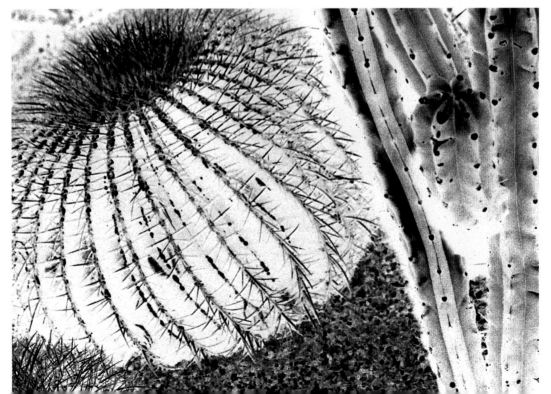

SPLIT TONING

Toning is a chemical-based technique for giving a tint of color to the silver of photographic prints by replacing it with other metals or compounds to produce a new image tone.

The exact tone resulting from this process depends on the chemical or metal used and also, to some degree, on the size of the particles produced by the process. Where there is variation in the size or density of silver particles, the image takes on variations in tint—from browns to coffee, for example—or contrasting tones, from pinks to azures. This variation is known as split toning and is caused by the chemical processes working at different rates with changes in grain density or size. Split toning is popular because it gives subtle tones with limited color variations in a monochrome image.

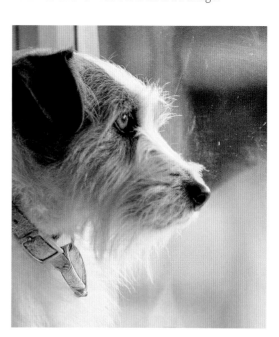

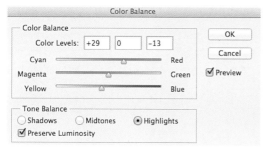

▲ Using Color Balance

The Color Balance control is the easiest way to create split-toning effects, working best with images that have well-separated tones. To add warm tones to the highlights in this portrait of a dog keeping watch, the Highlight button was clicked in the Color Balance panel and a touch of red added. Next, the Shadows button is activated and blue added to the control. Note Preserve Luminosity is checked, ensuring the image does not become darker with the addition of colors.

▲ Using Layer Blending Options

If you need to separate the brighter parts of the image from the darker ones, this can be achieved by duplicating the image into two layers, then blending them so that the darker areas of one layer show, and the light areas of the second layer show, too. First, duplicate the image into separate layers, apply the tints to the dark areas of one layer, and different tints to the second layer. Work with the sliders in Blending Options to create smooth transitions between the underlying blue and the reddish light tones.

Digital simulation

There are several ways to simulate split toning digitally. Any color control whose effect can be limited to shadows, mid-tones, or highlights may be used. This includes color-balance controls that work selectively: tone curves for color channels, adjustment layers with masks, or effects such as duotone or tritone (*see pp. 238–40*).

The first step is to turn your image from color to monochrome. For all methods apart from duotone, the image should be in RGB mode. When you apply the toning tints, the color should then appear. If you wish to apply duotone effects (to add up to four colors), the image needs to be in grayscale (no color information). After completing duotone work, you can turn the image back to RGB mode.

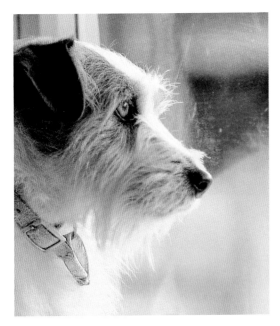

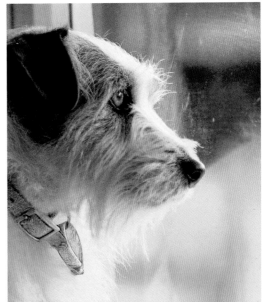

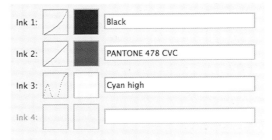

▲ Using Adjustment Layers

Adjustment layers applied with image masks offer the greatest control, and it is also easy to return and change the results if you change your mind. Create an adjustment layer—for instance, for Hue/Saturation—then mask the image using Apply Image. Duplicate this layer. Apply the colors: one color for the highlights in one layer, the other for the darker tones. Now apply tonal changes to the mask in the top layer. This allows the colors to reveal or mask those in the other layer and offers the most precise control.

▲ Using Duotone mode

The Duotone control allows you to add up to four different "ink" colors to a monochrome image with distribution controlled by curves. Here, we use the Tritone part of the Duotone options. The dialogue box (*above*) shows a normal curve for the black color. The second color, brown, is also set to normal, while the third color, a green-blue, is boosted in the light areas and reduced around the mid-tones. Without the addition of this third color, the mid-tones would look a little too weak.

SPLIT TONING CONTINUED

The original version of this portrait was full of the tropical colors of the location—Manila, in the Philippines—which competed with the depiction of a local beauty. However, removing the color entirely to neutral grays did a disservice to the subject, irrespective of the kind of conversion used (*see pp. 224-9*). A third option was split toning, or double toning: a warm tint, sympathetic to the mood of the light mid-tones, gives soft counterpoints to the hints of blue in the darker tones.

TECHNICAL INFO

CAMERA
Sony Alpha 7R

LENS
Canon 70–200 mm f/2.8
at 200 mm

SETTINGS
ISO 160 · f/2.8 · ½₅₀ sec

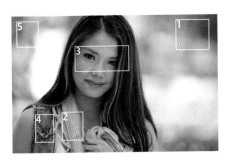

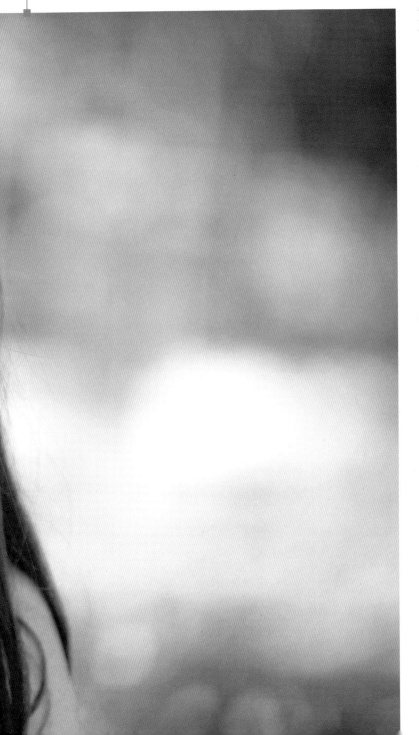

1 Smooth blur
The preferred image blur is smooth, with no fringing or sudden steps in tone or color. What is shown here results from a combination of top-quality lens design that allows good performance at full aperture, photographing at full aperture, and objects that are sufficiently distant to be rendered unrecognizable.

2 Deliberate blur
In the original image, the model's scarf and hand are rendered sharp because they lie on the same focus plane as her eyes. This presents a distraction from the model, so a small amount of blur was applied to reduce the impact of the sharply defined details seen in the weaving and the hand.

3 Sharp eyes
It is crucial that the model's eyes are sharp, while almost anything else can be unsharp. Catchlights—specular highlights reflecting sources of illumination—in her eyes bring animation to the face.

4 Controlled gray
In the conversion to black-and-white, the navy blue of the denim jacket has a tendency to be rendered too dark. To correct this, the area was dodged to lighten the shadows and help it slip into visual insignificance.

5 Double tint
The two-toned tinting was adjusted so that any darker shadows were lightly blue-tinted, and the somewhat lighter shadows were sepia-tinted. The subtle and shifting contrasts in hue give visual lift and a quiet dynamism to the background.

HAND TINTING

Digital hand coloring is altogether a different proposition from the old method of painting directly onto prints. It allows you risk-free experimentation, no commitment to interim results, and freedom from the mess of paints. The core technique is to apply, using a suitable Brush tool, the desired color values to the grayscale values of the image, leaving unchanged the luminance value of the pixels. That is the job of the Color or Colorize mode.

Techniques

The best way to imitate the effect of painting is to use the Brush set to Color mode and then paint directly onto your image. Set a soft edge for the brush, or use one that applies its effects in irregular strokes, like a true brush. You should also set the pressure and the flow to low values, so that application of the brush produces a barely visible change in the image.

Another method is to create a new layer set to Color mode above the image, and paint into this. This makes it possible to erase any errors without damaging the underlying image. You will also find it easier to see where you paint if you use strong colors, and then reduce the opacity afterwards. You may make extra layers

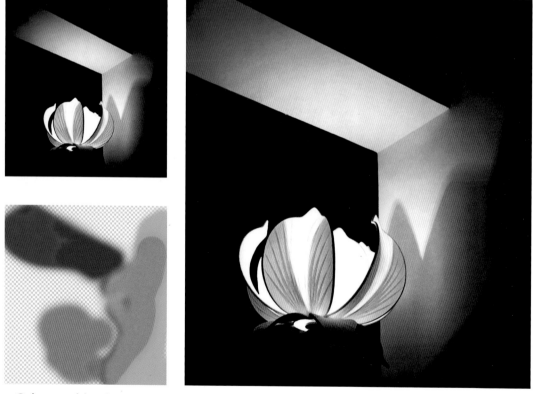

▲ **Color combinations**
To suit the strong shapes of the original image (*top*), equally strong colors were called for. You can work with any combination of colors, and it is worth experimenting—not only will some combinations look better, some will print more effectively than others. Bear in mind that a blank area will not accept color if the Color or Blending mode is set to Colorize. To give white areas density, go to the Levels control and drag the white pointer to eliminate pure white pixels. Once the pixels have some density, they have the ability to pick up color. To give black areas color, reduce the amount of black, again via Levels control. Although the "paint" is applied liberally (*above left*), note that in the finished print (*above*) color does not show up in the totally black areas.

to experiment with different strokes or even blend two or more layers.

Weak colors and pastel shades—that is, those of low saturation, with a lot of white—are often out-of-gamut for color printers and monitors (*see p. 61*), so you may need to bear in mind the limitations of the printed result while you work. As yet, the porcelainlike textured finish of a high-quality, hand-colored print is beyond the capabilities of ink-jet printers. The careful use of papers with tinted bases can help the effect, since the paper's background helps narrow the dynamic range and soften the image contrast.

Graphics tablet

The ideal tool for hand tinting is the graphics tablet, with its pen-shaped stylus. A standard mouse can position the cursor or brush with high precision and is useful if you need to leave the cursor in position, but with a graphics stylus you can vary the pressure with which you apply "paint," thereby affecting both the size of the brush and the flow of color. Some stylus designs also respond to the angle of the stylus. Another advantage of a stylus is that it is less tiring to use than a mouse. The downside is that a large graphics tablet requires far more desk space.

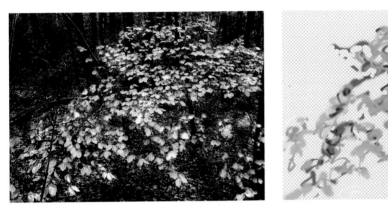

▶ Painting and opacity
You can apply the paint quite freely, using a range of colors—as in this image (*above right*) of the painted layer that lies above the base image. The spring foliage (*above*) was emphasized by a lot of dodging (*pp. 190-1*) to lighten individual leaves. To introduce some color, a new layer was created and its Blending mode set to Color, so only areas with density can pick up color (*above right*). The paint was then applied to this layer. Finally, the layer's opacity was reduced to 40 percent for the final image (*right*) to allow the foliage to show through the color overlay.

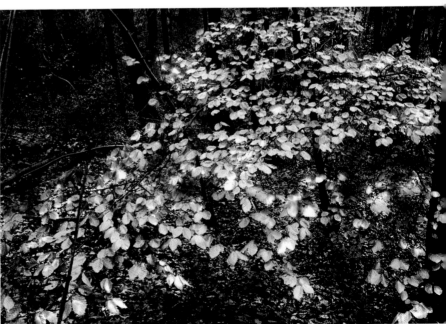

CROSS-PROCESSING

Of the numerous unorthodox ways to process color film, perhaps the most popular was developing transparencies in chemicals designed for color negatives, and processing color negatives in chemicals designed for color transparency film.

Cross-processing techniques made fundamental and irreversible changes to the image, so there is much to be said for simulating the effects using digital image-manipulation techniques. There is a further advantage to working digitally. Color negative film was overlaid with an orange-colored mask whose job it was to correct inherent deficiencies in the color separation or filtering process during exposure. Before the final print could be made, this mask had to be replaced or neutralized.

Color negative film to transparencies

Results from this type of cross-processing had flat tones and muted colors due to the fact that color negative film was low in contrast, and transparency processing chemicals compress highlights. Color was also unpredictable, resulting in color balance in the highlights being different from that in the lower mid-tones and shadows.

Digitally, the Curves control is the best way to simulate this effect, though do not be alarmed if your

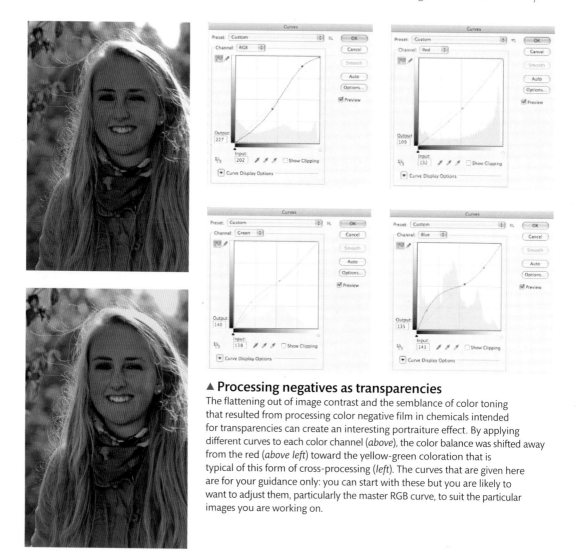

▲ **Processing negatives as transparencies**
The flattening out of image contrast and the semblance of color toning that resulted from processing color negative film in chemicals intended for transparencies can create an interesting portraiture effect. By applying different curves to each color channel (*above*), the color balance was shifted away from the red (*above left*) toward the yellow-green coloration that is typical of this form of cross-processing (*left*). The curves that are given here are for your guidance only: you can start with these but you are likely to want to adjust them, particularly the master RGB curve, to suit the particular images you are working on.

image becomes too dark or light—you can adjust overall brightness later. Another possible image outcome is posterization. If you find this effect unattractive, then the quality of the scan may not be good enough. If that is the case, your only option is to rescan the original image, possibly to a higher bit-depth (*see pp. 222–3*).

From transparencies to color negatives

Results from processing transparencies as color negatives were often contrasty, with color shifts toward cyan. They also had an open tonality, often with highlights reproducing as featureless white.

This occurred because of the need to print inherently high-contrast transparencies on paper meant for the lower contrast of color negatives.

The best way to create this effect digitally is to manipulate the separate channels in the Curves control. When you have a set of curves that work, you can save and reapply them to any image.

If you find it hard to concentrate on the overall lightness of the image while juggling with different channels, leave overall density to the end and work just on the colors and contrast. Once you are satisfied with these, call up the Levels control (*see pp. 188–9*) to adjust overall brightness.

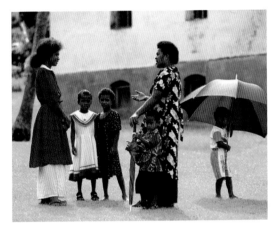

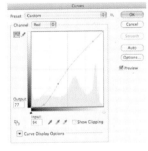

▲ Processing transparencies as negatives

The high-contrast effect that resulted from cross-processing color transparency film in color negative chemicals works with subjects that have strong outlines and punchy colors (*above left*). By applying the set of curves shown here (*right*), the result is brilliant color and the type of washed-out highlights typical of this form of cross-processing (*above right*). As the highlight areas are tonally balanced by the full shadows and strong colors, they are more acceptable than in an image with a normal tonal range. The curves are given here are for your guidance only: you can start with these but you are likely to want to adjust them, particularly the master RGB curve, to suit your particular images.

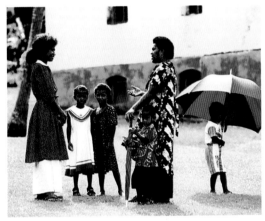

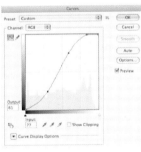

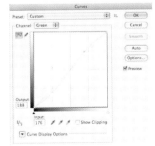

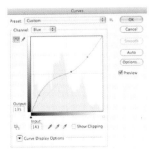

TINTS FROM COLOR ORIGINALS

It is not necessary for color images to be strongly colored in order to have impact. You can, for example, use desaturated hues—those that contain more gray than actual color—to make more subtle color statements. In addition, selectively removing color from a composition can be a useful device for reducing the impact of unwanted distractions within a scene (*see pp. 204–5*).

For global reductions in color, you need only turn on the Color Saturation control, often linked with other color controls, such as Hue, in order to reduce saturation or increase gray. By selecting a defined area, you can limit desaturation effects to just that part of the image.

Working procedure

While working, it may be helpful to look away from the screen for each change, since the eye finds it difficult to assess continuous changes in color with any degree of accuracy. If you watch the changes occur, you may overshoot the point that you really want and then have to return to it. The resulting shuffling backward and forward can be confusing. Furthermore, a picture often looks as if it has "died on its feet" when you first remove the color if you do it suddenly—look at the image again after a second or two, and you may see it in a more objective light.

For an extra degree of control, all image-manipulation software has a Desaturation tool. This is a Brush tool, the effect of which is to remove all color evenly as it is "brushed" over the pixels. Work with quite large settings—but not 100 percent—in order to remove color quickly while still retaining some control and finesse.

Another way of obtaining tints of color from your original is to select by color, or range of colors. If you increase the saturation of certain colors, leaving the others unchanged, and then desaturate globally, the highly saturated colors will retain more color than the rest of the image, which will appear gray in comparison.

Bear in mind that many pixels will contain some of the color you are working on, even if they appear to be of a different hue. Because of this, it may not be possible to be highly selective and work only over a narrow waveband. Photoshop allows you to make a narrow selection: you can use Replace Color as well as the waveband limiter in Hue/Saturation.

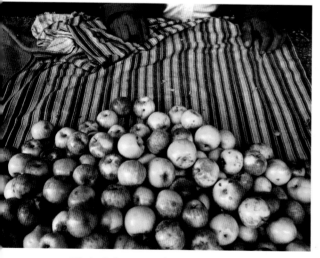 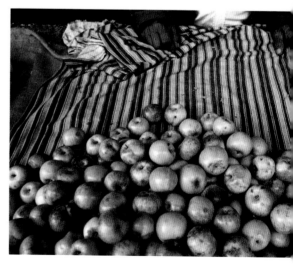

▲ Global desaturation

For a selective desaturation of the original (*above left*), the whole image was slightly desaturated, while ensuring that some color was retained in the apples and hands (*above right*). The process was paused so that the apples and hands could be selected, and then the selection was inverted, with a large feathering setting of 22. This is easier than selecting everything apart from the hands and apples. Desaturation was again applied, but this time just to the selected area.

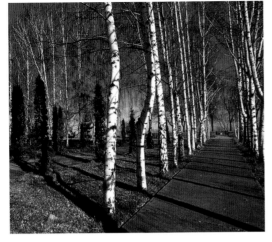
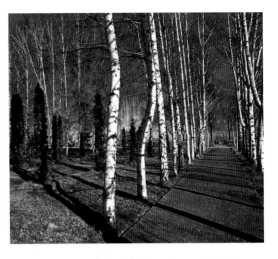

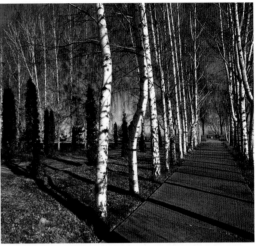

▲ Selective color

The original shot of a park in Kyrgyzstan (*above left*) was too colorful for the mood I wanted to convey. In preparation for a selective desaturation based on colorband, I first increased the blues to maximum saturation in one action by selecting blues in the Saturation sub-menu. Then I opened Saturation again and boosted yellows (in order to retain some color in the leaves on the ground and the distant trees in the final image). The result of these two increases produced a rather gaudy interpretation (*above right*). Normally, a 40 percent global desaturation would remove almost all visible color, but when that was applied to the prepared image, the strengthened colors could still be seen while others, such as greens, were removed (*right*).

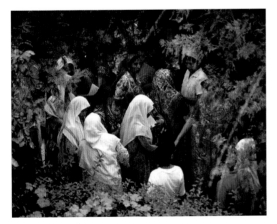
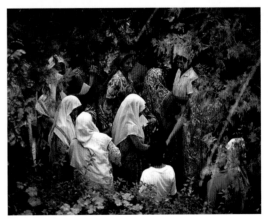

▲ Partial desaturation

The best way to desaturate the original highly colorful image (*above left*) was to use the Desaturation tool (also known as Sponge in the Desaturation mode), since it allowed the effects to be built up gradually and for precise strokes to be applied. Although the intention was to desaturate the trees completely, in order to emphasize the glorious colors of the women's clothes, as the strokes were applied it became clear that just a partial removal and toning down of the green would be more effective (*above right*). The image was finished off with a little burning-in to tone down the white clothing.

TINTS FROM COLOR ORIGINALS CONTINUED

Scenes that recall the past, such as this image of sheep herding in New Zealand, are ideal for soft tints that mimic the tonal and color rendering of color films of the past. For the easiest results, a filter created by analyzing the color, tonal, and grain characteristics of a specific color film can be applied to an image. Alternatively, as in this image, the greens and blues of the original full-color image can be reduced, and the picture overlaid with gold for a period-style glow.

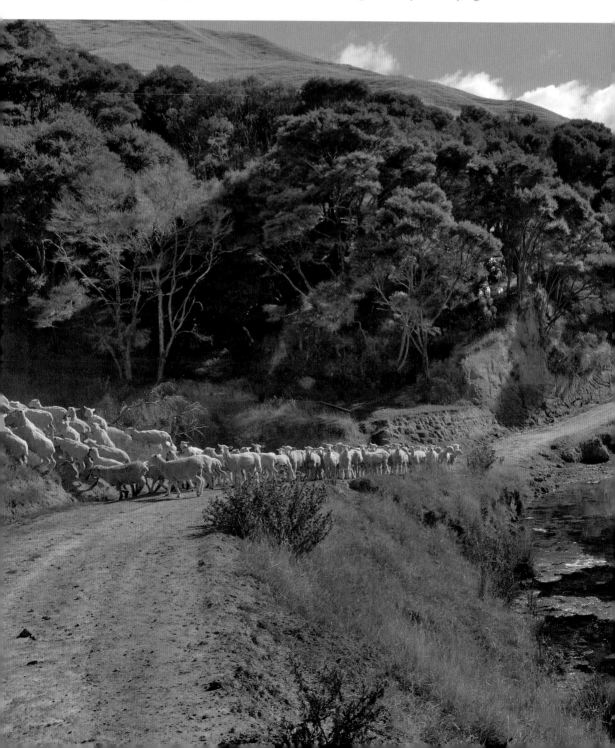

TECHNICAL INFO

CAMERA
Sony Alpha 900

LENS
Zeiss 24–70 mm f/2.8
at 70 mm

SETTINGS
ISO 100 • f/8 • ⅟₁₂₅ sec

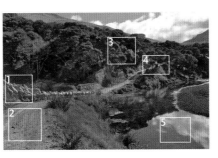

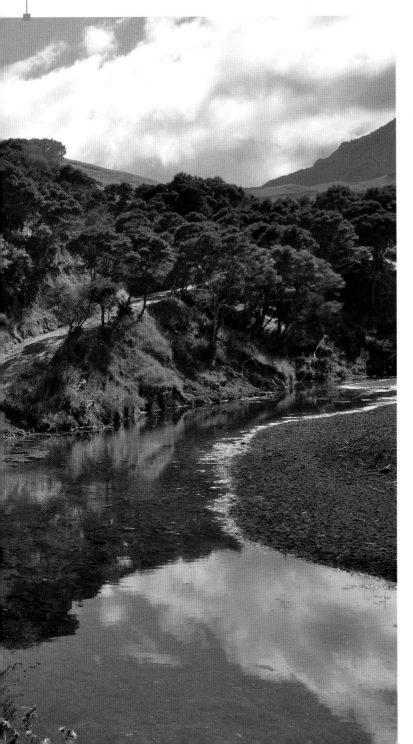

1 Exit stage right

The exit direction of the sheep tends to take attention to the left, out of the picture. This creates a tension because they are clearly avoiding the photographer standing in their path. This pastoral scene is not quite as peaceful as it may appear at first sight, which makes it more interesting than a country idyll.

2 Leading path

The path winds from the lower left-hand corner toward the upper right-hand corner, acting as a thread that holds the image together, a locus that is a reference for every other element. Its diagonal, climbing movement conveys more energy than a horizontal line would. Furthermore, as it winds away, it becomes narrower, thereby conveying the sense of receding distance.

3 Textured filler

This area is busy with tree forms, providing a counter to the static, flatter areas such as the water and bare hillside.

4 Clipped path

Vegetation overlapping the path helps define distances and also breaks up what would otherwise be an overly defined line, which would distract from the busy randomness of natural forms in the composition.

5 Calm waters

The overall mood of the image rests in the mirror-calm of the shallow summertime river. The water offers clear reflections of the hill, blue sky, and clouds, helping to establish the summeriness of the moment.

QUICK FIX BRIGHT LANDSCAPES

A landscape or city view in bright light or with a dramatic sky can look wonderful. Capturing the image calls for care in exposure control, as well as the best sensor technology, so you can be sure to capture the very wide range of exposures in the scene.

Problem: Skies in pictures are too bright, with little or no detail and lacking color. Or skies are well exposed, but the foreground is too dark. Either way, the tonal balance of the image is visually awry.

Analysis: The range of brightness on a sunny day means that the exposure for the brightest area detail may be more than 10 steps brighter than for the darkest area with detail. This range exceeds the capacity of all but the very best cameras, causing detail to be lost in either shadows or highlights, depending on the exposure used.

Solution: Many cameras offer features that balance exposures throughout the image in order to render both shadows and highlights well. These features are available only on JPEG images, not RAW.

If you are able to make only one exposure, you can use highlight and shadow controls in image-manipulation software to reduce brightness in highlighted areas and increase it in the shadows. Although they can be limited in effectiveness, these controls may be sufficient for your image. You may obtain the best results by recording in RAW format.

If you are able to, make three or more bracketing exposures (*see p. 76*), all identically framed—it is best to use a tripod for this. One should be exposed for the shadows, one for the highlights, and one for the mid-tone. Then open these files in an image-manipulation application that can merge them to ensure the whole image is made up largely of mid-tones. See also pp. 266–9.

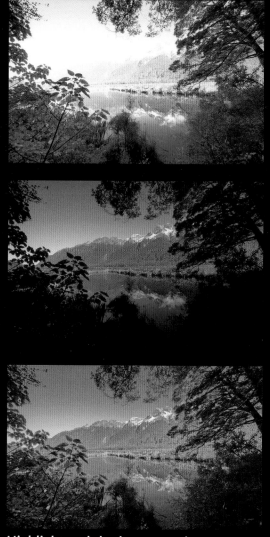

Highlight and shadow control

An exposure for the foreground (*top*) overexposes the background. Conversely, a beautifully rendered sky blackens the foreground (*middle*). We use this image because there is visible detail in the shadows. We apply a strong Shadow control to recover the color and tone in the dark leaves (*above*).

GRADUATED FILTERS

You can darken the sky by using a graduated filter; this is a filter that has the greatest density in its top half and becomes clearer toward the bottom. Adjust the position of the filter to suit the scene, then make a single exposure through the filter. For best results, you may use different density filters to match different scenes.

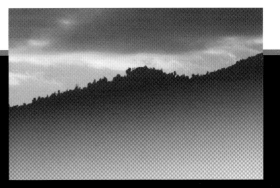

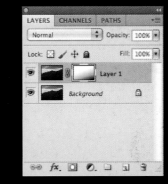

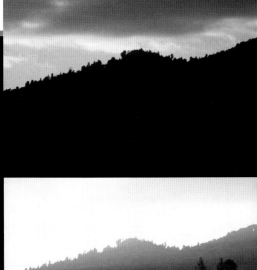

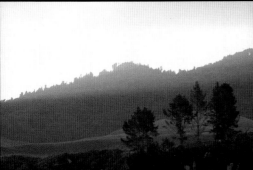

1 Masking overlays

The basis of this technique is to take two identically framed images—one exposed for the sky (*top*), the other exposed for the foreground (*above*)—and then composite them using a gradient or graduated mask to blend them smoothly. You need image-manipulation software that works with Layers and Masks (*see pp. 278–83*). This is easy for digital photographers but if you shoot on film, you can scan an original twice (once for highlights, once for shadows), ensuring the two are the same size, and copy one over to the other.

2 Making a gradient mask

Next, using the Layers control you have to create a gradient mask, which allows you to blend one image smoothly into the other (*top*). Notice that this entire image is slightly transparent: in other words, the whole image is masked but there is heavier masking in the lower half, as you can see in the dialog box (*above*). The overall effect of applying this mask is that the lower image will show through the top layer.

3 Final effect

Blending the two exposures and the mask produces an image that is closer to the visual experience than either original shot. This is because our eyes adjust when viewing a scene, with the pupil opening slightly when we look at darker areas and closing slightly when focusing on bright areas. A camera cannot adjust like this (although certain professional digital cameras can partly compensate). Image-manipulation techniques can thus help overcome limitations of the camera.

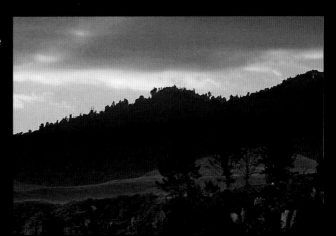

FILTER EFFECTS

One of the most alluring early advantages of digital photography was the ability to create fantastic visual effects at the touch of a button. These ranged from the visually dazzling to the faintly ridiculous. In time, it has become recognized that many special filter effects are solutions looking for visual problems. Filters are now, rightfully, part of a photographer's repertoire of techniques, but they are best reserved for a definite artistic objective. Therefore, it is important for a digital photographer to be familiar with the range of effects available in the software used.

Sharpness filters

The Sharpness filters are unlike other filters in that they are seldom used for special effects, but rather to improve the visual quality of the image by enhancing detail. They work by examining the edges of image detail: sharpening filters increase the brightness differences or contrast at these boundaries: the Unsharp Mask (USM) filter is an important tool for increasing image sharpness (*see pp. 196–9*).

Behind the scenes

Image filters are groups of repeated mathematical operations. Some work by focusing on small parts of an image at a time; others need to "see" the entire image at once. For example, the USM filter looks at blocks of up to 200 pixels square at a time, while Render loads the entire image into memory. A simple filter effect to understand is Mosaic. The filter takes a group of pixels, according to the size you set, and calculates their average value by adding them all and dividing by the number of pixels. It then gives all the pixels in the group the same value, so the pixels appear greatly enlarged. The filter then moves to the next set of pixels and repeats the operation. Most Mosaic filters can work on small image segments at a time, but some need to operate on the entire image for each calculation. These latter types require a great deal of computer memory and calculating power. Add all of these operations together and you obtain the pixelated effect of the Mosaic filter.

Distortion and Pixelate filters

Distortion filters change the shape of the contents of an image—either overall or small portions of it—by changing the relative positions of pixels, thus retaining overall color and tone. These can be very tricky to control and need to be used with moderation. Blur effects are similar to distortion except, of course, image detail is lost because the pixel data becomes mixed together. Pixelate filters, clumping pixels of similar color values into cells, represent another order of distortion.

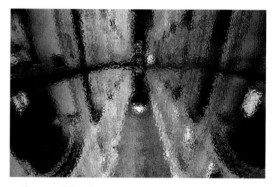

▲ **Ocean Ripple**
This filter adds randomly spaced ripples to the surface of the image so that it appears to be underwater. To make the effect more realistic, you can add surface reflections to separate the "water" from the image below the surface.

LEARNING TO USE FILTERS

- Practice on small files when experimenting with filter effects.
- Try the same filter on different styles of image to discover which filters work best on particular types of imagery.
- Filters often work best if applied to selected areas.
- Repeated applications of a filter can lead to unpredictable results.
- You usually need to adjust contrast and brightness after applying a filter.
- Reduce the image to its final size on screen to check the effect of filters.

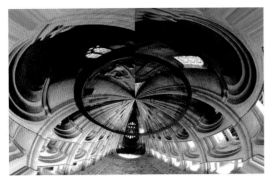

▲ Polar Coordinates

This extreme distortion is achieved by turning cartesian coordinates into polar coordinates, where positions are defined by their angle from a reference. The "anamorphic" result can produce surprising forms.

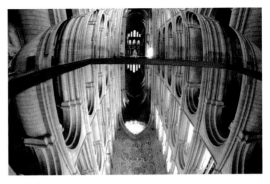

▲ Spherize

This imitates barrel, or pincushion, distortion, according to the setting. However, the effect is constrained by the canvas size, so to apply it over the entire image, you must first increase the canvas size, apply the filter, then crop.

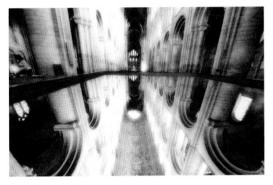

▲ Diffuse Glow

The effect of this filter is to render the image as though it were being viewed through a soft diffusion filter. The filter adds transparent white noise, with the glow fading from the center of the image or the center of a selection.

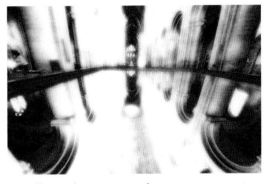

▲ Diffuse Glow repeated

A filter can be applied twice to an image for a cumulative effect. If the original effect is too weak, a second application can greatly improve it. Adjustments with Levels or Curves may still be needed, as here, to lighten the shadows.

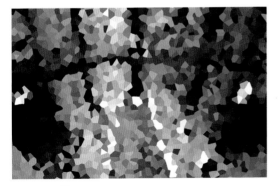

▲ Crystallize

The image is divided into areas, the size of which can be adjusted, then colored with the average of the hues within the area, creating clumps of even color. With limited color palettes, the effect can produce attractive abstracts.

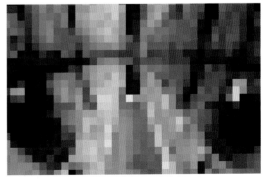

▲ Mosaic

This pixelate filter clumps the average colors together into squares of user-adjustable size. It appears to distort because the image boundaries are shifted when colors fill the large "pixels." This can be used to disguise detail in a selection.

FILTER EFFECTS CONTINUED

Artistic and Brush Strokes

Artistic filters in Photoshop, similarly to the artist brush effects in Corel Painter, simulate or replicate artists' materials. Effects such as colored pencils, charcoal drawing, or painting with dry or loaded brush strokes are available. They work by using the image information and combining it with local distortion effects programmed to mimic real artists' materials. Like the Artistic filters, the Brush Strokes filters give a painterly look using different brush- and ink-stroke effects, and the Sketch filters give similar effects but in monochrome.

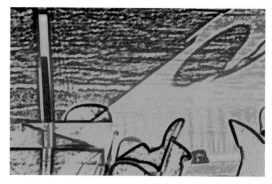

▲ Colored Pencil

In order to simulate a colored-pencil drawing, the boundaries of the main subject are given a rough crosshatch appearance, and the solid background color shows through the smoother areas with a texture resembling rough paper.

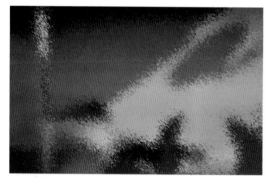

▲ Sprayed Strokes

This filter reduces an image to its essential shape. You can set the direction of the strokes, making it very versatile, but it often works best with low-contrast images. Here, the settings were: Stroke Length 6, Spray Radius 24, Left Diagonal.

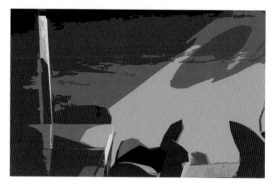

▲ Cutout

This filter quickly simplifies the image colors and shapes into blocks of uniform color based on averages taken over broad areas. Here, Levels were set to 5, with Edge Simplicity set to a medium 6, and Edge Fidelity to 2.

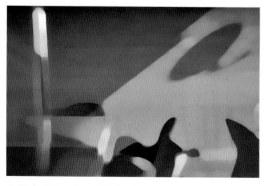

▲ Paint Daubs—Wide Sharp

Brush Size set to the maximum of 50 and Sharpness set to the minimum of 0 gives this edge-corrected blur, where the outlines of the image are recognized and their sharpness is preserved, but other details are blurred out.

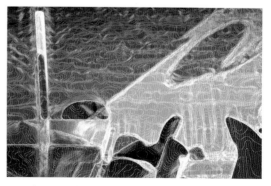

▲ Paint Daubs—Sparkle

Much more than mere daubing of paint, this filter adds false contour lines partially related to the underlying luminosity. It gives pleasing effects when the Brush Tips is set to Sparkle. Here, the settings were: Brush Size 26, Sharpness 32.

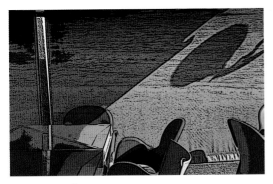

▲ Poster Edges

Giving a passably good imitation of comic-book or cartoon illustration, this filter exaggerates any texture and also outlines the edges of the image. For this result, Edge Thickness was set to 6, Edge Intensity to 5, and Posterization to 1.

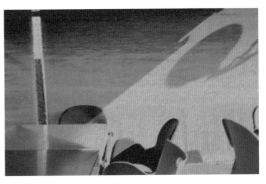

▲ Chalk & Charcoal

This filter readily produces images that are quite convincing in texture and tonality. It works well even with detailed originals. The Charcoal Area was set to a medium 8, the Chalk Area to a high 15, and the Stroke Pressure to the minimum of 0.

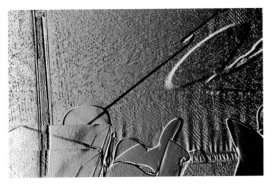

▲ Bas Relief

This filter raises a relief pattern on the image according to luminosity values. It can be very useful when combined with the original image, using Layers. Here, the Detail was set to 13, Smoothness to 3, with the Light coming from the left.

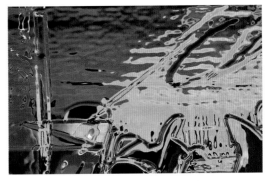

▲ Chrome

This filter applies a Liquify to the image, guided by local luminosity, so the areas with the greatest number of ripples are those with sharp luminosity gradients. Here, Detail was set to 3, and Smoothness to the maximum of 10.

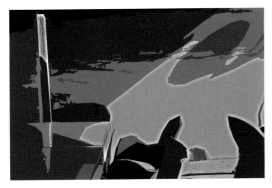

▲ Neon Glow

Effective for adding glowing edges to objects, this filter is useful for colorizing an image while softening its look. In Photoshop, the glow color can be selected from the Color Picker that is presented in the Filter Gallery.

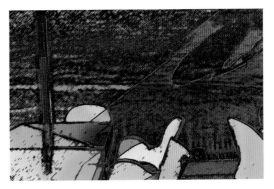

▲ Charcoal plus Difference mode

This image shows the result of applying the Charcoal filter to the original image, then merging it with a copy of the original, using the blend mode (*see p. 281*) set to Difference. (*See also Multiplying filter effects, pp. 264–5.*)

FILTER EFFECTS CONTINUED

Render, Stylize, and Texture

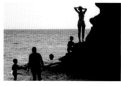

Render and Stylize filters simulate lighting effects in a scene, while Texture filters appear to raise the surface of an image to give it depth or an organic feel. All the filters in these families make heavy demands on the computer, and you may find large files take longer than usual to render. After using filters such as Find Edges and Trace Contour, which highlight edges, you can apply the Invert command to outline the edges of an image with colored lines or to outline the edges of a grayscale image with white lines.

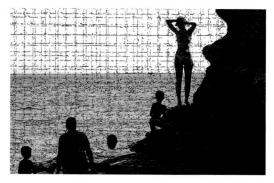

▲ Craquelure

This filter combines a texture change that replicates the cracks of an old oil painting with a little lighting effect. The image results from setting a low Spacing of 15, an average Crack Depth of 6, and a high setting for Crack Brightness, at 9.

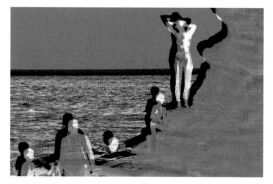

▲ Emboss

The Emboss filter can be effective for dramatic transformations of geometric shapes, its gray mask being helpful for further effects. Here, strong settings were used for all parameters: Angle -49°, Height 43 pixels, Amount 98%.

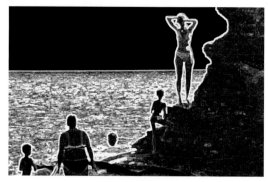

▲ Glowing Edges

While this is most obvious on large-scale boundaries, such as the rock, it also works on small-scale boundaries, dramatically changing the sea's color. Here, the settings used were: Edge Width 3, Edge Brightness 17, and Smoothness 4.

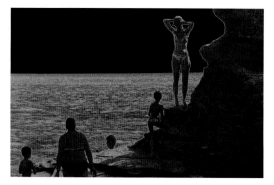

▲ Solarize

This reverses both tones and colors. It usually causes a drop in overall contrast and saturation because we prefer our images slightly darker than mid-tone. After application, it is usual to return contrast and saturation to normal levels.

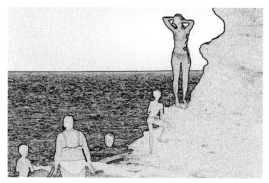

▲ Find Edges

Filters that define edges work at all scales of the image, so while their effect is predictable with large-scale boundaries, the surprises come with high-frequency, small-scale detail. Here, the sea is textured, while the figures are clearly outlined.

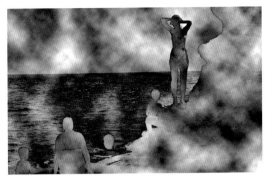

▲ Difference Clouds

Used alone, the Clouds filter randomizes luminance data to completely obscure image detail. The Difference Clouds filter combines Clouds with the Difference blend mode in one step. The results are unpredictable and often surprisingly good.

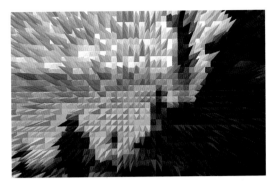

▲ Extrude

This is worth exploring for the strange effects it produces. You can define the type and size of extrusions and whether their depth is dependent or random. For this, Pyramids were chosen at a Size of 30 pixels, Depth of 30, and Random.

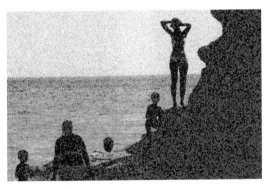

▲ Grain–Clumped

The Grain filter offers many different effects, or Grain Types, of which perhaps the most useful is Clumped. It appears similar to film grain and is a passable substitute. (For true film-grain simulation, use specific software such as DxO FilmPack.)

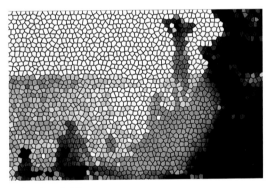

▲ Stained Glass

This filter is useful for defining the scale of important detail, and it also simplifies the color scheme. Adjust the size of the cells until they retain key subject detail. Here, the settings were: Cell Size 10, Border Thickness 4, and Light Intensity 3.

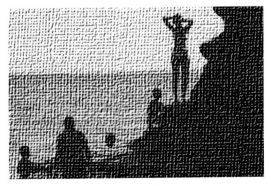

▲ Texturizer–Canvas

Another very useful filter is Texturizer. In Photoshop it offers four different textures, plus controls over the scale and relief, as well as the direction of lighting. The Canvas texture gives a good simulation of printing on canvas surfaces.

MULTIPLYING EFFECTS

To increase further the potential of filters:
- Apply filters to individual layers or several layers to build up the effects, altering blend modes as you go.
- Apply a sequence of different filters, then use the History Brush to blend the results.
- Apply filters to individual color channels with different settings for each.
- Create filter effects using Smart Filter to keep the filter effect editable for future alterations.
- Use masks or selections on layers to blend effects.
- Apply a filter to unrelated images to create a set.

MULTIPLYING FILTER EFFECTS

Filter effects have the overall effect of obscuring image details and outlines because they add textures or blur details directly (apart from the Sharpen filters, of course). The practical consequence is that the best images for use with filter effects are those with clear, simple shapes and good tonal contrasts—a landscape with trees or the silhouette of a building, for instance, or a leaf with an interesting shape. While the effects of filters on whole images are dramatic, as soon as you apply them selectively, the potential of the technique is multiplied many times.

If you have software, such as Adobe Photoshop, that allows editable filters to be applied, use them. This may slow down your working, but it allows you to adjust the settings to fine-tune results once you have designed the overall scheme of effects. Otherwise, save the various versions of your images as you experiment so that you can return to them if you decide you went too far when applying effects. You can always delete unwanted versions at the end of your project.

You can also work with filters applied to multiple layers and alter their blend modes (see pp. 278–83). This opens up your image-making to an infinite number of effects. To avoid being confused by all the choice, first learn your way around the filter effects, so that you can visualize their impact before applying any of them; then familiarize yourself with layer blend modes.

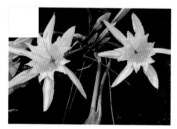

▲ Original image
In this image of dune lilies the flowers are well outlined, but the leaves are something of a distraction. By using filters, it is possible to separate out the different elements and bring the flowers to the fore.

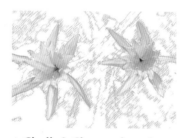

▲ Chalk & Charcoal + others
Cumulative filter effects are not always bold. Here, the combination of Chalk & Charcoal (which reduces contrast and color) with Sumi-e and Spatter (both of which also randomize detail) results in a minimal, high-key look.

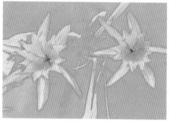

▲ Neon Glow
The flowers were first separated from the background using the Color Range control, then the selection was inverted. When Neon Glow was applied to the selected area—the background—a warmly high-key result was produced.

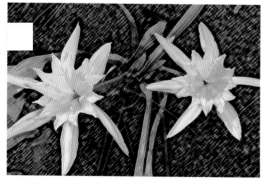

▲ Colored Pencil background
Going for minimal and moderate change, you can select the background and apply an Artistic or Brush Strokes type of filter to retain some original texture without large-scale alteration of color or exposure, as seen here with Colored Pencil applied.

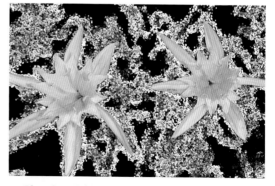

▲ Glowing Edges and Glass Spatter
With the flowers left out of the selection, the background was given two filter treatments. Glowing Edges increased contrast and color, while combining Glass and Spatter broke up the details into irregular clumps of color that contrast with the delicate lily petals.

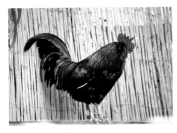

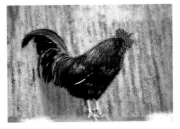

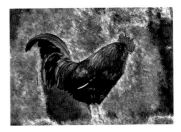

▲ Original image
This image of a cockerel was not sharp, but that does not matter, since the image will have filters applied that disrupt detail. To isolate the cockerel, it is easier to select it then invert the selection, so that the filter effects apply only to the background.

▲ Three filters together
The cockerel was first separated from his background, then three filters—Film Grain, Glass, and Spatter—were applied one on top of the other. The result retains the color but alters the overall texture of the background, and details of the background, to bring out the cockerel.

▲ Five filters together
With the cockerel separated out, five filters were applied to leave him unaffected. The result of any five-filter combination is hard to predict, but that is part of the fun. This used Glass, Glowing Edges, Chalk & Charcoal, Sprayed Strokes, and Angled Strokes.

CUMULATIVE FILTER EFFECTS

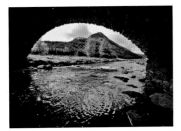

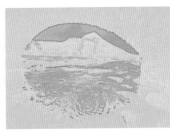

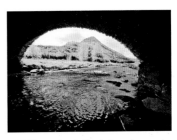

1 Original image
Let's suppose we decide to do something radical to this landscape. Taking inspiration from its composition and lighting, we will give the landscape a warm glow and bring some light into the dark area under the bridge.

2 Neon Glow
First, we duplicate the background layer, then select the new layer and apply Neon Glow. This fills dark areas with the color that is complementary to the purplish glow color. At the same time, it blurs image boundaries.

3 Soft Light blend mode
To blend the luminance of our source layer with the underlying layer, we experiment with the Overlay group blend modes. Soft Light looks best, but the main part of the image is too bright and has lost shadow detail.

4 Soft Light textured
We apply a mask to allow the Neon Glow layer to blend only with the underside of the bridge, with just a light effect on the main part of the landscape. We then texture the Neon Glow layer with a canvas surface to give it some "tooth" and adjust the final tonal balance using Levels.

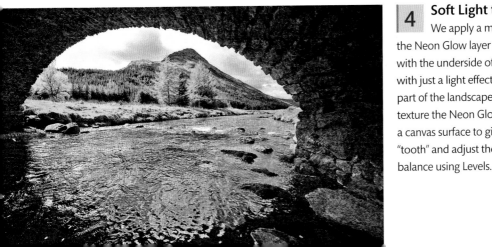

HIGH DYNAMIC RANGE

The dynamic range of a scene is the difference in brightness between its lightest (or brightest) part and the darkest (or blackest) shadow; formerly it was known as the scene luminance range. Dynamic range is high relative to the recording method we use: we say it is "high" where the scene's range of brightness is too large to record all the details we want, given the equipment being used. For this reason, a scene in which the dynamic range is "high" to a camera phone could be easily accommodated by a large-sensor SLR camera.

Capture range

Typical high-dynamic range (HDR) scenes are, for example, a landscape that contains bright sky or sun with deep shadows under trees, or a portrait by a window in which we wish to record skin tones in shadow as well as the sunlit garden beyond.

One way to consider a scene in which the dynamic range exceeds the recording capacity of our equipment is that the bright parts need one exposure setting, such as f/22 at 1/60 sec, while the darker parts need another, say f/2 at 1/15 sec. A full range of tones can be captured by blending two or more different exposures: one correctly exposed for the lower mid-tones and one for the upper high tones. There are various HDR techniques available, which calculate the blending in different ways, but the majority of "HDR images" are created through tone mapping. This compresses the range of tones

into the compass of a normal monitor or print image. At the same time, details can be smoothed, saturation raised, and curves adjusted to create an attractive image. These can range from the realistic in appearance to images that are strongly painterly, with bold colors expressed in only mid-tones.

HOW TO TONE MAP

To create tone-mapped images, you need to take a series of shots at different exposures that cover the dynamic range, without moving the camera between each. Note that tone mappping works best on static subjects.

- Set the exposure mode to Aperture Priority: this ensures there are no changes in focus or depth of field with each exposure.
- Lock the camera on a tripod, rest it on a stable surface, or turn on image stabilization.
- Set the camera to bracket exposures: best results come from making more exposures (5 is ideal, 3 is the minimum for good results), and having smaller differences between exposures (1 stop differences are better than 3 stops).
- Make the bracketing exposures: wait for a still moment when there is no wind or movement.
- Open the set of images in software such as Photomatix or Photoshop (File > Automate > Merge to HDR), and blend your images.
- Experiment with using different settings.

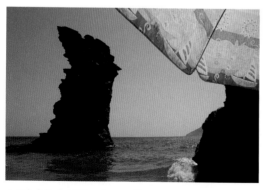

▲ Highlight/Shadow effect
By using controls that bring out shadow and highlight details, you can simulate the appearance of HDR; indeed, these controls work by compressing an

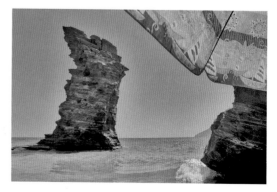

image's tonal range. However, the effect usually looks unnatural and is further marred by halos around the subject (*above*).

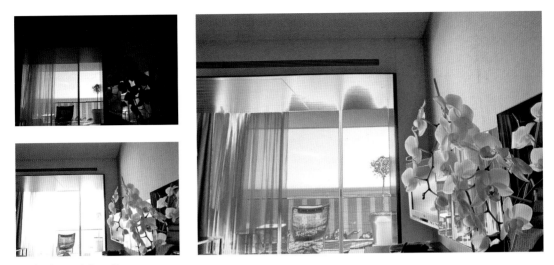

▲ Limits to blending

A raw image of an unlit room taking in the sunny view outside can be darkened to bring color to the window (*top left*), while another version may be lightened to bring out detail in the flowers in the foreground

(*above left*). Blending the images using Blend Options (*see p. 244*) partially succeeds (*above*), but transitional mid-tone areas, such as those around the window, are not well blended.

MERGE TO HDR

This shot of two friends by the sea originally came out as a silhouette, with poor details in the shadows. I wanted to retain some feeling for the silhouette, but extract some shadow detail, too. From the RAW file, I made some versions that darkened the bright light on the sea, and some that opened up the shadows. In Merge to HDR, the best result was from the Exposure and Gamma option. A little adjustment in Levels improved the overall contrast (*see below*).

In Photoshop, Merge to HDR offers four different algorithms for combining images: the "best" option depends on the characteristics of your image. In most cases, Exposure and Gamma is the most useful, and it offers fine-tuning controls that are not available in the other methods. Local Adaptations produces highly graphic results and offers radius-based fine-tuning.

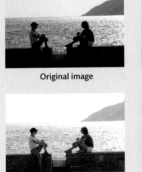

Original image

Underexposed 1 stop

Overexposed 1 stop

Underexposed 2 stops

Equalize Histogram

Exposure and Gamma

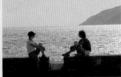

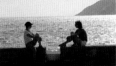

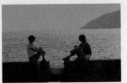

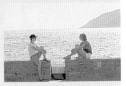

Highlight Compression

Local Adaptations

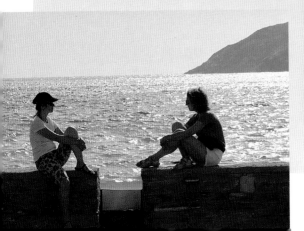

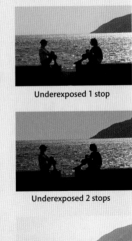

Constructured tones
Tone-mapped to ensure all tones approximate to mid-tone, the blending of images of moving waves adds a unique swirling blur to the rendering of the troubled seas.

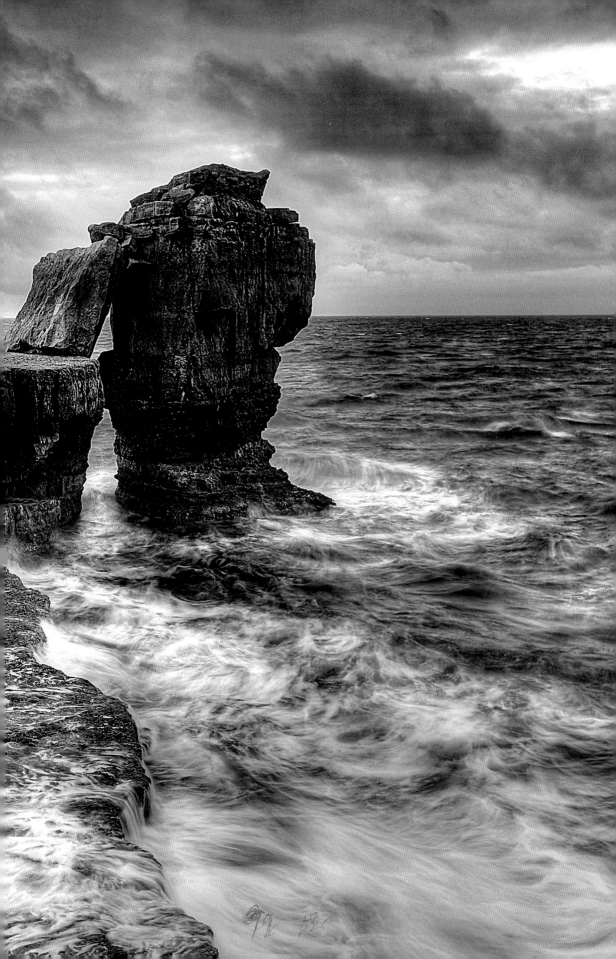

SELECTING PIXELS

There are two methods of localizing the action of an image-manipulation effect. The direct way is to use a tool that applies the effect to a limited area, such as the Dodge tool or any Brush. The other method is to first select an area or certain pixels within the image, then apply the effect. This ensures that only the selected pixels will be affected. Selection is founded on a continuous boundary of difference between two areas. This means that, with a bit of guidance from you, the software can compute the rest.

Masks and selections

It is important to understand that fundamentally there are two different ways of applying effects to a limited area of an image. Both define the areas that you can edit or in which you can apply an effect: these are called editable areas. A mask works by protecting an area from an effect—like an umbrella keeping you dry while all else gets rained on.

A selection does the opposite: it limits an action to the area it encloses—like watering only on a flower bed but not outside it.

There are also other differences. First, a selection is essentially a temporary mask—it disappears as soon as you click outside the selected area (some programs allow you to save a selection, to reapply it later or to use it on another image). If it can be saved for reuse, it is known as an alpha channel (technically a mask). Second, in software with Layers, the selection applies to any layer that is active. Third, you can copy and move selected pixels—something that cannot be done with a mask. In practice you will switch frequently between masks and selections.

Selections

A selection defines the border of the editable area, usually by showing a line of "marching ants" or moving dots. In fact the line joins the mid-points

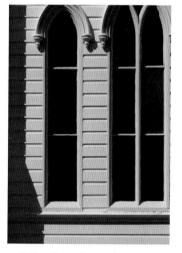

▲ **Selecting clean shapes**
This view of a church in New Zealand shows the clean lines of the wooden windows, but they look too dark and colorless. In order to make the windows lighter, but without affecting the pale wooden walls, we need to select the windows individually.

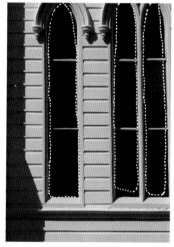

▲ **Making a selection**
Using Photoshop's Lasso, with a feathering width set to 11 pixels, I selected the dark glass within the window frames. To start a new area to be selected, hold down the Command key (for Macs) or the Control key (for PCs)—the selected area is defined by moving dashes, known as "marching ants." When the Levels command is invoked, settings are applied only to the selections.

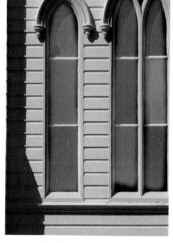

▲ **Final effect**
In some circumstances, the somewhat uneven result of using the Lasso selection can produce more realism than a perfectly clean selection would give. The dark areas remaining toward the bottom of the right-hand windows correspond to the area omitted from the selection in the previous image (*above left*).

← 97, 136, 146, 2cd

between pixels that are wholly selected and those that are fully ignored—others lie on a transitional zone, which is known as the "feather" region. It follows that selections are most accurate when the feather region is not wider than a few pixels; with a wide feather region it becomes difficult to know exactly where the editable area starts and stops. An important option is the ability to partially select a pixel near the edge of a selection. This is called "feathering." It creates a gradual transition across the boundary from pixels that are fully selected, through those that are partially selected, to those that are unselected, thus smoothing out the effect you apply. A feathering of 0 means that the transition will be abrupt; more than 1 pixel will give a more gradual transition. Note that the effect of increased feathering is to smooth out any sharp angles in the selection.

The appropriate feather setting depends on the subject and type of selection you want. Cleanly bounded subjects, such as buildings against the sky or a figure against a white background, benefit from a narrow feather range. On the other hand, a wide feathering suits images with blurred outlines due to limited depth of field.

Quick mask

When you make a selection it is very useful to be able to judge its effect—to see what has been blocked out and what is left in. The quick mask mode, available in many applications, switches between showing the selection and showing the equivalent mask—usually as a red overlay. In this mode, you can adjust the mask by erasing parts you wish the selection to reach, or painting to increase the reach of the selection.

Make a choice

There are two fundamentally different ways of making selections. Some, like the Lasso or Marquee

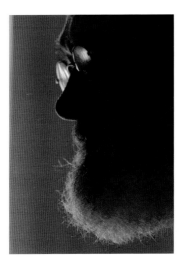

▲ **Selecting irregular shapes**
This back-lit portrait is rather harshly lit by the open window, although the darkness behind the curtains softly rim-lights the face. Clearly, removing the face from the background will be a challenge because of the man's beard.

▲ **Quick selection**
The Quick Selection tool in Photoshop selected the head swiftly, but as the darkness at the top blended into the background, the selection extended too far, so had to be reduced. Then, zooming in, a small Brush was used to apply Quick Selection to individual hairs. In Quick Mask mode you can see that the background will be removed so we can apply the face to a different background.

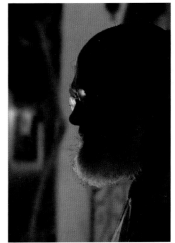

▲ **Layer over**
When you have masked away the original background, you are free to apply any other image as the background. An alley in Greece at night was chosen, as the lighting matches that of the portrait yet provides a much softer backdrop—one which makes the most of the sparkle in the eyeglasses.

SELECTING PIXELS CONTINUED

tool, indiscriminately gather up all the pixels within the area they define, taking no account of pixel values. On the other hand, value-sensitive selections, such as Magic Wand or Color Range, look at values and the location of pixels—for example, whether they are touching similar pixels or not—when calculating the selection.

The basic Lasso tool is best for selecting disparate areas with different colors and exposure. Where you have clearly defined objects that are distinguished by color and exposure from the background, Magnetic Lasso or the equivalent, is a good choice. If you need to select irregular areas with straight-line borders, the Polygonal Lasso is the obvious tool.

Tools that select like pixels include the Magic Wand tool; you can click directly on the image to select pixels that are similar to the sampled area. With the Color Range command you click on a preview to select all related pixels. The control is useful for locating out-of-gamut colors in order to bring them into gamut. More sophisticated tools can select pixels by computing their degree of similarity, which can give excellent results even for the unskilled.

Computed choice

Some boundaries are extremely complicated or subtle, or both, with hair and glass commonly regarded the trickiest subjects. Tools in software such as Topax Remask and Adobe Photoshop have eased the problem. All work by first defining a transition region, such as the edge of a wine glass. Then you define the region to keep and the region to cut. The boundaries do not have to be drawn with great precision, but the tighter and more accurately drawn the transition area—so that unwanted colors are not included—the more accurate the selection will be. The software then computes the mask to apply; the best create soft and hard edges as demanded by the image.

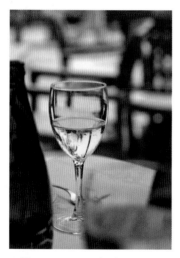

▲ **Transparent choice**
A wine-glass of water presents the paradox of a transparent edge. Color shows through the glass, but if we want to add another glass to the table we do not want to lose the edge. A combination of personal judgement and computation will be needed.

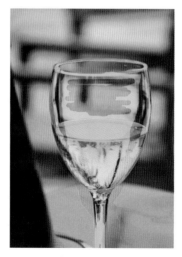

▲ **Remasking**
Using a masking plug-in such as Remask (illustrated) or Perfect Mask takes several stages. After defining the transition area—the areas to keep and areas to lose—you need to refine it. Here, parts of the glass will be lost (red) but other parts will be kept. The transition area is not perfect but computation will clean it up.

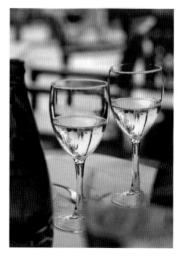

▲ **Double or dare**
The masked image is placed on a layer over the original, so it can be moved easily. Here, it was moved to occupy the empty space, the water was turned to wine with a brush loaded with yellow, and the glass was made a bit smaller than the original as it is a little further away.

HINTS AND TIPS

- Learn about the different ways of making a selection. Some are obvious, such as the Lasso or Marquee tool, but your software may have other less-obvious methods, such as Color Range in Photoshop, which selects a band of colors according to the sample you choose.

- Use feathered selections unless you are confident you do not need to blur the boundaries. A moderate width of around 10 pixels is a good start for most images. But adjust the feathering to suit the task. For a vignetted effect, use very wide feathering, but if you are trying to separate an object from its background, then very little feathering produces the cleanest results. Set the feathering before making a selection.

- Note that the feathering of a selection tends to smooth out the outline: sudden changes in the direction of the boundary are rounded off. For example, a wide feathering setting to a rectangular selection will give it radiused corners.

- The selected area is marked by a graphic device called "marching ants"—a broken line that looks like a column of ants trekking across your monitor screen: it can be very distracting. On many applications you can turn this off or hide it without losing the selection: it is worth learning how to hide the "ants."

- In most software, after you have made an initial selection you can add to or subtract from it by using the selection tool and holding down an appropriate key. Learning the method provided by your software will save you the time and effort of having to start the selection process all over again every time you want to make a change.

- Examine your selection at high magnification for any fragments left with unnatural-looking edges. Clean these up using an Eraser or Blur tool.

- Making selections is easier to control with a graphics tablet (*see p. 358*) rather than using a mouse.

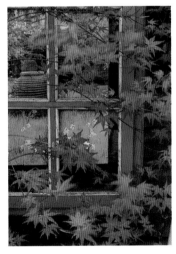

▲ Selecting like colors

The brilliant red leaves of this Japanese maple seem to invite being separated out from their background. However, any selection methods based on outlining with a tool would obviously demand a maddening amount of painstaking effort. You could use the Magic Wand tool but a control such as Color Range (*right*) is far more powerful and adaptable.

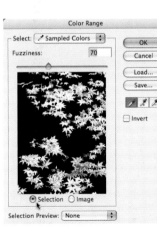

▲ Color Range screen shot

In Photoshop, you can add to the colors selected via the Eye-dropper tool by using the plus sign, or by clicking the Eye-dropper tool with a minus sign (beneath the Save button). However, you can refine the colors selected. The Fuzziness slider also controls the range of colors selected. A medium-high setting ensures that you take in pixels at the edge of the leaves, which will not be fully red.

▲ Manipulated image

Having set the parameters in the Color Range dialog box (*above left*), clicking "OK" selects the colors—in this case, just the red leaves. By inverting the selection, you then erase all but the red leaves, leaving you with a result like that shown here. Such an image can be stored in your library to be composited into another image or used as a lively background in another composition.

MASKS

Masks allow you to isolate areas of an image from color changes or filter effects applied to the rest of the image. Unlike real-life masks, digital types are very versatile: you can, for example, alter a mask's opacity so that its effects taper off allowing you to see more or less clearly through it. Using image-manipulation software you can alter a mask until you are satisfied with it and then save it for reuse. When you do so, you create what are known as "alpha channels," which can be converted back to selections. Technically, masks are 8-bit grayscale channels—just like the channels representing the colors—so you can edit them using the usual array of painting and editing tools.

If your software does not offer masks, don't worry—it is possible to carry out a good deal of work by the use of selections. But remember that selections are inclusive—they show what will be included in a change; masks work the opposite way, by excluding pixels from an applied effect.

Software takes two approaches to creating masks. First is Photoshop's Quick-mask, which gives direct control and allows you to see the effect of any transitional zones. Or, you can create a selection that is turned into a mask. This is quick, but transitional zones cannot be assessed.

Quick-mask

In Photoshop and Photoshop Elements you hit the Q key to enter Quick-mask mode. You then paint on the layer and hit Q again to exit, but in the process, you turn the painted area into a selection. You can also invert your selection (select the pixels you did not first select)—sometimes it is easier to select an area such as bright sky behind a silhouette by selecting the silhouette and then inverting the selection. You then turn the selection into a mask by adding a layer mask.

The layer mask makes all the underlying pixels disappear, unless you tell it to leave some alone. When applying a layer mask, you can choose to mask the selected area or mask all but the selected area. The advantage of Quick-mask is that it is often easier to judge the effect of the painted area than it is to make many selections. It also means that an accidental click of the mouse outside a selection does not cancel your work—it simply adds to the mask. Use Quick-masking when you have many elements to mask out at once.

Turning selections into masks

Some methods of selecting pixels have already been discussed (*see pp. 270–3*). If you need a sharp-

USING QUICK MASK

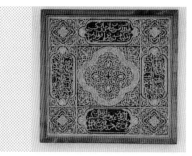

1 Bottom layer
Quick-mask, or any method where you "paint" the mask, is best when you are not attempting to enclose a clearly defined shape, such as a person's silhouette. It is best first to place the image that will be revealed under the mask—here, an Islamic painting.

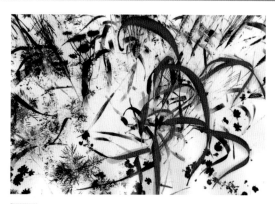

2 Creating the mask
Next, the mask is applied to the main leaves in this negative image. The red color shows where the freehand masking will be created. When it is turned into a mask, this is the area that will allow the base image to show through.

edged selection whose scale you can change without losing crispness of line, then you need to create a clipping path.

Although almost anything you can do with masks you can do with selections, it is convenient to turn a selection into a mask as it is then easier to store and reuse—even for other images. It is good practice to turn any selection you make into a mask (just in case you wish to reuse it), particularly if it took a long time to create.

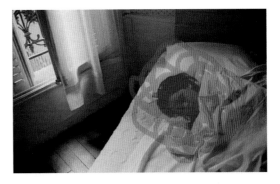

ALPHA CHANNELS

Alpha channels are selections stored as masks in the form of grayscale images. The convention is that fully selected areas appear as white, nonselected areas are shown black, while partially selected areas appear as proportionate shades of gray. In effect, an alpha channel is just like a color channel, but instead of providing color it hides some pixels and allows others to be visible. An alpha channel can be turned into a selection by "loading" the selection for that channel. The term "alpha" refers to a variable in an equation defining the blending of one layer with another.

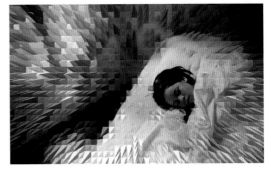

▲ Limiting filter effects
Here (*top*), the mask "protects" the child's face from the effect of the Stylize/Extrude filter. Note that when you turn the painted area into the selection, the mask would be applied only to that selection, so you have to invert the selection to take in everything but the face. When the filter was applied (*above*), it worked only on the pixels that were not protected.

3 **Quick-mask Layers screen shot**
This dialog box shows that the painting forms the bottom layer (but not the background, as masks cannot be applied to the background). The top layer consists of the grass and, to the right, the mask is also shown.

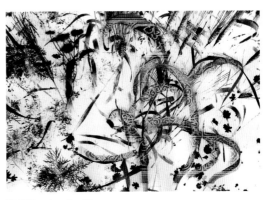

4 **Final effect**
You can move the underlying image around until you are happy with the results— in other words, when the most effective areas are showing through within the areas defined by the masking.

QUICK FIX REMOVING BACKGROUNDS

One of the most common image-manipulation tasks is the elimination of backgrounds. There are two main methods: one is to remove the background directly by erasing it (which is time-consuming); the other is to hide it under a mask.

Problem: The main problem is how to separate a foreground object from its background while retaining fine edge detail, such as hair, or maintain the transparency of a wine glass and retain shadows and blurred edges.

Analysis: Almost all edges in images are slightly soft or fuzzy—it is more the transitions in color and brightness that define edges. If a transition is more sudden and obvious than others in the locality, it is seen as an edge. If you select the foreground in such a way as to make all its edges sharp and well defined, it will appear artificial and "cut-out." However, much depends on the final size of the foreground: if it is to be used small and hidden by a lot of other detail, you can afford a little inaccuracy in the selection. If not, you must work more carefully.

Solution: Make selections with edge transitions that are appropriate to the subject being extracted. The usual selection methods—Lasso or Magic Wand—are sufficient most of the time, but complicated subjects will need special tools, such as Corel KnockOut, Extensis Mask Professional, or the Extract Image command in Photoshop.

HOW TO AVOID THE PROBLEM

With objects you expect to separate out, it is best to work with a plain backdrop. However, while a white or black background is preferable to a varied one, even better is a colored ground. The aim is to choose a color that does not appear anywhere on the subject—if your subject is blond, has tanned skin, and is wearing yellow, a blue backdrop is perfect. Avoid using rimlighting, as this imparts a light-colored fringe to the subject. In addition, avoid subject-movement blur and try to keep an extended depth of field so that any detail, such as hair behind the subject's head, is not soft or fuzzy.

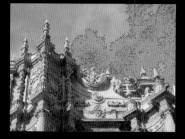

▲ Low tolerance

With simple tasks, such as removing the sky from this image, the Magic Wand or similar tool, which selects pixels according to their color and is available in almost all image-manipulation software, is quick to use. It has just one control—the tolerance—which allows you to set the range of colors to be selected. If you set too low a tolerance (here the setting was 22) you obtain a result in which only a part of the sky is selected, seen by the marching ants occupying just the right-hand portion of the sky and small, isolated groups.

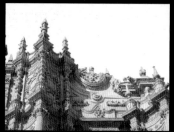

▲ Removing the sky

Adjusting the tolerance setting in small, incremental steps allows you to see when you have captured just the right area to be removed. Then, pressing "OK" removes your selection. The edges of the selection may be hard to see in a small image, but are clearly visible on a large monitor screen.

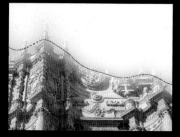

▲ High tolerance

If you set too high a tolerance, you will capture parts of the building where it meets the sky. Here, notice the result of setting a large feathering (111 pixels) to the selection—pixels a long way either side of a target pixel are chosen. As a result, the selection is smoothed out and the boundary is very fuzzy.

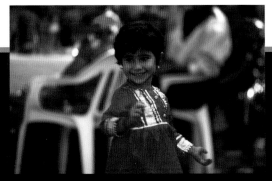

1 Original image
This original image of a young Afghan girl—an expert carpet weaver—shows her taking to the floor to dance. Unfortunately, the distracting background does not add to the image as a whole.

2 Defining fore- and background
Using Corel KnockOut, I drew inside the girl's outline to define the foreground and then outside it to define the background. Between is the transition area that allows soft boundaries to be smoothly masked.

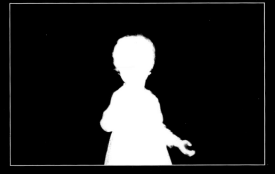

3 Making the mask
Using the information from step 2, a mask was created. This outlines the foreground and hides the background: the black shows the hidden area and the white where the image will show through.

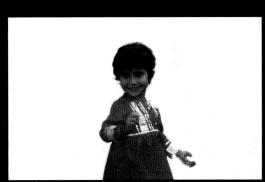

4 Knocking out the background
Now, while the mask hides part of the image on its own layer, it does not affect images on another layer (below left). Therefore, if you place an image behind the mask, you will see that image appear.

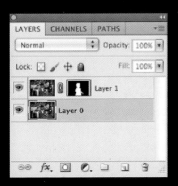

5 Layers screen shot
The Layers dialog box shows the girl and the associated mask lying over the introduced image. Because the mask was produced by extracting the girl, the original background is gone, awaiting a new background image to be introduced.

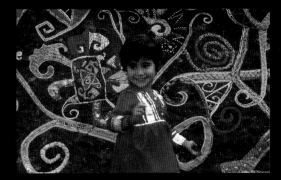

6 Masked combination
The background was lightened to tone in with the colors of the girl. The mask has preserved the softness of her outline, and now she appears to be in front of the wall-hanging. An extra refinement may be to soften the background so that it appears less sharp.

LAYER BLEND MODES

The "layers" metaphor is fundamental to many software applications, such as desktop publishing, video animation, and digital photography. The idea is that images are "laid" on top of each other, though the order is interchangeable. Think of layers as a stack of acetate sheets with images; where the layer is transparent, you see through to the one below. However, not all software layers have the same resolution, start with the same number of channels, or have the same image mode. The final image depends on how layers blend or merge when they are "flattened," or combined, for final output. Before then, however, they allow you to make changes without altering the original data, while each remains independent of the others.

Color as layers

A key point to remember is that the basic color image is comprised of red, green, and blue layers—normally called channels. In essence, the terms "layers" and "channels" are interchangeable. Masks, too, are channels, as they work with a layer to affect the appearance of an underlying layer.

By analogy, if you see a face through a layer of misted glass it looks soft or diffused. Now, if you clean off part of the glass, the portion of face lying directly under the cleaned-off area becomes clearly visible, without being obscured as it is under other parts of the glass. So the glass is a layer over the underlying layer—the face—and by doing something to part of it, but not the whole, you have applied a mask, which is, in effect, another layer.

Using layers

The main use for layers (also known as "objects" or "floaters" in some applications) is to arrange composite images—those made up of two or more separately obtained images. You can place images on top of one another—varying the order in which they lie; duplicate smaller images and place them around the canvas to create a new image; or change the size of the individual components or distort them at will. At the same time, the ways in which one layer interacts or blends with the underlying layer—known as the blend modes—can also be altered. Finally, you can control the transparency or opacity of the layers, too—from high opacity for full effect (or low transparency), to barely visible, when you set a high transparency (or low opacity).

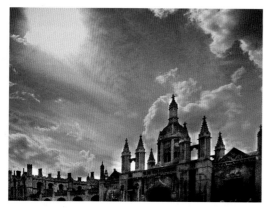

▲ **Original 1**
The dreamy spires of a Cambridge college in England offer the clean clarity of shape and line that are ideal for work with superimposing images. The actively clouded sky also adds variety without too much detail. Prior to use, the image had its colors strengthened by increasing saturation and the towers were straightened so that they did not lean backwards.

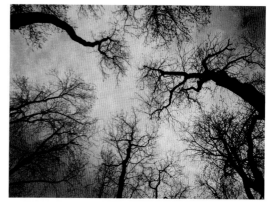

▲ **Original 2**
The outline of wintry trees in France provides fascinatingly complicated silhouettes for the image worker. Taken on a dull day, the sky was too even to be interesting for this exercise, so a rainbow-colored gradient was applied across the whole image. Finally, the colors were strengthened and the outline of the trees sharpened to improve their graphic impact.

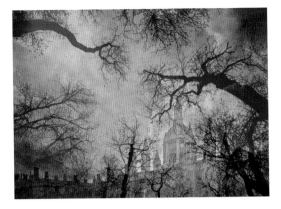

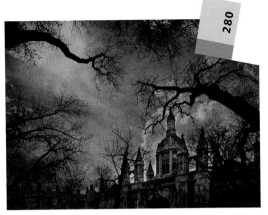

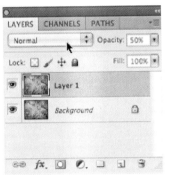

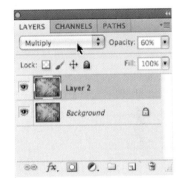

▲ Normal

The Normal blend is often ignored but it is a proper blending mode—provided you lower the opacity of the top layer below 100 percent, the lower layer then becomes progressively more visible. Here, the top layer at 50 percent shows a useful blend is possible—one that cannot be replicated by other blend modes—and it does not matter which is the topmost image.

▲ Multiply

This mode is the digital equivalent of sandwiching two color slides—densities multiply and the image darkens. Here, the upper layer was reduced to 60 percent opacity to stop the trees turning black. Multiply mode can be used to recover images that are too light (overexposed slides or underexposed negatives). Duplicate the image into another layer and set this new layer to Multiply.

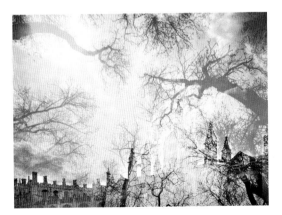

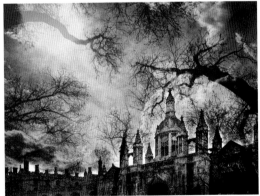

▲ Screen

Adding together the lightness of corresponding pixels is like projecting one slide from a projector onto the projected image of another slide—the result is always a lighter image. By reducing the opacity of the top layer, you control image darkness. This mode is useful for lightening an overly dark image (the opposite of Multiply). Simply duplicate the image onto another layer and set the top to Screen, then adjust opacity.

▲ Overlay

This mode is able to mix colors evenly from both layers, and is very responsive to changes in opacity. It works by screening light areas in the upper layer onto the lower and by multiplying dark areas of the upper layer onto the lower, which is the opposite effect of Hard Light (see p. 280). At lowered opacities, its effect is similar to that of the Normal blend but with more intense colors. It is useful for adding textures to an image.

LAYER BLEND MODES CONTINUED

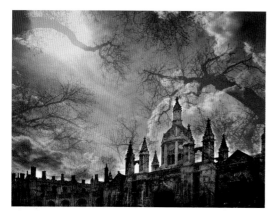

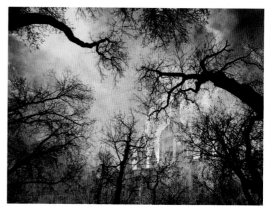

▲ Soft Light

Soft Light blending darkens or lightens image colors, depending on the blend color. The effect is similar to shining a diffused spotlight on the image. Now, painting with pure black or white produces a distinctly darker or lighter area but does not result in pure black or white. This is a very effective way of making local tonal adjustments. It is a softer, and generally more useful version of the Hard Light blending mode.

▲ Hard Light

This mode is similar to Soft Light: it darkens image color if the blend layer is dark, and lightens it if the blend is light, but with greater contrast. It simulates the contrasty projection of the image onto another image. It is generally less useful than Soft Light but can prove valuable for increasing local contrast—particularly if applied as a painted color at very low pressures and lowered opacity.

BLENDING MODES

Interactions between layers are tricky to learn, as their precise effect depends on the value of a pixel on the source (or blend, or upper) layer compared with the corresponding pixel on the destination (or lower) layer. The most often-used method is simply to try them out one by one (hold the shift key down and press "+" or "-" to step through the menu) until the effect looks attractive. This can distract from your initial vision by offering effects you had not thought of—but that is part of the fun of working with powerful software. With experience you will get to know the Blend modes that are most pleasing and plan your images with them in mind.

One key point to remember is that the effectiveness of a mode may depend to a great extent on the opacity set on the source layer—sometimes a small change in opacity turns a garish result into one that is visually persuasive. So if you find an effect that does not look quite right, change the opacity to see what effect this has.

Of the many blend modes available in such software as Adobe Photoshop or Corel Painter, some of the most useful are:

- **Soft Light:** Offers a useful approach for making tonal adjustments (*see above*).
- **Color:** Adds color to the receiving layer without changing its brightness or luminance—useful for coloring in grayscale images.
- **Difference:** Produces dramatic effects by reversing tones and colors.
- **Color Burn/Dodge:** Useful for greatly increasing contrast and color saturation or, at lower opacities, making global changes in tone and exposure (*see opposite*).

✓ Normal
Dissolve

Darken
Multiply
Color Burn
Linear Burn
Darker Color

Lighten
Screen
Color Dodge
Linear Dodge (Add)
Lighter Color

Overlay
Soft Light
Hard Light
Vivid Light
Linear Light
Pin Light
Hard Mix

Difference
Exclusion

Hue
Saturation
Color
Luminosity

▲ Interaction modes

The different ways in which layers can interact also apply to other situations, such as painting, fading a command, and cloning. Experience with different effects helps you to previsualize results.

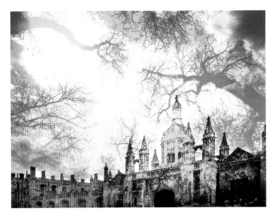

▲ Color Dodge

At first glance, Color Dodge appears like Screen mode (*see p. 279*) in that it brightens the image, but its effect is more dramatic. Black in the upper layer has no effect on the receiving layer, but all other colors will tint the underlying colors as well as increasing color saturation and brightness. This mode is useful when you want to create strong, graphic results. Note that when you change the order of the images you get markedly different effects.

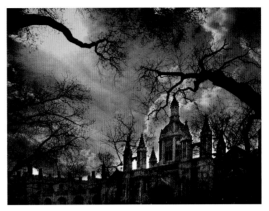

▲ Color Burn

This blend mode produces very strong effects as it increases color saturation and contrast. At the same time, it produces darkened images by replacing lighter underlying pixels with darker top pixels. Be aware that both Color Burn and Color Dodge modes often produce colors that are so extreme they cannot be printed—in other words, they are out-of-gamut for printers (*see p. 61*).

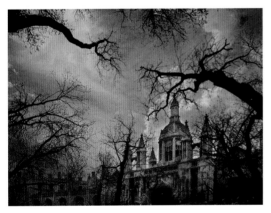

▲ Darken

The Darken mode applies only darker pixels from the top layer to the bottom layer. Here, the black branches of the trees overshadow anything that lies under them, showing the importance of using clear but interesting shapes. This mode does not strongly change colors. If, for example, there is no difference between the corresponding pixels on the top and bottom layers, there is no change—so this mode cannot be used to darken an image (*but see Multiply, p. 275*).

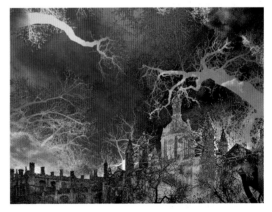

▲ Difference

The Difference mode is one of the most useful for giving dramatic and usable effects, since it reverses tones and colors at the same time—the greater the difference between corresponding pixels, the brighter the result will be. Notice how the dark forms of the trees are rendered in the negative, while the blues of the sky turn to magenta. Therefore, where top and bottom pixels are identical, the result is black, and if one is white and the other black, the result is white.

LAYER BLEND MODES CONTINUED

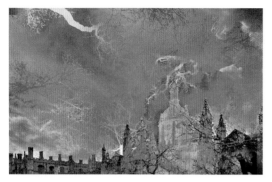

▲ Exclusion

A softer version of Difference mode (*see p. 277*), Exclusion returns gray to pixels with medium-strong colors, rather than strengthening the colors. A useful variant is to duplicate the top layer and apply Exclusion to the duplicate layer—now topmost. This creates something similar to the Sabattier effect (*see p. 242*).

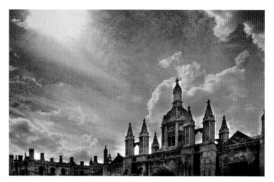

▲ Hue

In this mode the colors of the top layer are combined with the saturation and brightness (luminosity) values of the lower layer. The result can be a strong toning effect, as seen here, or it can be weak, depending on the images used. It is worth comparing the effect of this mode with that of the Color mode (*below*).

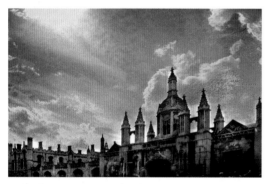

▲ Saturation

Here, the saturation of the underlying layer is changed to that of the corresponding pixel in the top, or source, layer. Where saturation is high, the lower image returns a richer color. It is useful where you wish to define a shape using richer or weaker colors: create a top layer with the shape you want and change saturation only within the shape, then apply Saturation mode.

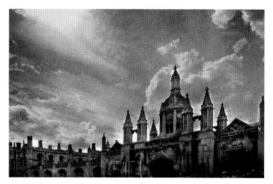

▲ Color

Both hue and saturation of the upper layer are transferred to the lower layer, while the luminosity of the receiving layer is retained. This mode simulates the hand-tinting effect of black and white prints. Note that the receiving layer does not have to be turned to a grayscale image for this mode to be effective. Compare this with Hue mode (*above*).

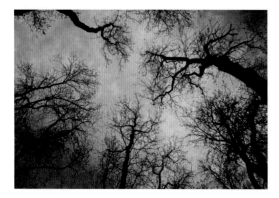

◀ Luminosity

This blend mode is a variant of Hue and Color: this time, the luminosity of the top layer is retained while the color and saturation of the underlying layer are applied. It is always worth trying the layers in different orders when working with these modes, particularly with this group consisting of Hue, Color, and Luminosity. In this image, reducing the opacity of the top layer produces a soft, appealing image, in contrast to the more high-contrast result when both layers are left at full strength.

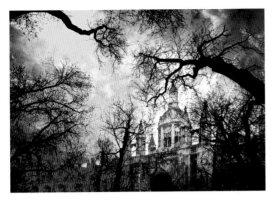

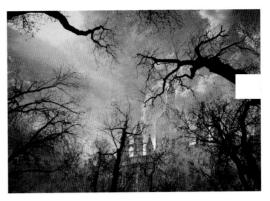

▲ Vivid Light

This both burns and dodges: lighter blend colors decrease contrast and lighten the receiving layer (dodges), while darker ones increase contrast and darken the lower color.

▲ Pin Light

Blend colors lighten or darken the underlying layer according to the blend color and underlying color. The results are tricky to predict, but visually appealing effects are often produced.

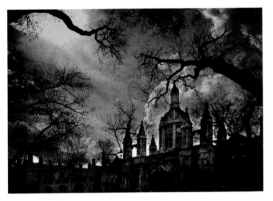

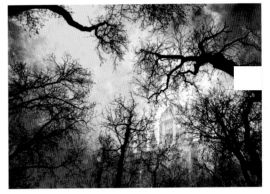

▲ Linear Burn

The receiving colors are darkened to match the blend color. This burns or darkens the image without increase in contrast. The strong darkening effect is best tempered through opacity control.

▲ Linear Light

Similar to Vivid Light, this burns or dodges in response to the blend color by changing brightness. Its effect is to increase contrast—as darker colors are darkened, lighter ones are lightened.

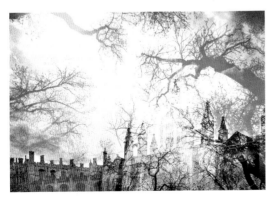

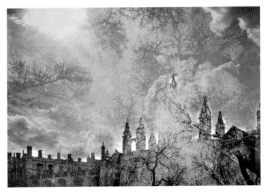

▲ Linear Dodge

Similar to Color Dodge (*see p. 277*), this blend mode brightens the base or receiving layer to match that of the blend layer, thus blends with black produce no change. It is an effective way of brightening an image to a high-key effect but has a tendency to produce too much blank white.

▲ Lighten

This mode chooses the lighter of the two colors being blended as the result of the combination. This blend tends to flatten or reduce contrast, but it is effective for producing pastel tones. Images that originally have subtle tones respond very well to this mode.

LAYER BLEND MODES CONTINUED

Blending layers with modes can produce startling results but may also be used to make more subtly intriguing images. Blending can easily create a level of complexity that would, in real life, be impossible. Here, three images of a misty morning in the Black Forest, Germany, were layered to create a forest that is even richer than in nature. The layer above the background was set to Luminosity, and the top layer to Hard Light. Highlights were given stronger colors to make them stand out as focal points.

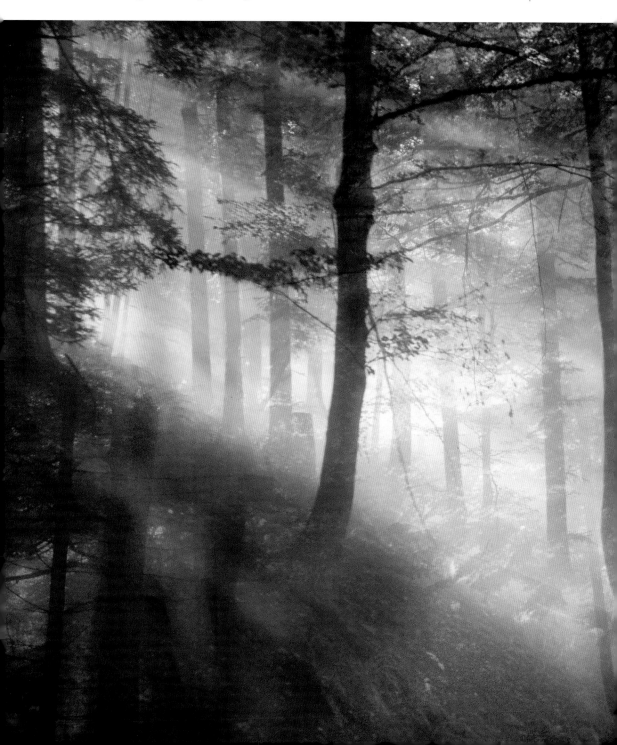

TECHNICAL INFO

CAMERA
Sony Alpha 900

LENS
Zeiss 24–70 mm at 50 mm

SETTINGS
ISO 400 • f/2.8 • ½₂₅₀ sec

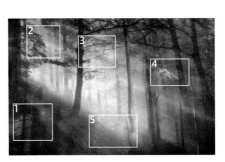

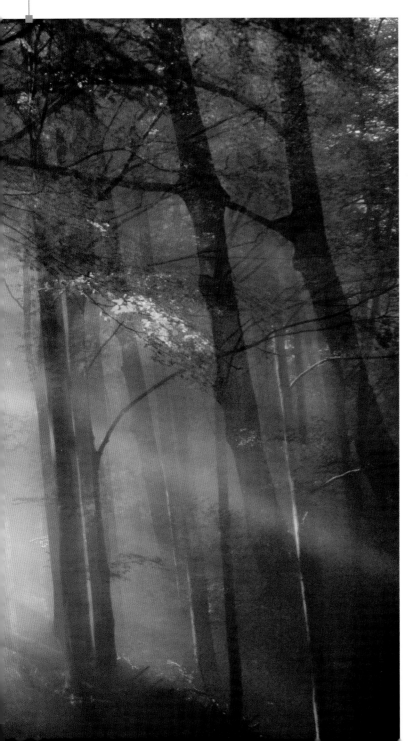

1 Ghostly trees

In two of the component images, this corner was dark and devoid of detail, but one of the images captured the main scene from a different angle, filling the corner with details. Some light was allowed through to keep this quadrant active with ghostly shadows.

2 Motivated light

Early morning sun streams through the low cloud forming a fog in the forest. Sloping through the picture in soft diagonals, it motivates the highlights of leaves and rays, showing how branches and trunks cast shadows in the sunlit fog.

3 Sky lights

The sky in one of the component images gives this part of the image its cool tones, which contrast well with the sunlit leaves and the carpet of brown foliage on the ground. It is tempting to increase the saturation, but a blue that is too strong would be distracting.

4 Sunny leaves

A vital element in the image is the sun on a few leaves that catch the sunlight to present an attractive array of colors. Their location off-center and in a relatively quiet portion of the picture rewards the viewer for exploring the image.

5 Leafy carpet

The covering of brown leaves on a path provides a quiet counterpoint to the rest of the image. It suggests movement into the foggy woods yet does not call attention to itself because it is not too busy with detail.

TEXT EFFECTS

Typefaces, also known as letterforms or fonts, can be treated in many unique ways using image-manipulation software. Letters can be made to flame up, for example, dissolve into clouds, recede and blur into the distance, or appear transparent over another image—the possibilities are truly unlimited. All image-manipulation applications offer at least a basic range of effects, but if they also accept Photoshop-compliant plug-ins, you can greatly extend your repertoire.

Note, however, that text can sit uncomfortably with image pixels. The reason is that type is best digitally encoded as "vector graphics," whereas photographic images are best encoded as "bitmap graphics" (*see below*). Nearly always, the text would have to be turned from vector into a set of bit-mapped pixels, resulting in a loss of clarity and sharpness. As a consequence, as you increase the size of an image that incorporates text, the letterforms quickly start to look ragged, with poorly defined outlines. More than anywhere else in image manipulation, if you work with text always work at the full output size; and avoid altering the image size after applying text to the image.

BITMAP AND VECTOR GRAPHICS

There are two classes of graphic image. Digital cameras all produce a bitmap type of image, also called a raster image, which is based on a grid of data (the colored pixels). Each pixel is placed in a specific location and given a color value. Image manipulation is all about altering pixels, and so such images are resolution-dependent—that is, they start with a fixed number of pixels and thus a change in image size alters the amount of detail that is available.

Vector graphics, also known as object-oriented images, are described according to their geometrical basics—lines, circles, and so on—with their location, together with operations such as stroke (to draw a line) or fill (to cover an enclosed area with color). Vector graphics are said to be resolution-independent—that is, they can be scaled to any size and printed at any resolution without losing sharpness, and so can always use the output device's highest resolution.

Vectors are best for designing text as well as graphics such as company logos, and are created by graphics software such as Macromedia FreeHand, Corel Draw, or Adobe Illustrator. You may discover that the more complicated letterforms, such as those with scrolls or long loops, may not print properly in your printer: if so, you may need to install special software to interpret the vector information, called a PostScript RIP (Raster Image Processor).

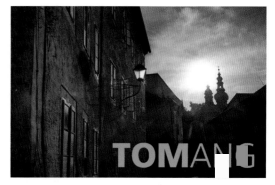

▲ **Display type**
If you wish to add effects to a typeface, it is advisable to start with a chunky display type such as Frutiger (shown here). With a color chosen to contrast with the rest of the image, the effect may be unattractive and garish, but it is easy to read at any size.

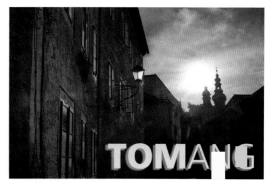

▲ **Drop shadow**
By asking the image-manipulation software to create a drop shadow, you make the letters appear as if they are floating above the image. The overall effect is of a poster. The color of the type was toned down to that of a tint of white: any light tint of white is likely to be an effective and safe choice of color for type.

HINTS AND TIPS

It is always best to check a typeface at full size by printing it out. Check again if you change the face: even at the same point size, different typefaces vary widely in legibility. Also consider the following:

- Use typefaces with narrow lines where they contrast well with the background; those with broad shapes should be used where the contrast is less obvious.
- You can use typefaces with narrow outlines if you create effects that separate the text from the underlying image, such as drop shadows.

- Use typefaces with broad lines if using them for masking or to allow images to show through.
- Avoid faces with narrow serifs—the little extensions to the end of a stroke in a letter—as these are easily lost into the underlying image. In addition, avoid letterforms with hollow strokes or those made up of double strokes for the same reason.
- Use only small amounts of text when combining it with images—at best a heading and at most a short block of text; but avoid using more than 50 words.

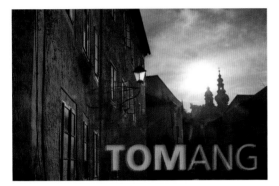

▲ Inner shadow
Here, an inner shadow in orange has been applied with a high level of noise, so creating the appearance of a rough texture. Drop shadows have been retained, but note that the "light" can be made to come from different directions.

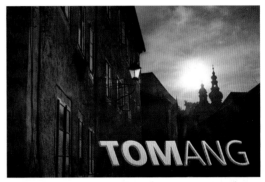

▲ Text warp
Distortion or unusual slant of text can be effective for drawing the viewer's attention. Here, the text has been slanted backwards. In addition, various stroke, bevel, and shadow effects were applied to make the type look 3D.

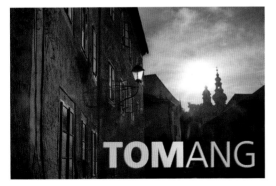

▲ Graduated overlay
Another way of making the type lively is to make the color appear graduated. Here, colors move between yellow and pale blue. The gradient chosen was sloped so that it runs across the type at an angle. With these effects you can produce comic-book effects that once had to be laboriously hand-painted.

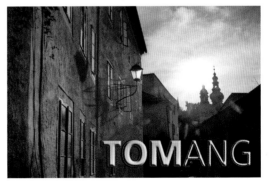

▲ Advanced effects
Tutorials can be found online showing you step-by-step techniques to create some quite advanced effects that add something special. The above effect makes the text appear to be metallic gold, and works well against the image that has been made black and white. Monotone images can take much brighter colors and bolder effects.

CLONING TECHNIQUES

Cloning is the process of copying, repeating, or duplicating pixels from one part of an image, or taking pixels from another image, and placing them on another part of the image. First, you sample, or select, an area that is to be the source of the clone, and then you apply that selected area where it is needed. This is a basic tool in image manipulation, and you will find yourself constantly turning to it whenever you need, say, to replace a dust speck in the sky of an image with an adjacent bit of sky, or remove stray hairs from a face by cloning nearby skin texture over them.

This is only the start, however. Such cloning makes an exact copy of the pixels, but you can go much further. Some applications, such as Corel Painter, allow you to invert, distort, and otherwise transform the cloned image compared with the source you took it from.

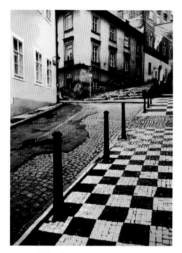

▲ Original image
An unsightly tarred area of road left by repairs marred this street scene in Prague. All it will take is a little cloning to bring about a transformation.

▲ History palette
The screen shot of the History palette shows the individual cloning steps that were necessary to bring about the required transformation.

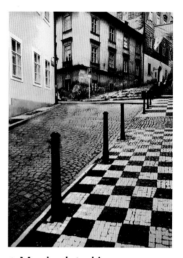

▲ Manipulated image
The result is not perfect, since it has none of the careful radial pattern of the original, but it is far preferable to the original image. It was finished off by applying an Unsharp Masking filter plus a few tonal adjustments.

HINTS AND TIPS

The following points may help you avoid some of the more obvious cloning pitfalls:

- Clone with the tool set to maximum (100 percent). Less than this will produce a soft-looking clone.

- In areas with even tones, use a soft-edged, or feathered Brush as the cloning tool; in areas of fine detail, use a sharp-edged Brush.

- Work systematically, perhaps from left to right, from a cleaned area into areas with dust specks—or else you may be cloning the specks themselves.

- If your cloning produces an unnaturally smooth-looking area, you may need to introduce some noise to make it look more natural: select the area to be worked on and then apply the Noise filter.

- You can reduce the tendency of cloning to produce smooth areas by reducing the spacing setting. Most digital Brushes are set so that they apply "paint" in overlapping dabs—typically, each dab is separated by a quarter of the diameter of the brush. Your software may allow you to change settings to that of zero spacing.

- If you expect to apply extreme tonal changes using, say, Curves settings, apply the Curves before cloning. Extreme tonalities can reveal cloning by showing boundaries between cloned and uncloned areas.

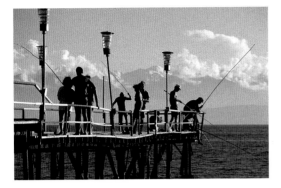

◄ Original image

Suppose you wished to remove the lamp on the far left of this image to show an uninterrupted area of sky. You could use the cloning tool to do this, but it would be a lot of work and there would be a danger of leaving the sky's tones unnaturally smoothed-out in appearance.

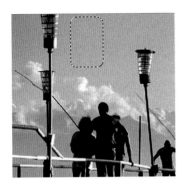

1 Marquee tool

The Marquee tool was set to a feather of 10 pixels (to blur its border) and placed near the lamp to be removed to ensure a smooth transition in sky tones.

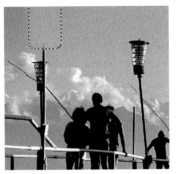

2 Removing the lamp

By applying the Marquee tool, you can see here how the cloned area of sky is replacing the lamp. Further cloning of sky was needed in order to smooth out differences in tone and make the new sky area look completely natural.

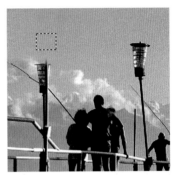

3 Looking at details

The final removal of the lamp was done with a smaller Marquee area, with its feather set to zero (as sharp as possible). Finally, the lamp behind the one removed was restored by carefully cloning from visible parts of the lamp.

4 Cleaned-up result

As a finishing touch, a small area of cloud was cloned over the top of the lamp and its lid was darkened to match the others left on the pier.

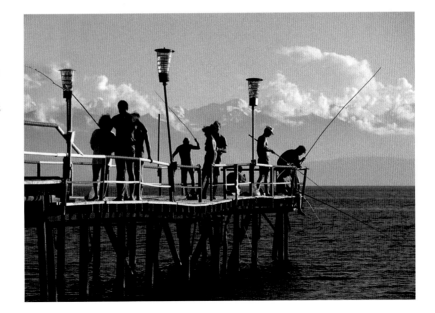

CLONING TECHNIQUES CONTINUED

Special cloning

In addition to the corrective type of cloning seen on pp. 288-9, it is possible to take the process further and use it creatively.

In most software, there are two main ways of applying a clone. The basic method is what is now known as nonaligned, or normal: the first area you sample is inserted to each new spot the Brush tool is applied to. The other cloning method keeps a constant spatial relationship between the point sampled and the first place the sample is applied to—in other words, an offset is maintained so that the clone is aligned to the source point.

However, software such as Corel Painter offers as many as nine other ways of aligning the clone to the source. You can distort, shear, rotate, mirror, scale up or down, and so on. The procedure is more complicated than with normal cloning because you need to define the original scale and position prior to applying the clone. You set the reference points in the source image, then set the transformation points; this can be either in the original image or in a new document. It is this latter feature that gives Painter's cloning tools tremendous power.

One interesting feature is that as your cloned image is being built up, it can, itself, become the source material for more cloning.

The examples below illustrate just how far it is possible to move away from the source material, as well as how diverse the results can be. Remember, though: with all cloning experiments, you should work on a copy of the original image.

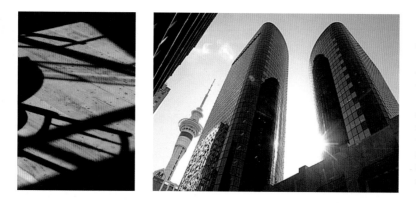

◀ Original images
Both of these originals (*left*) were taken in New Zealand. Note that images do not have to be the same size or shape for cloning to take place, but look for originals with strong, simple shapes. Sharpness and color were improved prior to the cloning: increasing sharpness after cloning can exaggerate the patches of cloned material.

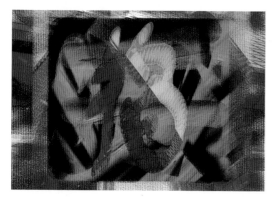

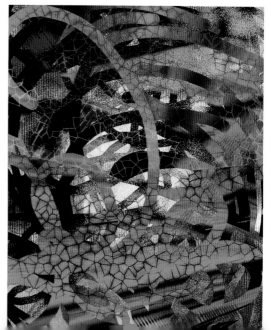

▲ Manipulated images
The originals were first cloned into a new file, but with added textures and overlaid with several layers. The first image (*above*) is intended to give a modern feel to the Chinese character "good fortune;" the other (*right*) has been given a distressed look.

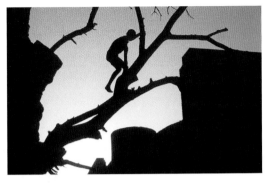

▲ Original image

Any original image can be cloned onto itself to make complexes of line and form. Starting with an image with clear-cut lines and simple colors, such as this, special cloning techniques can make images that are difficult to produce in any other way.

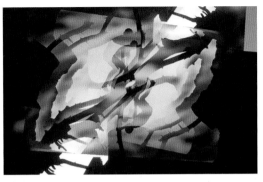

▲ Rotation and scale

Cloning with rotation and scale calls for two points to be set to define the source and a corresponding two points to determine the clone. By experimenting with different positions of the source and clone points, you can create a wide range of effects: here the boy appears to be spinning into an abyss.

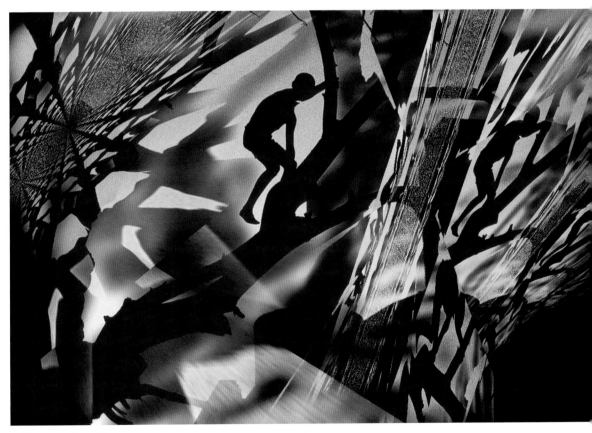

▲ Perspective tiling

Here, the boy was cloned with perspective tiling applied twice to different parts of the image. This requires four points to be set as the source, and four for the clone. By switching around the positions of the reference points, wild perspective distortions are produced, which could have come from a sci-fi comic.

Cloning yourself

Showing multiple versions or sides of yourself in one image is a fun concept. Shoot the elements against a plain, preferably green, background with a big depth of field for easy cloning.

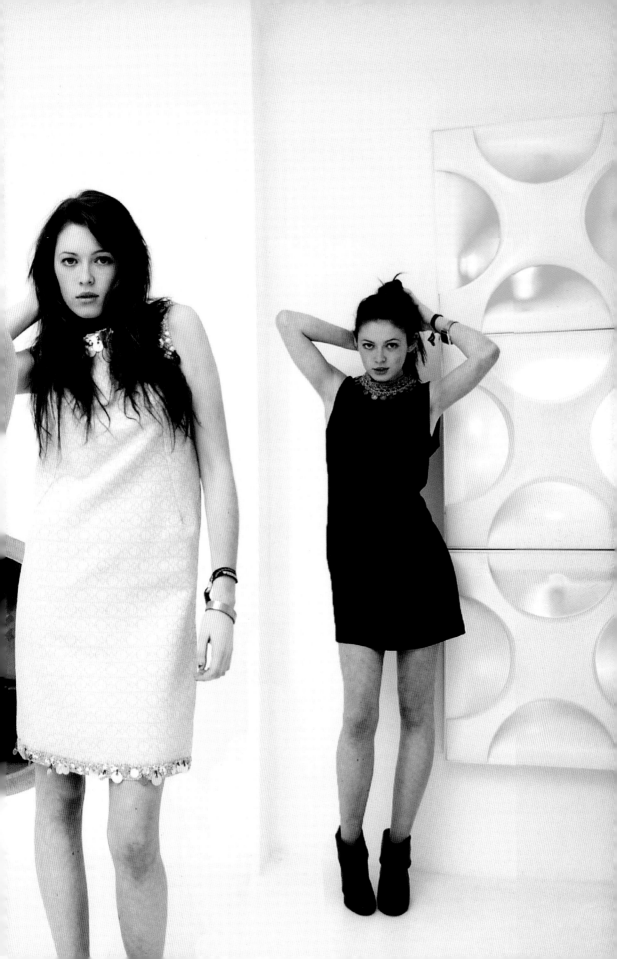

SIMPLE COMPOSITE

Composite images bring together disparate elements from different images. The resulting combination could be fantastical—an underwater tea party for lions—or it could be prosaic—a tea party on the lawn with a few extra people. Sketch out an idea in your mind before starting work. You will then find it easier to trawl your picture library for suitable elements. Before you start work, collect all the working images at their full size into one folder, then create a canvas of the size you wish to create.

Big match

Whatever kind of image you work on, the key to success is the match: the final image will work best when all the elements blend well. Images should share lighting (shadows should fall consistently), and tone and contrast should be appropriate—that is, elements that are further away should be lower in contrast. The detail resolution of different components should match, and, finally, color balance across the image should be consistent.

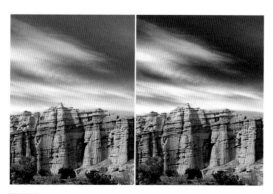

1 Original image
A rather lackluster image of the Plaza Blanca, New Mexico, USA, is asking for some added pizazz. The sky could be more exciting, and the foreground is woefully lacking in active interest.

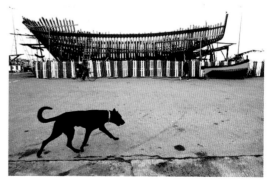

2 Choosing a dramatic sky
The skies of the American Midwest famously yield a rich variety of formations. The choice is restricted by the lighting in the original, in which the pale sun comes from the left of the image.

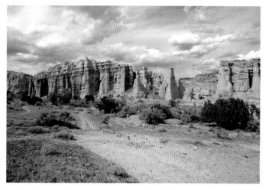

3 Cutting out
We could cut out the rocky skyline using a selection tool or, because it is a very easy outline, we can exploit the precision of the pen tool. We increase contrast and decrease exposure using an adjustment layer to give the sky more impact.

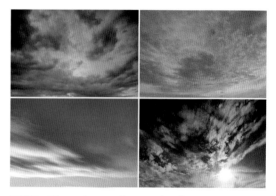

4 Finding a contrasting subject
A sleek dog strolling in the Moroccan port of Essaouira makes an outstanding candidate to occupy the foreground of the landscape. The shape is easily cut out, and the black color means there will be no problems with tonal matching.

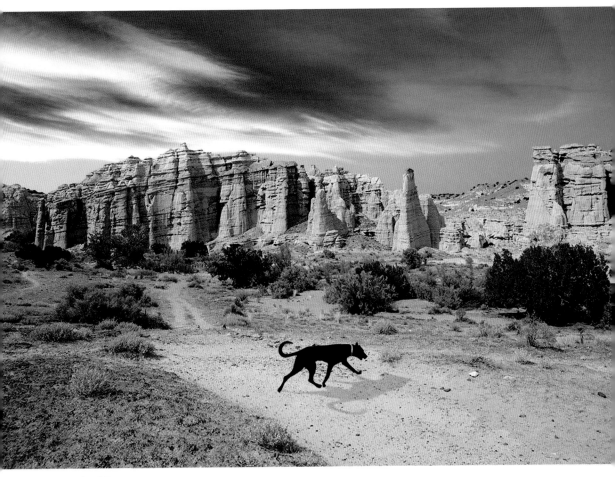

▲ FINAL SHOT

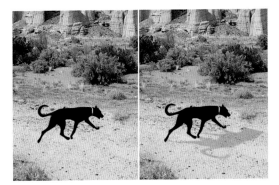

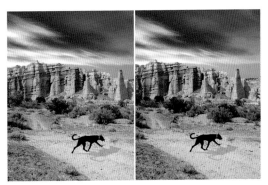

5 Adding in dog and shadow

We cut out the dog and paste it. We then select the dog's shape, then fill with black to make the shadow. We adjust opacity for a natural-looking density, then use the Free Transform tool to flip and position the shadow to make it look realistic.

6 Making color adjustments

Using adjustment layers for Hue/Saturation and for Color Balance, we tone down the colors to produce a soft, tinted look. The sky is masked in order to apply stronger adjustments to the foreground to subdue the strong orangey/pink color.

PHOTOMOSAICS

Since digital pictures are composed of an array of individual pixels, it is only a short step to making up an image from an array of individual pictures. This is the principle behind photomosaics: you can replace an image's pixels with tiny individual images, like the tiles of a traditional mosaic.

Preparation

The first thing you need to do is prepare the images with which to create the mosaic. The small "mosaic pieces" may be tiny versions of the larger one or different images. Photomosaic software treats individual pictures as if they are pixels, looking for best matches between the density and color of the small images to the pixel of the larger image that is to be replaced.

Speciality stand-alone photomosaic software usually provides libraries of mosaic pieces for you to work with, but it is more fun to create your own. However, the large numbers of images needed mean that this can be a lengthy process. Advanced users can create batch processing sets to automate the process of rendering files into the specific pixel dimensions needed for the mosaic pieces. Other sources are the thumbnails (small files) found in some collections of royalty-free CDs.

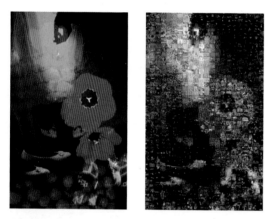

◄ Composite photomosaic
The original image was relatively complicated, but its clear lines and shapes, as well as the repeated elements it contained, made it a suitable candidate for photomosaic techniques. By selecting a small size for the mosaic "tiles" the resulting image still, overall, retains many details, but with an added richness of texture that invites closer inspection. The close-up view of the photomosaic (*below*) shows an intriguing mixture of images. Varying the component images is one way to produce an entirely different feeling to the image, while still retaining the outlines of the originals.

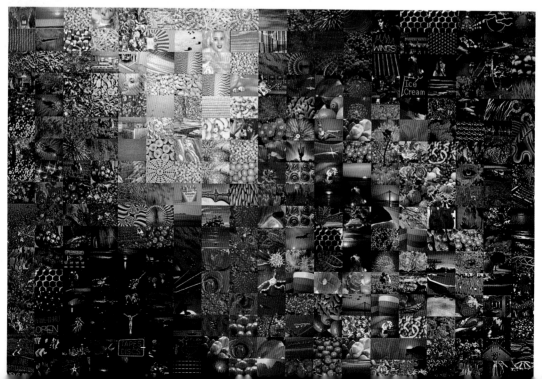

HINTS AND TIPS

If you are thinking of producing a photomosaic, bear the following points in mind.

- Provide a wide range of images from which to make up the mosaic pieces.
- Remember that smaller mosaic pieces produce finer, more detailed photomosaics.
- Use subjects with clear or recognizable outlines;

avoid complicated subjects lacking clear outlines as the process destroys all but the largest details.

- Bear in mind that if you create images in which a high level of detail is replaced with large mosaics, the resulting files will be very large.
- The rendering process that creates the photomosaic can take some time for your machine to handle.

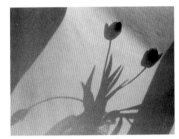

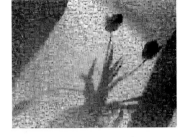

◀ **High-key photomosaic**

The large, even spread of tones presents a challenge to photomosaic software, as identical images next to each other must be avoided, or else false patterns are created. However, the photomosaic has superimposed an attractive texture over this image of tulip shadows. The close-up view (*below*) is richly rewarding.

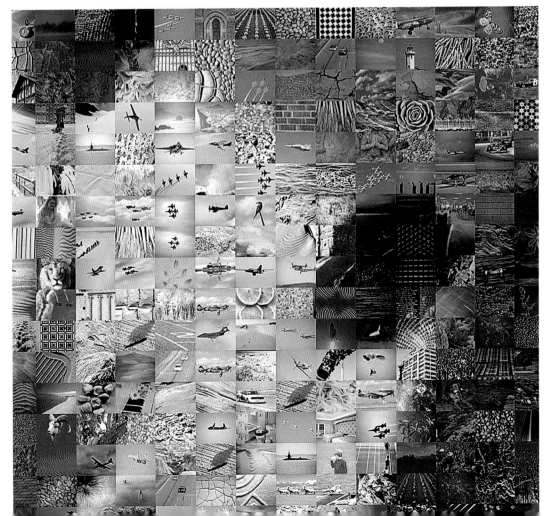

IMAGE STITCHING

Panoramic views can be created by "stitching," or overlaying, images side-by-side (*see pp. 150–1*). Essentially, a sequence of images is taken from one side of the scene to the other (or from the top to the bottom). The individual images are then overlapped to create a seamless composite.

You do not need special software to achieve panoramas if the original shots are taken with care. You simply create a long canvas and drop the images in, overlapping them. However, small errors in framing can make this a slow process, since you must blend the overlaps to hide the joins.

Appropriate software

Speciality panoramic software makes joining up component shots far easier, especially if they were taken without a tripod. The available software packages offer different approaches. Some try to match overlaps automatically and blend shots together by blurring the overlaps. The results look rather crude, but are effective for low-resolution use. Other software applications are able to recognize if the overlaps do not match and try to accommodate the problem—some by distorting the image, others by trying to correct perspective. Many digital cameras are supplied with panorama-creation software.

For more unusual effects, experiment with placing incongruous images together, or deliberately distort the perspective or overlaps so that the components clash rather than blend. There is a great deal of interesting new work still to be done.

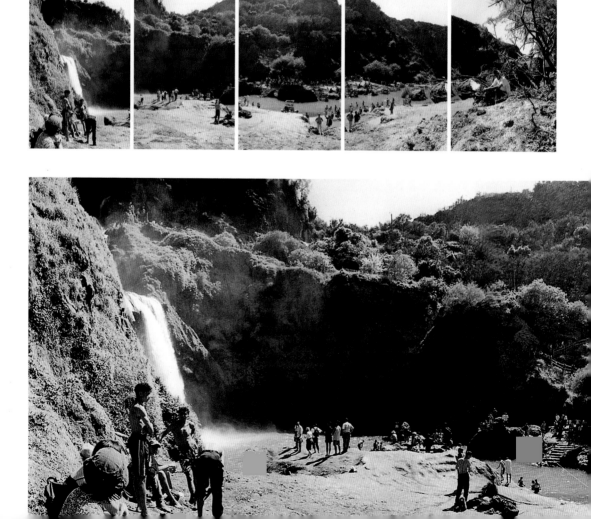

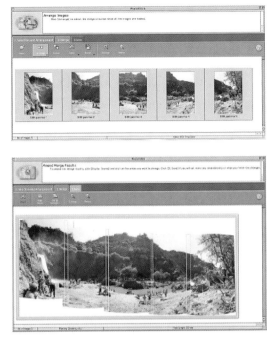

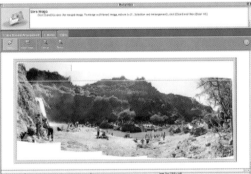

HINTS AND TIPS

- A panorama resulting from, say, six average-size images will be a very large file, so reduce the size of the component images first to avoid stretching your computer's capacity.
- If you want to create a panorama that covers half the horizon or more, it may be better to stitch it in stages: three or four images at a time, then stitch the resulting panoramas. Keep an eye on the image size.
- Place all the component images together into one folder: some software will not be able to access images if they are in different folders.

◄ Assembly

To start the assembly (*left*), move the component images into a single folder where the software can access them. With some software, you will be able to move images around to change their order, while in others you will have to open the images in the correct order. To merge the images, the software may need extra instructions, such as the equivalent focal length of the lens used.

▼ Final version

The component images show very generous overlaps, which make it easier for the software to create smooth blends. Once the component images are all combined on one canvas, you can use the facilities offered by the particular software to blend and disguise the overlaps to create a seamless, single image (*below*). Once you are happy with your work, save the file as a TIFF, not as a JPEG, for best-quality results.

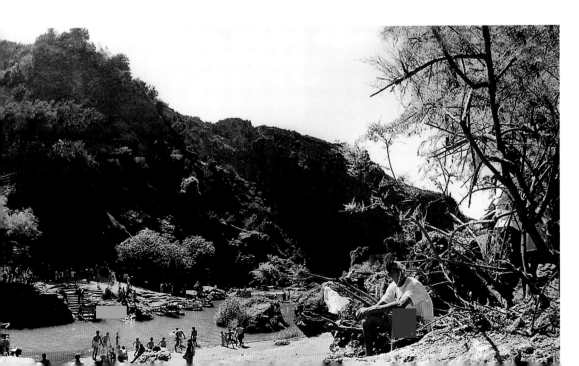

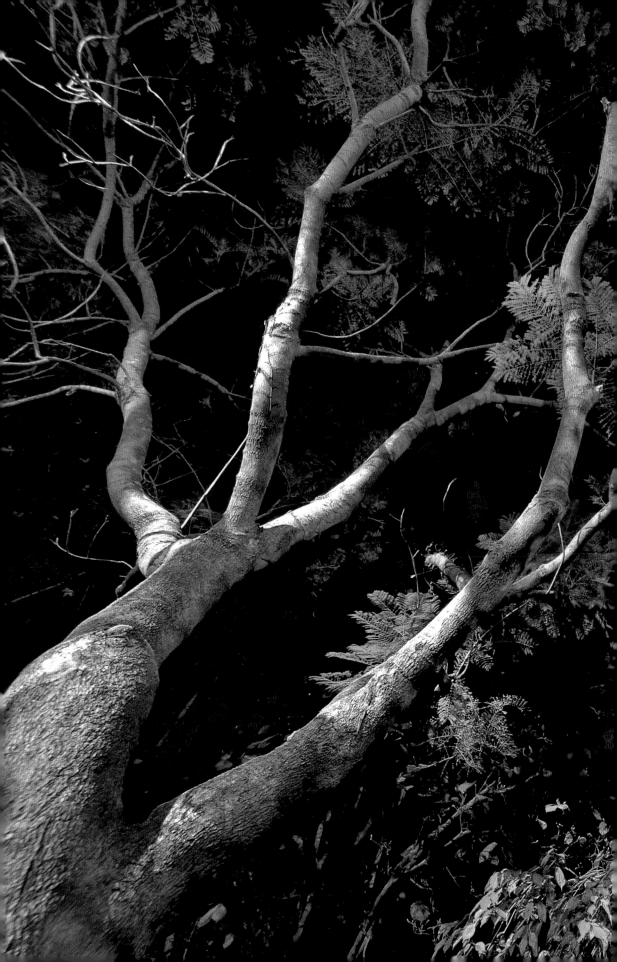

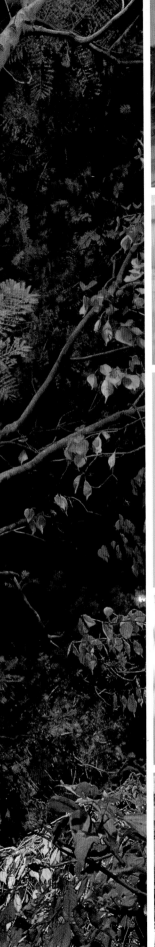
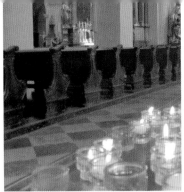
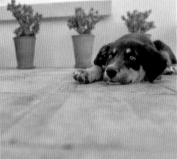

4 SHOWING AND SHARING

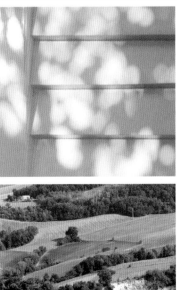

PROOFING AND PRINTING

It is an exciting moment. You have worked for hours at your computer, using all your know-how to create an image that looks just the way you want it, and now you are ready to print. You take a deep breath and press the button to send the file to the printer. If, then, the printer produces satisfactory results for most images, without any intervention on your part or setting up, you are lucky (make sure you note the settings in the printer driver for future reference). Unfortunately, a common experience for many photographers is that the results of printing will be disappointing.

No blame

An important point is that a mismatch between the monitor image and the printer is not, in the first instance, caused by any malfunctioning on the part of your printer or monitor. The basic problem is that the monitor produces colors by emitting a mix of red, green, and blue light, while a print reflects a mix of light to produce the colors you perceive. These fundamentally different ways of producing color lead to a difference in gamut, which is the range of colors that can be produced by a device (see p. 61).

There are two main approaches open to you. You can adjust the image to compensate for the differences between what you see on screen and the resulting print, then print again and again, repeating the process until the print is satisfactory. This is not only wasteful and unreliable, but the adjustments apply to only one image. A far better, and more methodical approach is to adopt a color-managed work-flow.

Printing with color management

The starting point for any image manipulation is the calibrated and profiled monitor (see pp. 182–3) as that is the way to be sure that the tones and colors that you see on screen are the tones and colors that you want to see on your print (or your website). Given the basis of a calibrated and profiled monitor, you can be confident that when you send color data to the printer, it will know how to interpret the data.

The basic idea is that you tell your printer what it needs to know to convert your image into the print: it needs to know the color space of your image—sRGB is a safe, reliable working color space, but you can use Adobe RG B (1998) if you really need a wide color gamut.

Next, the printer needs to know how to convert the image data into spots of ink so that the print looks the same as the image. This is job of the output profile; it is specific to the combination of printer, ink, and paper being used. For general purposes, generic output profiles give satisfactory results, but for exhibition and other demanding tasks, it is necessary to use bespoke profiles. These are created by printing a standard color pattern onto specific paper, then analyzing the color pattern: this gives excellent, reliable results. The task

▲ Color settings

The dialog box controlling color settings looks complex, and careful attention is needed to make full sense of it. However, there are many guides—such as those provided in printer and software manuals—that should help you master it. The crucial point to keep in mind is that, unless you are producing work to be printed by a commercial press for a mass market, you need not worry about these settings. You can get by without touching them: however, if you can control them, it will be far easier to obtain reliably good prints from your desktop printer.

```
┌─ Source Space ────────────────────────────────
│  ⦿ Document: Colorperfexion RGB
│  ○ Proof Setup: Offset B
└────────────────────────────────────────────────

┌─ Print Space ─────────────────────────────────
│  Profile: │ EPSON Stylus Photo EX  Photo Paper 1440 │ ⬍ │
│
│  Intent: │ ✓ Perceptual              │ ⬍ │
│            Saturation
│            Relative Colorimetric
│            Absolute Colorimetric
└────────────────────────────────────────────────
```

▲ Printer settings

A driver that complies with the ColorSync protocol for color management will offer a dialog such as that shown here. The Source Space is the color space or profile for the image: here I have specified a commercially defined standard, which defines an RGB space in a way that is optimized for print. The Print Space is not only that of the printer but of the paper and print quality being set. "Perceptual" has been chosen for the Intent, or preference for color conversions of colors that fall out of gamut, as that is most likely to give a photographically acceptable print.

WHAT IS POSTSCRIPT?

This is the most important of a range of programming languages that describe text and graphics on a page. PostScript breaks the most complex text and graphics into elementary components, such as lines or dots, and into basic operations, such as "stroke" (to draw a line) or "translate" (to turn a component). When a printer receives a PostScript file it has to interpret it in order to turn these commands into the correct output on the page. This can be done with software in the computer's operating system or through specialist PostScript RIPs (Raster Image Processors). Using a PostScript RIP is the best way of making sure that complicated graphics and text are properly printed out on the page.

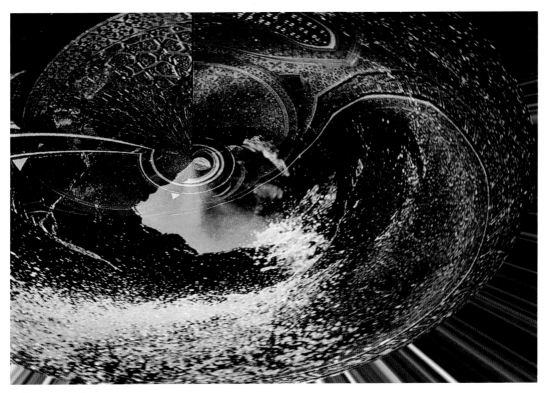

▲ Fantasy colors

When you produce highly manipulated images, even a large error in color accuracy is unlikely to damage the effectiveness of the image, since most viewers will not ever know what the right colors were supposed to be. Of course, for the sake of artistic integrity, you will strive to produce the exact color you have in your mind's eye, but the impact of images such as that shown here, with its artificial colors and fantasy content, does not depend on precise color reproduction.

PROOFING AND PRINTING CONTINUED

of managing the color data can be handled by image software such as Adobe Lightroom or Apple Aperture, or you can elect to have it managed by the printer. Results vary depending on software and printer, so it is best to try both strategies and gain experience with your own set-up.

Previewing

Making a print takes up valuable resources such as ink, paper and, above all, your precious time. Central to efficient printing practice is to soft-proof as much as possible—that is, check and confirm everything you can on the monitor screen (make preflight checks) before sending the image to the printer. Ensure first that you have the output profile for the paper and printer combination that you plan to use. Set this up, usually in the View menu, called "Proofing profile" or "Proof set-up," or similar.

In order to check exposure and color, set the software to Print Preview. There may be a change in the appearance of the image: if you have one with brilliantly bright colors, the soft-proof image may suddenly become dull and a little darker. If your image is not brilliantly colored, or is black and

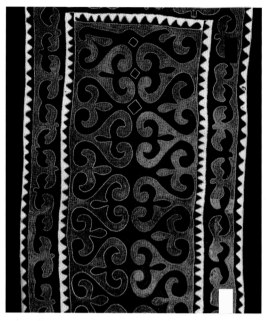

▲ Textile color

For accurate records of decorative objects, such as this piece of textile (above), precise color control is essential. Reds are visually very important but deep reds can vary considerably between monitor image and paper output. The subtle variations in deep tone are easily lost if a print-out is too dark.

WHAT ARE RENDERING INTENTS?

Converting from one color space to another involves an adjustment to accommodate the gamut of the destination color space. The rendering intent determines the rules for adjusting source colors to destination gamut: those that fall outside the gamut may be ignored or they may be adjusted to preserve the original range of visual relationships. Printers that are ColorSync-compliant will offer a choice of rendering intents that determine the way in which the color is reproduced.

- Perceptual (or image or photo-realistic) aims to preserve the visual relationship between colors in a way that appears natural to the human eye, although value (in other words, brightness) may change. It is most suitable for photographic images.
- Saturation (or graphics or vivid) aims to create vivid color at the expense of color accuracy.

It preserves relative saturation so hues may shift. This is suitable for business graphics, where the presence of bright, saturated colors may be important.

- Absolute Colorimetric leaves colors that fall inside the destination gamut unchanged. This intent aims to maintain color accuracy at the expense of preserving relationships between colors (as two colors different in the source space—usually out-of-gamut—may be mapped to the same color in the destination space).
- Relative Colorimetric is similar to Absolute Colorimetric but it compares the white or black point of the source color space to that of the destination color space in order to shift all colors in proportion. It is suitable for photographic images provided that you first select "Use Black Point Compensation".

white, you may see no difference. Check that the soft-proof image is acceptable: this helps manage your expectations about what will print, so you will not be disappointed at the loss of those deep purples and gorgeous reds—which can be seen on-screen but cannot be printed. Modern printers using up to 12 different inks are improving the range of colors which can be printed, but they still fall well short of what can be seen in real life.

Sizing up

Another basic preflight check is to ensure that the output size makes use full use of the paper, printing with the border suited for the end use, or borderless if your printer offers this feature. Image applications and printer drivers will show a preview of the size and position of the image on the page. Many printer drivers can automatically resize the image to fit the paper size you have chosen.

Some printers will warn you if the resolution of the image is insufficient for a top-quality print (missing the optimum resolution by a small amount is not fatal to print quality), or if the print is larger than the paper.

Summary of set-up

■ Working on a calibrated monitor, complete all post-processing. Check for defects such as spots by examining the print at 200 percent.

■ Soft-proof output: check that no important colors are compromised and that any highly saturated colors in the image are not posterized: reduce saturation locally if necessary.

■ Resize the image to fit the print size so that resolution is not more than 300 pixels per inch (120 pixels per cm) of output. Much lower resolutions are sufficient if you are printing on rough-textured papers such as watercolor rag, but you may wish to increase sharpening. Sending unnecessarily large files can slow down printing.

■ Command the software to print: check the preview for size and location of the print in relation to the paper used.

■ Insert the paper, ensuring that the correct side will be delivered to the ink. If you have not used the printer before, run a test—with some printers the paper comes out with the same side facing up as when it went in, with others the paper comes out the opposite way around.

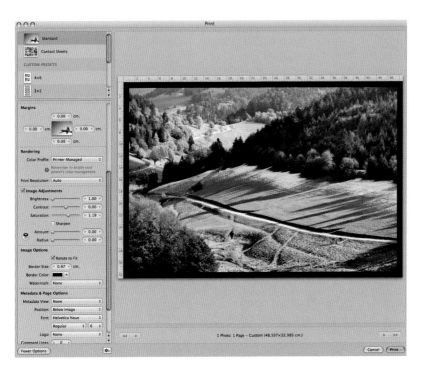

◀ Print preview

All digital images are virtual and thus they have no dimensions until they are sized for output. In this screenshot, from Apple Aperture, many controls for sizing and positioning the print on the paper, as well as different presentation styles (*top left*) can be seen. There are also controls for increasing brightness, saturation, and contrast, but it is best to give the printer a perfect image in the first place. Here, the print has been set up to print to the edge of the paper, with a black border.

OUTPUT TO PAPER

One great advantage of ink-jet printers is that they can print on a wide variety of surfaces. In fact, some desktop models will print on anything from fine paper to thin cardboard.

For the digital photographer, there are three main types of paper available. Most papers are a bright white or a near-white base tint, but some art materials may be closer to cream.

Paper types

Office stationery is suitable for letters, notes, or drafts of designs. Quality is low by photographic standards and printed images cannot be high in resolution or color saturation. Ink-jet paper that is described as 360 dpi or 720 dpi is a good compromise between quality and cost for many purposes.

Near-photographic quality is suitable for final print-outs or proofs for mass printing. These papers range from ultra-glossy or smooth to the slightly textured surface of glossy photographic paper. Paper thickness varies from very thin (suitable for pasting in a presentation album) to the thickness of good-quality photographic paper. Image quality can be the best a printer can deliver with excellent sharpness and color saturation. However, paper and ink costs may be high.

Art papers are suitable for presentation prints or for special effects and include materials such as handmade papers, watercolor papers, or papers with hessian or canvaslike surfaces. With these papers, it is not necessary to use high-resolution images or large files that are full of detail.

Paper qualities

If you want to experiment with different papers just ensure that the paper does not easily shred and damage your machine and clog the nozzles of the ink-jet cartridge. If using flimsy papers, it is a good idea to support them on thin card or a more rigid piece of paper of the same size or slightly larger. The main problem with paper not designed for ink-jets is that the ink either spreads too much on contact or else it pools and fails to dry.

Dye-sublimation printers will print only on specially designed paper—indeed some printers will even refuse to print at all when offered the wrong type of paper. Laser printers are designed only for office stationery and so there is little point in using other types of paper.

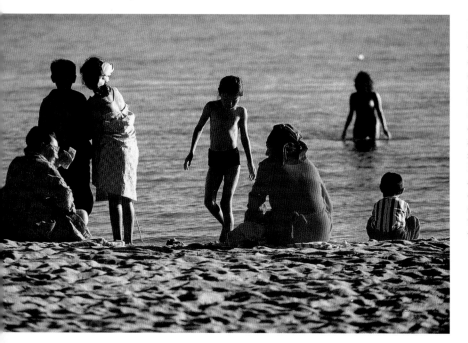

◀ Crucial color
Not only does the blue of this scene test the evenness of printing, it also tests color accuracy. Very slight shifts away from blue will make the image look unbalanced in color and distract the viewer's attention from the relaxed, sun-filled scene. In fact, blue ranks with skin tones as the most important of colors that must be correctly printed, or else the foundation of an image will be seen as unsound.

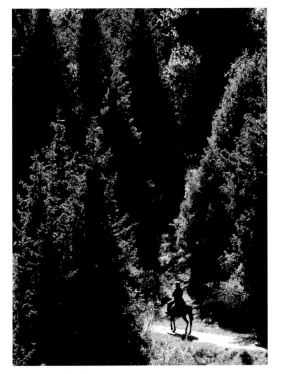

▲ Dark subjects

The blacker a color image, the more ink will be needed to print it. If your subject is full of very dark areas, such as this scene, the paper could easily be overloaded with ink. The ink may then pool if it is not absorbed and the paper could buckle or become corrugated. To minimize this problem, use the best quality paper and tone down the maximum of black as much as possible by reducing the black output level in the Levels control.

TRY THIS

To determine the minimum resolution that gives acceptable results on your printer, you need to make a series of test prints with the same image printed to the same size but saved to different resolutions. Start by printing out a good-quality image of about 8 x 10 in (20 x 25 cm) or letter size at a resolution of 300 dpi—its file size is about 18 MB. Now reduce resolution to 200 dpi (the file size will get smaller but the output size should be the same) and print the file, using the same paper as for the first print. Repeat with resolutions at 100 dpi and 50 dpi. Compare your results and you might be pleasantly surprised: depending on the paper and printer, files with low output resolution can print to virtually the same quality as much higher-resolution files. With low-quality or art materials, you can set very low resolutions and obtain results that are indistinguishable from high-resolution files. In fact, low resolutions can sometimes give better results, especially if you want brighter colors.

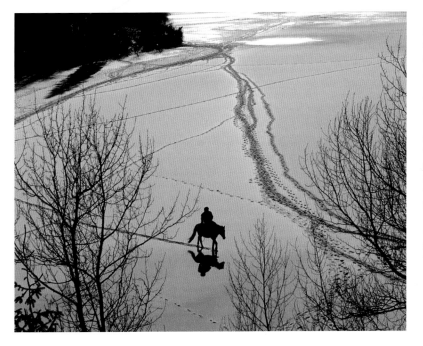

◄ Even tones

Subjects with large expanses of even and subtly shifting tone present a challenge to ink-jet printers in terms of preventing gaps and unevenness in coverage. However, in this image of a frozen lake in a Kazakh winter, the challenge is not so great as the color is nearly gray, which means that the printer will print from all its ink reservoirs. If there is only one color, most often the blues of skies, you are more likely to see uneven ink coverage.

Smoothly blurred
In this close-up of a pohutukawa flower, the sea in the background is blurred to perfect smoothness. Only printing at the highest resolution will preserve the delicate gradations and soft shades that are visible in the water.

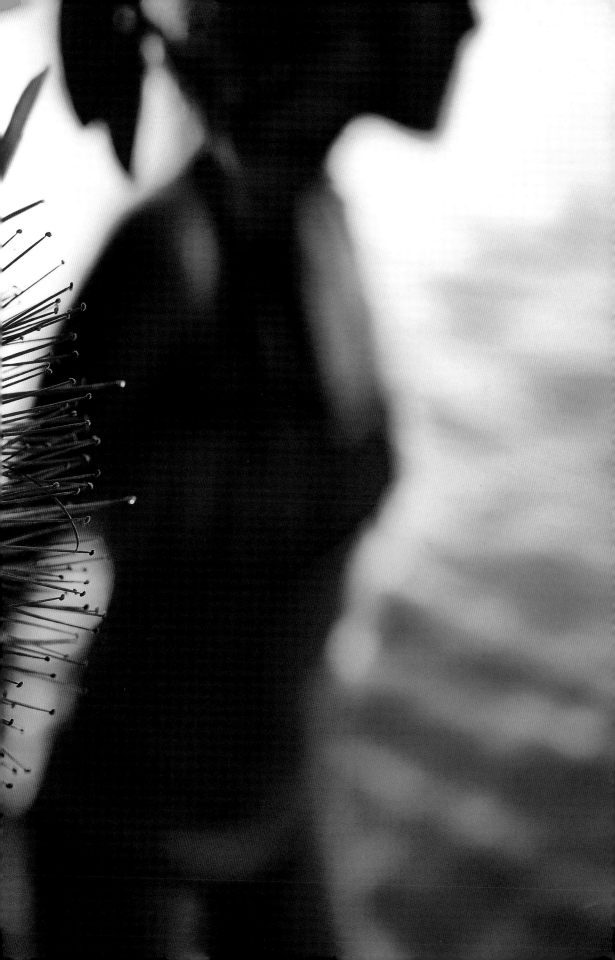

ART PRINTING

Fine-art printing calls for the consummate application of technical and artistic skill—in that order. Without technical skill in controlling color and ensuring exquisitely crafted prints, there is no chance for any artistry to make its way to public notice, let alone be acquired for a major collection.

High-quality prints

It is precisely because the technical hurdles are so substantial that there are now many bureaux that specialize in providing high-quality prints for artists and photographers.

Prints made on high-quality materials at high resolution for art or exhibition purposes have acquired the name "giclée," from the French word

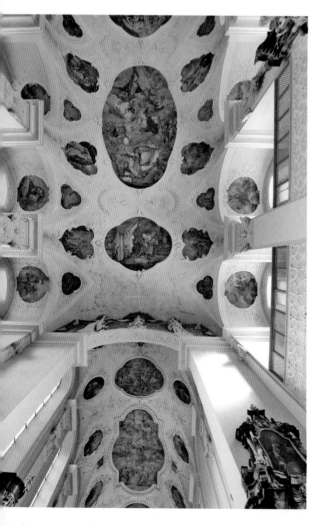

"gicler," meaning "to squirt, or spray." A giclée print should be made: on high-quality archival-grade paper; using pigment inks of high light-fastness; through an output profile specific to the printer/paper combination; at high resolution; and with repeatable results so that extra prints will be identical to the first.

If you make large prints only occasionally, a desk-top printer no larger than tabloid (A3) size, for proofing and making gifts, is all you need. For the occasions when you want poster-sized prints for exhibition or sale, send the image to a giclée bureau that specializes in exhibition-grade work. Their workload ensures that their printers are used regularly and are regularly calibrated, which helps to maintain consistency. Build a relationship with them, and do not hold back on insisting on top quality—that is what you are paying for.

Paper choice

When making prints for a fine-art market or for exhibition, the choice of paper is not only about its stability. The quality of the surface and its color is also of vital importance.

For fine-art photography, matt or semigloss surfaces are popular, and those that mimic silver-gelatin papers are especially sought after. Textured papers, such as hand-calendered watercolor board are also much favored. Collectors of fine-art photography usually prefer to have their giclée prints made on heavy papers—at least 200 gsm (grams per square meter).

The various base whites of paper also have an impact on the appearance of the print. Brilliant whites produce the greatest contrast and largest color gamut, but the result may look mechanical. Softer, off-white bases are most like photographic papers and can be used for a wide range of subjects, while creamy whites work well for monochrome landscapes, portraiture, and social photography.

◀ **Large scale**
Images have a natural size at which they should be viewed: monumental architecture, for example, can be printed as large as possible. Detail is not as important as the sense of space that comes with experiencing a large print.

ARCHIVAL STORAGE

There are two strategies for the archival storage of images. The first is to store prints in museum-grade conditions, that is: in total darkness, low humidity, chilled (close to, but not at, freezing point) with slow air circulation in archivally safe containers. These containers—boxes made from museum board—should emit no chemicals or radiation, be pH-neutral (neither acidic nor alkaline), and, preferably, incorporate a buffer (a substance that helps maintain chemical neutrality). These conditions are ideal for any gelatin-based film or ink-jet print.

The alternative strategy is to store images digitally, as computer files in archivally safe media. MO (magneto-optical) disks were once the favored option but have been supplanted by DVD and Blu-Ray. These are considered more durable than magnetic media such as tapes or hard disks. But you can never be absolutely sure: a fungus found in hot, humid conditions has developed a taste for a dye used in some types of CD, rendering these useless. Any digital medium relies on the non-obsolescence of machines able to read the data so, ironically, the best bet is to keep the image on film.

Preserving prints

In today's world, in which the still image has become the mobile image—jumping from one continent to another—the impermanence of printed pictures is seldom a problem. Long before an image in a portfolio starts to fade, it should be replaced with more recent work. And exhibited prints are rarely hung long enough to suffer fading. However, in a very small number of cases, for example, when prints are sold to collectors or museums or to clients who want to display the image for years on end, stability and archival permanence is important.

The materials involved in creating a print comprise the ink used to make the image and the paper or other supporting layer. Either or both of these will contribute to the impermanence of an

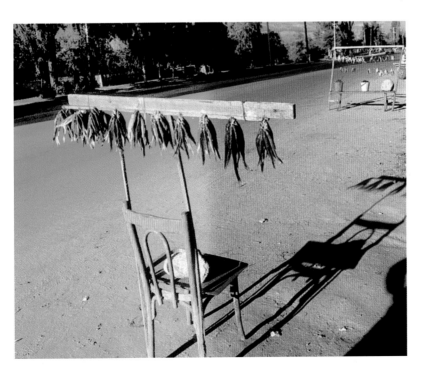

◀ **Faded print**
With half the print shielded, the exposed half faded after only one week's constant exposure to bright sunlight. Since some colors are more fast, or resistant to fading, than others, there will be a color shift in addition to an overall loss of density.

ART PRINTING CONTINUED

image. The best basis for ensuring the longevity of your printed images is to use the best materials: archival-grade papers and pigment inks. Some inks are made of dyes, which color by interacting with the paper: these are, in practice, less light-fast (that is, they are less fade resistant) in bright light. Inks that use pigments—solid materials that are themselves colored—have proven to be, in general, more permanent.

Black-and-white prints made from black and gray inks are likely to be the most stable, since degradation in ink density, unless extensive, will be difficult to detect. But if your black-and-white prints are made up of colored inks, even tiny changes in color balance caused by the fading of one color can create an apparent change.

Prints may also be coated with a clear varnish-like material to aid preservation, particularly to reduce the impact of ultra-violet light and atmospheric chemicals. Some printers apply the coating as part of the printing process, or you may spray it onto the print once the ink is dried.

Showing conditions

The other precondition for longevity is careful exhibition or storage conditions: with the right treatment even highly unstable images will retain the brilliance of their colors.

Ideally, you should hang your prints in cool, dark conditions with low, but not zero, humidity. A lamp may be turned on or a curtain drawn to admit light as needed. Of course, this is not always possible, or desirable, but at the very least you should ensure that your prints are not exposed to direct sunlight. Avoid exposure to high temperatures, high humidity, and chemicals such as those encountered in bathrooms, kitchens, and workshops: steam, oil vapor, and cleaning agents are enemies of image stability. Mounting prints behind UV-opaque glass will also help to preserve colors.

▼ Graphic works

The most demanding types of print are those that combine sharply defined graphics, such as calligraphy, with soft gradations against a neutral ground. Such work demands the highest resolution printing on semigloss paper.

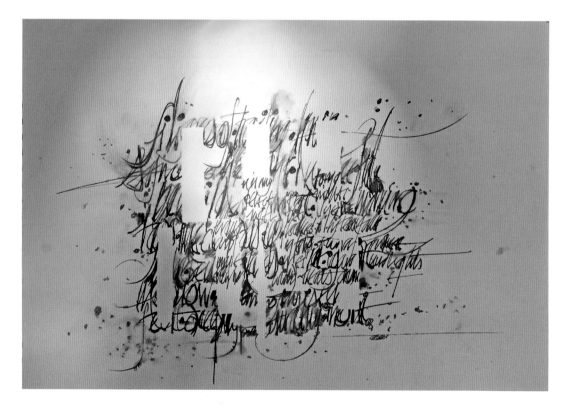

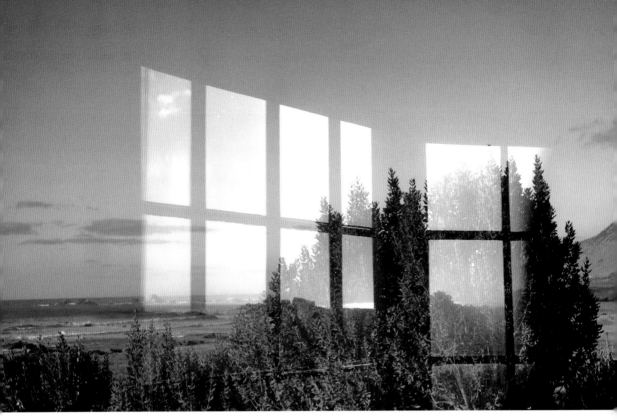

▲ Monochrome demands

Digital prints can now challenge the black-and-white darkroom print. While the utmost subtleties of silver gelatin print still elude ink-jet printers, the flexibility of toning and ease of production are far superior. The best results are obtained by combining black and gray inks—available as warm, neutral, or cold tone—with the lightest touch of color for tinting. Soft-proofing is often inadequate for such subtleties: you need to assess actual prints.

TILING A PRINT-OUT

One way to make prints larger than your printer can handle is to output the image in sections, or tiles. This is simple to do using desktop publishing applications: you simply create a large document size, set up the page for the available paper dimensions, and tell the software to print out each section on the paper supplied. You then trim the prints to remove the overlaps and butt the edges together to produce a seamless, large-size image. Or you can use your image manipulation software to enlarge the image to the size you wish, then crop overlapping sections to the paper size. Print these one by one, and again, trim and join the prints. When a large printer is unavailable, tiling is a very useful technique. Larger prints tend to be viewed from a distance, so small imperfections are acceptable.

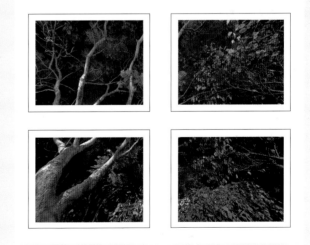

▲ Tiling option

Modern printers work with great precision and consistency, so it is possible to combine tiles almost seamlessly. Use heavier-weight papers, plastic, or film-like material to help retain shape. The overlaps need be only large enough to allow you to trim off the excess and butt the images together before fixing.

ONLINE PRINTING

Using online printing services, as opposed to your own desktop printer, is an excellent option if you only occasionally make prints or have irregular need for poster-sized prints. After a shaky start, the better-known services are now reliable, prompt, and easy to use, offering prices that can compete with running your own printer. However, you will miss out on the fun of watching your image emerge, line by line, from a printer.

Service emphasis

Websites for online printing are models of user-friendly design. If you come across one that is awkward to use, you can abandon it, safe in the knowledge that the next one will probably be easy to use. To order a print, you need only visit the website, upload your image and make the order confirming details of the print size and paper quality, and the quantity you want. Once your payment transaction is cleared (the print may have to go to the address registered to the payment method) you have only to wait for the print to be delivered.

Some services can optimize your images by adjusting contrast and color settings, applying text or borders, and other effects. Some services boast rapid turnaround and will send prints by courier. Some sites will mail abroad too, so you are not limited to services available in your own country.

Check the website for guarantees of satisfaction and whether they provide clear instructions regarding your image's color space, resolution, and format. Take deficiencies in these areas as a warning not to expect the highest quality. Also check what kinds of papers are used and any special claims made for them. High-quality services will print on giclée (exhibition-grade archival) papers and provide print profiles for you to soft-proof your images before ordering prints.

Photobooks online

It is astonishingly easy to design and print photographic books online and have them delivered to your door. The process calls for highly sophisticated technology that is easy for you to understand and use. The wide range of easy-to-use software enables you to make extremely desirable gifts that present your work in the best possible light with minimal effort.

CREATING A PHOTOBOOK

If you have never designed a book, a treat is in store for you. Photobook sites and software such as Apple Aperture provide professionally designed templates that make book creation ridiculously easy. You need only choose the type of page you want—a single picture, or a group of several images, with headings or captions—then fill the picture boxes with your images. To optimize your design you might try the following:

- Look at picture books you admire and note the design of pages that will work with your images
- Collect together all the images you wish to use in your book, and resize them if they are much larger than the book's overall size.
- The order and arrangement of your images, are important. If images are not shown in chronological order, think carefully about the flow or order in which the pictures appear.

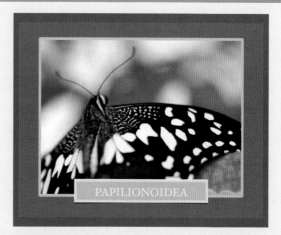

PAPILIONOIDEA

▲ **Cover design**
Work on the cover with a designer if possible: the image sets not only the subject of the book, but also its style, overall mood, and pace of delivery. The image may not need to be the most spectacular, but one that sets the stage for the rest of the book.

The process is a little more involved than printing single images, as you have first to design the book (although many applications automate even that, flowing images into pages). The vital first step is to organize your images, preferably in the order that you wish them to appear in the book. If possible, change their names to number them sequentially. Sketch out on paper how you want the pictures to appear in the book: some could stretch across the whole spread, others take up a page, while two or three may be grouped.

After reviewing the various services available, download the design software supplied by your chosen site (some services allow you to design the book online). Software such as Adobe Lightroom and Apple Aperture also provide photobook design modules. Decide the size of book you want and the type of binding—for example, with soft or rigid covers. Then design your book, placing pictures on to pages using the templates supplied. Upload your book to the website and make your order: multiple orders usually attract a discount. Within a few days you will receive a gorgeous book that will be expertly bound and presented.

BOOK RIGHTS

When you create a book of photographs and make it public by introducing it to a wider circle than your family, or if you offer it for sale, your work enters a public domain that can be tricky to negotiate. Use the following points to guide you:

- Ensure that you own the copyright of every image in the book, or that you have written permission to use any other images.
- Make sure you hold model releases from anyone who has posed for you.
- Ensure that you have property releases if you feature interiors of private property. Some outdoor artworks on public display, as well as certain buildings, restrict photography for professional purposes, but you may fall under their radar if you produce only a few books.
- Beware advertising your work using images from landmarks with photography restrictions.
- Bear in mind that when you create your book, you are creating a new copyright work comprising the book's layout, design, use of type, and pictures.

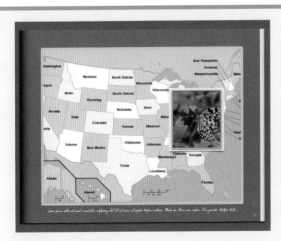

▲ **Section openers**
Break up your book into chapters to vary the pace and give a sense of progress: use maps, tickets, and pages from a passport, to show your location. The juxtaposition of graphics or text with a picture, even one at a token size, creates an invaluable change of rhythm and pace.

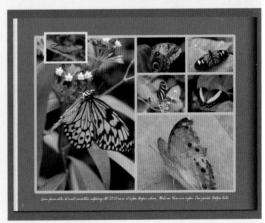

▲ **Busy contents**
Your layouts may be as simple as one image per page, or even one image over a spread of two pages; but a book of only big pictures lacks pace and rhythmic variety. Try making busy pages with multiple images where appropriate—several portraits together, abstract patterns seamlessly joined, and so on.

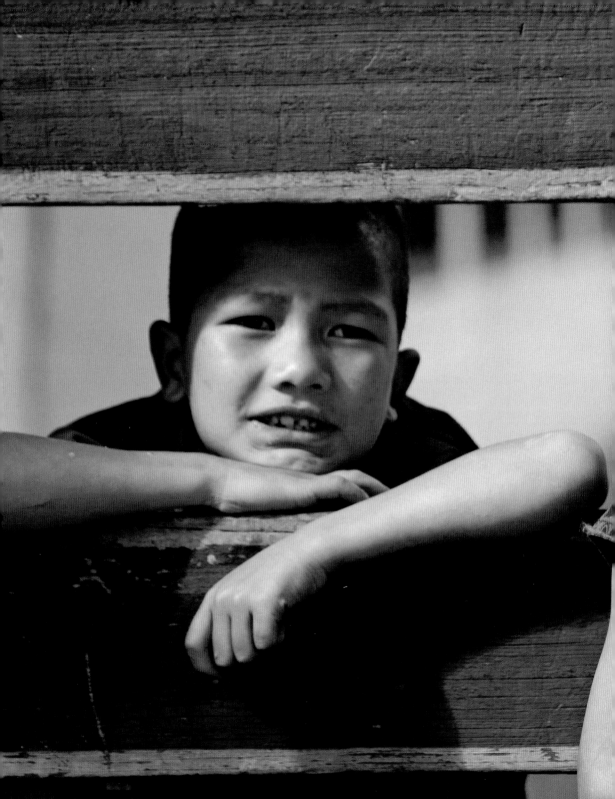

Accurate skin tones
When making prints with brilliant colors, it is tempting to allow the reds their full brilliance. But if skin tones are in view, they must be accurately rendered. The rest of the print will then fall into place.

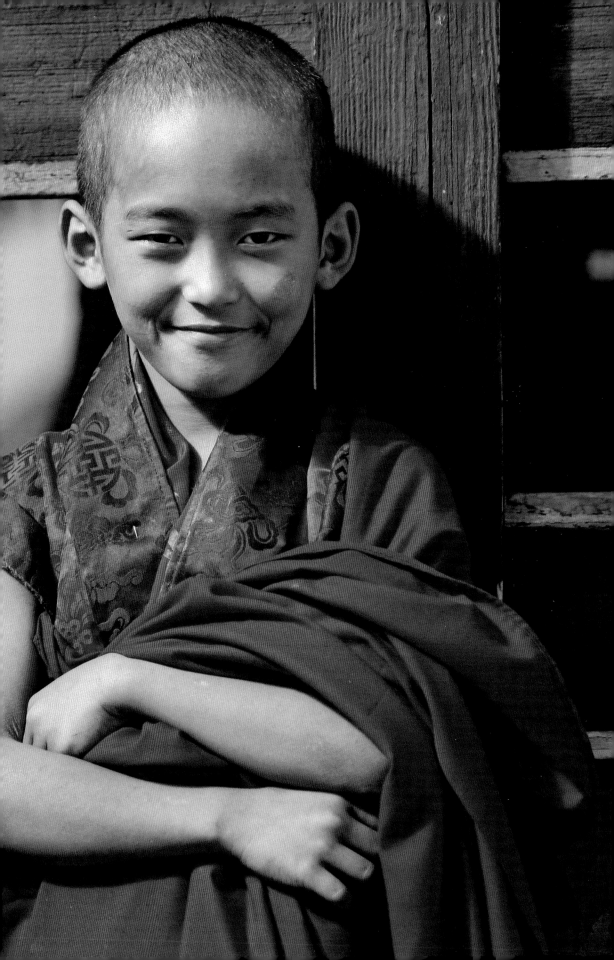

PRESENTING PRINTS

Digital photography hugely expands the options for presenting images. The choice ranges from a handheld tablet screen to single wall-sized prints. In between, you can create installations to present photocopied prints or frame them behind archival window mattes and glass. The biggest change is the ease with which you can turn still images into multimedia shows, adding moving transitions and soundtracks. The key is finding a style of presentation that is appropriate to your work and intentions.

Stages of show

There is a difference between preliminary and final presentations: current practice accepts small digital images for a first viewing. Ensure it is easy for people to view and assess the images quickly and easily.

When presenting personally, you may use a laptop, and one with 17-inch screen is ideal. Glossy screens deliver high-impact images, but reflections can be troublesome. For informal purposes, a tablet device is a good alternative. Art galleries and collectors may expect to see large unmounted prints. Publishers of books, magazines, and journals may ask to see prints up to tabloid size.

For the final display, remember that the color temperature of the illumination affects the final color of your print. If color accuracy is truly vital, you must take account of the lighting at the point of viewing when making the print. In practice, you need simply to ensure that your prints have the correct brightness and tonality, with correct white balance and pleasing colors. (*See also pp. 372–3.*)

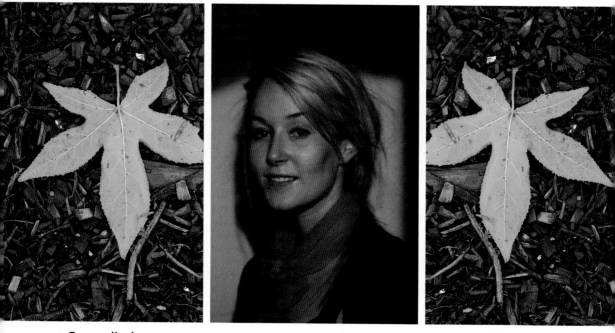

▲ **Group display**
Images are almost never seen singly: even when displayed one-by-one, you are aware of neighboring images out of the corner of your eye, or well inside your view. These juxtapositions create dynamic interactions between adjacent images, which is why the order in which images are shown is important. But you can be explicit about adjacency effects and show pictures in pairs—diptychs—or in threes—triptychs. As painters of the Italian Renaissance knew, three images grouped together are more powerful and resonant than the same images shown separately.

Presenting methods

Prints should be presented to help the viewer appreciate the images and to understand the message you wish to put across. Conventionally, this means that the prints should be at a comfortable eye-level (usually between 4 and 5ft above ground), be hung level, and be equally spaced in proportion to print size. And it should go without saying that the prints should be well lit.

There are many ways to counter the conventional. You can enclose small prints in the bottom of boxes, hang them on a single pin so that they flop about, wrap them around objects, and so on. Creating an installation for your images encloses them in an environment that removes them from normal exhibition space into a conceptual or critical orbit.

TRY THIS

If you have never combined images with sound, you may be in for a thrilling discovery. It is easy to create a multimedia show. Put your images into sequence: if your software does not do that for you, rename your images in order—for example, show01.jpg, show02.jpg. Start up a slide-show application such as Photostage or Photoshare, or a management software package, such as Apple Aperture or Adobe Lightroom. Create transitions between images if needed: usually the best is a simple fade from one to the next. Add the soundtrack by simply checking the soundtrack option and choosing from your collection of downloaded music. Try different tracks to experience the differences in their effect. The music gives depth and dimension to the slide-show.

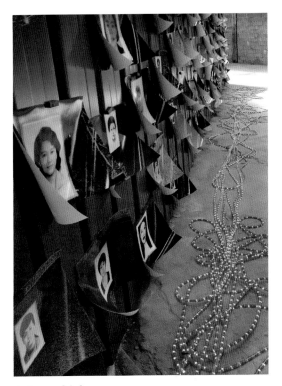

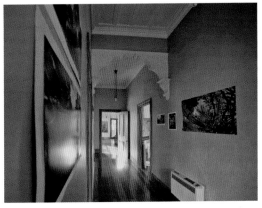

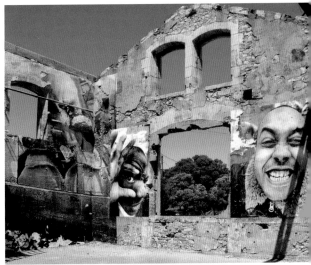

▲ **Any which way**
The display of prints is no longer confined to neatly trimmed, mounted, and glass-framed exhibits. These examples from formal events show that there are only practical limits and conceptual considerations. Feel free to experiment. Stick landscape images on the ground, put portraits on trees, put scenes on the ceiling. Take the view that if it works, it stays up.

SHARING IMAGES

Since the first websites dedicated to the public displaying of photographs started in 1999, photo sharing has become the most important and fastest growing way for images to be viewed. Photo-sharing sites are now truly gigantic, still growing in number, and all rapidly growing in size. It is one of the most feverishly active areas of photography. If you want a snapshot of what is going on in amateur photography, you need only visit a few photo-sharing websites.

Staggering figures

Photo enthusiasts all over the world upload millions of images every minute of the day, every day of the year. Between them, sites such as Webshots, Photobucket, Flickr, Snapfish, Kodak Gallery, and Windows Live Photos hold tens of billions of images. Their membership alone totals over 230 million—probably with insignificant overlap.

The reason for the popularity is that photo sharing enables photographers to join a community of people that share their passion for images. You can show off images that you are proud of, and receive praise. You can also show work to invite constructive criticism that can help you to improve your technique, composition, or general approach. Photo-sharing sites enable you to connect to a vast number of like-minded photographers: after a simple registration that takes a couple of minutes, you can suddenly reach millions of people. A picture uploaded to the site is exposed within seconds to a global community, and if it receives notice, will actually be seen by millions within days. The possibilities for self-promotion are heady.

Setting up

You will already have a collection of images that you want to share. Run an internet search for "photo sharing" or "picture sharing" and visit the many sites available. See which one you like the most and sign up or register. This is usually free, and enables you to view images, post comments, and upload a limited number of images: daily quotas vary but are ample for most purposes. If you wish to upload more images than the quota allows or larger images, and would like extra features such as building galleries and albums, you can subscribe for a higher level of membership.

Remember that an important part of uploading your images is ensuring that they carry useful tags

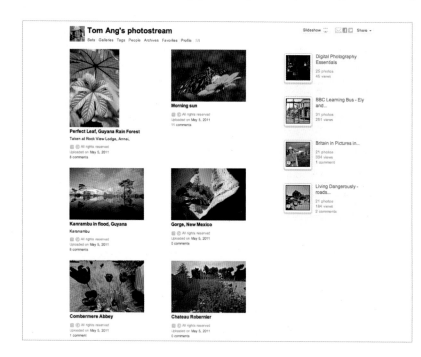

◄ Social tokens

Picture sharing admirably fulfills the needs for a virtual community. Images offer attractive tokens for social exchange—to be admired, to be tagged as "favorite," and to trigger invitations to join specialist groups. And in return, the images offer the photographer multiple opportunities to improve their status—the more people tag your images as favorites, or the more numerous the comments you attract, the higher rises your status in the group.

that key-word the image's content. Remember that within a day of being uploaded, your images will be "under" a pile millions of others that have been more recently uploaded, and therefore more likely to be seen. Even if your images are visually stunning, they are essentially invisible until they are found, and the easiest way for people to find your images will be for them to carry a tag that matches what someone is searching for.

Once able to access site features, you will find that not only can you post pictures and view others' work, but you have become part of a worldwide community humming with help, advice, information, and rumors. Furthermore, site members can be very generous with their assistance for beginners, so it is always worth asking for advice.

Storage and world access

Another useful but not often mentioned advantage of photo-sharing sites is that you are effectively backing up your portfolio of best work off-site—in fact your files exist in multiple locations all around the world. This is particularly valuable in the case of sites that accept large files, of 30MB or more in size. However, although the reliability of these sites is impeccable while in operation, there is always a danger that they will go out of business.

This back-up can be invaluable for professionals as it allows access to your image library from anywhere in the world. Any request for an image can be serviced wherever you are. One result is that photo-sharing sites have become an essential part of a photographer's marketing and operating "toolkit."

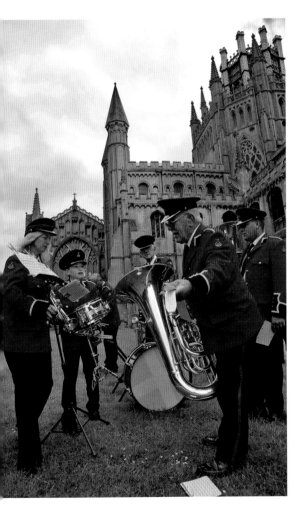

CODE OF COMMENT

The quality of comment, constructive criticism, and exchange of information is a vital element in the vigor of a photo-sharing site. You need to play your part by understanding a code of acceptable behavior that may or may not be unwritten, but is in common with codes elsewhere on the internet:

- Be fair and temperate in your comments.
- Compliments are always welcome but being specific is more helpful: "Lovely harmony of colors" is more informative than "Love it!".
- If you have critical but constructive comments to offer, it may be best to send a personal message to the photographer.
- Never shout by using CAPITAL LETTERS or strings of exclamation marks!!!!
- If you welcome critical comments, say so.

◄ **Ticking boxes**
Picture sharing is about social interaction, so images with identifiable people go down well. This image could easily be shared on social networks and could also be used in a guide to the region, as it shows a lively local event at a recognizable location—Lincoln Cathedral, England.

SHARING IMAGES CONTINUED

Shares management

Photo-sharing sites can be treated as data warehousing for your images. This is practicable if you have access to fast broadband free of quota limits. But before you gleefully upload your entire image collection online, it is wise to organize the material to suit internet use. You will not wish your high-resolution images to be freely available. If a publisher wants to use one of your images, you need them to pay you a licence fee before they have access to the high-resolution files. On the other hand, you need to ensure that all your images can be easily viewed by anyone.

Set up two types of viewing rights: some sites organize by albums or galleries, others by tagging individual images. For public viewing by anyone, use your smaller images; these can be reviewed quickly but the files are too small to be used for any purpose other than on a website. As a further precaution, images in this album may be watermarked (*see p. 376*). The high-resolution files reside in restricted, "invitation-only" albums or are tagged as "private." As the number of images can be overwhelming, the best way for a potential buyer to locate images is to search by tags. If you wish your images to be found it is essential that the caption is accurate and concise, and that your tagging is complete and skilful (*see p. 327*).

Preparing images

The size of the images you show on a website always depends on balancing quality with the speed of loading the web page. Quality depends on both the pixel dimension of the image and the level of compression: fewer pixels and higher compression make for smaller files and quicker loading; the downside is compromised image quality. Using high-quality images—measuring 1,024 pixels or more on the long side—may also expose your images to unlicensed use.

There are four main steps in preparing images for use on the web:

- **Evaluation:** Assess the image quality and content. If it is photographic, you can convert it to JPEG; if it is a graphic with few subtle color gradations, you can convert to GIF. Also adjust brightness and color so the image will be acceptable on a wide range of monitors.

- **Resizing:** Change the size of copies of the images (not the original files) to the viewing size intended, so that the file size is no larger than necessary. Images may be tiny, perhaps 10 x 10 pixels (for use as buttons), or large, say 640 pixels on the longest side (for displaying work).

- **Conversion:** Convert photographic images to JPEG. Set a compression slightly greater than you would like (the image is degraded just a little more than you would wish) to optimize loading speed. (*See also the box left.*)

- **Naming:** Give your files a descriptive name using letters and/or numbers. The only punctuation marks you should use, if desired for clarity, are dashes (-) or underscores (_). Always put a period before the jpg suffix (.jpg).

OPTIMIZING YOUR PICTURES ON THE WEB

You will want those who access your site to receive your images quickly and to have the best experience of your images the system permits. Here are some tips for optimizing your images on the internet.

- Use Progressive JPEG if you can. This presents a low-resolution image first and gradually improves it as the file is downloaded. The idea is that it gives the viewer something to watch while they are waiting for the full-resolution image to appear.

- Use the WIDTH and HEIGHT attributes to force a small image to be shown on screen at a larger size than the actual image size.

- Use lower resolution color—for example, indexed-color files are much smaller than full-color equivalents. An indexed-color file uses only a limited palette of colors (typically 256 or fewer), and you would be surprised at how acceptable many images look when reproduced even with only 60 or so colors (*see p. 222*).

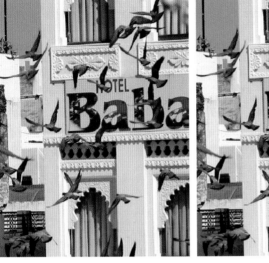

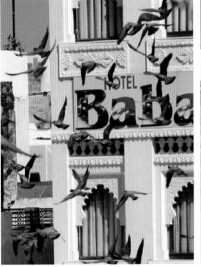

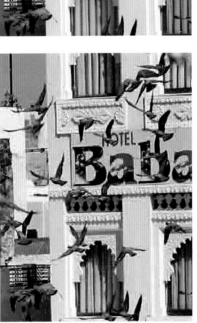

◄ JPEG compres

Maximum quality is the reward for minimum file compression. Even at high magnifications it is hard to see any loss in detail. At the magnification shown here you can just make out, with careful examination, a very slight blurring of detail in the right-hand image compared with the original on the left. The advantage, of course, is that the file is compressed from nearly 7MB to only about half the size, 3MB.

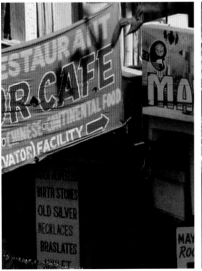

◄ Small file, low quality

At the minimum quality setting, the file size is pared down to an impressive 200K from 7MB—to some 3 percent of the original size. The loss of image quality is evident but only at high magnification: the clarity of the lettering and the pigeons' wings are now blurred and labor under artifacts. The evenness of tone of the wall is also broken. However, this is a 500 percent view, and the full image, at its normal size on screen, reveals none of these artifacts.

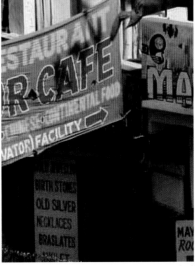

◄ Medium quality

With a medium-quality setting, here showing a different part of the same image, there is a substantial and useful reduction in file size—from nearly 7MB to just 265K—more than 25 times smaller, or 4 percent of the original file size. Download times are accordingly reduced by a large factor. Yet there is barely visible or practical loss of quality, even at high magnification. With the loss of resolution that accompanies printing, there will be no visible differences..

PHOTOS ON THE INTERNET

Photo-sharing websites such as Flickr and Instagram, as well as social media such as Facebook, make it very easy to publish images for worldwide viewing. However, these sites and services are essentially a collection of pictures: your work is presented on pages identical to millions of others, with only very limited features for personalizing page design. If you feel this is a constraint, you can easily create your own website instead. Bear in mind, though, that if you go solo, you lose the very considerable drawing power of the photo-sharing sites, with their tens of millions of visitors.

Hosting

There are hundreds of services that can host your site—that is, your files are physically located on their computers, which distribute pages to the visitors to your site. And there are hundreds that offer free hosting. Check the terms of service to make sure you will not have to carry advertisements and that you do not give away any rights to your pictures. You will also want secure ways in which people can communicate with you via the site. Ensure that the host has sufficient capacity to hold your pictures and that the monthly data-transfer limit is sufficient for your site's needs.

Site design

The advantages of running your own site include control over the look and feel, no restraints over use of your images (within legal limits), and the ability to organize the images however you like. The main disadvantage compared to picture-sharing sites is that you have to do quite a bit more work.

Nonetheless, there is a considerable amount of help available for the design and construction of your website. Free design applications can be downloaded; there are hundreds of web-based tutorials; and some services help you construct sites directly online. In addition, many image applications offer templates for site design. They also automate publishing of the site—that is, uploading the HTML pages and resources to your hosting server.

For more sophisticated sites on which you can present Flash or animated content with more features, the most popular solution is to use WordPress content-management software to create an entire site consisting of pages, blogs, and galleries, and to manage your content.

Once you have created your website, do not forget to tell everyone about it. Send links to all your friends and colleagues, asking them to spread the word, and post announcements on blogs.

PROFESSIONAL SITES

Websites such as Squarespace, 500px, SmugMug, and PhotoShelter provide paid-for picture hosting along with other features to suit markets as varied as photojournalism and wedding photography. In return for a fee, you can present a portfolio of work. Some will also store large numbers of high-resolution files as a backup to your own storage. Some sites may market your work by offering your images as part of the collective inventory of stock photography and may also handle management of the picture rights. There are, however, no shortcuts to the work needed to add keywords, captions, and tags to images, then uploading them all to the hosting site.

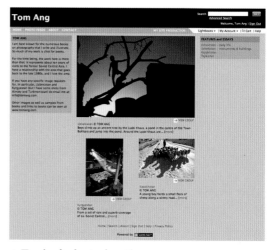

▲ Typical photo hosting

The home page of a photographer features details and links to other pictures in the photo collection. Visitors can click on an image to view an enlargement and search by keywords. If they wish to purchase usage rights, they can select the images and complete the whole transaction online.

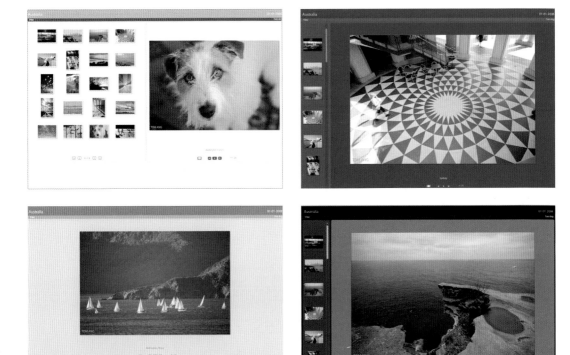

▲ Image export

Applications such as Adobe Lightroom offer features that automate the creation of web pages from predesigned templates. Other image-manipulation programs offer facilities that can automate the publication of images to sites such as Flickr and Facebook. This can be convenient if you publish many photos online.

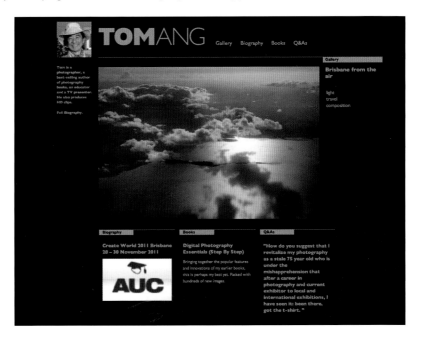

▶ Personal website

Even a simple personal site is effective in presenting yourself to the wider community. By showcasing your photographs and providing details of your interests, career, and availability, you allow visitors to learn about you at their convenience and to contact you through the site when they want.

SELLING YOUR PICTURES

There can be few photographers who would not be delighted to earn cash from their passion. It is possible to earn money through your photos, and there are some professionals who earn a comfortable living; but make no mistake, it is not easy. It is not only that digital photography has enabled millions of amateurs to produce work of professional standard. Thanks in part to the incredible ability of the internet to disseminate to the entire world at zero cost, the structure of the market for photography has been turned inside out and upside down. As a result, some old strategies work, others are hopelessly outmoded.

Cost and value

With so many photographers all around the world creating images of publishable quality, the unit cost of a picture taken of the west coast of Australia, for example, has been driven down to a small fraction of what it was in the days of film. So, while it may cost you a small fortune to equip yourself and travel to a location, the value of the resulting image is relatively low: hundreds, if not thousands, of other photographers have produced a similar shot.

However, you can drive up the value of your photographs by striving to meet specific needs: that is why you can charge more for photographing weddings, portraits, and products.

Microstock

The ready supply of highly competent photography has created the market formerly called "royalty free" but now more commonly referred to as "microstock." These are websites containing millions of images whose rights can be licenced for what amounts to loose change. These rights may cover virtually any use at all, including commercial, and last for the life of the licensee. In return, the photographer earns a royalty—around 30 percent of what the site receives for your image.

Many photographers earn from these sites, though making a living requires the submission of thousands of images. The best sites are the hardest to contribute to, but there are so many that there are even sites dedicated to their review. Once you have chosen a site you wish to work with, you will need to submit a small selection of images for initial review. If these pass for technical quality and saleability, you can submit freely. Your pictures will be reviewed, then posted on the site. Buyers visit the site in search of images: if they choose one of your pictures, they pay the site to download a

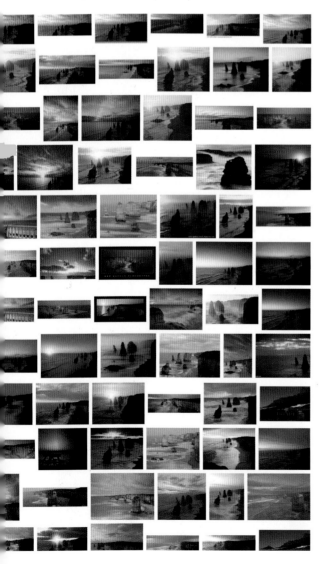

◀ Twelve Apostles

Even on the remote western coast of Australia, a popular landmark can attract thousands of photographs. Search engines reveal that there are over 700,000 images of this location alone—some are shown here. Your task is to make your shot a distinct and individual, yet truthful, depiction.

high-resolution copy of the image. You will then be credited with the royalty. This can be turned into cash, be used to top up your Paypal account, or be used to obtain rights to images.

Playing tag

The larger microstock sites hold tens of millions of images. One result is that it is easier to search for images by using words or tags. It follows that the key to making your image visible to searches conducted by potential clients is accurate, concise, and inclusive tagging of your images. In general, the more tags you can append to an image, the more likely it is to be found when someone searches.

▼ Topical coverage
The images most likely to sell are those that cover contemporary issues. Landscapes and views of famous monuments are least likely to sell. This image is clearly about modern transport and its effect on the environment, and gives an impression of the scale and numbers involved.

TAGGING PHOTOS

Tags are keywords that describe images in terms of their subject matter. Tags are different from the image caption which is a plain-language description of subject. Keywords in the caption should also be used as tags. A caption may say "Shadow of a Boeing 727 flying over Highway 66, Santa Fe, New Mexico, USA" (*see below*). The tags should include: "shadow," "aircraft," "flight," "highway," "road," "route," "cars," and "traffic." Other tags for the same image may include more abstract concepts such as: "sunny," "yellow-green," "aerial," "environment," "transportation," "greenhouse gas," and "global warming."

Tags can also be used to organize images: for example, all your images taken in New Mexico over a period of years can be quickly gathered together if all are tagged "New Mexico," even if they are kept in separate folders.

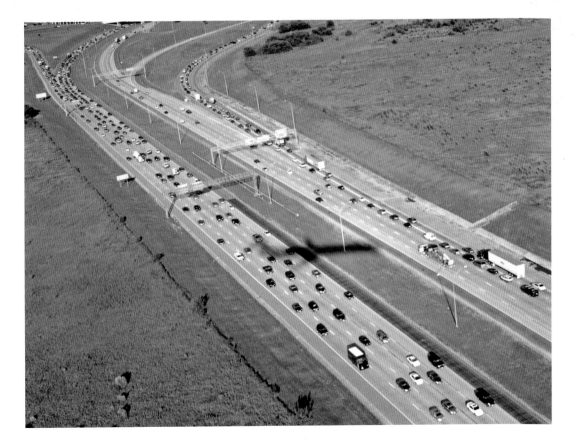

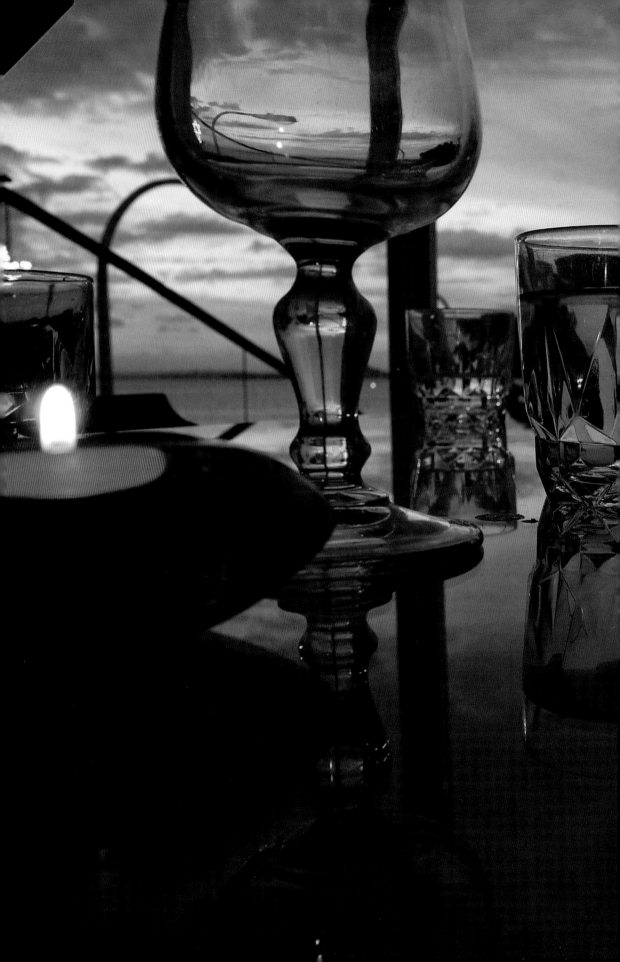

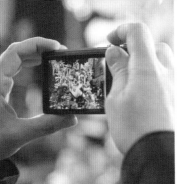

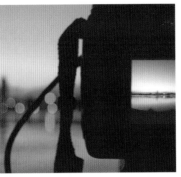

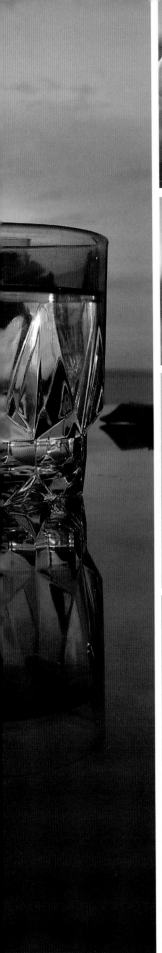

5 BUYING GUIDE

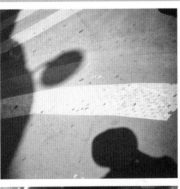

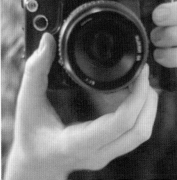

THE IDEAL CAMERA

There are many strategies for choosing the ideal camera. It is important to remember that the best camera in the world may not be the best for you, and that a camera that is easy to use may not be the best option when you want to experiment and improve your photography. In this day of innumerable equipment reviews and tests, it is not difficult to find guides to help you. In general, it is the higher-grade equipment that receives expert testing and review while cheaper point-and-shoot cameras are more superficially judged.

Matchmaking

The match between what you would like or need and the camera available is mostly a matter of common sense, and not different from any other purchasing decision. Set yourself a budget, not forgetting to include requisite accessories such as a protective filter (*see p. 347*), camera case, spare batteries, and memory cards. Review your current and projected uses of your photographs to work out which type of camera will best suit you. Consider the following points when making your choice:

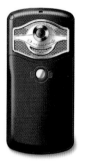

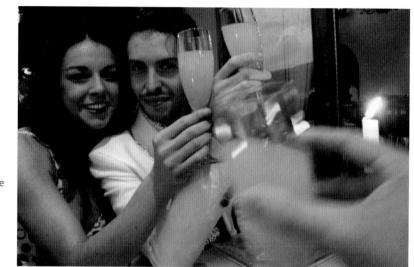

Reasons for choosing:
- With you most of the time
- Easy uploading to web
- Unobtrusive
- Inexpensive
- Easy to use

CAMERA PHONE

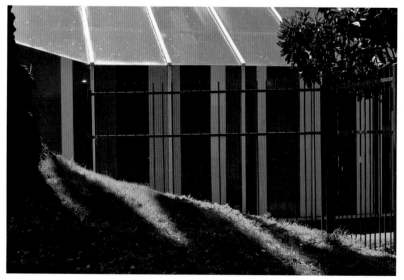

LOW-END COMPACT

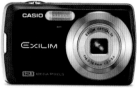

Reasons for choosing:
- Excellent introduction
- Easy to use
- Low cost
- Easy to carry
- Excellent image quality is possible

■ Compact point-and-shoot models are good for recreational and informal photography, and being lightweight, are good for traveling (*see p. 336*).

■ Enthusiast or advanced compacts (*see pp. 336–7*) are good for those needing higher image quality or more features; they offer more control and may be used as a back-up to a more serious camera.

■ Super-zoom or bridge cameras (*see p. 337*) are lightweight for traveling and good for enthusiast photographers on once-in-a-lifetime trips.

■ Compact interchangeable lens cameras are a good option for prosumer users (enthusiasts requiring professional quality) and those requiring access to specialist lenses.

■ Single-lens reflex cameras are good for those who need the highest standards in image quality, as well as control and versatility. The large dSLR models also offer the highest standards in reliability and durability. Models using APS-C sensors are good where extreme telephoto effects are needed. Models using a full 35mm format sensor are best for ultra-wide views.

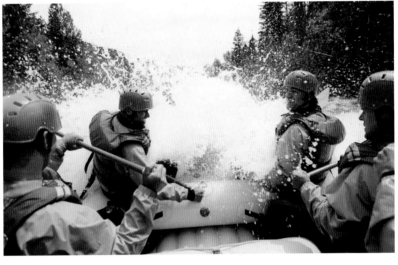

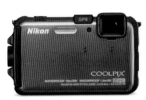

Reasons for choosing:
■ Waterproof
■ Dust-proof
■ Drop-proof
■ Compact
■ GPS tagging possible

RUGGED COMPACT

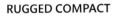

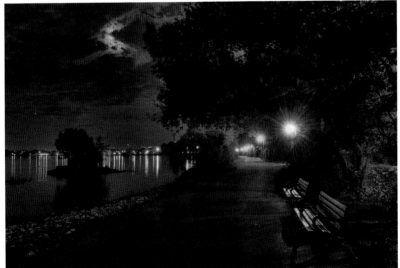

HIGH-END COMPACT

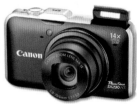

Reasons for choosing:
■ Lots of control
■ Excellent image quality
■ Good in low light
■ Many features
■ Recording in RAW

THE IDEAL CAMERA CONTINUED

The incredibles

You will be drowned in a welter of camera features, of which there are two kinds. First, there are those fashioned to help sell the camera: they allow words such as "amazing" and "incredible" to pepper sales talk, drive editorial interest, and separate the model from the dozen others that are essentially identical. A camera needs a repertoire of such features: the salesman or online site will offer them all in the hopes that one will have the "wow" factor to clinch the deal. Such features may include automatic panoramas, vintage effects, interval timing, face or smile detection, slide shows, in-camera manipulation, and many others. Impressive on paper, these features often turn out to be used once, then forgotten forever.

Rest assured that all modern cameras possess more than enough of the other, essential features and capabilities that you will use regularly. The issue is not their presence but the way in which you use them: do they work conveniently for you, and do they operate efficiently and smoothly? Convenience and handiness is a personal matter so, however detailed the reviews and tests, an important part of your research should involve handling different cameras yourself.

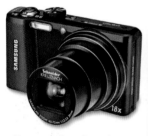

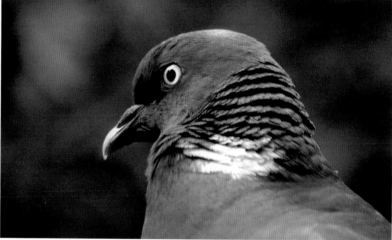

Reasons for choosing:
- Extreme telephoto
- Wide zoom range
- Compact
- High resolution
- Easy handling

SUPER-ZOOM

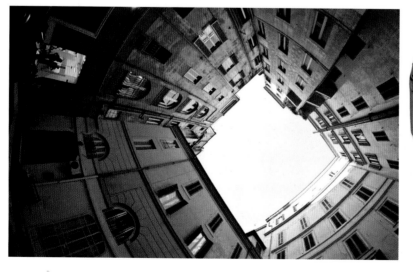

COMPACT INTER-CHANGEABLE LENS

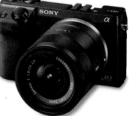

Reasons for choosing:
- Relatively large sensor
- High-quality lenses
- Flexible viewing options
- High resolution
- Compact

When comparing features, remember that you do not have to use them all—although having too many can be confusing. Ensure that the camera will work well for you should you have special requirements, such as needing a very wide-angle view, or if you are planning to copy paintings.

Two sizes

Of the two types of size you have to consider—camera size and resolution size—the most important is the size of the camera. You can boast the biggest resolution on the block, but if the camera is so large you have to make an effort to take it with you, you would be better off with a smaller camera that you take pleasure in carrying around and using.

Modern sensor resolutions are larger than needed by most people by a factor of several times. If you make pictures that you usually view on screen or post on social networks and picture-sharing sites, but you only occasionally make large prints, resolutions of around 6 megapixels are more than sufficient for 99 per cent of your photography. In fact it is now difficult to find a camera offering less than 10 megapixels. While the number of pixels does not fully assure image quality, it certain fills up memory cards and hard disk drives.

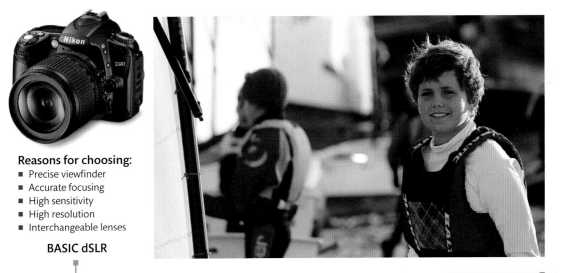

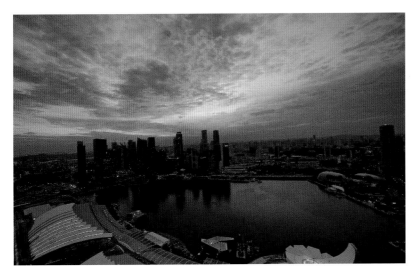

Reasons for choosing:
- Precise viewfinder
- Accurate focusing
- High sensitivity
- High resolution
- Interchangeable lenses

BASIC dSLR

ADVANCED dSLR

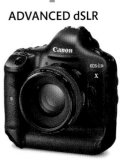

Reasons for choosing:
- Highly precise viewfinder
- High-speed operation
- Ultra-high sensitivity
- High resolution
- Excellent build quality

CAMERA PHONES

The capabilities of camera phones range from handsets that simply make phone calls and snap pictures to those that can apply image manipulations, upload images to remote websites, and more. The so-called "smartphone," with multimedia capabilities and multiple functions, is invariably equipped with a camera, and one with increasingly respectable performance that is able to rival that of simple point-and-shoot cameras.

The camera in your pocket

When the emphasis is on being ready to grab a shot whenever it may occur—particularly in a dramatic, once-in-a-lifetime situation—the best camera, without doubt, is the one that is in your pocket. That is most likely to be the camera on your phone.

The differences between camera phones and point-and-shoot cameras has narrowed to the extent that camera phones can start up, respond, and shoot almost as rapidly as point-and-shoot cameras. However, flash is much weaker on camera phones and they are not usually equipped with either fast (large-aperture) or zoom lenses. Low-light capabilities of camera phones are much weaker than those of compact cameras. Most use a combination of ISO selection and exposure time to adjust exposure.

The largest weakness of camera phones is their unprotected lens. Even when they are recessed for protection, lenses easily attract dust and fingerprints. Keep the lens clean by regularly using a microfiber cloth to remove grease and dust.

DIGITAL ZOOM

This feature takes the image produced by the lens's longest focal length setting and progressively enlarges the central portion. The camera appears to offer a zoom range that is longer than that of the lens alone, but this comes at the price of a reduction in image quality.

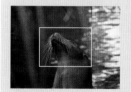
Longest zoom setting

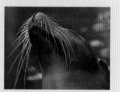
Digital zoom enlargement

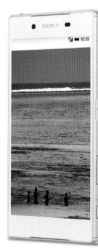

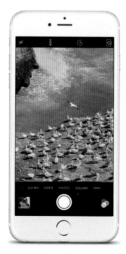

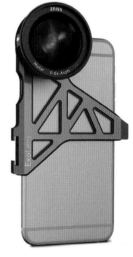

▲ High resolution
Camera phones offering high resolutions—of 23 megapixels or more—can make a good substitute for a point-and-shoot camera if they offer fast autofocus. Modern cameras can also record 4K (Ultra HD) video.

▲ Multifunction
Some designs are famed for the quality of their cameras, which may include image stabilization, as well as many built-in filters. High-end camera phones offer high-resolution screens and 4K (Ultra HD) as standard.

▲ Accessorizing
A camera phone's built-in lens may be supplemented by attaching converter lenses. Ranging from fish-eye lenses to telephoto, these vary greatly in quality, but generally speaking, the more you pay, the better the results.

Camera phone features

While a simple camera phone, offering essentially no more than a shutter button, may seem restrictive, many photographers enjoy the return to absolute basics. With nothing to adjust, you can concentrate fully on the subject and respond with uninhibited spontaneity. Many smartphones allow you to touch the screen to select the focus or exposure point, which is useful for back-lit conditions and off-center subjects. Some provide digital zoom to increase the reach of the view; these work best with high-resolution cameras (see box opposite).

Choosing your camera phone

Fitting a camera into the tiny space of a cellphone demands compromises, so it is best to look on the camera element as pared-down and simplified. Choose a phone that works well for you, before checking that the camera part performs well. You should be able to access the camera in a single movement; it should be able to take pictures at a rate of at least one frame per second; and uploading images to your computer should be easy—through USB or wirelessly through Bluetooth.

EXTENSION BY APP

A most significant aspect of camera phone technology is the ability to extend what they can do by downloading and installing applications on the camera phone itself. They do this by running with standard operating systems such as Android or iOS. Essentially they are computers that can be expanded if you supply more and more applications.

You can install applications that link GPS (Geographical Positioning Systems) data with your images, or that can even send the images to your computer or photo-sharing site automatically. There are numerous applications that make it easy to post-process your images, giving them vintage or other special effects. You can install apps to add grids to your screen to aid composition, add anti-shake features to reduce blurry pictures, or even add a self-timer. Other apps make it easy to share your images with social networks or dedicated photo-sharing sites. All these extend the feature-set of a camera phone without physically changing the phone.

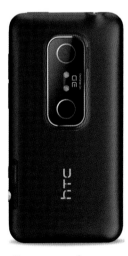

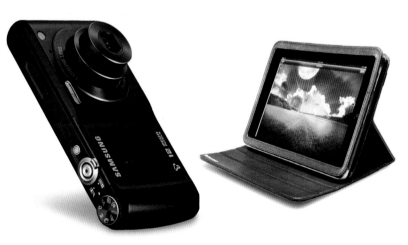

▲ **Stereoscopic**
Camera phones with two lenses can capture stills and video in stereo, and also play back in stereo. Modern systems do not need special glasses: the stereo effect is built into the screen, giving impressive results.

▲ **True zoom**
Some camera phones are true hybrids: cameras that can make phone calls, and vice versa. Equipped with a zoom lens, flash, and many camera-like controls, these may be ideal for the keen, connected photographer.

▲ **Tablets**
Many tablets are equipped with both backward- and forward-facing cameras but they do not make the most convenient cameras. They are ideal for showing pictures, and for monitoring views thanks to their large screens.

COMPACTS

Palm-sized and as easy to use as to carry around, compact point-and-shoot cameras did more than take photography to the masses—they took photography into every corner of modern life. From the most private and prosaic tasks, such as brushing your teeth or cooking last night's meal, to the most important occasions, from births to weddings, anything and everything was caught on camera.

Point-and-shoot cameras
Compact point-and-shoot cameras are so ubiquitous and widely used that it is easy to take them for granted. With more computing power and high-grade optics in each camera than took man to the moon, they are capable of amazingly good results in a wide range of conditions. And no longer are the color choices black or silver: many models offer body colors ranging from pink to purple through yellows and blues.

■ Ensure the camera is not too small: you should be able to use the controls while holding it.

■ Compacts are high-precision optical instruments: they will not survive for long in the bottom of a handbag, and will need to be looked after.

Enthusiast or advanced compacts
When images from camera phones can make it on to newspaper front pages and be seen all around the world, keen photographers should not dismiss simple point-and-shoot cameras too quickly. But if

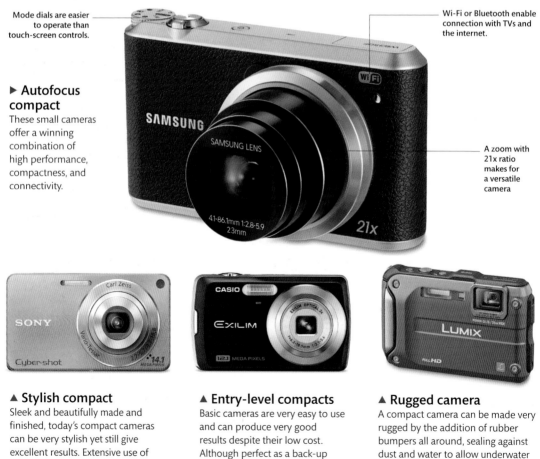

Mode dials are easier to operate than touch-screen controls.

Wi-Fi or Bluetooth enable connection with TVs and the internet.

▶ **Autofocus compact**
These small cameras offer a winning combination of high performance, compactness, and connectivity.

A zoom with 21x ratio makes for a versatile camera

▲ **Stylish compact**
Sleek and beautifully made and finished, today's compact cameras can be very stylish yet still give excellent results. Extensive use of touch-screen controls eliminates virtually all buttons, and compact dimensions make for easy portability.

▲ **Entry-level compacts**
Basic cameras are very easy to use and can produce very good results despite their low cost. Although perfect as a back-up camera, they may not be ideal for a beginner as their basic controls limit experimentation.

▲ **Rugged camera**
A compact camera can be made very rugged by the addition of rubber bumpers all around, sealing against dust and water to allow underwater operation, and with oversized controls to allow for use with gloves in cold weather conditions.

you enjoy cameras with many features, such as fully manual controls plus a choice of capturing in raw or JPEG, then enthusiast compacts will fit the bill. Some models offer zooms that are wider than usual (for example, 24mm or 25mm), some offer fast lenses with maximum apertures of f/2 or better and, as a class, every aspect of handling and image quality can be expected to be superior to that of less costly point-and-shoot models.

■ If you wish to shoot raw format images, check how quickly the camera works with the resulting large files.

■ If your camera is a back-up to a larger model, ensure that you can share the same type of memory cards and cables.

■ Check the availability of a hot-shoe if you may wish to use an accessory flash-gun.

Super-zoom cameras

Advances in lens technology have enabled extremely long-range zooms to be squeezed into very compact housings. Ranges of 20x are common, and 50x is possible. The wide-angle end is as short as 20 mm (usually 24 mm to 35mm), while the long end of the range can reach an amazing 1,000 mm or more. This means you can expect a lion's head to fill the frame at usual viewing distances on a safari.

To ensure that you can obtain sharp images at the longest zoom settings, built-in image stabilization is a must. Maximum apertures at the long end may be limited to as small as f/8; this is a severe limitation on working in low light or if you wish to obtain short depth-of-field effects. These cameras are ideal for travel and vacation photography as they are very compact yet highly versatile.

■ Check the sturdiness of the lens housing at full extension: it will be a little loose, but should not bend visibly.

■ Limit use of the zoom in very dusty conditions to avoid sucking up dust into the mechanism.

RESOLUTION AND QUALITY

The word "resolution" is used in several different senses in photography. Applied to camera sensors, it measures the number of photo-sites used to capture the image. The resolution of the image itself is often equated with image size, or its number of pixels. In the context of lens performance or image quality, it is a measure of how well a system separates out fine detail.

These measures are related, but not directly. For example, the resolution of a sensor sets the upper limit of image quality, but not the lower limit: a high-resolution sensor may deliver a poor-resolution image if the quality of capture, lens, or image-processing is poor.

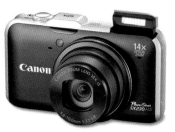

▲ **Enthusiast zoom**
Even in a compact body, modern cameras can offer extensive zoom ranges of 14x or greater. However, maximum aperture at the telephoto end may be limited to f/8 or less, which restricts photography in low-light conditions.

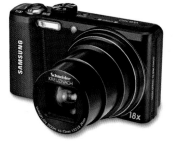

▲ **Super zoom**
By compromising on a slightly larger camera, the lens can be of larger aperture and focal range. Modern super-zooms offer very wide-angle performance, for example from 24mm to 350mm extreme telephoto with full camera controls.

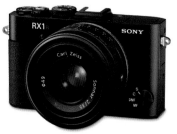

▲ **Prime-lens compact**
For the enthusiast or purist who does not need a zoom lens, a compact such as this model, with a fixed zoom (28 mm or 35 mm equivalent), may be an acceptable option. It is easy to operate and places an emphasis on the quality of image capture.

MIRRORLESS COMPACTS

Within a few years of its introduction in 2010, the mirrorless interchangeable lens compact camera proved to be an innovative development. By disposing of the mirror used by SLR cameras (*see pp. 340–1*), this new design could be made slimmer and more compact. By offering an interchangeable lens mount that is very close to the sensor, these cameras can offer compact lenses of their own and also make use of virtually any lens in existence simply by fitting an appropriate lens adapter to interface between lens and camera.

The right camera for the job

Mirrorless cameras exploit a range of sensor sizes—from Nikon's 13.8 x 10.4 mm, through the popular Micro 4/3 and 4/3 sizes, to "full-frame" 24 x 36mm. If you need the most compact designs, choose cameras fitted with smaller sensors. The lenses will also be more compact than those for larger sensors. If you fit a lens designed for a larger sensor, you will multiply the effective focal length, giving extra telephoto reach but reducing wide-angle views (*see also p. 343*).

Multiple modes, overrides, and many menu options give versatility.

The high-resolution electronic viewfinder (EVF) is ideal for accurate framing.

▶ Full-frame compact

A relatively small body equipped with a 35mm format sensor offers a winning compact but high-quality package taking a vast range of interchangeable lenses. Compromises come with reduced battery life and sturdiness.

A cover hides and protects sockets for HDMI, USB, and other cables.

Zoom or fixed-focal length lenses can be fitted.

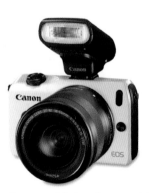

▲ Compact interchangeable

By including an APS-C sensor size and only a rear LCD screen, models of this type can be very light and compact. Interchangeable lenses—ranging from wide angles to long zooms—and flashes extend its versatility.

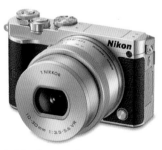

▲ Modern retro

The controls may look old-fashioned, but their chunkiness improve handling and usability, complementing touch-screen controls. These compact and light cameras use a CX-format sensor (just 14 mm on longest side).

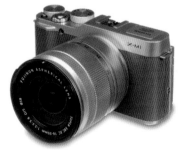

▲ Top-end siblings

You don't have to pay big money to benefit from the superior technology of top-end models. By sacrificing a few features, such as optical rangefinder, you can still capture high-quality images with a mid-budget camera.

Picture quality is not necessarily inferior with smaller sensors, given the high quality of modern signal processing. For the best compromise between size and image quality, choose cameras with APS-C sized sensors or similar—that is, about 24 x 15 mm.

These cameras are all absolutely packed full of functions, so they offer users extreme versatility. Their capabilities may be extended by installing apps from the internet, and many models offer the ability to connect wirelessly to the Web or to computers and printers.

Using the EVF

In addition to the monitor screen included on the backs of all cameras, the more advanced models offer users an electronic viewfinder (EVF). This is a small but very high-resolution screen that is looked at through an eyepiece. The EVF gives you the best image for evaluating and framing your subject. It works well in the dark and can give fairly accurate representations of color balance and exposure override, as well as special effects. The EVF can display camera settings clearly, too, so you do not need to take your eye away from the viewfinder in order to check the camera's settings.

Interchangeable lenses

As sensors improved in quality, the search began for camera designs that could combine the image quality and versatility of single-lens reflex (SLR) cameras with the compactness and portability of point-and-shoot models.

The 4/3 (Four Thirds) format is an open standard for single-lens reflex cameras—they have a mirror box and reflex optical viewfinder behind a standard lens mount. The sensor has an imaging area of 17.3 x 13.0 mm (21.63 mm diagonal), with a 4:3 aspect ratio. This results in a focal-length factor of 2x—for example, a 25 mm lens on 4/3 format is equivalent to a 50 mm lens on full-frame (*see p. 340*).

Video capable

Almost all modern models are capable of capturing video, and when possible they will capture HD (high definition). Some can even record at 4K (Ultra HD). These cameras can produce footage of film-studio quality and are, indeed, even used in the motion-picture industry. These cameras helped revolutionize independent filmmaking. For best results, ensure you equip the camera with high-quality, high-speed memory cards.

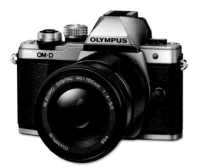

▲ SLR look-alike
It may seem like an SLR, but this model is considerably smaller and lighter. Thanks to its Micro 4/3 lens mount, it accepts a wide range of excellent optics to give professional-grade imaging in the mid-price range.

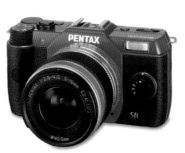

▲ Compact capable
Cameras that do not offer the highest resolution or fastest lenses benefit users who wish to balance high quality with convenience and speedy operation. These cameras are also suited to smaller budgets or those just starting out.

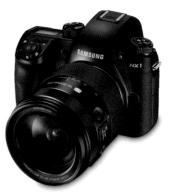

▲ Advanced CIL
High-specification compact interchangeable lens (CIL) cameras with APS-C sensors bridge the gap between truly professional models and others. The most recent models also offer 4K video recording.

SLRs

At one time, the dominance of the digital single-lens reflex (SLR) camera seemed unassailable. It gives the clearest, most precise view of the subject with accurate feedback on focus. But the SLR has lost ground to compact interchangeable lens cameras using high-resolution electronic viewfinders.

lenses and accessories that can be used on larger SLRs but are smaller, lighter, and generally offer lower specifications than their professional equivalents. Therefore, they make good back-ups to professional gear. All current models offer HD video recording in addition to a full range of stills settings.

Entry-level SLRs

The entry-level SLR is fully capable of professional quality results but is built to offer many features at low cost, using the APS-C or Four Thirds sensors. These cameras will accept most, if not all, of the

Professional SLRs

There is no clear line between entry-level SLRs and professional-level SLRs, as different models are used by both amateurs and professionals. The larger cameras—such as the EOS-1D series from Canon,

▶ SLR

The most reliable, sturdy, and consistent performance can be expected from today's SLR cameras. All the technology used is highly refined and all controls are easy to access, allowing for fluid, versatile photography at professional levels for affordable prices.

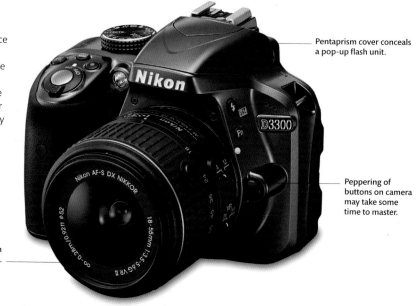

Pentaprism cover conceals a pop-up flash unit.

Peppering of buttons on camera may take some time to master.

Some systems offer more than 50 interchangeable lenses.

SENSOR SIZE AND FIELD OF VIEW

A camera lens projects a circular image. The sensor captures a rectangular area centered on this image. If the rectangle extends to the edge of the circle of light, the sensor captures the full field of view. But if the capture area falls short of the edge, the field of view is smaller. Many SLR cameras accept conventional 35mm format lenses but use sensors that are smaller than the 35mm format (around APS, or about 24 x 16mm). The result is that the field of view is reduced, which in turn means the focal length is effectively increased, usually by a factor of around 1.5x. This means that a 100mm lens used on full-frame 35mm is effectively a 50mm lens when used with an APS-sized sensor. The convention is to relate the actual focal length to the 35mm format equivalent.

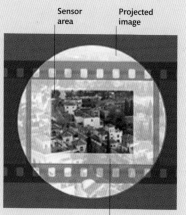

Sensor area

Projected image

35mm film area

the D3 series from Nikon, and certain models from Sony and Olympus—are designed for the professional. They feature high-specification shutters, a sturdy build, seals against dust and moisture, as well as a superior-quality viewfinders and features. Some cameras use a full-frame, 36 x 24mm sensor; others use smaller ones, with resolutions ranging from 10 MP (megapixels) to 25 MP or more, depending on whether the emphasis is on quality or speed of operation.

Choosing an SLR

For the beginner, the best-value cameras are those that have been supplanted by a new model or two. Their price will be much lower than when they were first introduced, yet their performance will be more than satisfactory. This is because, by 2010, technological development had reached a plateau with all camera models capable of producing image quality that easily matched the professional levels of a few years earlier.

- Choose a camera that you find easy to hold, comfortable to use, and easy to set up.
- You almost certainly do not need the highest resolution camera: 12MP is ample for most image uses, such as in websites and publications.

LIVE-VIEW AND VIDEO

The normal way to view through an SLR is to examine the image reflected onto the focusing screen by the mirror. In some models, you can view the image via the LCD display, just like using a compact camera: this is called live view, and it gives you more viewing options. To enable this, either the mirror is raised and the shutter is opened, to allow light to fall on the sensors, or the focusing screen image is reflected onto a sensor.

When live view is enabled, the sensor receives light continuously. This makes it possible for the sensor to record video—an advantage fully exploited by today's cameras. The result is that modern SLRs can now capture high-definition video—of 720 or 1080 lines in resolution. However, SLR lenses are not as well made as cinematic lenses, so zooming, aperture control, and focus are not as smooth. SLR cameras also capture lower-quality sound than professional HD video cameras. Furthermore, SLR cameras tend to capture highly compressed video, which limits post-processing. However, video quality can be excellent, and at a fraction of the cost of professional HD cameras.

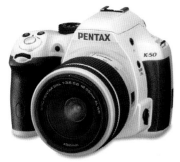

▲ Entry level

SLR cameras designed for amateurs are the best value cameras ever made. They deliver excellent-quality images with accurate focus, color, and tonality while being able to accept a wide range of new and older lenses.

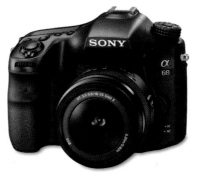

▲ Multifunction

Cameras that use semi-reflecting mirror technology can capture high-definition video with full autofocus conveniently—that is, without having to flip up the mirror. High-resolution still images can also be captured at fast frame rates.

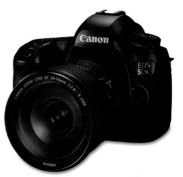

▲ Large professional

Top-resolution cameras are not necessarily large and heavy. Models offering over 50 MP sensors can be similar in size to other SLR cameras. Some offer very high-quality video capture at 4K (Ultra HD) resolution.

CHOOSING LENSES

Modern camera lenses benefit from the adoption and merging of several technologies to deliver high performance with good quality in compact form and at low prices. Nonetheless, it remains as true now as ever that larger lenses with heavier construction, modest specifications, and built from costlier materials will perform better and more reliably than small, lightweight lenses or those with ambitious specifications. The most popular type of lenses are made to zoom—that is, to be able to vary their focal length (*see opposite*) while remaining focused on the image. Lenses are also designed with fixed focal length (prime lenses), wide aperture, extreme focal length, or with an emphasis on speciality use.

Fixed lenses

Compact cameras and many EVF (electronic view-finder) cameras use a permanently mounted lens. This arrangement saves weight, allows a compact design, and virtually eliminates problems from dust

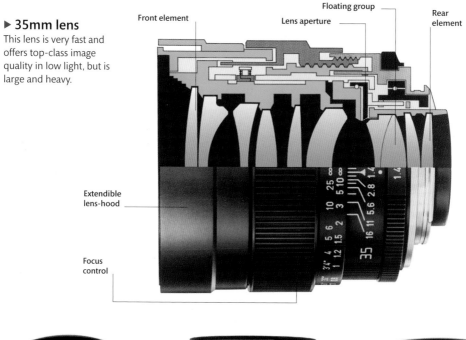

▶ **35mm lens**
This lens is very fast and offers top-class image quality in low light, but is large and heavy.

Front element

Floating group

Lens aperture

Rear element

Extendible lens-hood

Focus control

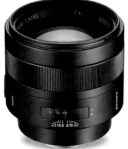

▲ **Ultra-fast telephoto**
Fixed focal length lenses, such as this 85mm optic offering an ultra-fast f/1.4 full aperture, can produce fine effects with superb quality but at premium costs.

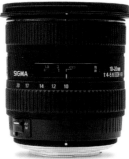

▲ **Ultra wide-angle**
An ultra wide-angle lens for APS-sized sensors must offer very short focal lengths, such as this 10–20mm optic, but can be surprisingly bulky due to complicated construction.

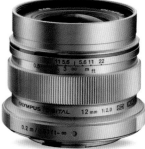

▲ **Standard lens**
A growing appreciation of the value of fixed focal length lenses has given rise to exquisitely compact, high-quality lenses for compact interchangeable lens camera systems.

on the sensor. While it is tempting to opt for a fixed lens with a very large zoom range, such as 26–520mm, bear in mind that more modest ratios are likely to give higher overall image quality, with less vignetting at long focal lengths (see p. 45) and less distortion at wide-angle settings.

Lens specifications

The main specification for a camera lens is its focal length, or range of focal lengths if a zoom. Focal length measures the distance between the point from which the image is projected by the lens to the sharp image at the sensor, where the subject is very far away (at infinity). In practice, we use it to indicate the magnification and field of view of the lens: longer focal length lenses magnify a small portion of the view, whereas shorter focal lengths reduce a larger portion of the view.

Zoom lenses shift elements within the optics to change the focal length without changing the focus setting. From this we obtain the zoom range, or ratio, measuring the longest to shortest focal length, or vice versa. For example, a 70–210mm lens offers a zoom ratio of 1:3.

EQUIVALENT FOCAL LENGTH

The focal length of a photographic optic tells you if a lens is wide-angle, normal, or telephoto. A "normal" lens is one in which focal length is about equal to the length of the diagonal of the format. With the 24 x 36mm format, the diagonal is about 43mm, which is usually rounded up to 50mm. Because the sizes of sensors, and therefore format, of digital cameras vary so greatly, the accepted approach is to quote the equivalent focal length for the 35mm format (35efl). For example, on one camera the 35efl of a 5.1mm lens is 28mm, but it may be 35mm on another. The equivalence is only an approximation, because the proportions of picture rectangles also vary.

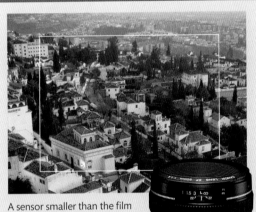

A sensor smaller than the film format for which a lens is designed takes in a view smaller than that projected by the lens.

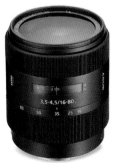

▲ **High-quality standard zoom**
For a standard lens—such as this zoom covering the 35mm equivalent of 24–120mm—you should buy the best quality you can afford, because you will use it extensively.

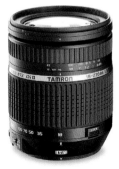

▲ **High-ratio zoom**
A zoom lens that offers high ratios between wide and telephoto settings, such as the 15x of this model, is a tempting option, but performance may be compromised for convenience.

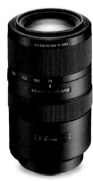

▲ **Telephoto zoom**
A zoom limited to the telephoto range, such as this 70–300mm model, can produce results almost equal to those of fixed focal length lenses but with greater versatility.

CHOOSING LENSES CONTINUED

The other key measure is the maximum aperture. Lenses with a large maximum aperture—such as f/1.4—are said to be fast. They collect more light than lenses with a small maximum aperture—for example, f/4—allowing for shorter exposure times.

Comparing focal lengths

As a result of the earlier dominance of the 35mm format, the focal length of a lens is usually related to that of the equivalent 35mm format lens. For example, the 35mm equivalent of a 10–22mm lens for APS format is 15–33mm. Note that the maximum aperture of the lens does not change; only the field of view changes. Therefore, a 135mm f/1.8 lens for 35mm is effectively a 200mm f/1.8 lens for APS-format sensors. (*See also the box on p. 343.*)

Match to format

The growth of SLR cameras using APS-sized sensors (around 24 x 16mm) has resulted in the development of two lines of interchangeable lenses. Generally, full-format (also called full-frame) lenses—that is, those designed for the 35mm format—can be used on APS-sensor cameras, but not vice versa. Some full-frame cameras automatically match the active sensor to the type of lens in use. The Four Thirds

---

POINTS TO CONSIDER

- Use a lens hood: stray non-image-forming light within the many internal lens elements can seriously degrade otherwise excellent image quality.
- Avoid using the maximum aperture or the minimum aperture. With most zoom lenses, at least one stop less than maximum is required to obtain the best image quality.
- Adjust focal length first and focus on the subject just before releasing the shutter. Avoid altering focal length after you have focused as this can cause slight focusing errors to occur.
- When using a wide-ranging zoom remember that a shutter setting that will ensure sharp results at the wide-angle setting may not be sufficiently short for the telephoto end of the range.

WHAT IS LENS APERTURE?

The terms lens aperture, f/number, and f/stop all mean roughly the same thing: they measure the size of the aperture sending light to the film or sensor. The actual size of the aperture depends on a control called a diaphragm—a circle of blades that open up to make a large hole (letting in lots of light) or overlap each other to reduce the aperture and restrict (stop down) the amount of incoming light. The maximum aperture is the setting of the diaphragm that lets in the most light. Lens aperture is measured as an f/number and is a ratio to the focal length of the lens. For example, with a lens of 50mm focal length, an aperture of 25mm gives f/2 and an aperture of 3.125mm gives f/16.

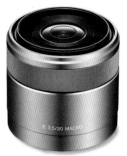

▲ Macro lens
Invaluable not only for close-up work and copying flat originals, macro lenses offer the very best image quality, with high resolution, excellent contrast, and freedom from distortion.

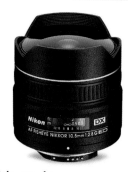

▲ Fish-eye lens
An ultra wide-angle lens that distorts any line not running through the center of the lens, the fish-eye is excellent for special effects. The most useful type fills the frame with the image.

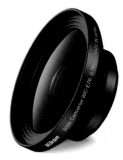

▲ Converter lens
The focal length range of permanently attached lenses can be increased by using a coverter lens. The telephoto increases, and the wide type decreases, the basic focal length settings.

format is a third line of interchangeable lenses, and it uses its own unique mount.

Lens accessories

The zoom ranges of permanently attached lenses may be extended by using supplementary lenses. Those marked, for example, 1.7x will increase the zoom-set focal length by 1.7x to improve telephoto reach. Those marked 0.6x will decrease it by 0.6x, with the effect of increasing wide-angle views.

Interchangeable lenses accept accessories such as filters that mount on the front of the lens, as well as accessories that mount between camera and lens. Converters, also called extenders, are rear-mounted accessories that multiply the focal length of a lens. A 2x extender doubles the focal length of the lens—from 135mm to 270mm, for example, or giving a 100–300mm zoom a 200–600mm capability. But light transmission is also reduced: a 2x extender causes a 2-stop loss in aperture. Extension rings are just like converters but without a lens: they increase the focusing extension of the lens so that it can focus on very close subjects.

Speciality lenses

Lenses can be designed for special photographic tasks such as close-up dental photography, architectural or photogrammetric (measuring) work.

Lenses offering shift and tilt movements are very useful tools. Shifting allows you to reduce or increase, say, foreground coverage without moving the camera. Tilting the lens allows you to position the plane of best focus, to give very deep or shallow depth of field, without adjusting the aperture—ideal for architectural and landscape work, and invaluable for still lifes and portraiture.

The most popular speciality lens is the macro lens, designed for high-performance close-ups. A 50mm macro lens is good for copying work; the 100mm focal length is useful for general macro photography. A long telephoto lens is essential for photographing wildlife from a distance.

HIGH IQ

The three main ways to ensure high image quality from your lens is steadiness during exposure, accurate focus, and use of the optimum lens aperture. Focus manually with SLRs, guided by the focusing screen. Manual fine-tuning as a supplement to auto-focus gives good results. All but the best lenses perform only adequately at full aperture and provide sharpest results two to four aperture stops smaller. For example, if the full aperture is f/4, best results are found between f/8 and f/11. With smaller apertures, quality falls. Shooting the same target at different apertures will soon show you the best apertures to use.

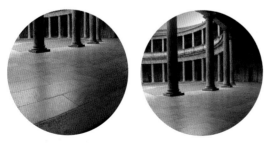

▲ **Moving views**
With the camera held level, the use of lenses with tilt or shift or swivel joints allows you to move the lens assembly to point at and focus on different parts of the image.

▶ **Adjustable lens**
The Lensbaby mounts a lens on a swivel joint allowing you to point the lens freely to produce tilt and unusual blur effects with a wide range of lens mounts.

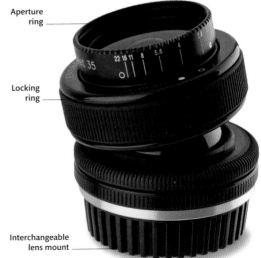

Aperture ring

Locking ring

Interchangeable lens mount

PHOTOGRAPHIC ACCESSORIES

Carefully chosen accessories can make a big difference to the quality and enjoyment of your photography. It is very tempting to load up with numerous accessories, but too many items can slow you down more than they aid you.

Tripods

Tripods can make the biggest single contribution to improving the technical quality of your photography. The best are heavy, large, and rigid, while small, lightweight ones can be next to useless. As a rough guide, a tripod should weigh twice as much as the heaviest item you put on it.

Carbon-fiber tripods offer the best balance between weight and rigidity, while aluminium alloy models are heavier but less expensive. Models that telescope with four or more sections are very compact when folded but less rigid when extended compared to those with fewer sections. Collars that twist to lock a section are compact, and do not snag on clothes, but slower to use than lever locks.

Very small tabletop tripods are handy for steadying the camera on flat surfaces. Where space is limited, and you need to be able to move easily, the monopod is a popular compromise: the single leg helps steady the camera, reducing movement in two axes, and it also helps take the weight of the equipment. Shoulder stocks, which enable you to brace the camera against your shoulder, can help reduce camera shake and work well in combination with a monopod.

Tripod head

The choice of tripod head is as important as the choice of tripod itself. Choose one that is quick and easy to use but that holds the camera firmly.

Ball-and-socket heads are quick to adjust with smaller cameras and lenses as you have to control just one locking knob. The most convenient also feature a panning lock, allowing you to turn the head about the vertical axis.

3-D heads are easy to adjust with fair precision but are slow to operate, as you have three separate movements to control and lock down. However, the handles improve leverage on the head when equipment is larger or heavier. The slowest heads to

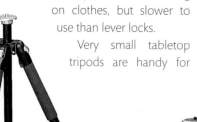

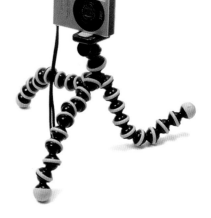

▲ **Telescopic tripod**
A bulky and heavy tripod is the best way to ensure that images are free from camera shake. Carbon-fiber models are expensive but lighter than metal types.

▲ **Travel tripod**
A lightweight, compact tripod is useful for lighter equipment and to supplement supports such as table tops. Press the camera down on the tripod to improve stability.

▲ **Gorillapod**
Unconventional supports, such as this design with flexible legs or those using clamps, are handy for compact cameras and quick set-ups that do not call for long exposures.

operate are those driven by gears, but the reward is very precise adjustment. For extremely heavy lenses, use center-of-gravity pivots or gimbal heads such as the Wimberley head. The camera and lens assembly is balanced so that only finger-tip pressure is needed to adjust the aim and tilt of the camera.

Quick change

Attach your camera to the tripod head with a quick-release mount: this is a plate locked to the camera that "mates" with a trap on the tripod. The result is the swift and sturdy interchange or disassembly of cameras. While adding the plate adds a little to the weight and bulk of the camera, it can help improve hold on the camera and also protects the base. Ensure the plate is big enough for your largest equipment. For heavy lenses, affix the plate directly to the lens. There are many designs on the market; the Arca-Swiss is widely used, and excellent versions are available from Gitzo and Manfrotto.

LENS FILTERS

Filters that attach to the front of lenses are not obsolete in the era of image manipulation. At their simplest, a plain or UV filter protects the vulnerable front element from dust and scratches. Plastic molded filters with prismatic or diffraction lines can give special effects that are very hard to recreate in post-processing. Graduated filters—with denser color at the top fading to clear at the bottom—help to capture landscape images that reduce the need for highlight/shadow or tone-mapping manipulations. Polarizing filters can reduce reflections and intensify sky colors. When you need to reduce the light entering the lens to work at full aperture, you can use a neutral density filter.

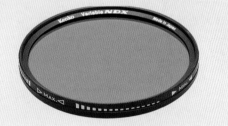

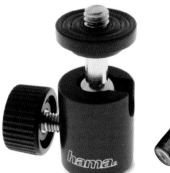

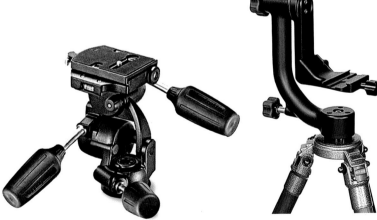

▲ Ball-and-socket head
Lightweight versions are ideal for travel where long exposures are not needed. For more serious work and heavier equipment, use heavy-weight models that work very smoothly.

▲ 3-D head
Excellent for the flexible control of a heavy camera and lens combination, a 3-D head is easy to control and easiest to use with a quick-release plate. Some models are equipped with levels.

▲ Gimbal head
An off-axis head balances extreme telephoto lenses and large cameras, making it effortless to line up shots. But the units themselves are large, heavy, and almost as expensive as a tripod.

PHOTOGRAPHIC ACCESSORIES CONTINUED

Exposure control

Image previewing on digital cameras has not made separate light meters obsolete. The best practice is to make exposures as accurately as possible, which reduces the time needed to make post-processing corrections. Handheld meters are also the best way to make incident-light readings—that is, readings of the light falling on the subject. Some handheld meters also offer far greater accuracy, especially in low-light conditions. And spot meters, which read reflected light from a very narrow field of view—commonly 1° or less—offer unsurpassed accuracy in tricky lighting.

Flash meters enable speedy work in the studio, without the need to refer to previews again and again. Most modern handheld meters can measure flash exposures as well as ambient light and, indeed, indicate the balance between the two. A flash meter is an essential accessory for serious still life and portrait work.

Another aspect of exposure control is the use of standard targets such as gray cards, standard color targets, and other aids. By including these in a test shot under the same lighting as the subject, you create an invaluable reference of guaranteed neutral tones and colors which improve the accuracy of any post-processing.

TIMER REMOTE RELEASE

The mechanical cable release to trip the shutter without disturbing the camera has been replaced by the electronic switch. These range from models that simply trip the shutter to those that can open the shutter for a preset time, which is useful for making accurately timed exposures. More sophisiticated models also work as intervalometers: you set a time interval—for example, 5 seconds—and every 5 seconds the timer makes exposures as the basis for creating time-lapse movies. Some releases are corded and plugged into a camera; more recent models use wireless connections, such as Bluetooth or radio.

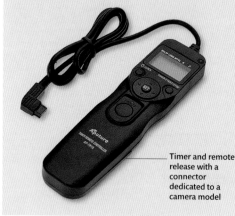

Timer and remote release with a connector dedicated to a camera model

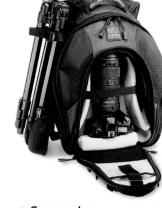

▲ Neutral target

This ingenious target, from Datacolor, combines specular highlight (top) and deep shadow (bottom) with five neutral gray tones.

▲ Advanced exposure meter

Professional exposure meters can measure flash as well as ambient light, and some models also function as a spot meter.

▲ Camera bag

Backpack designs are best for comfort and carrying awkward loads, but are slower to use than shoulder-hung models.

Bags

Modern, padded soft bags combine high levels of protection with lightweight construction. Bags hung over the shoulder are easiest to access but can be tiring to carry for long distances. Shoulder bags tend to be the lightest designs, so may be best for use as cabin luggage.

Backpack styles are easy to carry for long distances, and comfortable even with quite heavy and awkward loads such as a tripod. However they tend to be slower to use as you have to take them off your back before getting into them.

A working compromise is to use a shoulder bag with a waist-strap that is tightly strapped to your body. This displaces some mass onto the hips and relieves your shoulders.

For work in highly challenging conditions, or if you fear your precious lenses and laptop might have to travel in cargo holds or be slung into the backs of trucks, a hard case with a waterproof and dustproof seal is essential. However, even when empty they are heavy, so expect to have to pay excess-baggage charges.

Waterproofing

A waterproof camera housing is not only needed if total immersion is likely, but also in situations such as shooting from a canoe or when sailing. Camera housings are also ideal for particularly dusty conditions, such as industrial sites and deserts. Housings vary from flexible plastic cases for shallow water, to sturdy cases for deep water. They are available for compact cameras through to professional models, but they may cost at least as much as the camera they are made to protect. The key to their maintenance and longevity is to keep the O-ring seals meticulously clean and lubricated with silicone grease.

CAMERA RAINCOAT

For sports and nature photographers, the invention of camera raincoats has been a boon. There are generic models and those made for specific cameras, and they usually come in plain gray or in camouflage patterns.

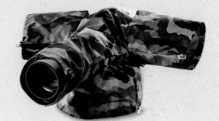

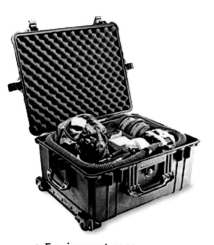

▲ **Equipment case**
Rigid cases can be waterproof and provide sturdy protection for rough conditions. Rolling models equipped with wheels are easiest to transport.

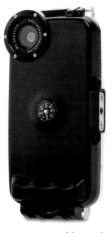

▲ **Waterproof housing**
Extend the life of your camera by protecting it from the elements. Use a waterproof housing specific to your camera to ensure watertightness.

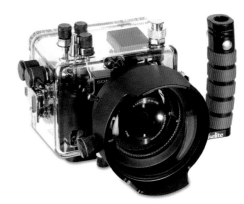

▲ **Underwater housing**
For serious diving, an underwater housing keeps your camera safe and offers the best image quality, as well as access to all necessary controls.

DIGITAL ACCESSORIES

The modern digital camera has to work with a retinue of digital accessories to ensure that it is powered and has the capacity to record images.

Memory cards

Memory cards use banks of memory registers that hold their state—on or off—without needing power. They can hold data indefinitely yet can easily write new or altered data. Their compact size, low power requirements, and large capacity make them ideal for image data. When an image is written to them, the registers are flipped on or off according to the data. To read the memory, the registers are turned into a stream of data. Modern cards can hold more than 100 GB of information and read or write 300x faster than a standard CD.

There are many card types in circulation: some are extra-compact for use in cell phones, others are optimized for speed or sturdiness. If you own more

CARD CARE

- Keep memory cards well away from magnetic fields, such as in audio speakers.
- Keep cards dry.
- Keep cards away from extreme heat.
- Keep cards dust-free.
- Keep cards in protective cases when not in use.
- Do not bend or flex cards.
- Avoid touching the contacts with your fingers.

MEMORY CARD READERS

There are two ways of transferring images taken on your digital camera to your computer. You can connect the camera to your computer and instruct the camera's software to download images, or you can take the memory card out of the camera and read it to the computer. To do this, you need a memory card reader, a device with circuitry to take the data and send it to the computer, via a USB or FireWire cable. There are many card readers on the market that can read almost every type of memory card.

Multitype
card reader

▶ Using a reader
When slotted in, the reader opens the card as a volume or disk. You can then copy images straight into the computer.

CompactFlash
card reader

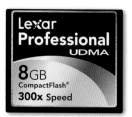

▲ CompactFlash
Very widely used in dSLR cameras and others, this is a sturdy card in a range of capacities, up to at least 100 GB, and read/write speeds to suit different budgets and camera requirements.

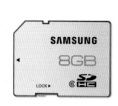

▲ Secure Digital
Very widely used in compact and dSLR cameras, SD (and SDHC) cards are very small yet offer capacities of 64 GB and over with low draw on current. They are also sturdy and reliable.

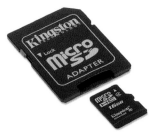

▲ Micro SD
These cards are widely used in cell phone cameras but their small size restricts capacities from reaching over 64 GB. Via an adaptor, they can also be used in devices that take the larger Mini SD and SD cards.

▲ MemoryStick
Proprietary to Sony, this family of cards is used in a variety of digital equipment, including Sony video cameras, allowing interchange with good capacities and performance.

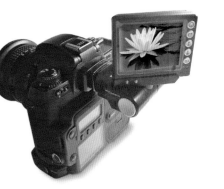

Video viewfinder
Video viewfinders use a tiny camera to capture the image of the focusing screen to display on a larger, outside screen. They can also be used for automatic remote release: the system trips the shutter when it detects movement in the image.

than one camera or want to use another device, try to ensure intercompatibility.

CompactFlash and SD
The most widely used memory cards for digital photography are the CompactFlash (CF) and Secure Digital (SD) cards. SD cards are more compact and less prone to failure as the pins are flat and less numerous than those in CF cards. You can remove the card from the camera at any stage before it is full and slot it into a reader to transfer files to a computer, but do not remove it while the camera is trying to read the card, usually indicated by a red light blinking. You can also erase images at any time to make room for more.

Digital image storage
When traveling with a digital camera it is often impractical, and always inconvenient, to carry a laptop computer for storing image files. One option is what is essentially a portable hard disk equipped with an LCD screen and card-reading slots. The screen may be color for reviewing images on the device, or it may simply show the copying status and basic file data. Some of these units can hold several terabytes (TB) of data and are equipped with slots for reading memory card devices. Data can be copied straight from the card devices onto the drive, then the drive can be connected to your computer to transfer your images once you are back at home.

Viewing images
It is as important to view and show images as it is to capture them. You can use tablets, such as the iPad, and photo frames to display your images, and use simple transitions such as fading between images and even add a suitable soundtrack.

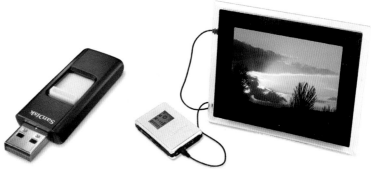

▲ **Mobile storage**
Freeing you from taking a computer outdoors, these small hard disk drives allow you to back up photos and so continue using your memory cards. They also allow you to review and show images as you shoot.

▲ **USB drive**
As small as a key ring, a USB drive is a most convenient way to transfer quantities of files from one machine to another. USB drives are solid-state memory devices with storage capacities of 64 GB and more.

▲ **Photo frame**
These devices display a single image or a slide show of images downloaded from a memory card or picture store. They are useful for personal use, such as in living rooms, or for store displays and gallery exhibitions.

ELECTRONIC LIGHTING

The invention of portable flash had a tremendous impact on photography: it opened the night world to the camera, with compact, easily carried equipment. Today, electronic flash is standard to all compact digital cameras, found on many cell phone cameras, and fitted to the majority of dSLRs. However, the position of the fitted flash is just about the worst possible, in terms of the quality of lighting. Accessory lighting units are a necessity for versatile and attractive lighting.

Power and recycling

A further problem is that flash built into a camera relies on the camera's own batteries for power. To curb their hunger for energy, built-in flashes are designed to be low-powered—usually sufficient to light to a distance of 3–7ft (1–2m) but little further. In addition, the recycling rates—how quickly the flash can be fired in sequence—is also limited.

Flash power

Portable, or accessory, flash units overcome the limitations of built-in flash by carrying their own power and circuitry; this makes the units much larger than compact cameras. Accessory flash units

also offer more control over flash power, direction of flash, and angle of coverage.

Accessory flashes fit onto the hot shoe, which combines electrical contacts with a slot that "mates" with a corresponding, locking part on the bottom of the flash unit. While the majority of cameras use a standard hot-shoe design, the contacts may be specific to the camera producer, and some manufacturers—such as Sony—use proprietary hot-shoe designs.

Adjustable angle

Many portable flash units place the flash on a swiveling turret so that it can be directed to the sides, or even backward, according to the nearest surface for bounce flash (*see pp. 82–9*). Some offer a tilting head so that you can point the flash upward, or downward for close-up work. A fully adjustable head increases flexibility, so is a must for wedding and paparazzi photography.

Adjustable coverage

On many flash units you can also adjust the coverage, or the angle over which light is spread. This ensures that when you use a wide-angle lens or

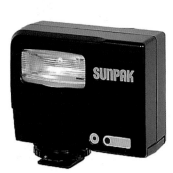

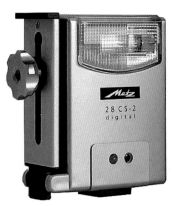

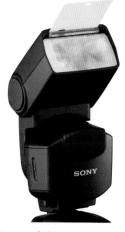

▲ Small supplementary flash
Units like this can augment the power of built-in flash units. It is triggered by the camera's own flash, so it does not need a hot shoe, and adds its output to that of the camera's unit. It is an inexpensive solution to lighting problems, but control is limited.

▲ Slave flash unit
Slave units can add to the power of built-in flash units. This unit synchs with the on-camera flash for the most accurate exposure, after which operation is fully automatic. Position it to one side of the camera to improve modeling effects.

▲ Powerful on-camera flash
Accessory flash mounted on a camera's hot shoe can be sufficiently powerful for all normal needs, offering a tilt-and-swivel head for bounce, multiple-exposure facilities, and focusing aids for working in complete darkness.

setting, the flash coverage is sufficient to light the angle of view: this causes a lowering in the maximum power of the flash. When you make a telephoto setting or use a long focal length lens, the coverage is narrowed to match, approximately, the angle of view. This causes a gain in the maximum power of the flash, since the light is concentrated into a narrower beam.

Adjustment may be carried out automatically, with the camera instructing the flash according to the zoom setting on the lens, or it can be manually set. Zoom-like optics in the flash tube alter coverage, and a diffuser may be used for ultra wide-angle coverage.

Red-eye

The unsightly red dot in the middle of eyes lit by flash—commonly known as red-eye—is caused by two factors: the flash being so close to the optical axis that the light reflects off the blood-rich retina of the eye, while, at the same time, the eye's pupil is dilated in dark conditions. Accessory flash mounted on the hot shoe or to one side moves the source of flash relatively far from the optical axis, with the result that red-eye is avoided.

GUIDE NUMBER

The light output of accessory flash units is usually measured by the Guide Number (GN). The figure is for a specific film/sensor speed—usually ISO 100—in either feet (ft) or meters (m), and for a specified angle of coverage. The GN for a unit will be higher for narrow coverage—suitable for medium-telephoto lenses—and lower for wide coverage—suitable for wide-angle lenses. A Guide Number may be quoted as, for example, GN45 (m), indicating the distance scale is meters. A typical small camera GN is 5–10 (m); accessory flash units offer 30–50 (m). The standard practice is that that the GN figure is quoted for the coverage of a standard lens but may be inflated in specifications by being quoted for a narrow coverage. The Guide Number scale is defined:

Guide Number = subject distance x f/number

The f/number for a correct exposure is the result of dividing the GN of your unit by the distance between the flash/camera and the subject. Using GN to set an f/number is generally more accurate than relying on automatic systems.

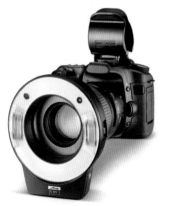

▲ Macro ring-flash
For shadowless flash photography of insects, flowers, and other small objects, a ring-flash is ideal. The brief flash can stop inadvertent movement, and very small apertures can be set for maximum depth of field.

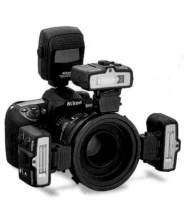

▲ Adjustable macro flash
For controlled lighting in macro work, units with two or more small flash units that can be set to different positions around the lens give the most flexibility. They can be set to different power levels and point in different directions.

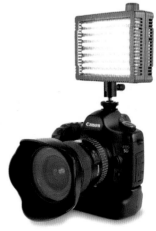

▲ LED unit
Lightweight LED lights produce a daylight-balanced, continuous beam of light that is ideal for video recording. But it also provides a source of easy visible light that can be used off-camera and precisely positioned to control modeling.

LIGHTING ACCESSORIES

If photography is writing with light, then lighting accessories are your fountain pens. You can shape and articulate the light from even the harshest compact camera flash with accessories. These can range from the humblest—a paper handkerchief or piece of paper—to precision polished light-shapers and fold-away reflectors.

Reflectors

The most inexpensive and effective way to soften the hard light from small light-sources such as portable flash is to use reflectors. These range from models with shiny, silvered surfaces to dull, matt surfaces. Light bounced from shiny surfaces is harder, with more contrast, than that from matt surfaces. The color of the surface can range from cool silver to warm gold or copper tones, which tints the color of the bounced light.

Look for models that are compact when folded, but expand to three or more times their size when unfolded. The most versatile feature different surfaces on each side—for example, silver on one side and gold on the other. Those that attach to a light stand make you independent of an assistant to hold and position the reflector.

Light shapers

The main requirement with portable flash is not to focus light more strongly but to diffuse it to soften the modeling it produces. You may attach reflectors directly to the flash head and aim it to bounce into the reflector. Or you may attach soft-boxes: these range from relatively large light tents, which attach to the flash by way of an arm articulated on a light stand, or smaller models that fit onto the flash. One popular model is blown up like a balloon to keep its shape, then strapped to flash head. It is a lightweight solution and it folds into a very compact package when not being used.

Ring-flash adaptor

Another type of light shaper is the ring-flash adaptor. This attaches to a portable flash with the lens viewing through the central hole. The several designs on the market all achieve the same basic result: the light source is circular, so it produces a shadowless effect as the shadow from one part of the circle is reduced by the light from the opposite side. The effect is popular in portraiture and fashion. Proper ring-flash units are very costly but they produce much more power than ring-flash adaptors.

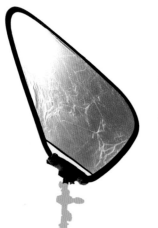
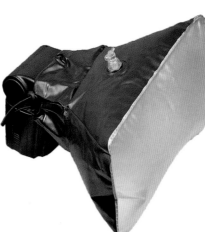
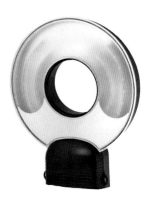

▲ **Reflectors**
Used to send fill-in light from the main light into unlit areas to relieve shadows, reflectors, when carefully placed, allow you to work with just a single light source. The colors of different surfaces tint the fill-in light.

▲ **Light shaper**
Detachable light-boxes or diffusers are very effective at reducing the harshness of small flash units. They save you from having to look for surfaces to bounce off, and keep color temperature constant.

▲ **Ring-flash**
Ring-flash attachments almost turn your portable flash unit into a new flash-gun, giving effects impossible to simulate. Ideal for some types of portraiture, fashion, and close-ups of tiny animals and small objects.

Home studios

You can easily convert any space into a studio for still lifes or small objects: it takes only a table and large sheets of card or foam-core board. You can also create light tents for very low cost by draping translucent material around a frame cut from a large cardboard box. Alternatively, there are several models of custom-made light tents that are easy to erect and pack away compactly. These light tents are ideal for photographing highly reflective objects such as cameras, glassware, and metalwork.

To use a light tent, you can shine any lamp or flash onto the tent while the camera lens pokes through a small hole. A light tent produces an inherently beautifully soft light but you can vary the position of the hot-spot by the position of the main light and how closely you hold it to the light tent.

For larger spaces, the easiest way to create a studio environment is by controlling the background. The classic method is to spool off a sheet of paper from a large roll: the paper can be any color, but the most versatile are warm grays or whites. You can create your own painted background by painting pale washes on a canvas sheet: you do not have to be very artistic as you need to create only a blurry effect. There are also many prepared backgrounds on the market.

PHOTOGRAPHING AUCTION ITEMS

Millions of members of the public have become advertising photographers. Needing to sell used or unwanted items on auction websites, they must present their goods in the best possible light to attract vigorous bidding. It is a highly technical exercise, but a rewarding one, to photograph an item objectively yet to present it attractively.

- Show small items against a plain background from different angles so that every detail can be clearly seen.
- Focus accurately, with maximum depth of field and sharpness.
- Expose accurately with accurate white balance.
- Keep contrast medium to low, and do not exaggerate colors.
- Include boxes and instructions if available.
- If accurate measurement is important, include a ruler or coin in one of the shots.
- Remove specks of dust and fine hairs using image manipulation software, but do not be tempted to alter any other defects such as scratches or other damage.

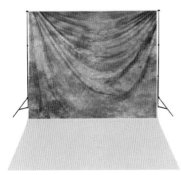

▲ Background systems
You can drape a background across a wall to turn a living room instantly into a studio. For more flexibility, use a background system consisting of a horizontal rail held up by stands: you can unroll paper or painted canvas.

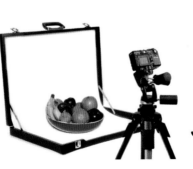

▲ Tabletop set-up
Photography for online auctions is now well catered for by tabletop backgrounds such as this. They are suitable for small objects and can be folded and packed away after use. It is best to use a soft-box for lighting.

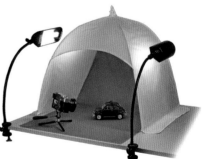

▲ Light tents
Any lamp is turned into the softest of light-sources. A large aperture for the camera creates a large dark patch on reflective surfaces. Control the position of the lamps to vary the location of hot-spots and reflections

COMPUTERS

The serious digital photographer spends at least as much time at the computer as he or she does taking pictures. Not only has the computer replaced the darkroom, it is now effectively the photographer's library as well as their communication and media center. The computer will also drive the scanner, printer, and perhaps the camera, too.

What to look for

All modern computers can work with digital images. The differences lie in three main areas: the operating system, the system performance (which depends on video graphics and memory), and the storage capacity. The latest operating system may offer the most features, but other software and hardware upgrades may need to be updated to work with them, and they may need extra RAM to run digital photography software. You should consider 2GB of RAM to be the minimum.

Mouse and keyboard

The quality of the mouse and keyboard can make a big difference to your enjoyment and comfort. If the keyboard is not to your liking or you find the mouse uncomfortable to use, change them. Such replacements are inexpensive, and if made at the time of purchase, they may even be cheaper.

Software packages

When budgeting, do not forget software costs. A full suite of software for image manipulation as well as desktop and web publishing can cost more than a computer, so use modest applications until your skills develop. Professional software can be very hard to master, while simpler, cheaper packages still produce good results (*see pp. 360–61*).

Connections

When buying a computer, ensure its interfaces match those of the equipment you wish to use. Note that you may need to install some software to make a connector work.

■ Universal Serial Bus (USB) is widely used in its various forms for data transfer between computers and hard disk drives, card readers, and cameras. Note that some peripherals, such as keyboards and screens, may offer USB connections. To be most useful, these should be powered but many are unpowered, which limits the accessories that can be used.

■ FireWire is a high-speed standard suitable for professional work. It offers an excellent choice for removable drives, extra hard disks, and digital cameras. FW800 is comparable to USB 3.0 for speed of data transfer.

CONTROLLING REFLECTIONS

Sidelight reaching monitors can reflect into the user's face, causing uncomfortable glare (left). The use of a deep hood (right) reduces this problem.

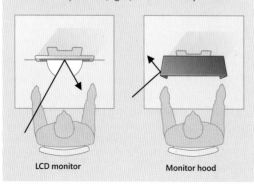

LCD monitor   Monitor hood

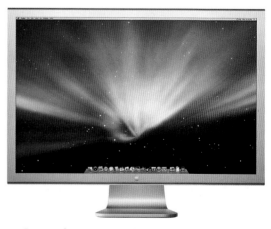

▲ **General-purpose LCD monitor**
High-quality modern LCD screens offer the best balance of ergonomic features and image quality, as well as minimizing eye-strain. Images are stable, geometry perfect, and color rendition sufficient for most color-checking needs.

- eSATA (External Serial Advanced Technology Attachment) connects external drives to computers and is up to twice as fast as USB 2.0 or FW800. Cable length is limited to 7ft (2m).

Laptop or desktop?

Desktop machines may cost less than laptops, but can offer more power in return for the loss of portability. However, modern laptops have more than enough power for digital photography. Some, like the Apple MacBook Pro, are not only more powerful than many desktop computers, their screens are also of sufficient quality and large enough for serious work. The best Windows machines also make excellent workhorses for digital photography. Against the premium cost of miniaturizing is the convenience of a computer that takes up no more desk space than an open magazine. Laptops are essential for the digital photographer on the move. At base, they can be supplemented by attaching a large monitor.

Monitors

Except for color specialists, LCD or LED monitors are universally used in photography. Modern LCD monitors are backlit (a panel of light shines through the LCD) to improve visibility and contrast. Screens using LEDs (Light Emitting Diodes) as the backlight are energy-efficient and provide excellent color reproduction. Both types of screen can be slim, consume little electricity, cause minimal eyestrain, and are suitable for all but the most color-critical viewing.

For image manipulation, the minimum screen size recommended is 12in (50cm). The screen resolution should be 1,600 x 1000 pixels or better. All modern monitor screens can display millions of colors, but the accuracy and extent of the color gamut varies considerably. Broadly speaking, you need to spend more for colorcritical work. The surface of LCD screens may be matt or glossy. Matt screens are less prone to stray reflections and display images similar to print reproduction. Glossy screens give much better image quality but are prone to stray reflections.

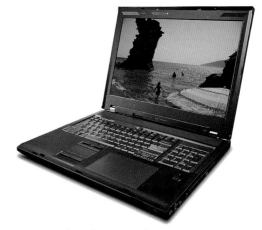

▲ Laptop for photographers
Widescreen laptops with 17-in (43-cm) screens and powerful graphics are ideal for digital photography. More power may mean less compact, but they can easily replace a desktop machine.

MONITOR CALIBRATION

As viewers, we are tolerant of quite wide variations in color balance in an image. However, to make the most of the superb images produced by today's digital cameras, you should work with a calibrated monitor.

Modern operating systems offer software calibration as part of the setting up. For Apple Mac, the calibration process is in the Displays section of System Preferences: select Color and click on the Calibrate button, then follow the instructions. There are different approaches for Windows users, according to the version installed. Windows Vista uses a new, powerful color-management system that addresses limitations of older systems. The best solution is to use a hardware calibrator. This instructs the monitor to display standard colors, which are measured and compared with the target values: the differences between actual and target values enables a monitor profile to be created. (*See also pp. 182–3 on color management.*)

Monitor calibrator

COMPUTER ACCESSORIES

As your expertise in digital photography increases and the quantity of images you produce grows, you will wish to invest in accessories that make life easier and increase your enjoyment.

Mobile storage

Digital photography produces vast amounts of data, and removable media provide the essential storage space you need. In general, the greater the capacity of the device, the cheaper is the cost per gigabyte of available space.

Portable hard disk drives are, all around, the best solution for the digital photographer. Not only are their capacities ample for most workers—offering up to 1 TB and more—they are also very cost effective and can transfer files rapidly. Models of about the size of electronic personal organizers are extremely portable and ideal for working on location with a laptop computer, since they can be powered from the laptop.

There are two types of hard disk drives: those specifically designed for transferring and storing digital images, with their own card reader and controls (*see also pp. 350–1*); and drives that require the use of a computer. Drives use different interfaces, such as USB 3.0 or FireWire, so make sure you select the type that connects with and best suits your computer. The most versatile offer two ports—for example, one USB 2.0 and one FireWire; the second port enables you to connect another device while the drive is hooked up.

Larger, desktop hard disk drives are the fastest and can offer capacities over 3 TB (3 terabyte, or 3,000 GB) yet, at the size and weight of this book, are still relatively portable; however, this type does need a separate power supply.

For heavy-duty work and the highest reliability, consider using RAID (Redundant Array of Inexpensive Disks), in which data is copied or striped over two or more disks so that if one should fail, data can be easily be recovered from the other drives. NAS (Network Attached Storage) is also invaluable when more than one person in a studio needs access to the image data.

Removable media

Optical disk media such as CD and DVD offer reliable storage that can be universally accessed. The CD, with its 650 MB capacity, is still used for small-scale transfer, while DVD, carrying up to about 7.5 GB in dual-layer form, is the current standard for large amounts of data. In 2008, Blu-ray

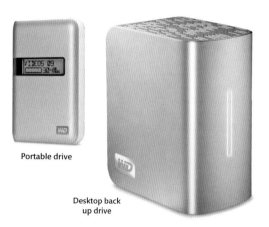

Portable drive

Desktop back up drive

▲ Hard disk drives
Portable hard disk drives are becoming smaller and lighter with capacities of 1 TB or more, but their desktop cousins offer even greater storage. Portable disks are powered from your laptop via their USB or FireWire port but they do run slower than corded desktop units.

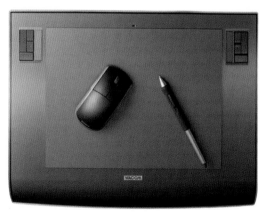

▲ Graphics tablet
Graphic tablets come in a range of sizes—starting with models smaller than a mouse mat—to suit different ways of working. Large sizes can take up the entire desk area. The pen and mouse tools also cover a range, from simple devices to those sporting several buttons to access various functions.

Disk (BD) won the high-density format war with HD-DVD. A BD carries up to about 48 GB in dual-layer form and will increasingly be the standard for archiving data. However, in comparison with hard-disk drives, optical media are slow to write and slow to access.

Graphics tablet

These input devices are an evolutionary step up from the mouse. Comprising a flat tablet, like a solid mouse mat, and a pen-like stylus, graphics tablets give you excellent control over hand-drawn lines because of their high spatial resolution—that is, they can detect tiny changes in position. They also allow you to increase the width of a line or the depth of a color by varying the pressure of the stroke—something that is impossible to do with a mouse. A tablet can be small, about the size of a mouse mat, or large enough to need a desk to itself. It is good practice to interchange the use of graphics tablet and mouse to help avoid repetitive strain injuries—for example, by using the graphics tablet for image manipulation and the mouse for the internet and word processing.

UPS, SURGE PROTECTORS, ADAPTORS, AND CABLES

Computer systems are highly susceptible to even very small fluctuations in the amount of electrical current powering them. Because of this, you may want to consider protecting your equipment from power surges and failures—something that is even more worthwhile if you live in areas with uncertain power supplies. Saving your work frequently as you go ensures that, if the worst happens and your machine does crash, then at least not too much of it will be lost. However, apart from the frustration and wasted time involved in restarting your computer, an uncontrolled shut-down does carry with it the risk of damage to your hard drive. To safeguard against this, an uninterruptible power supply (UPS) is essential, although they can be expensive to buy. This is a battery that powers the computer and monitor for a short period in case of a power loss, giving you time to quit the application and shut the computer down safely.

Another useful piece of equipment is a surge protector, which prevents sudden rises in power from damaging your delicate equipment. This is well worth its relatively low cost.

Other accessories that you will accumulate are cords to connect devices to your computer and to each other, and adaptors that allow older equipment, such as those based on SCSI, to be used with newer systems, such as FireWire.

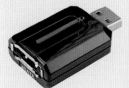

eSATA to USB adaptor

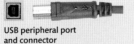

USB peripheral port and connector

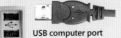

USB computer port and connector

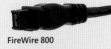

FireWire 800

FireWire 400

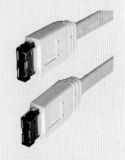

▲ Adaptors
With the multiplicity of different standards, there is an accompanying proliferation of adaptors that convert one to another, such as eSATA to USB.

▲ USB ports
USB (Universal Serial Bus) is a widespread protocol allowing devices to be plugged straight into a working computer and be recognized and connected.

▲ FireWire cables
Second to USB in popularity, FireWire is equally easy to use and carries power, but connectors come in many different shapes and sizes.

▲ eSATA cable
SATA drives are designed for high data throughput—up to three times that of FireWire 400. eSATA connectors are used to connect SATA drives to other devices but do not carry power.

CHOOSING SOFTWARE

Your choice of software for digital photography is akin to your choice of camera: it should meet your current and future needs without being too costly or over-burdened with features that are difficult for you to use. Professional software may offer all the features you could ever need, but if you find the learning curve of finding your way around is too steep, you will not exploit all the features you have paid for. On the other hand, you should not feel constrained by cost either, for easily available free or shareware software can perform all the tasks a professional needs.

Multiple functions

A generation after the birth of digital photography, software is now expected to do more than simply manipulate the image. On top of image editing functions many applications can also organize images, add tags and other data, upload them to social networking and picture-sharing sites, as well as order printed books online. All of this means that there can be lots to master with new software, and one may long for the limitations of early software.

When you first install your software it is important to remember that you will not harm anything by trying every option and setting available. You will learn to use the software most rapidly by trying out all the features and options, checking their effects and playing with every control and slider.

- Create a folder of small images for learning.
- Explore the menu options systematically: start with the File, then Edit menus and so on.
- Start learning the keyboard short-cuts: where available, these are shown together with the pull-down menu options.
- Use the built-in and online support whenever something does not work as you expect.

Multiple platforms

Software for digital photography is not limited to personal computers: you can install applications for smartphones and tablet devices that can manipulate images, post the results on picture-sharing sites or send them to other devices. Some, such as Photoshop Express, are pared-down versions of software packages, but others, such as Instagram and Hipstamatic, closely integrate smartphone features with picture effects and social networking. Remember that sending images may use up your online data quota quickly: if your contract sets limits, exceeding them may be costly.

Direct or proxy

Photographers who produce large numbers of images—a thousand or more a week—but do not need extensive manipulations will find that image management applications are their first priority. There are two approaches. Simple image review and

CHECKLIST

When purchasing software, particularly the professional applications with more advanced feature sets, you should check the following:

- **Operating system required:** If you do not have the latest computer, check that your version of the operating system will run the software. You may need to download updates to your operating system first.
- **Minimum RAM:** Check how much RAM the software needs to run efficiently. One advantage of entry-level software is its modest demands for RAM.
- **Online registrations:** Some applications require you to be online in order to activate or register

the software. An online connection may even be obligatory for programs that are cloud-based.

- **Minimum hard disk space:** Check how much hard disk space the software needs. In addition to the space for the software itself, it will need space to store temporary working files—the larger your files, the greater the amount of space that will be needed.
- **Drive type:** You may need to use a CD reader to install files, and some software is delivered on DVD, although most are online. An internet connection may be needed to download updates or bug fixes.

management such as that offered by Photo Mechanic or ACDSee works with the image files themselves. Photo Mechanic is popular with photojournalists because of its small RAM footprint and very rapid operation. ACDSee is slower in operation but more versatile as it is a RAW converter and can also be used for basic image enhancements.

Software such as Adobe Lightroom, Capture One, and Apple Photos work on proxy files rather than directly on the image itself, so they are able to organize very large numbers of images. Lightroom and Capture One are also powerful RAW converters. However, before you can work on any images, each must be registered or imported into the software, either as part of the download process or separately, from a folder containing images. You can also use some applications to add data, design photobooks, and even create websites and slide shows, complete with a soundtrack. Lightroom and Capture One match each other well for features, so the choice between them is largely down to personal preferences and the type of work you do.

If you generate a relatively small number of images—up to a few hundred in a year—the most appropriate workflow is to work directly on copies of your images. For this, use software such as Photoshop Elements, Affinity, Pixelmator, Paintshop Pro, Corel Photo-Paint, or Photoscope. Many image-manipulation applications are free, the most powerful being GIMP (GNU Image Manipulation Program).

If you have reliable access to the internet, you can use web-based, online editors such as Google Picasa, Pixlr, and Adobe Photoshop Express. You access the application from your usual web-browser. These are free to use, and some allow you to store your images on remote websites, leaving your computer free of clutter.

Tablet apps

A separate category of image applications are built for tablets and smartphones using portable operating systems such as iOS, Android, and Windows Portable. These apps are slimmed down in terms of features, but still very useful. You can manipulate and manage images right on the camera phone or tablet in which you made the picture. There are also portfolio and slide show applications. The power of these applications surpasses that of early image manipulation software, but all contained in the smartphone or tablet.

RAW converters

Some RAW converter packages are produced by camera manufacturers specifically for their cameras. These are usually supplied free with purchase of the camera, but their features may be limited. Others are written by independent manufacturers, such as DxO OpticsPro, to work with a wide range of cameras. In either case, you may need to update the software to accommodate new camera models that generate new types of RAW file. RAW converters open the actual RAW file but save a "sidecar" data file of manipulation instructions, such as color and exposure settings. When you are ready to export the image, you can do so in a variety of formats, leaving the original RAW file untouched. DxO OpticsPro is one of the most powerful RAW converters, with large libraries of convenient processing presets.

INTERNET DEPENDENCE

Software used to be installed only through media such as CDs or DVDs, but installation by download over the internet is cheaper, more convenient, and uses fewer resources. Some software is exclusively installed by download, and many applications need an internet connection to unlock or register the installation, and to download updates or fixes. If your desired software requires large downloads of 1 GB or more, it is essential to have access to a fast internet connection.

- The majority of installations by download allow a free trial period: make full use of that by timing your installation when you have leisure to trial it.

- Download only from trusted sites.

- Choose quiet periods to download software to avoid interruption of the data stream.

PRINTERS AND OTHER DEVICES

With the demise of film and the attendant redundancy of the darkroom, photographers need few items to supplement their camera equipment. And with the growth of online services, from printing to file archiving, it is not obvious that equipment such as printers or even hard disks are necessary. While owning your own equipment allows you to work at your own convenience, it does mean that you have to maintain it, which can be costly in the case of printers.

Printers

Desktop ink-jet printers are able to match the quality of color prints of the past when used with high-quality papers. There is a slight loss in subtlety of shading and delicacy of hues compared to a laboratory color print, but that is fully compensated for by the convenience of being able to print directly from your computer. If you make prints for presents or to display, it is worth buying the best printer you can afford that prints at the size you require. Printers for tabloid size (11 x 17 in) offer a good balance between being able to output usefully large prints, purchase and running costs, and the amount of desk area they take up. If you only occasionally make poster-size prints, it is more economical to order these online (*see also pp. 314–5*).

Check that the printer takes separate ink cartridges for each color and uses a minimum of six different colors. If you intend to make black-and-white prints, look for printers using gray and black inks. A paper path that is straight—feeding from the back to the front of the machine—will be able to accept thick papers such as watercolor or hand-made papers. If the printer can accept rolls of paper, you can make banner or panoramic format prints easily. Before you purchase a printer, try to examine prints that it has made on papers that you like: choice of printer can be a matter of personal preference.

Other printers

The smallest, most compact printers—ideal for making cards and small gifts when traveling or at a party—are dye-sublimation (dye-sub) printers. These use a cartridge that contains colored ribbons and special receiving paper, and are usually powered by battery for maximum portability. They deliver excellent, lively results.

Desktop color laser printers are suitable for producing multiple copies of color images quickly, but image quality lags a long way behind that of ink-jet or dye-sublimation printers. Industrial-scale laser printers are widely used to print photobooks (*see also pp. 314–5*).

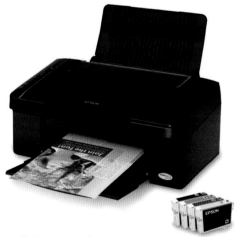

▲ **All-in-one printer**
A combined scanner, copier, and printer is capable of producing excellent prints for day-to-day use. Larger ink-jet machines are best for exhibition-quality prints.

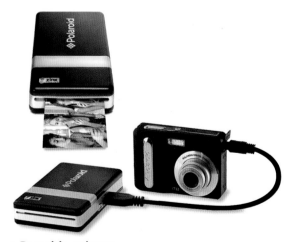

▲ **Portable printer**
Printers such as this model, hardly any larger than the prints it produces, are ideal for use on location and at social events, but need regular supplying with paper and charge.

HALF-TONE CELLS

Printers can lay more than 2,000 dots of ink per inch (dpi) but since no printer can change the strength of the ink and not all can vary dot size, not all dots are available for defining detail. Thus, printers use groupings of dots—half-tone cells—to simulate a grayscale. At least 200 gray levels are needed to represent continuous tone. Therefore, a printer must control a large number of ink dots just to represent gray levels, reducing the detail that can be printed. In practice, detail resolution above 100 dpi meets most requirements. Now, if a printer can lay 1,400 dpi, it has some 14 dots to use for creating the effect of continuous tone. If you multiply together the four or more inks used, a good range of tones and colors are possible.

▶ Filling in cells

Each cell accepts up to 16 dots—counting a cell with no dot, 17 grayscale levels are thus possible. Cells should be randomly filled. Here, they have a regular pattern, so when cells are combined a larger pattern emerges. The device resolution is used to place more dots in each cell.

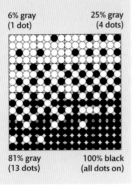

6% gray
(1 dot)

25% gray
(4 dots)

81% gray
(13 dots)

100% black
(all dots on)

Scanners

Flatbed scanners look and work like small photocopiers, but they output image files instead of printed copies. They are useful when you need to turn many drawings, documents, or prints into digital form. The maximum size of the original is usually letter (A4), with well-regarded models made by Epson, Canon, and Hewlett Packard. If you do not need the highest quality or need to make only a few copies, you can photograph the original. Should you wish to turn text on documents into editable text, you can pass the images to optical character recognition (OCR) applications such as Omnipage.

Film scanners are the best way to digitize 35mm film such as legacy collections, or film from Holga cameras, giving resolutions up to 4000 lines per inch. If you wish to scan medium-format film (6 x 4.5cm and larger) a flatbed scanner may provide acceptable quality. Within fewer than fifteen years after the rise of digital photography, only a handful of film scanners remain in production. Nikon and Imacon models provide the best quality but are very costly. Less costly models and flatbed scanners can fulfil less demanding standards. Second-hand film scanners from Nikon, Minolta, Canon, Microtek, and Kodak, can offer good buys, but spare parts and servicing are problematic.

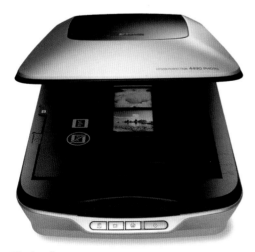

▲ Flatbed scanner
Modern flatbed scanners produce excellent results from prints. With a transparency adaptor in place, good-quality scans can be obtained from film.

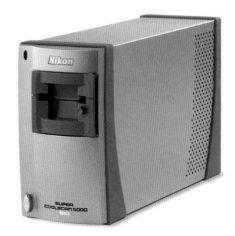

▲ Film scanner
A high-quality film scanner is necessary for turning legacy film-based material into digital form. The majority of models accept 35mm film, but some accept medium-format.

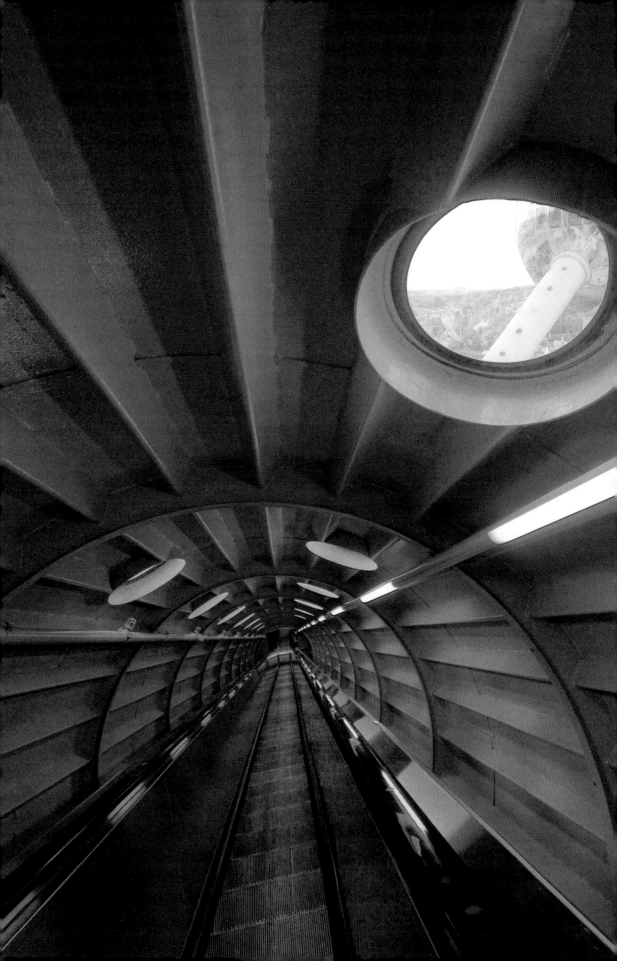

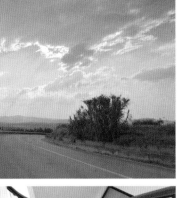

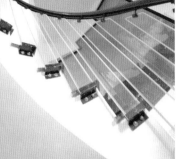

6 GOING FURTHER

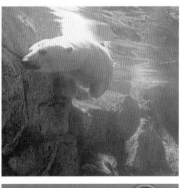

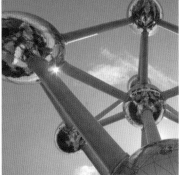

LEARNING MORE

With the vast quantity of information available it is relatively easy to find out all you need to know about the many aspects of digital photography. There are numerous sources of information on the web—although these vary in both quality and depth, the best-known sites have excellent, in-depth and up-to-date information on photography, image manipulation, and equipment. There are also videos and online courses that guide you step-by-step, and there are also numerous books, some of which you will find listed in Further Reading (*see pp. 398–9*). The best way to learn from these sources is usually to have a specific task to complete: having a clear direction in mind, rather than just picking up unrelated snippets of information, will greatly speed up your learning.

Another option to help you go further is to attend a training course. Many are available, but the most cost-effective are usually those offering intensive or residential tuition. These are often run as summer schools in which you immerse yourself in a completely "digital" environment. Such courses will enable you to concentrate on problem-solving, and being able to ask for help from experts at the immediate time that you need clarification can greatly accelerate the learning process. However, if you do not have the equipment to continue at the same level once you return home, you may quickly forget all you have learned. To make the most of immersion teaching, you need to continue using your newly acquired skills. To check if an intensive or residential course is suitable for you, ask these questions when you speak to the administrator or when you read through the prospectus.

■ Do the fees include all materials, such as paper, ink, and removable media?

■ Will there be printed information to take home and keep?

■ Which software, and version, will be taught?

■ Which computer platform will be used?

■ Do students have individual computers to work on or will you have to share?

■ What standard is expected at the start; what standard is to be attained by the end?

■ What are the qualifications of the instructors?

■ You will gain most from any course if you first thoroughly prepare yourself. Having a project or two in mind to work on prevents your mind going blank when you are asked what you would like to achieve. And take along some image files or a scrapbook of pictures to use or to scan in. The best way to learn how to use computer software is to have a real task to complete—this might be a poster for a community event you are involved in, making a greeting card, or producing a brochure for a company.

Courses and qualifications

If you want more in-depth training and a broader educational approach to the subject of digital photography and image manipulation, then higher or further education courses at a college or university are the best route. They are good for meeting other

---

GETTING ON A COURSE

To help ensure that you get onto the course of your choice, consider the following points.

■ **Plan ahead:** most courses recruit and interview only at certain times of the year.

■ **Prepare a portfolio** (see pp. 370–1).

■ **Read up:** if the course contains elements you are not familiar with, such as art history, media theory, and so on, check that you are interested in them before applying. Further, if you know what the course objectives are, you will then know that what you want to do is in line with what the institution wants to achieve. This is important for you—and it is likely to impress the interviewer.

■ **Check on any formal requirements:** some colleges insist that you have certain minimum educational qualifications before you are considered. You may need to attend an introductory course before entering college.

■ **Plan your finances:** attending a course affects your ability to earn and can itself be a financial drain. Calculate the course fees, then add the materials, equipment, and travel costs to your living expenses to work out how much you need to put aside.

like-minded individuals: over a period of a few years you can make lasting friends and valuable contacts, and a shared course of study also makes it far easier to share interests and solve problems. A longer period of study also gives you time to work out future plans and develop in-depth projects.

In some countries you may need a qualification in order to gain a licence to work professionally—in which case completing a formal course is a necessity. In the English-speaking world, qualifications are seldom a prerequisite for professional practice unless you wish, for example, to teach digital photography in college. Indeed, formal qualifications may even be discouraged in some sectors of practice. Don't be afraid to ask local professionals for their advice—most will recall their own initial struggles and will be prepared to help others.

If undertaking a college-based course is not possible, then you may want to consider some type of distance-learning or online study. In these, you communicate with your tutor by mail or email, working with printed materials or from a website, or you can work by yourself. A distance-learning course enables you to be flexible about your rate of progress and when you work, and so is ideal for fitting into a busy schedule, but it can be a lonely process. You may have no contact with fellow students or teaching staff beyond brief summer seminars.

Multi-skilling

Digital photography is just one expression of an enormous growth in employment and career opportunities based on new technologies that has taken place. One important feature of these recent developments is that the need to have multiple skills makes it relatively easy for, say, competent digital photographers to transfer to print publication, or for people talented in the field of page design to transfer their skills to internet-based work.

Careers in digital photography

Working as a digital photographer is not solely about the glamorous areas of fashion, advertising, photojournalism, or celebrity portraiture. Many varied and satisfying ways of doing what you enjoy and earning a living are available.

Those, for example, who have some sort of speciality interest—say, archaeology, architecture, music, or natural history—may find work with institutions relevant to their interests, such as museums, heritage-preservation organizations, humane societies, and so on. In such an environment, a likely job description will require not only photographic skills but also an enthusiasm for and knowledge of the subject. Other career opportunities could take you in the direction of becoming an in-house photographer for speciality magazines—those covering an industry or particular sport, such as sailing, fishing, or biking. If you like working with animals, you might want to consider offering a photographic service to pet owners by taking their animals' portraits in an inventive and creative way (*see pp. 140–3*).

Those who enjoy photography may also find work in the background to other activities—for example, as technicians in laboratories, manufacturers, or universities. This type of work often has the advantage of letting you do the things you enjoy—perhaps scanning and then the digital manipulation of pictures—without the stresses associated with working as an independent professional photographer. At the same time, you may enjoy access to the type of equipment that only large organizations can afford—astronomical telescopes or electron microscopes, for example.

Another burgeoning area of photographic interest is in the field of scientific and medical imaging. This ranges from remote satellite sensing to unraveling the secrets of the atom. The work is highly technical but could perfectly suit those with physics or medical degrees who have an interest in both digital photography and aspects of computer technology.

Those with the requisite depth of knowledge and industry experience can also find a welcome in teaching and training institutions: it is widely recognized in many countries that high-technology industries and service providers are being held back by a skills shortage. If you are an experienced

LEARNING MORE CONTINUED

photographer or a designer who has developed a professional grasp of key applications—including Photoshop, Aperture, Lightroom, InDesign, web-authoring applications such as Flash and Dreamweaver, or vector-based graphics software such as Adobe Illustrator—then there are many opportunities for training the thousands of people who need to learn how to use these computer programs.

Finally, the digital photographer is but a step away from working with time-based media, such as animations and video. Indeed, Photoshop was originally invented to clean up images for the film industry, and today the distinction between software for stills images and software for moving images is becoming increasingly blurred, especially with the internet carrying more and more moving imagery.

Another dimension of time-based media is multimedia production, whether for computer games, websites, or educational presentations. All of these career applications have an enormous appetite for well-made pictures.

Career advice
The key requirement for a career in digital photography today is versatility: having a wide range of skills covering diverse fields and the willingness to apply them to different and sometimes untried ends. You need to be competent in photography—to understand lighting, exposure, composition, and the nature of the recording medium. You need to be comfortable with computers and working with varying pieces of hardware to get the most out of them: the more extensive your technical experience, the easier it will be to solve production problems. And you need an understanding of how images work in contemporary society and the wider cultural context in which they operate. A base in visual and contemporary culture and an awareness of art history are great assets.

Needless to say, you have to be competent with software. This means more than being able to use standard software; rather, you have to be able to obtain the results you want effortlessly and rapidly so that your thinking and creative processes are not hampered by imperfect knowledge or lack of experience. All professional imaging artists use only a fraction of the capabilities of their software—just as photographers use a very limited range of equipment—but their command of what they use is so fluent that the software becomes almost an extension of their thinking. Much of today's professional work is the creation of a visual solution to a conceptual or communication problem, so it helps to understand how to translate abstract concepts into an attractive, eye-catching image.

And because operating professionally means working successfully in a commercial environment, you need some business sense, or at least access to good advice, as well as a desire to act professionally—to commit yourself to working to the highest standards, to work honestly, and to take your commitments, such as keeping to agreed deadlines, seriously.

Digital photographers may, therefore, have graphics, illustration, design, or photography backgrounds. While the list of competencies may seem demanding, the good news is that the need is growing much faster than the supply. Anybody who offers technical skills combined with artistry, creativity, and business acumen will be kept busy.

Turning professional
Having the right attitude and doing your homework are essential if you are thinking of turning professional. Here is a basic checklist of points to consider before taking the plunge.
■ Be positive, decide what you really want to do, and decide that you are going to do it.
■ Be prepared to start small, with work you may not want to do long-term, to gain experience, build confidence, and provide the capital reserves to take you in the direction you really want to go.
■ Check out the competition: if you want to be a portrait photographer, then you need to know if there are already two other portrait photographers in your immediate locality.
■ Decide what to charge for particular types of

work: it is embarrassing to be asked "How much will it cost?" when you cannot give a quick answer.

■ Consider a loan to finance your start-up: this means preparing a business plan (see below).

■ Check any legal and local regulations: do you need to register with an authority; are you allowed to carry on business on your property; do you have to insure against third-party claims?

■ Check your supply lines: can you get materials quickly or rent equipment if you need something more specialized than you already own?

■ Raise your profile: make sure local newspapers and magazines know you are in business.

■ Prepare a portfolio (see pp. 370-1)—potential clients will want to see what you can do—and other advertising, such as a website or posters for your local library and meeting places.

■ Consider joining a professional organization or Chamber of Commerce to network with others.

■ Above all, you will have to work hard. Adopt a work ethic that does not allow you to stop trying.

Preparing a business plan

A business plan makes you consider whether you have a viable prospect. It makes you think about what you want to do and if you have the means to do it, in terms of money and management skills. Just as important, a business plan demonstrates to your bank manager or accountant that you should be taken seriously. It is no exaggeration to say that merely possessing a well-presented, clearly argued business plan takes you half way to the finances your business might need.

The business plan is a report: it summarizes your aims and objectives while honestly presenting your strengths and weaknesses. It should assess the competition and market to arrive at an honest appraisal of your chances of success. The plan also presents a cashflow forecast of how your business will develop over the first two years or so.

A typical cashflow will show that in the early months more money will be spent than income is earned. As the business becomes established, income increases while overheads (rent, heating, utilities) remain steady: your business is starting to make money. But at predictable times during the year—when insurances need renewing, perhaps—there will be heavy costs, and these might coincide with times when business is slow. By working this out, you know when to expect a few tricky months and can warn the bank in advance. This confirms your financial competence and makes it easier to obtain short-term loans or an extended overdraft. The cashflow will also show when an injection of extra cash may be needed to take on more people or invest in new equipment.

All banks give advice or literature on writing a business plan and constructing cashflow forecasts. These may be alien concepts, but you should keep in mind that they are essentially works of fiction—they mix a good deal of fact with the potential and the probable. They should not, however, be works of fantasy, which combine the improbable with the potential. Finally, bear in mind that as your work develops it may move away from the projected business plan. But with it written, at least you know you are changing direction. A business plan is a map—drawn by you—by which you can plot your future.

KEEPING RECORDS

Good records are essential for a well-run business, minimizing the time involved in completing tax returns, dealing with the bank, or setting prices for particular types of work. Keep a diary. Try to make a brief note of the phone calls you make and receive, and keep a book on the projects you work on. In addition, keep a note of everything you are paid and of everything you spend. Good records keep you on the right side of the law and tax authorities. They also put you in a good position if you are ever involved in litigation—you can refer to your notes and give times and dates on what was discussed and agreed. Good records will also lower your accountancy costs. Accurate financial records enable you to regulate your cashflow and the resulting soundness of your money affairs will also lower bank and other finance charges.

PORTFOLIO TECHNIQUE

A portfolio is a selection of your best work brought together to show to a potential client, gallery owner, or employer. "Selection" indicates the need to be selective: you show the type of material that best improves your chances of getting the work, and only that. "Best" means that you select only from the work in which you have complete confidence: work that pleases you and that you wish to be known for.

Painful choices

In order to arrive at your best work, you will have to make many choices, some of which will not be easy. Take comfort in the fact that you have already made many thousands of choices—deciding what not to photograph. Now, you need to make some tougher decisions—to reject images you have captured, some at great expense and trouble.

The golden rule here is that if there is any doubt—the slightest doubt—the picture is out. If sticking to this rule means that you end up with a paltry two or three images, congratulations! You are making sound choices. If you need more pictures, you will have to create more, not become less selective. Conversely, if your final selection is of thirty or more images, there is no doubt you are being soft on yourself.

Storytelling

When you show your work, it is most likely to be viewed sequentially, with one picture following another. This sequence is more or less linear. A viewer may flick back to remind themselves of an image they've seen, but usually, they will look at pictures one after another. This has two important consequences. The most important is that the order of images is a vital part of your presentation technique. You can leave your very best images until last, so you build up to a crescendo of stunning work. Alternatively, you may place your images in chronological order. Of course the most appropriate sequence depends on your subject—landscapes may be presented in a seasonal sequence, portraits from full-length to close-up, and so on.

Not only is the overarching sequence important, it is also helpful to ensure that the relationships between any pair of images contribute to their impact on the viewer. Jarring contrasts or sudden changes from one subject or treatment to another—for example from saturated colors to black and white or from a sensual nude to a warts-and-all character portrait—can ruin the effectiveness of both images involved.

Another consideration, which may or may not be important to you, is that Middle Eastern and Far Eastern cultures read from right to left, so many of their books open from what would be regarded as the back of the book by Western, left-to-right reading cultures. It may be a small point, but arranging your images to suit the culture you are working in demonstrates cultural sensitivity.

How many?

It is also crucial to choose the right number of images to show. Too few—say, under ten images—suggests a struggle to gather enough material. But too many—more than about twenty—may allow weak images to dilute the effect of stronger ones. In general, the qualities of a photographer should be evident by the time the first five images have been evaluated; the rest confirm the opinion of the reviewer and fill gaps in coverage.

Pitching ideas

In many areas of photography, such as magazines, journals, galleries, and agencies, it is not sufficient to simply be a superb photographer; you have to surpass the thousands of competitors with equally fine skills. With magazines, newspapers, or websites you will be expected to have your own ideas, and to suggest subjects, stories, or innovative approaches. Keep up with current affairs and world news as well as news in your area; research potential ideas and be prepared to pitch them when you meet clients: this shows them that you can make an active contribution to the editorial content.

It is natural to feel that the ideas you have are unique and to be afraid to share them in case they are stolen. If you have invested a great deal of research in a story, write down the outline in detail, date it, and submit the idea in writing.

Portfolio tips

Your portfolio and its presentation is one element of a carefully thought out process. Consider everything, from the way you dress to the words you use, from the way you mount or display your prints to the style of your business cards. All are designed to make exactly the right impression. Imagine the person you are showing your work to has challenged you with the words "You have three minutes, impress me," and bear in mind the following advice:

▪ Show only the kind of work that you want to be commissioned to photograph: don't show portraits if you wish to work on interiors or gardens. If you have not shot the subjects the client works with, then make the effort to do so. For example, if you want to shoot fashion but have no examples to show, engage a stylist to pull together a model and clothes for a fashion shoot just for your portfolio.

▪ Show enough to make it clear you are talented and capable, but no more: showing too many images demonstrates a lack of confidence and poor judgement.

▪ Talk about your images or explain the thinking behind them only as much as you are invited to: talking too much about your work could, again, suggest a lack of confidence.

▪ Allow the people reviewing your work to look through it at their own pace. Most professionals sort pictures very rapidly—pausing for perhaps barely a second on each image. This can be very disconcerting, but is normal. When they pause, you know you have their attention.

▪ Dress to match the culture. If your client is in the media you may generally dress more informally than when meeting a financial or industry client. Awareness of dress codes is not about conformity, it is about understanding the needs of clients.

▪ Be polite. You may be rejected today, but you may want to return another day or approach a different part of the company.

▪ Leave contact information—preferably a good quality picture or print, or at least a business card.

▪ Try to leave with a lead. Ask for suggestions of who else to visit—other magazines or companies that may be interested in your work, for example.

METHODS OF PRESENTATION

▪ **Screen-based presentation:** Using tablets or laptop computers is the most convenient and flexible way to show your work. Move between images by manual control or with a slide-show that can be stopped or speeded up as required. Avoid using transitions or a music track unless these are specifically called for.

▪ **Unmounted prints:** This is the cheapest method but these are recommended only for very informal presentations. Prints easily become damaged when they are handled.

▪ **Mounted prints:** These are still relatively inexpensive but the prints do receive some protection. They may need interleaving or window-mattes (cards with window apertures to reveal the image) for best protection. Being bulky and heavy, over-sized mounts (larger than tabloid size) are not popular with commissioners. Generally, it is best to mount prints singly, rather than arrange them in groups.

▪ **Mounted color transparencies:** This is a fairly costly solution but it means you can show many images at once, although you will need a lightbox and magnifier.

▪ **Large-format transparencies:** These are very costly but can be highly impressive: they tend to make any image look rather good. However, you need a light box to view them properly. For a long time this was the favored method of presentation in advertising and commercial photography.

▪ **CD/DVD:** Reliable media whenever you have to leave a large number of images with a client, but the majority will prefer images sent to their FTP (File Transfer Protocol) server or by email.

▪ **Website:** Very inexpensive and easy to set-up, a website allows anyone, anywhere in the world, 24-hour access to view your pictures. Provide links to your site in all your communications. If you work in very different genres, such as glamour and antiques, and do not want your clients confused, set up different websites, for example, www.tomang.body.com and www.tomang.collectibles.com.

BUILDING UP YOUR BUSINESS

Your aim as a photographer is to provide a service for potential clients: in short, people will offer you work if you give them what they want. To that end, you need to bring all your photographic skill, inventiveness, flexibility, and professionalism to bear on the task, as well as honesty and as much charm as you can muster under what will sometimes be very testing circumstances. The qualities that help you attract business in the first place are the same ones that help you retain and build up your client base.

Promotion and marketing

One of the keys to building a successful business is good communication. To start with, clients must be able to find you, and to find you they must first know about you. This is the task of promotion and marketing. Start small—perhaps by placing advertisements locally in community newspapers and magazines, cards or posters in store windows or library noticeboards, even leafleting homes and businesses in your neighborhood. Visit local businesses and leave contact details—preferably a promotional card featuring a picture of yours. If there is any interest, be prepared to show your portfolio (see pp. 370-1): pay particular attention to businesses that are likely to be visually more aware, such as architects, real estate agents, interior designers, garden architects, and, of course, local publications. Remember, there is no shame in starting by visiting homes to take pictures of babies before making your move on the competitive world of celebrity portraits; hone your skills on interiors of homes for sale or flower arrangements before tackling a multinational's annual report. And, of course, the web is an increasingly important place for self-promotion, and a natural choice for the digital photographer. A web presence has to be supported by targeted marketing, however, such as mailings of your photographic calling card or sending out CDs of work.

Once you have made contact with potential clients, you then need to enter into discussions with them to help bring about a successful conclusion to the exercise.

WHAT IS A CONTRACT?

A contract creates legal relations between two parties in which one offers to carry out some work or service and the other party accepts an obligation or liability to pay for that work or service. The contract may not have to be a formal legal document: an exchange of letters, even a conversation, may be sufficient to form a contract and, with it, corresponding legal obligations (depending on local law: ask your lawyer if you are not sure). However, in general, both parties must want to enter into a relationship. This may carry with it conditions that both sides agree. In addition, a contract is generally legally binding only if it is possible to carry it out, is not illegal, and is not frustrated by circumstances beyond the control of either party. Many photographers do not realize that when they are commissioned to carry out work to an agreed specification, they are legally bound to do so: artistic licence and freedom of expression do not come into the debate. By the same token, if a client commissions a photographer to take ten portraits, to ask in addition for shots of the building is to vary the contract. It is reasonable for other terms, such as payment, to be renegotiated. An important issue is who retains copyright on a commission: in some countries, national law allows copyright to be assigned from the creator to the commissioner; but in other countries, copyright is held to be an inalienable right of the artist and cannot be assigned to anybody else.

Clarity

Be specific (not "as soon as possible," but "within five working days"); be precise (not "digital images," but "high-resolution 10 x 8 images at 300 dpi"); be straight (not "of course I can do it" when you don't really know, but "I'll shoot a free test and you can see how it works").

Honesty

Evaluate your skills objectively. Certainly you can take risks and push yourself, but don't let others down—in the end you only damage yourself. If you don't like something—perhaps an element of the commission is dangerous or unethical—then say so (and the sooner the better).

Repetition

Summarize the conclusions after any discussion has taken place; summarize and agree the action points; repeat and agree the schedule with everybody concerned; and repeat and agree all task allocations and responsibilities.

Follow-up

Construct a paper trail with a written or emailed note after all meetings. Record phone conversations pertinent to a commission, particularly if detailed changes are being discussed. Keep records of what you do, why you're doing it, and how much it is costing you. If, right from the beginning, you make a habit of keeping good records, even with small jobs, you will be able to cope better with the larger ones.

Legality

Introduce into the discussion anything to do with copyright, licensing, or other legal aspects of the commission that may concern you as soon as they become relevant. Doing this will add to, rather than detract from, the air of professionalism you project. And more often than not, the client will be pleased to know about any possible legal complications at the earliest possible point.

Finances

Talk about money—fees, day rates, equipment rental charges, and any associated charges that will affect the final bill—early on. You will not seem greedy by doing this; you will look more professional. And if you don't think that the money is right, then tell your client. If the finances are going to be a sticking point, then the sooner you know about it the better.

Repeat business

Clients will appreciate any sign of your involvement in the project over and above that engendered by the fee. For example, suggesting new approaches to the task, offering additional shots that were not specified, or trying out different angles or a more interesting and creative approach all represent "value-plus" from a client's point of view while, in fact, costing you very little.

CALCULATING YOUR DAY RATE

The basic day rate is your benchmark for survival: it measures the average cashflow (*see p. 369*) you need to keep going. After all, the fees you charge must at least pay for your survival. If you hit the rate, you can survive, but your profits will be minimal.

The first step is to add up your living expenses, including your rent or mortgage, the cost of any loans or rental purchase, utilities and food bills, and business overheads, such as insurance, bank charges, loan charges, driving and travel expenses, and so on. These are the expenses you must meet before you can move into profit. Don't forget to add depreciation of capital items, such as your camera equipment and car: you will need money to pay for their replacement.

The next step is less objective—you need to evaluate how many chargeable days you wish for and can reasonably expect to work in a year. Be realistic, so allow yourself vacations, days off for illness, and other days on which you may not be earning any money but you will still be working—going to meetings, for example, researching new projects, taking your portfolio around. A figure of around 100–150 non-chargeable days per annum is not an unreasonable figure.

Now, simply divide the figure for total costs by the number of chargeable days. Many photographers arrive at a figure much higher than they expected. To this, of course, must be added your profit element, without which a business cannot grow and improve. An alternative approach, having worked out how much you need a year, is to divide the figure by the day rate you think the local market will bear: that will tell you how many days you need to work.

MOUNTING AN EXHIBITION

After spending some time taking photographs and accumulating images, the urge to show your work to people beyond your immediate circle of family and friends may start to grow and gnaw at you. The first thing you must do is banish from your mind any doubts that your work is not good enough to show to the wider public. An exhibition is exactly that: you make an exhibit of yourself. People will not laugh, but they may admire. If you have the drive and the ambition, then you should start planning now—you cannot start this process too early.

Turning a dream into reality

You may feel that you are not ready to mount an exhibition just yet. If so, then perhaps you had better get on with the task of building up a library of suitable images. At some point in the future you will know you have the right material and that the time is right.

Now try to imagine in your mind's eye what the show will look like: visualize how you would light it, how you will position your images for maximum impact, how to sequence photographs to create a particular atmosphere, and create a flow of meaning or narrative. Picture to yourself the size of the prints,

how they will glow in the light. This will help to focus your mind and guide your energies as well as act as a spur to your picture- or print-making. Here are some other pointers you might want to consider.

■ Choose your venue well in advance, as most of the better-known galleries are under a lot of pressure and have to plan their schedules at least a year ahead. Other galleries may call quarterly or half-yearly committee meetings to decide what to show in the following period. At the other end of the scale, venues such as a local library or a neighborhood community hall may be prepared to show work at very short notice. In any event, you will want to give yourself the time necessary for your plans to mature and to give the venue the opportunity to tie something in to the exhibition, such as a concert or lecture (depending on the subject matter of your imagery).

■ Choose your venue creatively. Any public space could be a potential exhibition venue—indeed, some seemingly improbable spaces may be more suitable for some types of work than a "proper" gallery. Bear in mind that the very presence of your work will transform the space into a "gallery," whether it is on the top deck of a bus, in a shopping mall, or on a pedestrian walkway.

■ Budget with your brains, not your heart. Put on the best show you can afford, not one that costs more than you can afford. The point of an exhibition is to win a wider audience for your work, not to bankrupt you or to force you to call in financial favors that you might need at some time in the future.

■ Once you have decided on the space you want to use and have received all necessary permissions, produce drawings of the layout of the entire venue. This will also involve you in making little thumbnail sketches of your prints in their correct hanging order: it is easier to visualize the effectiveness of picture order this way.

SELLING PRINTS

Remember that silver-based prints will continue, for a long time yet, to sell for higher prices than any digitally produced print. Here are some hints for ensuring good, continuing relations with buyers.

■ Don't make unsubstantiated claims about the permanence of printed images.

■ Give people advice about how to care for the prints, such as not storing them in humid conditions or where they will be exposed to bright sunlight.

■ Never exceed the run when you offer limited-edition prints—produce the specific, guaranteed number, and not one more.

■ Print on the best-quality paper you can afford or that recommended by the printer manufacturer.

Timing

Mounting an exhibition requires very careful planning on many different levels if you want your show to look professional, so don't leave any

DRAWING UP A BUDGET

When budgeting for the costs of an exhibition, take into account not only your direct photographic expenses but also the range of support services. These include the costs of electricians to light your work, picture-framing, public-liability insurance, the building (or renting) of "flats" to break up the exhibition space and provide extra surfaces on which to hang your work. Here are some cost categories to consider.

- Direct photographic costs—including making prints or slide duplication if projected images form part of your show.
- Indirect photographic costs—including retouching, mounting, frame-making, and rental equipment, such as projectors.
- Gallery costs—including venue rental, deposits against damage or breakages, and the renting of flats or similar.
- Publicity—including the cost of producing and mailing out invitations, advertising in trade or local journals or newspapers, as well as the production of an exhibition catalog.
- Insurance—budget for the costs of insuring your work, public liability, and any possible damage to the venue.
- And don't forget—no matter what your final budget figure is, there will always be out-of-pocket expenses you cannot identify beforehand. At the last minute, for example, you might decide you want flowers for the opening night. So, as a precaution, add a 15 percent contingency to the final budget figure.

important carpentry, electrical, picture-framing, or similar work to, say, a long weekend or holiday period when you might not be able to gain access to key personnel should something go critically wrong. And you should always count on the fact that something will go wrong.

Looking at sponsorship

One way to offset some of the costs of mounting an exhibition is by sponsorship. The key to success is persuading a potential sponsor that the likely benefits from the relationship will flow both ways. It is obvious that you will benefit from the deal by being offered the use of equipment you might not otherwise be able to afford perhaps, or complementary or discounted print-making, but what do the other parties get?

The best approach to sponsorship involves you persuading potential benefactors that by making equipment or services available to you they will receive some boost to their business or that their public profile will be somehow enhanced by the association. It could be that, for example, sponsoring individuals, companies, or organizations will receive coverage in trade newspapers or journals as a result of their help.

As a rule, it is always easier to obtain services or products than it is cash. Printing materials, exhibition space, scanning, processing, even food and drinks for the opening night are all possible, but cash is unlikely. And remember to make your approach in good time—organizations have budgets to maintain and once sponsorship allocations have been made, often there may be nothing left until the next financial year.

Finally, even if the answer from a potential sponsor is "no," you can still ask for something that may be even more valuable—information. So ask for suggestions about which other companies or organizations might be interested in helping.

An exhibition is your chance to get your work known by a wider audience, so make full use of the opportunity if it arises by telling everybody you know about it, and encouraging them to spread the word to their contacts.

Finally, mounting a photographic exhibition brings together many different people and skills. They are your sponsors just as much as any commercial contributor, so always take the trouble to acknowledge their invaluable help and contributions, for without them your show might never have got off the drawing board.

COPYRIGHT CONCERNS

Copyright is a vital subject, as it regulates the intellectual content of digital media and all information. Different traditions of copyright law in different countries lead to variation not only in the detail but also in the entire approach to this subject, but the broad outlines are regulated by international treaty and, for the web, by usage. The following are some frequently asked questions and answers framed to have as wide an applicability as possible. However, always seek professional advice if you are not sure what your rights are or how you should proceed. You may not need to hire a lawyer, as many photographic organizations provide basic copyright advice. Other sources of help can be found online (*see pp. 392–4*).

Do I have to register in order to receive copyright protection?

No, you do not. Copyright in works of art—which includes writing, photographs, and digital images—arises as the work is created. In more than 140 countries in the world, no formal registration is needed to receive basic legal protection.

Can I protect copyright of my images once they are on the web?

Not directly. This is because you cannot control who has access to your website. Make sure you read the small print if you are using free web space. You may be asked to assign copyright to the web server or service provider. Do not proceed if you are not happy with this condition.

Do I have to declare copyright by stamping a print or signing a form?

In most countries, no. Copyright protection is not usually subject to any formality, such as registration, deposit, or notice. It helps, however, to assert your ownership of copyright clearly—at least placing "© YOUR NAME"—on the back of a print or discreetly within an image on the web, such as in a corner.

What is a "watermark"?

It is information, such as a copyright notice or your contact details, incorporated deep in the data of an image file. The "watermark" is usually visible but it may be designed to be invisible. In either case, watermarks are designed so that they cannot be removed without destroying the image itself.

Can I be prosecuted for any images I place on the web?

Yes, you can. If your pictures breach local laws—for example, those to do with decency, pornography, or the incitement of religious or racial hatred, or if they feature illegal organizations—and if you live within the jurisdiction of those laws, you may be liable to prosecution. Alternatively, your Internet Service Provider (ISP) may be ordered to remove them.

Is it wrong to scan images from books and magazines?

Technically, yes, you are in the wrong. Copying copyright material (images or text) by scanning from published sources does place you in breach of copyright law in most countries. However, in many

CAN I PREVENT MY IDEAS FROM BEING STOLEN?

There is no copyright protection covering ideas to do with picture essays, for example, or magazine features or books. The easiest way to protect your concept is by offering your ideas in strict confidence. That is, your ideas are given to publishers or editors only on the condition that they will not reveal your ideas to any third party without your authorization. Your idea must have the necessary quality of confidentiality—that is, you have not shared the information with more than a few confidants—and the idea is not something that is widely known. The most unambiguous approach to this issue is to require your publisher or the commissioning editor to sign a nondisclosure agreement—a written guarantee. However, this may be an unduly commercial-strength approach. You may preface your discussions with a "this is confidential" statement. If the person does not accept the burden of confidentiality, you should not proceed.

countries you are allowed certain exceptions—for example, if you do it for the purposes of study or research, for the purposes of criticism or review, or to provide copy for the visually impaired. Bear in mind, though, that these exceptions vary greatly from country to country.

If I sell a print, is the buyer allowed to reproduce the image?

No—you have sold only the physical item, which is the print itself. By selling a print, you grant no rights apart from the basic property right of ownership of the piece of paper—and an implied right to display it for the buyer's personal, private enjoyment. The buyer should not copy, alter, publish, exhibit, broadcast, or otherwise make use of that image without your permission.

What are "royalty-free" images?

These are images that you pay a fee to obtain in the first instance, but then you do not have to pay any extra if you use them—even for commercial purposes. With some companies, however, certain categories of commercial use, such as advertising or packaging, may attract further payments. Royalty-free images can be downloaded from websites and also come on CDs.

How is it possible for images to be issued completely free?

Free images found on the internet can be an inexpensive way for companies to attract you to visit their site. You can then download these images for your own use, but if you wish to make money from them, you are expected and trusted to make a payment. This fee is usually relatively small, however, so you are encouraged to behave honestly and not exploit the system.

Does somebody own the copyright of an image if that person pays for the film or the rental of the equipment?

In most countries, no. In some countries, if you are employed as a photographer then it is your employer who retains copyright in any material you produce; in others, however, it is the photographer who retains the copyright. In any circumstance, the basic position can be overridden by a local contract made between the photographer and the other party prior to the work being carried out.

What is the Creative Commons?

This is a type of licence designed to allow a flexible range of protections and freedoms for authors, artists, and educators to encourage wide use of intellectual property while discouraging abuse. Works can be used provided: the author is credited, the use is not for commercial purposes, and no derivative works are made. This allows a widespread sharing of creative and other works without loss to the copyright owners by those who otherwise would not be able to benefit from the works. It is in widespread use in the photo-sharing community. See creativecommons.org.

If I manipulate someone else's image, so that it is completely changed and is all my own work, do I then own the copyright in the new image?

No. You were infringing copyright in the first place by making the copy. And then, altering the image is a further breach of copyright. Besides, the new image is not fully all your work: arguably, it is derived from the copy. If you then claim authorship, you could be guilty of yet another breach—this time, of a moral right to ownership.

Is it okay to copy just a small part of an image—say, part of the sky area or some other minor detail?

The copyright laws in most countries allow for "incidental" or "accidental" copying. If you take an insignificant part of an image, perhaps nobody will object, but it is arguable that your action in choosing that particular part of an image renders it significant. If this is accepted, then it could be argued that you are in breach. If it makes no real difference where you obtain a bit of sky, then try to take it from a free source.

SHOPPING FOR EQUIPMENT

Purchasing all the equipment needed for digital photography can be either bewilderingly off-putting or delightful fun and full of new things to learn. There is undoubtedly a lot to consider, but if you are not lucky enough to have a knowledgeable friend to help, don't worry. A lot of information is available on the web—and all of it is free.

Where to look for help

The web is the prime resource for information about equipment, followed a long way second by printed magazines. Web sources fall into four broad categories: large retail stores such as B&H (bhphotovideo.com); review sites such as dpreview.com; general photographic websites or web versions of printed magazines, such as What Digital Camera; and manufacturer's websites.

Large retailers with a web presence are a good starting point for information on photographic equipment. Their websites may even be superior to the manufacturer's own sites for quality and ease of access to information, and you can easily compare specifications of different models. Of course, you can learn about prices, too.

Review sites are numerous. Some do little more than take the camera out of the box and describe it, while others perform exhaustive technical checks. The quality of information, and the depth of knowledge applied, is variable. It is unfortunate but inevitable that only the more glamorous models tend to be reviewed in depth. Obtain a consensus from as many sources as possible.

Other photography websites offer large amounts of information and are constantly updated; they may know more about new products than retailers do. Again, the quality is variable, since they may be written by people who are journalists first and photographers second. Also, magazines may come under pressure to say good things about a product, so you may have to read between the lines.

The manufacturers' websites can offer useful information and other resources such as tips on photographic technique or features on the technology of digital cameras.

Buying online

Online purchases can be safe, efficient, and economical. The sensible precautions for online transactions apply equally for photography. Buy from sites that: guarantee secure transactions; you know about or have been recommended; offer guarantees that cover your purchase, particularly if you are buying abroad. Note that equipment purchased from a foreign website may have instructions in a language other than your own. If possible, use a credit card that protects against fraud. Always print and retain transaction details.

Beware of items that are much cheaper from one source than any others. The importer may not be officially recognized, the guarantee might not cover your region, or the language of the instructions—even on the camera itself—may be foreign to you.

Buying secondhand

The rise of digital photography has helped create

RENTING EQUIPMENT

Do you ever need expensive equipment but cannot really afford it or would use it only occasionally? You may, for example, need a super-long telephoto lens for a safari trip, a data projector for a talk, a superior-quality scanner, or a replacement computer while yours is under repair. One answer is to rent items you need—you will save on the purchase price, pay only when the item is really needed, and the rental cost should be fully tax deductible if you are in business. Note the following points.

- Research possible equipment sources and set up account facilities. Some companies will send items if you live far from them if you are a known customer, while new customers may need to provide a full-value cash deposit.
- Contact the supplier to reserve the item as soon as you think you might need it.
- Try to pick up the item a day or two early so that you can familiarize yourself with it and fully test it.
- Ensure your insurance covers any rented items.

a swollen market for secondhand film-based cameras; even professional-grade models can be bought at bargain prices. The rapid development of digital cameras has also created a burgeoning supply of keenly priced digital equipment. Make sure that digital cameras are sold complete with all original software, chargers, and cables, since some use nonstandard items that could be difficult to source.

The world's largest market for secondhand or pre-used equipment is eBay, online at ebay.com. This site offers copious help for the uninitiated, but local retailers are likely to offer stocks of equipment that you can examine in person and return easily if found to be faulty.

Shopping for specific interests

Today's photographer is spoilt for choice, thanks to the numerous camera models with features for every occasion. However, it can take a good deal of research to find the right camera for you.

Challenging conditions: Cameras should be sealed against dust and rainfall, and have a rugged construction. Cameras with minimal moving parts are best, and avoid those with lenses that zoom forward on turning on.

Collections: Modern digital cameras offer excellent close-up qualities, but many distort the image. Choose an SLR with a macro lens, and avoid zoom lenses. For flat objects where precision is essential, such as coins or stamps, use a flatbed scanner.

Nature: Electronic-viewfinder (EVF) or micro 4/3 digital cameras are good for nature photography: some offer focal lengths of 400mm or more, allowing high-magnification images of distant animals. A tripod will be invaluable.

Low light: Fast lenses—that is, those with a large maximum aperture—are limited to costly prime optics for SLRs. A cheaper solution is to use the highest ISO setting available, and select cameras with image stabilization.

Portraiture: Use fast, high-quality lenses. If possible, use full-frame sensors, as digital cameras with small sensors suffer from excessively large depth of field.

Sports: Rapid response and long lenses are essential. Many EVF cameras give fair results in

SHOPPING CHECKLIST
- Try to shop with somebody knowledgeable.
- Write down the details of your computer model, operating system, and the other equipment that needs to work with the item you need.
- If it is secondhand, check that the equipment appears to have been well treated.
- If it is secondhand, enquire about the history of the equipment—for what purpose was it used, and for how long?
- Check that there is a guarantee period and that it is long enough for any likely faults to appear.
- When buying computer peripherals, make sure they will work with your exact computer model and operating system. You may, nonetheless, still need to test equipment at home with your computer, so if any compatibility problems arise, make sure the store will provide you with free technical support. If these problems prove to be insurmountable, enquire about the store's policy regarding refunds.
- Ask about anything that may be causing you confusion. You will not look foolish—the only foolish thing is to pay for equipment that later proves useless.

good lighting. If lighting is poor, you may need an SLR and fast, long focal length lenses with large maximum apertures, and a monopod or tripod.

Still life and studio: Ensure your digital camera can synchronize with studio flash. Some cameras may be controlled from a computer, and some can even send pictures direct to the computer.

Travel: EVF cameras offer a winning combination of compact, lightweight bodies, with extensive versatility and freedom from dust. Cameras that use standard AA batteries free you from worries about power, but try to choose cameras with long-lived batteries. For wide-angle views, you may need supplementary lenses—awkward on location.

Underwater: Housings are available for several models—from entry-level to professional—allowing you to reach all controls. The least expensive are flexible plastic bags but access to controls is limited.

GLOSSARY

2D Two-dimensional, as in 2D graphics. Defining a plane or lying on one.

3D Three-dimensional, as in 3D graphics. Defining a solid or volume, or having the appearance of a solid or volume.

4/3 Four thirds. Format of sensor size 18 × 13.5 mm, with associated camera and lens systems.

24x speed The device reads or writes data at 24x the basic rate for the device—for CDs and memory cards, 150 KB per second. DVDs read and write at a basic speed about 9x greater than CDs.

24-bit A measure of the size or resolution of data that a computer, program, or component works with. A color depth of 24 bits produces millions of different colors.

35 mm equivalent 35mm equivalent focal length. A digital camera's lens focal length expressed as the equivalent focal length for the 35mm film format.

36-bit A measure of the size or resolution of data that a computer, program, or component works with. In imaging, it equates to allocating 12 bits to each of the R, G, B (red, green, blue) channels. A color depth of 36 bits gives billions of colors.

5,000 The white balance standard for pre-press work. Corresponds to warm, white light.

6,500 The white balance standard corresponding to normal daylight. It appears to be a warm white compared with 9,300.

9,300 The white balance standard close to normal daylight. It is used mainly for visual displays.

A

aberration In optics, a defect in the image caused by a failure of a lens system to form a perfect image.

aberration, chromatic An image defect that shows up as colored fringes when a subject is illuminated by white light, caused by the dispersion of white light as it passes through the glass lens elements.

absolute colorimetric A method of matching color gamuts that tries to preserve color values as close to the originals as possible.

absolute temperature A measure of thermodynamic state, used to correlate to the color of light. Measured in Kelvins.

absorption Partial loss of light during reflection or transmission. Selective absorption of light causes the phenomenon of color.

accommodation An adjustment in vision to keep objects at different distances sharply in focus.

achromatic color Color that is distinguished by differences in lightness but is devoid of hue, such as black, white, or grays.

ADC Analog-to-Digital Conversion. A process of converting or representing a continuously varying signal into a set of digital values or code.

additive A substance added to another, usually to improve its reactivity or its keeping qualities, especially in lengthening the life span of a print.

additive color synthesis Combining or blending two or more colored lights in order to simulate or give the sensation of another color.

address Reference or data that locates or identifies the physical or virtual position of a physical or virtual item: for example, memory in RAM; the sector of hard disk on which data is stored; a dot from an ink-jet printer.

addressable The property of a point in space that allows it to be identified and referenced by some device, such as an ink-jet printer.

algorithm A set of rules that defines the repeated application of logical or mathematical operations on an object: for example, compressing a file or applying image filters.

alias A representation or "stand-in" for the continuous original signal: it is the product of sampling and measuring the signal to convert it into a digital form.

alpha channel A normally unused portion of a file format. It is designed so that changing the value of the alpha channel changes the properties— transparency, for example—of the rest of the file.

analog An effect, representation, or record that is proportionate to some other physical property or change.

antialiasing Smoothing away the stair-stepping, or jagged edge, in an image or in computer typesetting.

aperture The hole in the lens that is letting

light through. *See* f/numbers.

app A commonly used abbreviation for application software.

array An arrangement of image sensors. There are two types. **1** A two-dimensional grid, or wide array, in which rows of sensors are laid side by side to cover an area. **2** A one-dimensional or linear array, in which a single row of sensors, or set of three rows, is set up, usually to sweep over or scan a flat surface—as in a flatbed scanner. The number of sensors defines the total number of pixels available.

aspect ratio The ratio between width and height (or depth).

attachment A file, such as a PDF or JPEG, that is sent along with an email.

autoexposure Automatic exposure setting achieved by the camera balancing ISO, aperture, and shutter setting against the brightness of subject.

autofocus Automatic focusing carried out by the camera to ensure the lens projects sharp images.

B

back-up To make and store second or further copies of computer files to protect against loss, corruption, or damage of the originals.

bandwidth **1** A range of frequencies transmitted, used, or passed by a device, such as a radio, TV channel, satellite, or loudspeaker. **2** The measure of the range of wavelengths transmitted by a filter.

beam splitter An optical component used to divide rays of light, such as a semi-reflective mirror.

bicubic interpolation A type of interpolation in which the value of a new pixel is calculated from the values of its eight near neighbors. It gives superior results to bilinear or nearest-neighbor interpolation, with more contrast to offset the blurring induced by interpolation.

bilinear interpolation A type of interpolation in which the value of a new pixel is calculated from the values of four of its near neighbors: left, right, top, and bottom. It gives results that are less satisfactory than bicubic interpolation, but requires less processing.

bit The fundamental unit of computer

information. It has only two possible values—1 or 0—representing, for example, on or off, up or down.

bit-depth Measure of the amount of information that can be registered by a component: hence, it is used as a measure of resolution of such variables as color and density. 1-bit registers two states (1 or 0), representing, for example, white or black; 8-bit can register 256 states.

bit-mapped **1** An image defined by the values given to individual picture elements of an array whose extent is equal to that of the image; the image is the map of the bit-values of the individual elements. **2** An image comprising picture elements whose values are only either 1 or 0: the bit-depth of the image is 1.

black **1** Describing a color whose appearance is due to the absorption of most or all of the light. **2** Denoting the maximum density of a photograph.

bleed **1** A photograph or line that runs off the page when printed. **2** The spread of ink into the fibers of the support material. This effect causes dot gain.

BMP Bitmap. A file format that is native to the Windows platform.

bokeh The subjective quality of an out-of-focus image projected by an optical system—usually a photographic lens.

bracketing To take several photos of the same image at slightly different exposure settings, to ensure at least one picture is correctly exposed.

brightness **1** A quality of visual perception that varies with the amount, or intensity, of light that a given element appears to send out, or transmit. **2** The brilliance of a color, related to hue or color saturation—for example, bright pink as opposed to pale pink.

brightness range The difference between the lightness of the brightest part of a subject and the lightness of the darkest part.

browse To look through a collection of, for example, images or web pages in no particular order or with no strictly defined search routine.

Brush An image-editing tool used to apply effects, such as color, blurring, burn, or dodge, that are limited to the areas the brush is applied to, in imitation of a real brush.

GLOSSARY CONTINUED

buffer A memory component in an output device, such as printer, CD writer, or digital camera, that stores data temporarily, which it then feeds to the device at a rate the data can be turned into, for example, a printed page.

burning-in 1 A digital image-manipulation technique that mimics the darkroom technique of the same name. **2** A darkroom technique for altering the local contrast and density of a print by giving specific parts extra exposure, while masking off the rest of the print to prevent unwanted exposure in those areas.

byte Unit of digital information: 1 byte = 8 bits. A 32-bit microprocessor, for example, handles four bytes of data at a time.

C

C An abbreviation for cyan. A secondary color made by combining the two primary colors red and blue.

cache The RAM dedicated to keeping data recently read off a storage device to help speed up the working of a computer.

calibration The process of matching characteristics or behavior of a device to a standard.

camera exposure The total amount of the light reaching (in a film camera) the light-sensitive film or (in a digital camera) the sensors. It is determined by the effective aperture of the lens and the duration of the exposure to light.

camera phone Cellular or mobile telephone that is equipped with a digital camera.

capacity The quantity of data that can be stored in a device, measured in MB or GB.

cartridge A storage or protective device consisting of a shell (a plastic or metal casing, for example) enclosing the delicate parts (film, ink, or magnetic disk, for example).

catch light A small, localized highlight.

CCD Charge Coupled Device. A semiconductor device used as an image detector.

CD Compact Disk. A storage device for digital files invented originally for music and now one of the most ubiquitous computer storage systems.

characteristic curve A graph showing how the density of a given film and its development relate to exposure.

chroma The color value of a given light source or patch. It is approximately equivalent to the perceived hue of a color.

CIE LAB Commission Internationale de l'Éclairage LAB. A color model in which the color space is spherical. The vertical axis is L for lightness (for achromatic colors) with black at the bottom and white at the top. The a axis runs horizontally, from red (positive values) to green (negative values). At right angles to this, the b axis runs from yellow (positive values) to blue (negative values).

clipboard An area of memory reserved for holding items temporarily during the editing process.

CLUT Color Look-Up Table. The collection of colors used to define colors in indexed color files. Usually a maximum of 256 colors can be contained.

CMOS Complementary Metal Oxide Semiconductor. Construction of sensor used in cameras in phones, as well as digital cameras.

CMYK Cyan Magenta Yellow Key. The first three are the primary colors of subtractive mixing, which is the principle on which inks rely in order to create a sense of color. A mix of all three as solid primaries produces a dark color close to black, but for good-quality blacks, it is necessary to use a separate black, or key, ink.

codec co(mpression) dec(ompression). A routine or algorithm for compressing and decompressing files; for example, JPEG or MPEG. Image file codecs are usually specific to the format, but video codecs are not tied to a particular video format.

cold colors A subjective term referring to blues and cyans.

colorize To add color to a grayscale image without changing the original lightness values.

ColorSync A proprietary color-management software system to help ensure, for example, that the colors seen on the screen match those to be reproduced by a printer.

color 1 Denoting the quality of the visual perception of things seen, characterized by hue, saturation, and lightness. **2** To add color to an image by hand—using dyes, for example—or in an image-manipulation program.

color cast A tint or hint of a color that evenly covers an image.

color gamut The range of colors that can be reproduced by a device or reproduction system. Reliable color reproduction is hampered by differing color gamuts of devices: color film has the largest gamut, computer monitors have less than color film but more than inkjet printers; the best inkjet printers have a greater color gamut than four-color CMYK printing.

colour management The process of controlling the output of all devices in a production chain to ensure the final results are reliable and repeatable.

color picker The part of an operating system (OS) or application that enables the user to select a color for use—as in painting, for example.

color profile The way one device—screen, scanner, printer, etc.—handles color as defined by the differences between its own set of colors and that of the profile connection space.

colour sensitivity A measure of the variation in the way in which films and sensors respond to light of different wavelengths.

color space Defines a range of colors that can be reproduced by a given output device or be seen by the human eye under certain conditions. It is commonly assigned to manage the color capture and reproduction of each photo image.

color synthesis Recreating the original color sensation by combining two or more other colors.

color temperature The measure of color quality of a source of light, expressed in Kelvins.

complementary colors Pairs of colors that produce white when added together as lights. For example, the secondary colors—cyan, magenta, and yellow—are complementary to the primary colors—respectively, red, green, and blue.

compliant A device or software that complies with the specifications or standards of a corresponding device or software to enable them to work together.

compositing A picture-processing technique that combines one or more images with a basic image. Also known as montaging.

compression 1 A process by which digital files are reduced in size by changing the way the data is coded. **2** A reduction in tonal range.

continuous-tone image A record in dyes, pigment, silver, or other metals in which relatively smooth transitions from low to high densities are represented by varying amounts of the substance used to make up the image.

contrast 1 Of ambient light: the brightness range found in a scene. In other words, the difference between the highest and lowest luminance values. High contrast indicates a large range of subject brightnesses. **2** Of a light source or quality of light: the difference in brightness between the deepest shadows and the brightest highlights. Directional light gives high-contrast lighting, with hard shadows, while diffuse light gives low-contrast lighting, with soft shadows. **3** Of color: colors positioned opposite each other on the color wheel are regarded as contrasting—for example, blue and yellow, green and red.

CPU Central Processor Unit. The part of the computer that receives instructions, evaluates them according to the software applications, and then issues appropriate instructions to other parts of the computer system.

crash The sudden and unexpected nonfunctioning of a computer.

crop 1 To use part of an image for the purpose of, for example, improving composition or fitting an image to the available space or format. **2** To restrict a scan to the required part of an image.

cross-platform Application software, file, or file format that can be used on more than one computer operating system.

curve A graph relating input values to output values for a manipulated image.

cut and paste To remove a selected part of a graphic, image, or section of text from a file and store it temporarily in a clipboard ("cutting") and then to insert it elsewhere ("pasting").

cyan The color blue-green. It is a primary color of subtractive mixing or a secondary color of additive mixing. It is also, the complementary color to red.

GLOSSARY CONTINUED

D

D65 The white illuminant standard used to calibrate monitor screens. It is used primarily for domestic television sets. White is correlated to a color temperature of 6,500 K.

daylight **1** The light that comes directly or indirectly from the sun. **2** As a notional standard, the average mixture of sunlight and skylight with some clouds, typical of temperate latitudes at around midday, and with a color temperature of between 5,400 and 5,900 K. **3** Film whose color balance is correct for light sources with a color temperature between 5,400 and 5,600 K. **4** Artificial light sources, such as light bulbs, whose color-rendering index approximates to that of daylight.

definition The subjective assessment of clarity and the quality of detail that is visible in an image or photograph.

delete **1** To render an electronic file invisible and capable of being overwritten. **2** To remove an item, such as a letter, selected block of words or cells, or a selected part of a graphic or an image.

density **1** The measure of darkness, blackening, or "strength" of an image in terms of its ability to stop light—in other words, its opacity. **2** The number of dots per unit area produced by a printing process.

depth **1** The sharpness of an image—loosely synonymous with depth of field. **2** A subjective assessment of the richness of the black areas of a print or transparency.

depth of field The measure of the zone or distance over which any object in front of a lens will appear acceptably sharp. It lies both in front of and behind the plane of best focus, and is affected by three factors: lens aperture; lens focal length; and image magnification.

depth perception The perception of the absolute or relative distance of an object from a viewer.

digital image The image on a computer screen or any other visible medium, such as a print, that has been produced by transforming an image of a subject into a digital record, followed by the reconstruction of that image.

digital zoom Enlarging or zooming into an image by cropping toward the center.

digitization The process of translating values for the brightness or color into electrical pulses representing an alphabetic or a numerical code.

display A device—such as a monitor screen, LCD projector, or an information panel on a camera—that provides a temporary visual representation of data, such as an image.

distortion, tonal A property of an image in which the contrast, range of brightness, or colors appear to be markedly different from those of the subject.

dithering Simulating many colors or shades by using a smaller number of colors or shades.

d-max **1** The measure of the greatest, or maximum, density of silver or dye image attained by a film or print in a given sample. **2** The point at the top of a characteristic curve of negative film, or the bottom of the curve of positive film.

dodging **1** A digital image-manipulation technique based on the darkroom technique of the same name. **2** A darkroom technique for controlling local contrast when printing a photograph by selectively reducing the amount of light reaching the parts of a print that would otherwise print as too dark.

down-sampling The reduction in file size achieved when a bitmapped image is reduced in size.

dpi Dots per inch. The measure of resolution of an output device as the number of dots or points that can be addressed or printed by that device.

driver The software used by a computer to control, or drive, a peripheral device, such as a scanner, printer, or removable media drive.

drop-on-demand A type of inkjet printer in which the ink leaves the reservoir only when required. Most inkjet printers in use today are of this type.

drop shadow A graphic effect in which an object appears to float above a surface, leaving a fuzzy shadow below it and offset to one side.

drum scanner A type of scanner employing a tightly focused spot of light that shines on a subject that has been stretched over a rotating drum. As the drum rotates, the spot of light traverses the length of the subject, thus scanning its entire area.

duotone **1** A photomechanical printing process in which two inks are used to increase the tonal range. **2** A mode of working in image-manipulation software that simulates the printing of an image with two inks.

DVD-RAM A DVD (Digital Versatile Disk) variant that carries 4.7GB or more per side that can be written to and read from many times.

dynamic range **1** The measure of spread of the lowest to the highest energy levels in a scene. **2** The range that can be captured by a device, such as a camera or scanner.

E

effects filters **1** Lens attachments designed to distort, color, or modify images to produce exaggerated, unusual, or special effects. **2** Digital filters that have effects similar to their lens-attachment counterparts, but also giving effects impossible to achieve with these analog filters.

electronic viewfinder (EVF) An LCD or LCOS screen, viewed under the eyepiece and showing the view through a camera lens.

engine **1** The internal mechanisms that drive devices such as printers and scanners. **2** The core parts of a software application.

enhancement **1** Change in one or more qualities of an image, such as color saturation or sharpness, in order to improve its appearance or alter some other visual property. **2** The effect produced by a device or software designed to increase the apparent resolution of a TV monitor screen.

EPS Encapsulated PostScript. A file format that stores an image (graphics, photograph, or page layout) in PostScript page-description language.

erase To remove, or wipe, a recording from a disk, tape, or other recording media (usually magnetic) so that it is impossible to reconstruct the original record.

EV Exposure value. A measure of camera exposure. For any given EV, there is a combination of shutter and aperture settings that gives the same camera exposure.

exposure **1** A process whereby light reaches a light-sensitive material or sensor to create a latent image. **2** The amount of light energy that reaches a light-sensitive material.

exposure compensation Altering autoexposure setting to suit the subject or creative intention.

exposure factor The number indicating the degree by which measured exposure should be corrected or changed in order to give an accurate exposure.

F

f/numbers Settings of the lens diaphragm that determine the amount of light transmitted by a lens. Each f/number is equal to the focal length of the lens divided by diameter of the entrance pupil.

fade The gradual loss of density in silver, pigment, or dye images over time.

fall-off **1** The loss of light in the corners of an image as projected by a lens system in, for example, a camera or a projector. **2** The loss of light toward the edges of a scene that is illuminated by a light source whose angle of illumination is too small to cover the required view. **3** The loss of image sharpness and density away from the middle of a flatbed scanner whose array of sensors is narrower than the width of the scanned area.

feathering The blurring of a border or boundary by reducing the sharpness or suddenness of the change in value of, for example, color.

file format A method or structure of computer data. It is determined by codes—for example, by indicating the start and end of a portion of data together with any special techniques used, such as compression. File formats may be generic—shared by different software—or native to a specific software application.

fill-in **1** To illuminate shadows cast by the main light by using another light source or reflector to bounce light from the main source into the shadows. **2** A light used to brighten or illuminate shadows cast by the main light. **3** In image manipulation, to cover an area with color—as achieved by using a Bucket tool.

GLOSSARY CONTINUED

filter 1 An optical accessory used to remove a certain waveband of light and transmit others. **2** Part of image-manipulation software written to produce special effects. **3** Part of application software that is used to convert one file format to another. **4** A program or part of an application used to remove or to screen data—for example, to refuse email messages from specified sources.

fingerprint Marking in a digital image file that is invisible and that survives all normal image manipulations, but one that can still be retrieved by using suitable software.

fixed focus A type of lens mounting that fixes a lens at a set distance from the film. This distance is usually the hyperfocal distance. For normal to slightly wide-angle lenses, this is at between $6\frac{1}{2}$ and 13ft (2 and 4m) from the camera.

flare A nonimage-forming light in an optical system.

flash 1 To provide illumination using a very brief burst of light. **2** To reduce contrast in a light-sensitive material by exposing it to a brief, overall burst of light. **3** The equipment used to provide a brief burst, or flash, of light. **4** The type of electronic memory that is used in, for example, digital cameras.

flat 1 Denoting a low-contrast image in which gray tones only are seen. **2** The lighting or other conditions that tend to produce evenly lit or low-contrast image results.

flatbed scanner A type of scanner employing a set of sensors arranged in a line that are focused, via mirrors and lenses, on a subject placed face down on a flat, glass bed facing a light source. As the sensors traverse the subject, they register the varying light levels reflected off the subject.

flatten To combine multiple layers and other elements of a digitally manipulated or composited image into one. This is usually the final step of working with Layers prior to saving an image in a standard image format; otherwise, the image must be saved in native format.

focal length For a simple lens, the distance between the center of the lens and the sharp image of an object at infinity projected by it.

focus 1 Making an image look sharp by bringing the film or projection plane into coincidence with the focal plane of an optical system. **2** The rear principal focal point. **3** The point or area on which, for example, a viewer's attention is fixed or compositional elements visually converge.

font A computer file describing a set of letter forms for display on a screen or used for printing.

foreground 1 The part of scene or space around an object that appears closest to the camera. **2** The features in a photographic composition that are depicted as being nearest the viewer.

format 1 The shape and dimensions of an image on a film as defined by the shape and dimensions of the camera's film gate. **2** The dimensions of paper on which an image is printed. **3** The orientation of an image: for example, in a landscape format, the image is oriented with its long axis running horizontally, while in a portrait format the image is oriented with its long axis running vertically.

fractal A curve or other object whose smaller parts are similar to the larger parts. In practice, a fractal displays increasing complexity as it is viewed more closely and where the details bear a similarity to the whole.

frame 1 A screen's worth of information. **2** An image in a sequence replicating movement.

G

gamma In monitors, a measure of the correction to the color signal prior to its projection on the screen. A high gamma gives a darker overall screen image.

GIF Graphic Interchange Format. This is a compressed file format designed for use over the Internet. It uses 216 colors.

grain The texture of a print paper's surface.

graphics tablet An input device allowing fine or variable control of the image appearance in an image-manipulation program. The tablet is an electrostatically charged board connected to the computer. It is operated using a pen, which interacts with the board to provide location information, and instructions are issued by providing pressure at the pen tip.

greeking The representation of text or images as gray blocks or other approximations.

grayscale The measure of the number of distinct steps between black and white that can be recorded or reproduced by a system. A grayscale of two steps permits the recording or reproduction of just black or white.

H

half-tone cell The unit used by a half-tone printing or reproduction system to simulate a grayscale or continuous-tone reproduction. In off-set lithography, the half-tone cell is defined by the screen frequency: continuous tone is simulated by using dots of different sizes within the half-tone cell. With desktop printers, the half-tone cell consists of groups of individual laser or inkjet dots.

hard copy A visible form of a computer file printed more or less permanently onto a support, such as paper or film.

HDR High Dynamic Range. This usually refers to a tone-mapped image.

highlights The brightest (whitest) values in an image or image file.

hints Artificial intelligence built into outline fonts, which turn elements of a font on or off according to the size of the font. Intended to improve legibility and design.

histogram A statistical, graphical representation showing the relative numbers of variables over a range of values. Usually used in image-manipulation software, histograms are also available to view on many digital cameras.

HLS Hue, Lightness, Saturation. A color model that works well for representing a visual response to colors, but one that is not satisfactory for other color reproduction systems. This model has been largely superseded by the LAB model.

hot-pluggable A connector or interface, such as USB, that can be disconnected or connected while the computer and machine are still powered up.

hue The name given to the visual perception of a color.

I

IEEE 1394 A standard providing for the rapid communication between computers and devices, and between devices without the need for a computer, such as between digital cameras and CD writers. It is also known as FireWire and iLink.

ILC Interchangeable Lens Compact. A type of digital camera design without a mirror.

image aspect ratio The comparison of the depth of an image to its width. For example, the nominal 35mm format in landscape orientation is 24mm deep by 36mm wide, so the image aspect ratio is 1:1.5.

indexed color A method of creating color files or defining a color space based on a table of colors chosen from 16 million different colors. A given pixel's color is then defined by its position, or index, in the table (also known as the "color lookup table").

inkjet Printing technology based on the controlled squirting of extremely tiny drops of ink onto a receiving layer.

intensity **1** A measure of energy, usually of light, radiated by a source. **2** A term loosely used to refer to the apparent strength of color, as in inks or the colors of a photograph.

interpolation The insertion of pixels into a digital image based on existing data. It is used to resize an image file, for example, to give an apparent increase in resolution, to rotate an image, or to animate an image.

ISO International Organization for Standardization. Most exposure indices or film speeds today are described by the ISO system, which uses the same numeric values as the old ASA system—that is, ISO 100, 400, 800, etc. Digital cameras have sensitivity adjustments that are essentially equivalent to ISO film speed.

JK

jaggies The appearance of stair-stepping artifacts.

JPEG Joint Photographic Expert Group. A data-compression technique that reduces file sizes with loss of information.

GLOSSARY CONTINUED

k **1** An abbreviation for kilo, a prefix denoting 1,000. **2** A binary thousand: in other words, 1024, as used, for example, when 1024 bytes is abbreviated to KB. **3** Key ink or blacK—the fourth color separation in the CMYK four-color print reproduction process.

Kelvin (K) A unit of temperature that is relative to absolute zero, and is used to express color temperature.

kernel A group of pixels, usually a square from 3 pixels up to 60, that is sampled and mathematically operated on for certain image-processing techniques, such as noise reduction or image sharpening.

key tone **1** The black in a CMYK image. **2** The principal or most important tone in an image, usually the mid-tone between white and black.

keyboard shortcut Keystrokes that execute a command.

L

layer mode A picture-processing or image-manipulation technique that determines the way that a layer, in a multilayer image, combines or interacts with the layer below.

light **1** That part of the electromagnetic spectrum, from about 380–760nm, that stimulates the receptors of the retina of the human eye, giving rise to normal vision. Light of different wavelengths is perceived as light of different colors. **2** To manipulate light sources to alter the illumination of a subject.

light box A viewing device for transparencies and films consisting of a translucent, light-diffusing top illuminated from beneath by color-corrected fluorescent tubes in order to provide daylight-equivalent lighting.

lightness The amount of white in a color. This affects the perceived saturation of a color: the lighter the color, the less saturated it appears to be.

line art Artwork that consists of black lines and black and white areas only, with no intermediate gray tones present.

live view In SLR cameras, viewing by raising the mirror and feeding the image on the sensor to the rear LCD screen.

load To copy enough of the application software into a computer's RAM for it to be able to open and run the application.

lossless compression A computing routine, such as LZW, that reduces the size of a digital file without reducing the information in the file.

lossy compression A computing routine, such as JPEG, that reduces the size of a digital file but also loses information or data.

lpi Lines per inch. A measure of resolution or fineness of photomechanical reproduction.

LZW Lempel-Ziv Welch compression. A widely used computer routine for lossless file compression of, for example, TIFF files.

M

Mac Commonly used term for Apple Macintosh computers and their operating system (OS).

macro **1** The close-up range giving reproduction ratios within the range of about 1:10 to 1:1 (life-size). **2** A small routine or program within a larger software program that performs a series of operations. It may also be called "script" or "action."

marquee A selection tool used in image-manipulation and graphics software.

mask A technique used to obscure selectively or hold back parts of an image while allowing other parts to show.

master **1** The original or first, and usually unique, incarnation of a photograph, file, or recording: the one from which copies will be made. **2** To make the first copy of a photograph, file, or recording.

matrix The flat, two-dimensional array of CCD sensors.

matte **1** The surface finish on paper that reflects light in a diffused way. **2** A box-shaped device placed in front of camera lens to hold accessories. **3** A board whose center is cut out to create a window to display prints. **4** A mask that blanks out an area of an image to allow another image to be superimposed.

megapixel A million pixels. A measure of the resolution of a digital camera's sensor: a 7-megapixel camera has a 7-megapixel sensor.

metering Assessment by a camera of the brightness of a scene, or by a flash for the purpose of making an exposure.

micro 4/3 A type of 4/3 camera that uses a mirrorless design.

mirrorless Type of camera design similar to SLR but without a mirror, using interchangeable lenses.

moiré A pattern of alternating light and dark bands or colors caused by interference between two or more superimposed arrays or patterns, which differ in phase, orientation, or frequency.

monochrome An image made up of black, white, and grays, which may or may not be tinted.

N

native **1** The file format belonging to an application program. **2** An application program written specifically for a certain type of processor.

nearest neighbor The type of interpolation in which the value of the new pixel is copied from the nearest pixel.

node **1** A computer linked to others in a network or on the Internet. **2** A word or short phrase that is linked to other text elsewhere in a hypertext document.

noise Unwanted signals or disturbances in a system that tend to reduce the amount of information being recorded or transmitted.

Nyquist rate The sampling rate needed to turn an analog signal into an accurate digital representation. This rate is twice the highest frequency found in the analog signal. It is applied to determine the quality factor relating image resolution to output resolution: pixel density should be at least 1.5 times, but not more than 2 times, the screen ruling. For example, for a 133 lpi screen, resolution should be between 200 and 266.

O

off-line A mode of working with data or files in which all required files are downloaded or copied from a source to be accessed directly by the user.

online A mode of working or operating with data or files in which the operator maintains continuous connection with a remote source.

opacity The measure of how much can be "seen" through a layer.

operating system The software program, often abbreviated to OS, that underlies the functioning of the computer, allowing applications software to use the computer.

optical viewfinder A type of viewfinder that shows the subject through an optical system, rather than via a monitor screen.

out-of-gamut The color or colors that cannot be reproduced in one color space but are visible or reproducible in another.

output **1** The result of any computer calculation—any process or manipulation of data. Depending on the context, output may be in the form of new data, a set of numbers, or be used to control an output device. **2** A hard-copy printout of a digital file, such as an inkjet print or separation films.

override Control for increasing or decreasing autoexposure setting.

PQ

paint To apply color, texture, or an effect with a digital brush or the color itself.

palette **1** A set of tools, colors, or shapes that is presented in a small window of a software application. **2** The range or selection of colors available to a color-reproduction system.

peripheral A device, such as a printer, monitor, scanner, or modem, connected to a computer.

photodiode A semiconductor device that responds very quickly and proportionally to the intensity of light falling on it.

photograph A record of physical objects, scenes, or phenomena made with a camera or other device, through the agency of radiant energy, on sensitive material from which a visible image may be obtained.

photomontage A photographic image made from the combination of several other photographic images. Also known as a composite.

PICT A graphic file format used in the Mac OS.

pixel The smallest unit of digital imaging used or produced by a given device. An abbreviation of "picture element."

GLOSSARY CONTINUED

pixelated The appearance of a digital image whose individual pixels are clearly discernible.

platform The type of computer system, defined by the operating system used—for example, the Apple Macintosh platform uses the Mac OS.

plug-in Application software that works in conjunction with a host program into which it is "plugged," so that it operates as if part of the program itself.

posterization The representation of an image using a relatively small number of different tones or colors, which results in a banded appearance in flat areas of color.

PostScript A programming language that specifies the way in which elements are output: it uses the full resolution of the output device.

ppi Points per inch. The number of points seen or resolved by a scanning device per linear inch.

prescan In image acquisition, it is a quick view of the object to be scanned, taken at a low resolution for the purposes of, for example, cropping.

primary color One of the colors (red, green, or blue) to which the human eye has peak sensitivity.

prime lens A fixed focal length lens, in contrast to a zoom lens.

process colors Colors that can be reproduced with the standard web offset press (SWOP) inks of cyan, magenta, yellow, and black (CMYK).

proofing The process of checking or confirming the quality of a digital image before final output.

quality factor The multiplication factor—usually between 1.5 and 2 times the screen frequency—used to ensure a file size that is sufficient for good-quality reproduction.

R

RAM Random Access Memory. The component of a computer in which information can be temporarily stored and rapidly accessed.

raster The regular arrangement of addressable points of any device, such as scanner, digital camera, monitor, printer, or film writer.

read To access or take off information from a storage device, such as a hard-disk, CD, or DVD.

refresh rate The rate at which one frame of a computer screen succeeds the next. The more rapid the rate, the more stable the monitor image appears.

res The measure of the resolution of a digital image expressed as the number of pixels per side of a square measuring 1 x 1mm.

resampling The addition or removal of pixels from an image by sampling or examining the existing pixels and making the necessary calculations.

resize To change a file's resolution or size.

RGB Red Green Blue. A color model that defines colors in terms of the relative amounts of red, green, and blue components they contain.

RIP Raster image processor. Software or hardware dedicated to the conversion of outline fonts and vector graphics into rasterized information—in other words, it turns outline instructions such as "fill" or "linejoin" into an array of dots.

S

scanner An optical-mechanical instrument for the analog-to-digital conversion, or digitization, of film-based and printed material and artwork.

scanning The process of using a scanner to turn an analog original into a digital facsimile—in other words, a digital file of specified size.

screengrab An image file of the monitor display or part of it. Also called a screenshot.

scrolling The process of moving to a different portion of a file that is too large for it all to fit onto a monitor screen.

selfie Self-portrait made while holding the camera at arm's length or at the end of a "selfie stick."

shadows The dark (or black) areas of an image.

shutter lag Time between pressing a shutter button fully and the exposure being made: 0.075 seconds is just perceptible and acceptable for professional use.

shutter time Duration of exposure of film or sensor to light.

soft proofing The use of a monitor screen to proof or confirm the quality of an image.

stair-stepping A jagged or steplike reproduction of a line or boundary that is, in fact, smooth.

subtractive color synthesis Combining of dyes or pigments to create new colors.

SWOP Standard Web Offset Press. A set of inks used to define the color gamut of CMYK inks used in the print industry.

system requirements The specifications defining the minimum configuration of equipment and operating system needed to run application software or a device. It usually details the type of processor, amount of RAM, free hard-disk space, oldest version of the operating system, and, according to the software, any specifically needed device.

T

thumbnail The representation of an image in a small, low-resolution version.

TIFF A widely used image file format that supports up to 24-bit color per pixel. Tags are used to store such image information as dimensions.

tint **1** Color that is reproducible with process colors; a process color. **2** An overall, usually light, coloring that tends to affect areas with density but not clear areas.

tone-mapped A type of image created by blending two or more differing exposures of the same scene, "mapping" the scene's dynamic range to predominantly mid-tones.

transparency **1** Film in which the image is seen by illuminating it from behind—color transparency film, for example. Also known as a slide. **2** In image manipulation, the degree to which background color can be seen through the foreground layer.

transparency adapter An accessory light source that enables a scanner to scan transparencies.

TWAIN A standardized software "bridge" used by computers to control scanners via scanner drivers.

UVWZ

undo To reverse an editing or similar action within application software.

upload The transfer of data between computers or from a network to a computer.

USB Universal Serial Bus. A standard for connecting peripheral devices, such as a digital camera, telecommunications equipment, or a printer, to a computer.

USM UnSharp Mask. An image-processing technique that has the effect of improving the apparent sharpness of an image.

variable contrast A coating formula that mixes emulsions of different speeds and sensitivities to light, with the effect that the mid-tone contrast can be varied by changing the spectral qualities of the illumination.

vignetting **1** A defect of an optical system in which light at the edges of an image is cut off or reduced by an obstruction in the system's construction. **2** Deliberately darkened corners—used to help frame an image or soften the frame outline.

VRAM Video random access memory. Rapid-access memory that is dedicated for use by a computer or graphics accelerator to control the image on a monitor.

warm colors A subjective term referring to reds, oranges, and yellows.

watermark **1** A mark left on paper to identify the maker or paper type. **2** An element in a digital image file used to identify the copyright holder.

write To commit or record data onto a storage medium, such as a CD-R or hard disk.

zoom **1** Type of lens that can vary its focal length (field of view) without changing the focus. **2** To change the magnification for onscreen viewing.

WEB RESOURCES

www.bjphoto.co.uk
The website of The British Journal of Photography has a wide mix of free and subscriber-only content covering news, reviews, and feature articles.

www.bobatkins.com
Mixed bag of reviews, technical articles, and links. Generally high-quality information and many interesting discussions. Worth dipping into.

www.creativepro.com
One of the best sources for news, techniques, issues of image manipulation, digital photography, design, and graphics. Also software and hardware reviews. Highly recommended.

www.dcresource.com
Digital Camera Resource is dedicated to thorough reviews of consumer cameras and also features useful comparison charts. An enormous number of cameras are covered. An excellent resource.

www.digicamhelp.com
Full of helpful advice, but particularly useful as a portal for downloading camera manuals.

www.diwa-awards.com
The Digital Imaging Websites Association features camera reviews carried out by 12 (at the time of writing) digital photography sites all over the world, following common formats and shared procedures.

www.dpreview.com
Leading site for highly detailed camera and lens reviews and industry news. Also hosts lively discussion fora.

www.ephotozine.com
General digital photography website with serious content and useful news, reviews, and help pages.

www.fredmiranda.com
Lively reviews and discussions for the technically inclined, plus illustrated articles.

www.idigitalphotography.com
Beginner-friendly site covering topics on request, with blogs and the most comprehensive and authoritative photography dictionary on the web.

www.informit.com/articles
Extracts from a wide range of sources, including technology books, many with high-quality content.

www.jackspcs.com
Jack's Photographic and Chemistry Site offers concise information on chemicals, with formulary for developers, toners, and so on, as well as links.

www.lens-reviews.com
Reviews contributed by users. A useful resource for potential buyers.

www.letsgodigital.org
Extensive news and reviews of equipment, as well as a regularly up-dated picture gallery.

www.lightstalkers.org
Extensive, lively, and broad-ranging debate and exchange in a community site dedicated to photography in all its aspects. Worth regular visits.

www.luminous-landscape.com
High-quality, varied content, with some substantial essays on a wide range of photographic topics and detailed, considered reviews. Worth a leisurely visit.

www.normankoren.com
Dedicated to the technically inclined photographer, this site offers much to ponder on: from printing to scanning and digital photography, with good links.

www.pdnonline.com
This online resource from Photo District News magazine offers lively, rich, and wide-ranging news and features. The site complements the print version and is well worth regular visits.

www.photodo.com
News on lenses, as well as reviews—both technical and user-based—of a wide range of lenses.

www.photographydirectory.org
Portal for thousands of sites for photographers, photography agencies, clubs, and manufacturers.

www.popphoto.com
The home of venerable and much-respected photography magazines Popular Photography and American Photo. Excellent for news, features, and reviews. Well worth frequent visits.

www.retrophotographic.com
The technical section of this commercial outpost of darkroom practice offers a valuable compendium of data sheets and processing guides.

www.shuttertalk.com
Lively, busy, and extensive photography community with articles, galleries, resources, and news. Worth making regular visits.

www.steves-digicams.com
Well-known site with a large amount of information on many subjects, as well as reviews, technical features, and news. Worth bookmarking.

www.the-digital-picture.com
Content-rich site with reviews, hints, and tips.

www.travelphotographers.net
Travel Photographers Network is a specialist site offering illustrated travel features, equipment reviews, and technical advice aimed at travel photographers, with image and discussion fora.

SOURCES OF HISTORY AND INSPIRATION

www.colorsmagazine.com
Super collection of powerful, imaginative, emotive imagery of great editorial intelligence. Must visit.

www.foto8.com
Website of the eponymous magazine, which is the leading showcase for contemporary photojournalism and documentary photography. Should be bookmarked by any photography lover.

www.getty.edu
Authoritative references on digital collections, including book-length introduction to digital imaging—highly educational. Also, a collection of marvelous photos and artwork.

www.photography-museum.com
A treasure trove of great images collected thematically with informative historical notes. Like any good museum, well worth the occasional visit.

TECHNICAL RESOURCES AND STANDARDS

www.color.org/iccprofile.html
The website of the International Color Consortium explains everything you need to know about color profiles, their applications, and details of software that complies with the specifications.

www.dofmaster.com
This site offers free, easy-to-use calculators for depth of field and hyperfocal distance, useful articles, and software for Windows, Palm, and iPhone.

www.edmundoptics.com
Primarily a corporate site for an optics supplier, but informed with clear FAQs and articles on optics, as well as an excellent list of web links. For those interested in applied photography and optics.

www.hugsan.com/EXIFutils
EXIF Utilities is an application for editing, correcting, and altering the EXIF and IPTC data saved in image files by digital cameras.

www.iptc.org/IPTC4XMP/
The International Press Telecommunications Council's standards for image metadata: technical documentation, tutorials, and samples.

www.photoattorney.com
A valuable blog from an attorney specializing in representing photographers, covering copyright, trademark, contracts, privacy, and other legal issues. Has broad relevance despite being US-based, since much contemporary media law is led by US judgments.

www.schneiderkreuznach.com
The Know How section contains valuable and authoritative (technical but approachable) essays on lens coatings and lens design, among other things.

www.schorsch.com
A lighting-design corporate website with a useful knowledge base, offering a range of information for anyone interested in light and lighting.

www.tawbaware.com/maxlyons/calc.htm
Handy calculators for depth of field and angle of view sit alongside a number of other utilities.

www.updig.org/guidelines
Here you will find the universal photographic digital imaging guidelines for best practice in the creation, supply, and transmission of digital image files. Essential reading.

www.wilhelm-research.com
An essential resource on printing and print permanence, print care, and storage, supported by test data.

WEB RESOURCES CONTINUED

SOFTWARE RESOURCES

www.imatest.com
Imatest is used to test all major aspects of lens performance in digital cameras—widely used in the industry. It is worth using the evaluation runs on your digital camera. Windows only.

http://photoshopnews.com
A heavyweight site with high-quality material on many issues relating to the Photoshop user, covering not only the software but technical, market, and legal issues, as well as news and web links.

www.photoshopsupport.com
This valuable beginner's resource offers numerous tutorials and free resources such as brushes, fonts, actions, and so on. Also, links to plug-ins, video training, and extracts from Photoshop books. Supports other software, such as Lightroom and Dreamweaver, too.

www.photo-software.com
Douglas Software offers tools for calculating camera and lens details, as well as sun and moon positions.

www.pluginsworld.com
Comprehensive and constantly up-dated listings of plug-ins for Photoshop and other software.

www.versiontracker.com
The best site for keeping your software up-to-date and for trying out new software, with useful user reviews. Essential to bookmark.

PICTURE HOSTING AND SHARING

The internet allows anyone to place hundreds of their images onto photo-sharing websites for friends, family, and prospective clients. These sites operate as online, off-site storage for images, so your images are backed up in secure storage and can be accessed at any time from anywhere in the world.

www.500px.com
Picture-sharing and photography community.

www.flickr.com
One of the most popular picture-sharing sites, offering good image management and low prices.

www.fotki.com
One of the largest social networking sites hosting images and videos for sharing.

www.photobucket.com
Offers a hybrid of community and picture-hosting features, catering for popular and social imagery.

http://pa.photoshelter.com
Picture-hosting photography site with a range of contemporary work. Strong North American bias.

http://picasa.google.com
Picasa's software integrates well with Google accounts and offers low-cost picture storage.

www.shutterfly.com
Unlimited uploads and many offers to make prints, books, and so on.

www.smugmug.com
Picture sharing of professional-quality images.

www.webshots.com
Low-cost picture storage on an easy-to-use site.

ONLINE PHOTO EDITING

These and similar sites allow you to enjoy image manipulation without buying your own software.

www.picnik.com
www.photoshop.com/express
www.fotoflexer.com
www.phixr.com

MANUFACTURERS

Many of the multinational manufacturers host different websites for each of their sales regions. It may be worth visiting those outside your region, since the quality and information can vary between sites: some, for example, simply present pages of their product catalogs, while others offer practical tips and technical resources, as well as product information. The following is a selection of photographic manufacturers, but inclusion does not imply recommendation.

Apple Computers, displays, software
  www.apple.com
Canon Cameras, lenses and accessory systems, printers, scanners, data projectors
  www.canon.com
Eizo LCD monitors
  www.eizo.com
Epson Printers, scanners, picture storage
  www.epson.com
Fujifilm Cameras and accessories
  www.fujifilm.com
Hasselblad Medium-format cameras, lenses, accessory systems, scanners, software
  www.hasselblad.com
Hewlett-Packard Printers, scanners, computers
  www.hp.com
Jobo Picture storage, digital display, darkroom and other accessories
  www.jobo.com
Kodak Cameras, film, papers, printers
  www.kodak.com
LaCie Hard-disk drives and media, displays
  www.lacie.com
Leica Cameras, lenses, accessory systems
  www.leica.com
Lexar Memory cards and readers for digital cameras
  www.lexar.com
Lexmark Printers
  www.lexmark.com
Microtek Scanners
  www.microtek.com
Nikon Cameras, lenses, accessory systems, film scanners
  www.nikon.com

Olympus Cameras, lenses, printers, removable storage
  www.olympus.com
Panasonic Cameras, lenses, data projectors
  www.panasonic.com
Pantone Color control, color-matching systems
  www.pantone.com
Pentax Cameras and lenses, medium-format cameras and lenses
  www.pentax.com
Phase One Digital backs and medium-format camera systems and software
  www.phaseone.com
RH Designs Enlarger timers, densitometers, and other darkroom aids
  www.rhdesigns.co.uk
Ricoh Digital cameras
  www.ricoh.com
Rollei Medium-format, speciality, and consumer digital cameras; medium-format film cameras; lenses
  www.rollei.com
Samsung Cameras and SLR lenses, projectors
  www.samsungcamera.com
Sandisk Memory cards, readers
  www.sandisk.com
Sekonic Exposure meters
  www.sekonic.com
Sony Digital cameras, SLR systems and accessories, data projectors, computers
  www.sony.com
Studioflash Generic studio flash accessories: reflectors, soft-boxes, stands
  www.studioflash.co.uk
Tamron Interchangeable lenses for SLR cameras
  www.tamron.com
Tokina Interchangeable lenses for SLR cameras
  www.tokinalens.com
X-Rite
Color-management solutions: software, hardware, and support
  www.xrite.com

SOFTWARE RESOURCES

IMAGE-MANIPULATION SOFTWARE

Despite the dominance of Photoshop, there are many software applications that are capable of excellent results. The simpler programs are better suited to the beginner or those who do not wish to commit a large amount of time to learning how to use the software.

Photoshop This is the industry-standard software package due to its many features, such as color management, and a vast range of elements that can be expanded with the widest range of plug-in software. However, it can be difficult to master and is burdened by some weak features. Mac and Windows.

www.adobe.com

Affinity Photo

Powerful and capable, closely following Adobe Photoshop with its shortcuts and functions but with improvements in many areas, such as RAW conversion. Inexpensive considering its power.

www.affinity.serif.com

Photoshop Elements

An extremely capable image-manipulation program that is easy to use and comes with many presets and templates. Suitable for the majority of digital photographers. Mac and Windows.

www.adobe.com

GIMP

The GNU Image Manipulation Program is a free, powerful application for image enhancement and compositing. Mac and Windows.

www.gimp.org

Painter

Enormous range of Brush tools (more than 30 categories, with innumerable options), with highly controllable painting effects and powerful cloning tools. An excellent supplement to Photoshop. Mac and Windows.

www.corel.com

Paint Shop Pro

Affordable, powerful software with good Layers features and excellent support for RAW formats. It is suitable for most requirements, including web work. Windows only.

www.corel.com

PhotoImpact

Very good range of tools, strong on features for web imagery, in an affordable package. Useful for graphics to video. Includes cut-down version of Corel Painter. Windows only.

www.ulead.com

Photo-Paint

Powerful, comprehensive features, with good Layers and cloning elements. Windows only. Not to be confused with the low-cost image editor Ability Photopaint (www.ability.com).

www.corel.com

PhotoSuite

Inexpensive, tutorial-based software with a good range of tools and Layers handling, together with good functions for web work and creating slide shows on DVD. Windows only.

www.roxio.com

WORKFLOW SOFTWARE

These applications aim to provide all you need for a digital image workflow—from uploading of images and adding metadata, to image enhancement and management, to output as books, prints, or to the web.

ACDSee

This has been refined over the years as an efficient tool for the whole digital image workflow, with excellent support of RAW formats and the ability to apply adjustments selectively.

www.acdsee.com

Adobe Lightroom

This offers powerful RAW conversion, with good image-management features and excellent enhancement tools and metadata handling, but the workflow methodology is rigid. It has a good range of web-page options and controls over printing.

www.adobe.com

Phase One Capture One

Powerful image-management, manipulation, and capture software widely adopted by professionals. Flexible RAW conversion, batch processing, and cataloging features.

www.phaseone.com

IMAGE MANAGEMENT
FotoStation
Simple and effective tool for creating sets of pictures and management, with multiple printing and web-page output options. Mac and Windows.

www.fotoware.com

Photo Mechanic
Very speedy picture management, aimed at digital photographers. Easy to use. Mac and Windows.

www.camerabits.com

Portfolio
Powerful tool for the management of picture libraries, with the ability to publish on the internet. Suitable for use over networks. Mac and Windows.

www.extensis.com

PLUG-INS
Plug-in software adds functions to the prime software, appearing in its own dialog box for settings to be made. Many of these will work with applications such as Painter, which accepts Photoshop-compatible plug-ins. Check with the supplier prior to purchase.

Alien Skin
Offering numerous filters effects, as well as plug-ins for enlargement, enhancement, and correction—one of the best collections of Photoshop plug-ins.

www.alienskin.com

Andromeda 3D
Powerful and able to wrap images around basic 3D objects, but tricky to learn.

www.andromeda.com

Genuine Fractals
Industry-standard image-enlargement software.

www.onOnesoftware.com

KPT
Kai's Power Tools offers powerful special-effects filters. It can be tricky to use but is worth exploring.

www.corel.com

NIK
A range of well-regarded tools: Silver Efex for black-and-white images, Color Efex for special effects, Dfine for noise reduction, and Viveza for selective image enhancement.

www.niksoftware.com

Noise Ninja
Powerful and effective reduction of noise, with a high level of control.

www.picturecode.com

DESIGN AND OTHER SOFTWARE
BBEdit
HTML editor with many features invaluable for programming; beloved of web-authoring experts. The Lite version is available as freeware. Mac only.

www.bbedit.com

Canvas
Integrates illustrations with graphics for publishing, supporting a wide range of formats with image-enhancement filters. One version works with GIS (Geographical Information Systems). Windows only.

www.acdsee.com

Dreamweaver
Full-featured WYSIWYG (what you see is what you get) software for designing web pages and managing websites. Mac and Windows.

www.adobe.com

Flash
Software for drawing, animation, and multimedia creation. Flash animation is widely readable on the internet. Mac and Windows.

www.adobe.com

InDesign
Very powerful page-design software with excellent feature set. Mac and Windows.

www.adobe.com

Mask Pro
This software offers highly controllable tools for masking difficult objects such as hair and glass. Mac and Windows.

www.onOnesoftware.com

QuarkXPress
Well-established page-design application. Mac and Windows.

www.quark.com

FURTHER READING

Tom Ang:
Digital Photography Essentials
DK Publishing
A reader-friendly book reflecting all the latest advances in digital photography. Covers basic principles and techniques. Answers the most frequently asked photography questions.

The Complete Photographer
DK Publishing
With broad scope and appeal, this book is based around tutorials on 10 different genres, covering both technical and creative aspects of photography. Behind-the-scenes features introduce the work of 20 top international photographers, showing in step-by-step detail how an idea progresses from concept stage to final image.

Digital Photography Masterclass
DK Publishing
Organized as one-on-one lessons, with practical assignments, examples from contributing photographers, and inspirational interviews with up-and-coming photographers.

How to Photograph Absolutely Everything
DK Publishing
Step-by-step solutions for numerous picture-making opportunities and packed with examples. Designed for beginners, but also being used by more experienced photographers.

Digital Photography Month by Month
DK Publishing
Inspiration and ideas for capturing the moments and moods of every season throughout the year. With exercises, tips, and picture analysis.

Photography: The Definitive Visual History
DK Publishing
Lavishly illustrated history of photography featuring hundreds of great photographers and examples of their work, with a uniquely full treatment of the history of technology and the impact it has had on photography.

Peter Burian:
National Geographic Photography Field Guide
National Geographic Society
Concise, clear guide to practical photography, with excellent instruction, examples, and interviews.

Steve Caplin:
How to Cheat in Photoshop CC
Focal Press
Clear instructions for elaborate techniques that lay the foundations for a wider range of effects.

Michael Freeman:
Mastering High Dynamic Range Photography
Ilex
Comprehensive, detailed treatment of HDR photography, with high standard of illustration. Very technical in parts. Overall, recommended.

The Digital SLR Handbook (revised 2nd edition)
Ilex
Sound and accurate advice covering many aspects of digital SLR photography and software use. Recommended.

Mark Galer & Les Horvat:
Digital Imaging
Focal Press
Uneven in quality and coverage, but containing much useful information. Worth a browse.

Roger Hicks & Frances Schultz:
Quality in Photography
David & Charles
Valuable approach to photography, concentrating on technical work, perhaps somewhat to the detriment of visual quality, but many tips and advice offered.

The Adobe Photoshop Lightroom Book for Digital Photographers
Peachpit Press
Thorough, clear introduction to efficiency in Adobe Lightroom, which is rapidly becoming an essential item on a digital photographer's computer.

Michael Kieran:
Photoshop Color Correction
Peachpit Press
Excellent, thorough, authoritative coverage of color correction and management. Invaluable.

Peter Krogh:
The DAM Book: Digital Asset Management for Photographers
O'Reilly Media
Comprehensive coverage of an important field, covering workflows, archiving, and software.

Michael Langford:
Basic Photography
Focal Press
Patchy, and lacking in digital matters, but the coverage of fundamentals and analog photography is peerless and thorough. For selective reading.

Barbara London et al:
Photography
Pearson Education
A comprehensive, albeit basic, voluminous introduction to photography—perhaps the best modern treatment. Fully illustrated.

Dan Margulis:
Photoshop LAB Color
Peachpit Press
Insightful treatise on color correction. A little long-winded, but essential for the advanced worker.

Professional Photoshop
Peachpit Press
A classic on image manipulation, full of insight on topics such as tone and color correction, color spaces, sharpening, resolution, and blends. A must.

William Mitchell:
The Reconfigured Eye
MIT Press
An art-critical approach to image manipulation, looking at the impact of digital technologies on art.

David Okuefuna:
The Wonderful World of Albert Kahn
BBC Books
A truly inspirational collection of fascinating autochrome images.

Sidney F Ray:
Photographic Imaging & Electronic Photography
Focal Press
More encyclopedia than dictionary, this book is strongest on its longer entries.

Photographic Technology & Imaging Science
Focal Press
Good on photographic technology, but not so hot on the imaging science.

Andrew Rodney:
Colour Management for Photographers
Focal Press
Comprehensive treatment of color management. Invaluable for the advanced photographer.

Graham Saxby:
The Science of Imaging
Institute of Physics
This is the best modern, all-around introduction to the science of photography.

Uwe Steinmueller & Juergen Gulbins:
Fine Art Printing for Photographers (2nd edition)
Rocky Nook
Sound presentation of color management needed for producing high-quality ink-jet prints.

Ron White:
How Digital Photography Works
Que
Clear illustrations of digital camera operations.

INDEX

ACKNOWLEDGMENTS

From the author

The sixteen years and six editions of this book have run concurrently with almost the whole life of digital photography itself. That the book has grown and developed to keep up with changes in technology and photographic practice is entirely thanks to its readers. My first and biggest thanks are to you: thank you for buying this book (especially to those of you who—I know—purchase new editions to replace their old ones).

I am also delighted to record my thanks to readers from around the world who have written to me over the years to encourage me, to suggest changes, to point out errors, and to share ideas. This book, and my other titles, are much improved for your input. Do keep writing—there is plenty of room for improvement!

This book has steadily improved and adapted itself to changing circumstances over its several editions, thanks to the keen attention of my senior editor, Nicky Munro. Sadly for us, Nicky is now happily reading in a greater library in the sky, so this edition is the first not to benefit from her razor-sharp editorial eye for style and detail. But she continues to hover at my shoulder, and I'm sure even this edition is all the better for that.

Finally, as the original dedicatee of the first edition, my wife Wendy continues to deserve the dedication and biggest acknowledgment, remaining a steadfast source of inspiration, strength, and good sense.

Tom Ang
Auckland, 2016
info@tomang.com

From the publisher

Many thanks also to David Summers and Hugo Wilkinson for editorial assistance, and Margaret McCormack for compiling the index.

Picture credits

Dorling Kindersley would like to thank the following for their kind permission to reproduce their photographs:

(Key: a-above; b-below/bottom; c-center; f-far; l-left; r-right; t-top)

118 Corbis: Disc Pictures / AsiaPix (br). 119 Corbis: (clb, crb). 123 Joe Munro (br). 155 Getty Images: Naki Kouyioumtzis / Axiom Photographic Agency (br). 158 Wendy Gray. 159 Getty Images: Shelley Corinne (tr); eva serrabassa (bl); DOF-PHOTO by Fulvio (br). 160 Corbis: Gadd (bl). 161 Corbis: Ariel Skelley / Blend Images (br). 162 Getty Images: Thomas Barwick (tc). 163 Getty Images: baranova_ph (tr). 168 Paul Self. 202 Getty Images: Heinrich van den Berg (cla). 268–9 Paul Self. 292–3 John Munro. 329 Getty Images: Jessamyn Harris (bc); Photo Nadieshda (tc); weechia@ms11.url.com.tw (ca). 331 Corbis: David Madison (cr). Getty Images: Brook Tyler Photography (bl). 332 Getty Images: Marco Poggioli (bl)

All other images © Tom Ang.